The Domestic Assault of Women

Donald G. Dutton

The Domestic Assault of Women: Psychological and Criminal Justice Perspectives

Revised and Expanded Edition

UBCPress / Vancouver

Printed in Canada on acid-free paper ∞

ISBN 0-7748-0462-9

Canadian Cataloguing in Publication Data

Dutton, Donald G., 1943-
The domestic assault of women

Includes bibliographical references and index.
ISBN 0-7748-0462-9

1. Wife abuse – Psychological aspects. 2. Wife abuse –
Investigation. 3. Abused wives. I. Title.
HV6626.D87   1994   362.82'92   C94-910881-2

UBC Press gratefully acknowledges the ongoing support to its publishing program from the Canada Council, the Province of British Columbia Cultural Services Branch, and the Department of Communications of the Government of Canada.

UBC Press
University of British Columbia
6344 Memorial Road
Vancouver, BC V6T 1Z2
(604) 822-3259
Fax: 1-800-668-0821
E-mail: orders@ubcpress.ubc.ca

Credits: Figure 5.3 © 1994, American Psychiatric Press, Inc. (reprinted by permission); Figures 5.4 and 9.5 © 1994, American Psychological Association (reprinted by permission); Table 2.4 © 1994, American Psychological Association (reprinted by permission).

To my father, George, and my wife, Marta –
two of my favorite people

Contents

Preface

Since the first edition of this book was published in 1988, there has been an explosion of research interest in family violence. Researchers 'discovered' family violence in the sense that Columbus 'discovered' America, although the discovery was no news to those who already lived there. However, the fact that wife assault is more common than was believed twenty years ago, that police now routinely respond to wife assault calls, that shelter houses are more abundant than before, and that court-mandated treatment groups are now commonplace all testify to the productivity of a social response to family violence generated largely by the women's movement. There is now a dawning recognition that family violence and wife assault are not 'family problems' but problems for all society. Children who grow up in abusive homes are more at risk for committing violence themselves, both within and outside their own families.

Arrest and treatment combinations still seem the best bet to reduce recidivism, but the success of these depends on conditions in the broader social fabric: the victim's willingness to report the abuse, the willingness of the police to make arrests, and the man's willingness to complete group treatment and to stop his violence. In the absence of these factors, a criminal justice system solution will not succeed.

The explosion of research made the process of updating *The Domestic Assault of Women* a challenge. What I tried to do was to add the methodologically most strong research on the major questions posed in the first edition. Do men become violent out of power or powerlessness? Is intimate violence inherited? Is there a personality type associated with intimate violence? Why do battered women stay with their oppressor? Does arrest reduce repeat violence? Do treatment groups work? What does the future hold? Although the conclusions do not differ strongly from the first edition, the evidence presented is much firmer.

Chapter 1 of the present edition contains an expanded history of social policy towards family violence. Elizabeth Pleck's brilliant work, *Domestic Tyranny*, which forms the basis for this expansion, was not available at the time the first edition was written. Its chronicling of social policy from the time of the Puritans to the present provides an essential antidote to the ahistorical approach to the problem. It is indeed common wisdom that if we forget history, we are surely doomed to repeat its mistakes.

I have added a new chapter on the abusive personality (Chapter 5) which summarizes current research on the central role that a personality constellation, called borderline personality organization, plays in abusiveness. My thesis is that growing up in an abusive home can do more than provide an opportunity to model actions, it can influence a sense of self and an entire set of perceptions and expectations that are manifested in intimate relationships. The upshot of this work points to the radical thesis that persons growing up in abusive homes may develop two personalities: one public and one private. The breakthrough research of Phillip Shaver on adult attachment patterns has been incorporated into our work on origins of intimate assaultiveness.

Similarly, new empirical studies of the immediate effects of abuse victimization on battered women serve as the basis for a new chapter on traumatic bonding and the battered woman syndrome (Chapter 7). Since this now constitutes a legal defence in most North American courts, the overlap of psychology and law becomes crucial.

Some important new research has surfaced on the efficacy of arrest and treatment since the original edition. This work seems to qualify rather than negate the conclusion that arrest-treatment combinations effectively reduce recidivism. What becomes clear with the new studies is how social factors set limits on the effectiveness of criminal justice solutions. When men have nothing to lose through arrest, arrest loses its ability to deter. Employment and social cohesion provide the 'something' that can be lost.

While trends still show gradual declines in wife assault incidence, the data from dating relationships are troubling. The next generation seems to be in serious need of effective secondary intervention. We have the ability to do this, although whether we have the political will remains a question.

This book is the product of twenty years of experience working with batterers, battered women, police, and academic researchers. My sense of family violence as a serious social issue is no less diminished. To the contrary, I think we are just beginning to see that numerous social costs are driven up by what I call the 'original problem.' When abuse is encountered at a vulnerable early age, it creates a lifelong problem for many. Nothing short of a revolution of values will finally end the problem.

Acknowledgments

I would like to acknowledge the following intellectual debts: Ernest Becker and Eric Fromm for the breadth and depth of their vision in understanding human motivation, Murray Straus for his pioneering studies on wife assault incidence, J.Q. Wilson for his critical thinking about the function and limits of law, Anne Ganley for her pioneering work on treatment groups. I would also like to thank Linda Graham, for her support. They are independent and critical thinkers, all.

Several other people made major editorial efforts on this book: Barbara McGregor made stylistic comments on the first draft, Ardis Krueger carefully compiled the subject and author indexes, Ehor Boyanowsky made several helpful critical comments, and Andrew Starzomski did virtually all the statistical analyses in Chapter 5. They have all assisted greatly.

The Domestic Assault of Women

1

History and Incidence of Wife Assault

> How vast is the number of men, in any great country, who are a little
> higher than brutes ... This never prevents them from being able, through
> the laws of marriage, to obtain a victim ... The vilest malefactor has some
> wretched woman tied to him against whom he can commit any atrocity
> except killing her – and even that he can do without too much danger of
> legal penalty.
>
>   – John Stuart Mill, *The Subjection of Women* (1869)

Wife assault refers to any physical act of aggression by a man against a
woman with whom he is in an intimate (i.e., sexual-emotional) relationship. Researchers (e.g., Schulman 1979; Straus 1979) typically define *severe
assault* as actions with a relatively high likelihood of causing injury to the
victim. Hence, kicking, biting, hitting with a fist or object, beating up, or
using a weapon against a victim are all actions regarded as constituting
severe assault. These actions are likely to carry medical consequences for
the victim; and they are actions that, in practice, are considered grounds
for arrest. Other assaultive acts (e.g., slapping, pushing, shoving, grab-
bing, throwing objects at the victim) are less likely to invoke medical or
criminal justice consequences.

Some might object that this classification system does not pay enough
attention to the effects of the actions it classifies. Shoving someone down
a flight of stairs, for example, may have more serious consequences than
hitting him or her with a rolled up newspaper. However, since we will be
making use of research that has followed this convention of classifying
violent acts (using the Straus *Conflict Tactics Scale* [*CTS*]), and since we
wish to connect our understanding of the psychology of such actions to
the criminal justice policy used to reduce their likelihood, we will use it
throughout this book.

Figure 1.1

Straus (1979) *Conflict Tactics Scale*

No matter how well a couple gets along, there are times when they disagree on major decisions, get annoyed about something the other person does, or just have spats or fights because they're in a bad mood or tired or for some other reasons. They also use different ways of trying to settle their differences. I'm going to read a list of some things that you and your (spouse/partner) might have done when you had a dispute, and would first like you to tell me for each one how often you did it in the past year.

	You								Partner						
Frequency of:	1	2	5	10	20	+20	Ever?		1	2	5	10	20	+20	Ever?
a. Discussed the issue calmly.	1	2	3	4	5	6	X		1	2	3	4	5	6	X
b. Got information to back up (your/his/her) side of things.	1	2	3	4	5	6	X		1	2	3	4	5	6	X
c. Brought in or tried to bring in someone to help settle things.	1	2	3	4	5	6	X		1	2	3	4	5	6	X
d. Argued heatedly but short of yelling.	1	2	3	4	5	6	X		1	2	3	4	5	6	X
e. Insulted, yelled, or swore at other one.	1	2	3	4	5	6	X		1	2	3	4	5	6	X
f. Sulked and/or refused to talk about it.	1	2	3	4	5	6	X		1	2	3	4	5	6	X
g. Stomped out of the room or house (or yard).	1	2	3	4	5	6	X		1	2	3	4	5	6	X
h. Cried.	1	2	3	4	5	6	X		1	2	3	4	5	6	X

i. Did or said something to spite the other one.	1	2	3	4	5	6	X	1	2	3	4	5	6	X
j. Threatened to hit or throw something at the other one.	1	2	3	4	5	6	X	1	2	3	4	5	6	X
k. Threw or smashed or hit or kicked something.	1	2	3	4	5	6	X	1	2	3	4	5	6	X
l. Threw something at the other one.	1	2	3	4	5	6	X	1	2	3	4	5	6	X
m. Pushed, grabbed, or shoved the other one.	1	2	3	4	5	6	X	1	2	3	4	5	6	X
n. Slapped the other one.	1	2	3	4	5	6	X	1	2	3	4	5	6	X
o. Kicked, bit, or hit with a fist.	1	2	3	4	5	6	X	1	2	3	4	5	6	X
p. Hit or tried to hit with something.	1	2	3	4	5	6	X	1	2	3	4	5	6	X
q. Beat up the other one.	1	2	3	4	5	6	X	1	2	3	4	5	6	X
r. Threatened with a knife or gun.	1	2	3	4	5	6	X	1	2	3	4	5	6	X
s. Used a knife or gun.	1	2	3	4	5	6	X	1	2	3	4	5	6	X
t. Other _____	1	2	3	4	5	6	X	1	2	3	4	5	6	X

e - k, verbal aggression   j - k, direct verbal and symbolic aggression   l - n, physical aggression   o - s, severe aggression

A second objection to limiting the study of violence towards wives to discrete physical actions is that they are only part of what is experienced in wife assault. Physical assault may be accompanied by verbal abuse, psychological abuse, and threats or destructive actions aimed at children, pets, and personal property. This constellation of destructive actions more fully represents a continuum of coercive control and, some would argue, therefore constitutes the proper subject matter for a psychology of interpersonal violence. This argument is an important one and we will return to it at various times. But since our explanation for wife assault is related to social intervention, we are primarily interested in focusing on those behaviors that society agrees are unacceptable and that require the intervention of agents from outside the family.

While there is some disagreement over how society should control wife assault, there is no agreement whatsoever over social intervention vis-à-vis family conflict. Whatever our philosophical and political beliefs tell us about the pathological nature of power imbalances and coercion in social systems, it is rare that social agents will become involved in altering the use of coercion in families until that coercion involves physical force or threats of physical force (see also Steiner 1981). By concentrating on physical assault, we can develop an explanation which will have the greatest utility for deciding when to intervene in dysfunctional families. At the same time, we must remain aware that wife assault may have a common psychological substratum with other, less dramatic, coercive actions. Our definition of wife assault, then, is chosen with a view to intervention, and the questions we will pose about the causes of such assault will bear on the strategies a society might invoke to reduce its incidence.

Incidence of Wife Assault: The Magnitude of the Problem

The distinction between use and effects of violence made in the last section has implications for the importance we attach to the incidence of various types of violence. As Straus (1980) points out, the national 'speed limit' on marital violence is that it must be severe enough to cause an injury requiring medical treatment in order for police intervention to lead to arrest. The distinction between the Violence Index and the Severe Violence Index on the Straus *CTS* reflects this attitude: actions such as slapping or shoving are less likely to produce injury than are punching, beating, or using a weapon. Exceptions exist, of course, as in our example of shoving someone down a staircase, but in general the *CTS* ranks actions according to potential physical injury. Similarly, although slapping or pushing someone is technically an assault, in practice, police in most jurisdictions would not arrest unless an action corresponding to those listed in the Severe Violence Index had occurred. Accordingly, in reviewing the incidence of wife assault, we will focus on the actions that entail the greatest potential for injury.

Estimating the incidence of wife assault presents a problem in that, by definition, the event occurs in private. For different reasons, two general measures of wife assault are of interest. The first is an actual estimate of the frequency and incidence of wife assault in a general population. This is obtained by a victim survey which entails interviewing a representative sample drawn from a general population about any experiences they have had with being victimized by violence. Several such surveys have been completed. They are:

- a nationally representative sample of 2,143 interviewed in 1974 by Response Analysis Corporation (Straus, Gelles, & Steinmetz 1980)
- a survey of spousal violence against women in Kentucky that interviewed 1,793 women (Schulman 1979)
- a second national survey completed by Straus and Gelles (1985, 1986)
- a sample of 1,045 for Alberta (Kennedy & Dutton 1989).

All the above are *conflict tactics* surveys which use the *CTS*. In addition, there are two crime victimization surveys:

- the National Crime Survey of victimization, based on interviews conducted during 1973-6 with 136,000 people across the US (US Department of Justice 1980)
- the Canadian Urban Victimization Survey of 61,000 homes in seven Canadian cities (Solicitor General of Canada 1985).

The second general measure is the proportion of a social service agency's client population that has been generated by family violence. Stark, Flitcraft, and Frazier (1979) determined what proportion of clients for urban hospital emergency services were assaulted women, and Levens and Dutton (1980) determined what proportion of clients for police service were the result of domestic disputes. Contrasting these two types of data suggests that although a small percentage of all assaulted women make use of hospital or police services, they still constitute a sizeable proportion of the entire hospital or police client population. This finding underscores the seriousness of wife assault and the considerable costs associated with it. We first turn our attention to the victim surveys.

Surveys of Incidence

Conflict Tactics Surveys
As described above, two general types of incidence surveys exist – what we shall term conflict tactics surveys and crime victim surveys. The former

ask people what actions they have taken to resolve family conflicts, the latter ask people by what crimes they have been victimized. The oft-cited Straus survey (Straus et al. 1980), the Kentucky survey (Schulman 1979), and the Alberta survey (Kennedy & Dutton 1989) used the Straus *CTS* to measure the type of actions used to resolve family conflicts. This common measure enables some direct comparison between these surveys. The National Crime Survey (NCS) and the Canadian Urban Victimization Survey (CUVS) used different questions and definitions, thus making data comparison more difficult.

The Straus, the Kentucky, and the Alberta surveys, for example, use Straus's definition of severe assault as anything from item O on the *CTS* (kicked, bit or hit you with a fist) to item S (used a knife or fired a gun). Using this definition, the victimization rates for husband-to-wife violence on the two surveys were 8.7% (Schulman) and 12.6% (Straus et al.). Corresponding rates, using the more inclusive measure of any violent husband-wife acts (including slapping, pushing, and shoving), were 21% (Schulman) and 27.8% (Straus et al.). These rates refer to the use of violence at any time in the marriage. In Chapter 10 we will examine the results of the 1985 national survey (Straus & Gelles 1985, 1986), which indicated a decrease in incidence of wife assault in comparison to the 1975 data.

The Kentucky survey reported single versus repeat assault in its data, specifically asking respondents the number of times they had been assaulted in the past twelve months. These data bear on an issue we will consider in more detail in Chapter 2: wife assault as a repeated, self-sustaining habit. Table 1.1 shows the percentage of women in the Schulman survey reporting single or repeated victimizations in the prior twelve

Table 1.1

Percentage of women reporting single or repeated victimization in prior year (*n* = 1,793) on Schulman (1979) survey

	Single	Repeated	Total	Probability action repeated
Violence items (L-N)	2.0	3.40	5.4	63%
Severe violence items (O-S)	.6	1.04	2.0	63%
Comparable estimates from Straus et al. (1980) for 1975				
Violence items (L-N)			9.00	66%
Severe violence items (O-S)			2.24	66%

months. These data indicate that, about 63% of the time, if assaults occur once, they are likely to be repeated.

Kennedy and Dutton (1989) used a combination of face-to-face and random digit-dialling techniques to survey 1,045 residents in Alberta. Respondents were asked to report violence for the year preceding the survey. Since this survey also used the Straus *CTS*, it led to a comparison of US and Canadian rates of wife assault. These data are reported in Table 1.2. The minor violence rates for the two countries are virtually identical, but the severe violence indexes were quite different. In effect, as the acts became increasingly violent, the Canadian incidence rates fell further below the US rates. For kicking and hitting (items O and P) the Canadian rates were 80% of the US rates, for beating up (item Q) they were 25%, and for threatening with or using a gun/knife they were 17%.

Table 1.2

Incidence rates found in US and Canadian surveys

	US rates			Canadian rates
	Schulman (1979)	Straus, Gelles, & Steinmetz (1980)[a]	Straus & Gelles (1985)	Kennedy & Dutton (1989)[b]
Any violence ever	21.0%	28.0%	22.0%	19.0%
Severe violence ever	8.7	12.1	11.3	7.8
Repeat severe violence ever	5.9	8.0	7.7	5.4
Severe violence/past year	4.1	3.8	3.0	2.3
Repeat severe violence/ past year	2.5	2.5	2.0	1.5

[a] Data collected in 1975.
[b] Data collected in 1987.

By way of comparison with these North American data, Kim and Cho (1992) report family violence rates for Korea, also using the *CTS*. Whereas Straus et al. reported an 11.6% incidence rate of wife assault (any violence) in the past year, the Korean rate was 37.5%. The severe violence wife assault rate in the US for the past year was 3.8-3.0%, whereas in Korea it was 12.4%. Hence, Korean society appears to be more violent than US society.

If we combine the estimate of repeated violence in about two-thirds of marriages (Schulman 1979; Straus et al. 1980) with Straus et al.'s and

Schulman's estimates for severe violence ever occurring in a marriage (12.6% and 8.7%, respectively), we obtain the estimate that severe repeated violence occurs in about 7.2% of all marriages in the US and in 5.4% of all marriages in Canada.

Alternately, we could look at the number of repeatedly assaultive men in a population. In both Canada and the US about 22.5% of the entire population is male, married or separated, and over the age of 15. This translates into about 6,210,000 men in Canada and 62,210,000 in the US. From Table 1.2 we see that 2.5% of these men are repeatedly severely assaultive to women in any given year. This means that about 155,000 men in Canada and 1,550,000 in the US present the core problem for the criminal justice system. One could argue that unmarried men are also part of the problem. If we include all men over 15, married or not, the core problem numbers jump to 260,000 and 2,600,000, respectively, in Canada and the US. However, these figures are not yet age-adjusted. If we dropped men over 55 from the sample because, statistically, they are less risky, the numbers are cut by over 25% to 182,000 and 1,820,000, respectively (the median age for wife assault is 31; as we depart from that age the statistical chances of a man being assaultive decrease – see Turner, Fenn, and Cole [1981] and Chapter 10). Any way you present them, these are large numbers.

It is these men and incidents that, arguably, represent the major challenge to the criminal justice system, since single assaults are unlikely to be preventable via police intervention. As we shall see in Chapter 8, police typically respond after an assault has occurred. Hence, police intervention might be most effective in preventing future assaults. An understanding of the repeat assaulter will require analysis, not only of the circumstances of the initial assault, but also of the mechanisms that sustain an assaultive habit.

Crime Victim Surveys
The Canadian Urban Victimization Survey (CUVS) (Solicitor General of Canada 1985) generated a subsample of 10,100 incidents of wife assault. Six per cent of these were series assaults (five or more) by the same offender; 45% were reported to police either by the woman or a third party; 51% of the women were injured – 27% required medical treatment, and 52% lost time from their job. The 6% series assault rate is very close to the 6.8% rate generated by the Straus and Schulman studies.

The National Crime Survey (NCS) in the US used a stratified multi-cluster sample design. The Bureau of the Census selected a rotating sample of 72,000 households that were representative of the entire population of

the US (US Bureau of the Census 1979). Of these, 60,000 yielded interviews. Sample households were interviewed every six months until seven
interviews had been completed in each household. At each interview,
respondents were asked to recall incidents of crime that occurred during
the previous six months.

As with the CUVS, the NCS was not specifically designed to answer certain questions that are especially important to family violence research.
Spouse or ex-spouse was a single category used to define the victim's relationship to the offender, so no reliable distinction could be made between
assaults that occurred while the victim was married to the offender and
those that occurred after separation (Gaquin 1977). The NCS survey
revealed that 32% of assaults by a spouse/ex-spouse were repeated three or
more times, but it did not ask questions about how victim reactions may
have affected and/or accounted for repeater/non-repeater differences.

For a total of 1,058,500 victimizations recorded by the NCS study,
injuries resulted in 56.8%, medical care was required for 23.7%, and hos-
pitalization for 14.3%. Twenty-one per cent of the victims lost one or
more days from work as a result of the attacks, and 55% reported their
victimization to the police. In surveys such as the CUVS and the NCS,
which are defined to the victim as crime surveys, report rates to police for
assaults by husbands are relatively high and are comparable to other types
of assault (CUVS = 37%, NCS = 55%) (Dutton 1987b). In surveys of family
conflict resolution which measure spousal violence per se (e.g., Schulman
1979; Straus & Gelles 1985), rates of reporting serious assaults (defined by
the *CTS* subscale) to the police are only 14.5% (17% and 10%, respectively, weighted by sample sizes). One interpretation of this discrepancy is
that many violent interspousal acts of violence are not considered criminal by the victim. To the extent the victim considers the action criminal,
she is more likely to report it to police and more likely to report it to an
interested interviewer. To the extent that the victim does not consider the
action criminal, she is less likely to report it in a crime survey and more
likely to report it in a conflict-resolution survey (see Table 1.3).

Surveys of Client Populations
By coding 174 hours of taped calls for police services in an urban setting,
Levens and Dutton (1980) determined that 17.5% of all calls were for
family disputes, and that 13.5% of all calls were specifically for husband-
wife disputes that frequently involved wife assault. In Chapter 8, when we
consider policy issues for controlling wife assault, we will have to consider
the huge demand which family disputes place on police resources (see
Figure 1.2).

Table 1.3

Likelihood of reporting wife assault to police as a function of seriousness of assault

Survey	Sample size	Per cent reporting severe violence	Per cent reporting to police
A. Conflict Tactics Surveys			
Schulman (1979): State of Kentucky	1,793 women	8.7	17
Straus et al. (1980): US National Sample	1,183 women	12.1	n/a
Straus & Gelles (1985): US National Sample	6,002 households	11.3	10

Survey	Sample size	Item	Per cent reporting to police
B. Crime Victim Surveys			
National Crime Survey (US) (1980)	72,000 households	Spouse/ex-spouse assaults	54.8 (56.8)[a]
Canadian Urban Victimization Survey (1983)	61,000 people	All assaults against women	44.0
		Last in a series of assaults against women	48.0
		All assaults by relatives (on victims of both genders)	38.0
		All assaults against men	32.0
		All robberies	45.0
		All crimes	48.0

[a]Gaquin (1977) reports 54.8%; the US Department of Justice (1980) reports 56.8% for the same data.

Figure 1.2

Relationship of total estimated incidence of wife assault to demand for police intervention

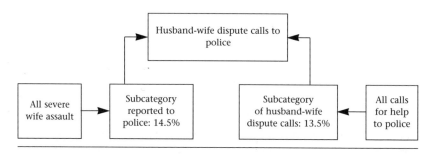

Similarly, family disputes resulting in wife assault place heavy demands on hospital resources. Schulman's (1979) respondents reported requiring medical attention for 15% of the serious assaults against them. In urban areas, this usually means emergency-room care (62% of all hospital treatment). The NCS survey respondents reported receiving medical attention in 23.7% of spouse/ex-spouse incidents (Gaquin 1977), and the CUVS reported that 27% of women attacked by their spouses required medical treatment. Again, most of this attention (53.2%) consisted of hospital emergency care.

Viewing the demand for hospital service as another social cost of wife assault, Stark, Flitcraft, and Frazier (1979) examined hospital records for an urban emergency room and concluded that 33.2% of all injuries presented by women were probably caused by assaults by intimates, and that 22.5% were definitely caused by such assaults. The Schulman (1979) survey found that injuries inflicted by a male partner resulted in 4.4 physician visits per year per 100 women. Two-thirds of these were emergency-room visits. A survey of 1,210 women in Texas found a 1% per annum rate of injuries which required medical treatment (Teske & Parker 1983). Straus (1986) pointed out that if one extrapolated the Kentucky and Texas results to the entire US population, about 1.5 million women per year receive medical attention because of assaults by their male partners. Despite this absolute number, only 7.3% of severe assaults result in any medical attention (the most common being an emergency-room visit), 19% result in time off work, and 43.9% result in increases in psychosomatic symptoms (Stets & Straus 1990). Even though only a fraction of all assault victims make use of hospitals, the drain on resources is extremely high.

Measuring Abuse

There have been some criticisms of the *CTS* (Straus 1992a, 1992b, 1992c). These include the critique that (1) the *CTS* ignores the context in which violence occurs; (2) differences in size between men and women make acts scored the same on the *CTS* quite different; and (3) impression management or social desirability factors may preclude people from answering the *CTS* accurately. Straus's (1992c) response to (1) is that, as there are too many potential context variables to fit within the *CTS* as a generic measure, assessment of context should be done separately. The *CTS* is designed to allow for the easy addition of any special set of context questions. This is also true for questions about the *consequences* of assault (e.g., whether anyone was injured, the nature of the injury, whether the police were called, etc.) With respect to (2), Straus argues that, while it is possible to weight actions by differences in size between perpetrator and victim (or, similarly, to construct an upper limit after which slapping gets counted as severe violence), such weightings have rarely led to changes in research results. With respect to (3), a study by Dutton and Hemphill (1992) correlated scores on two measures of social desirability (the tendency to present a perfect image on self-report tests) and scores on the *CTS*. Social desirability is measured by a test called the *Marlowe-Crowne Social Desirability Scale* (*MC*) (Crowne & Marlowe 1960), which assesses the tendency to present the self in a socially acceptable manner. *MC* scores did correlate significantly (and negatively) with perpetrators' self-reports of verbal abuse. The higher their social desirability score, the lower their reported rates of verbal abuse. However, it did not correlate with their reports of physical abuse or with any reports of abuse (verbal or physical) made against them by their partners. Hence, it seems that reports of physical abuse are largely uncontaminated by social-desirability factors. This means that the incidence survey rates are probably fairly accurate as far as image management is concerned. Of course, whether or not respondents remember all abuse continues to be an issue.

Some newer scales have been developed that are of central importance to family violence researchers. One is the *Severity of Violence Against Women Scale* (*SVW*) developed by Linda Marshall (1992). A parallel form, the *Severity of Violence Against Men Scale*, also exists. The *SVW* assesses forty-six acts in the following categories: symbolic violence; threats of violence (mild, moderate, and severe categories); acts of mild violence (minor, moderate, and severe categories); and sexual violence. For each action, Marshall had two groups of women (university undergraduates and a community sample) rate the severity of each action for both physical and emotional harm. The resulting weightings can be used to multiply

Figure 1.3

Severity of Violence Against Women Scale (Marshall 1992)

You have probably experienced anger or conflict with your partner. Below is a list of behaviors you may have done during the past 12 months. For each statement, describe how often you have done each behavior by writing the appropriate number in the blank.

1	2	3	4
never	once	a few times	many times

_____ 1. Hit or kicked a wall, door, or furniture
_____ 2. Threw, smashed, or broke an object
_____ 3. Drove dangerously with her in the car
_____ 4. Threw an object at her
_____ 5. Shook a finger at her
_____ 6. Made threatening gestures or faces at her
_____ 7. Shook a fist at her
_____ 8. Acted like a bully toward her
_____ 9. Destroyed something belonging to her
_____ 10. Threatened to harm or damage things she cares about
_____ 11. Threatened to destroy property
_____ 12. Threatened someone she cares about
_____ 13. Threatened to hurt her
_____ 14. Threatened to kill yourself
_____ 15. Threatened to kill her
_____ 16. Threatened her with a weapon
_____ 17. Threatened her with a club-like object
_____ 18. Acted like you wanted to kill her
_____ 19. Threatened her with a knife or gun
_____ 20. Held her down, pinning her in place
_____ 21. Pushed or shoved her
_____ 22. Grabbed her suddenly or forcefully
_____ 23. Shook or roughly handled her
_____ 24. Scratched her
_____ 25. Pulled her hair
_____ 26. Twisted her arm
_____ 27. Spanked her
_____ 28. Bit her
_____ 29. Slapped her with the palm of your hand
_____ 30. Slapped her with the back of your hand
_____ 31. Slapped her around her face and head
_____ 32. Hit her with an object
_____ 33. Punched her
_____ 34. Kicked her

(continued on next page)

Figure 1.3 (continued)

Severity of Violence Against Women Scale (Marshall 1992)

_____ 35. Stomped on her
_____ 36. Choked her
_____ 37. Burned her with something
_____ 38. Used a club-like object on her
_____ 39. Beat her up
_____ 40. Used a knife or gun on her
_____ 41. Demanded sex whether she wanted it or not
_____ 42. Made her have oral sex against her will
_____ 43. Made her have sexual intercourse against her will
_____ 44. Physically forced her to have sex
_____ 45. Made her have anal sex against her will
_____ 46. Used an object on her in a sexual way

frequency scores. As a result, more finely honed scores in each of the nine subscales can be obtained (see Figure 1.3).

The *Psychological Maltreatment of Women Inventory* (*PMWI*) (Tolman 1989) is designed to focus more comprehensively on emotional abuse than does the *CTS*. The version of the *CTS* shown in Figure 1.1 has only six items that count in the Verbal/Symbolic Abuse Scale (e,f,g,i,j, and k). The *PMWI*, on the other hand, has fifty-eight items that fall into two distinct categories: dominance/isolation and emotional/verbal abuse. The former is made up of items such as 'monitored her time,' 'did not allow her to leave the house,' 'did not allow her to work,' and 'restricted use of car.' In general, these have to do with male control of the woman's use of space, time, and social contacts. The second category is made up of items such as 'blamed her when upset,' 'said something to spite her,' 'treated her like an inferior,' and 'swore at her.' These really have to do with acts designed to hurt the woman's feelings. A background of emotional abuse often accompanies physical abuse and acts as part of the context for violence (see Figure 1.4).

The net or cumulative effect of repeated physical and emotional abuse can be great. Consequences include injuries and health problems, days lost from work, and general social withdrawal. A variety of trauma symptoms also develop with chronic abuse. The third related scale, the *Trauma Symptom Checklist* (*TSC-33*) (Briere & Runtz 1989) can be used to assess these long-term consequences. The *TSC-33* is a 33-item scale that assesses depression, anxiety, sleep disturbance, dissociation (spacing out), and other experiences that can result from trauma in the family (see Figure 1.5).

Figure 1.4

Psychological Maltreatment of Women Inventory (Tolman 1989)

For each of the following statements please indicate how frequently *your partner* did this to you during the last year by circling the appropriate number.

0	1	2	3	4	5
not applicable	never	rarely	occasionally	frequently	very frequently

1. My partner put down my physical appearance. 0 1 2 3 4 5
2. My partner insulted me or shamed me in front of others. 0 1 2 3 4 5
3. My partner treated me like I was stupid. 0 1 2 3 4 5
4. My partner was insensitive to my feelings. 0 1 2 3 4 5
5. My partner told me I couldn't manage or take care 0 1 2 3 4 5
   of myself without him. 0 1 2 3 4 5
6. My partner put down my care of the children. 0 1 2 3 4 5
7. My partner criticized the way I took care of the house. 0 1 2 3 4 5
8. My partner said something to spite me. 0 1 2 3 4 5
9. My partner brought up something from the past to
   hurt me. 0 1 2 3 4 5
10. My partner called me names. 0 1 2 3 4 5
11. My partner swore at me. 0 1 2 3 4 5
12. My partner yelled and screamed at me. 0 1 2 3 4 5
13. My partner treated me like an inferior. 0 1 2 3 4 5
14. My partner sulked or refused to talk about a problem. 0 1 2 3 4 5
15. My partner stomped out of the house or yard during
    a disagreement. 0 1 2 3 4 5
16. My partner gave me the silent treatment, or acted
    as if I wasn't there. 0 1 2 3 4 5
17. My partner withheld affection from me. 0 1 2 3 4 5
18. My partner did not talk to me about his feelings. 0 1 2 3 4 5
19. My partner was insensitive to my sexual needs
    and desires. 0 1 2 3 4 5
20. My partner demanded obedience to his whims. 0 1 2 3 4 5
21. My partner became upset if household work was not done
    when he thought it should be. 0 1 2 3 4 5
22. My partner acted like I was his personal servant. 0 1 2 3 4 5
23. My partner did not do a fair share of household tasks. 0 1 2 3 4 5
24. My partner did not do a fair share of child care. 0 1 2 3 4 5
25. My partner ordered me around. 0 1 2 3 4 5
26. My partner monitored my time and made me
    account for where I was. 0 1 2 3 4 5
27. My partner was stingy in giving me money. 0 1 2 3 4 5
28. My partner acted irresponsibly with our financial
    resources. 0 1 2 3 4 5

(continued on next page)

Figure 1.4 (continued)

Psychological Maltreatment of Women Inventory (Tolman 1989)

29. My partner did not contribute enough to supporting
    our family.   0 1 2 3 4 5
30. My partner used our money or made important
    financial decisions without talking to me about it.   0 1 2 3 4 5
31. My partner kept me from getting medical care that
    I needed.   0 1 2 3 4 5
32. My partner was jealous or suspicious of my friends.   0 1 2 3 4 5
33. My partner was jealous of friends who were of his sex.   0 1 2 3 4 5
34. My partner did not want me to go to school or other
    self-improvement activities.   0 1 2 3 4 5
35. My partner did not want me to socialize with my same
    sex friends.   0 1 2 3 4 5
36. My partner accused me of having an affair with
    another man/woman.   0 1 2 3 4 5
37. My partner demanded that I stay home and take care
    of the children.   0 1 2 3 4 5
38. My partner tried to keep me from seeing or talking
    to my family.   0 1 2 3 4 5
39. My partner interfered in my relationships with other
    family members.   0 1 2 3 4 5
40. My partner tried to keep me from doing things
    to help myself.   0 1 2 3 4 5
41. My partner restricted my use of the car.   0 1 2 3 4 5
42. My partner restricted my use of the telephone.   0 1 2 3 4 5
43. My partner did not allow me to go out of the house
    when I wanted to go.   0 1 2 3 4 5
44. My partner refused to let me work outside the home.   0 1 2 3 4 5
45. My partner told me my feelings were irrational or crazy.   0 1 2 3 4 5
46. My partner blamed me for his problems.   0 1 2 3 4 5
47. My partner tried to turn our family, friends, and/or
    children against me.   0 1 2 3 4 5
48. My partner blamed me for causing his violent behavior.   0 1 2 3 4 5
49. My partner tried to make me feel like I was crazy.   0 1 2 3 4 5
50. My partner's moods changed radically, from very calm
    to very angry, or vice versa.   0 1 2 3 4 5
51. My partner blamed me when he was upset about
    something, even when it had nothing to do with me.   0 1 2 3 4 5
52. My partner tried to convince my friends, family, or
    children that I was crazy.   0 1 2 3 4 5
53. My partner threatened to hurt himself if I left him.   0 1 2 3 4 5

(continued on next page)

Figure 1.4 (continued)

Psychological Maltreatment of Women Inventory (Tolman 1989)

54. My partner threatened to hurt himself if I didn't do   what he wanted me to do.   0 1 2 3 4 5
55. My partner threatened to have an affair with someone   else.   0 1 2 3 4 5
56. My partner threatened to leave the relationship.   0 1 2 3 4 5
57. My partner threatened to take the children away from me.0 1 2 3 4 5
58. My partner threatened to have me committed to a mental   institution.   0 1 2 3 4 5

A Brief Social-Legal History

The development of social history methodology in the last twenty years has provided the means for studying the life of average citizens in various historical periods. We now have available studies of the social evolution of love (Hunt 1959), sex (Taylor 1954; Tannahill 1980), sex and power (de Reincourt 1974), manners (Elias 1978), folly (Tuchman 1984), and even torture (Peters 1985). A comprehensive social history of wife assault remains to be written, largely because, due to the private nature of the event, historians have problems gaining access to adequate data.

What little historical work has been done has focused on misogyny, especially in theological tracts such as the *Malleus Maleficarum* (Summers 1928), *Gratian's Decretum* (Davidson 1977), and the writings of St Paul and St Augustine (Daly 1973, 1978), as well as on the legal sanction of wife assault. The theological tracts are of relevance because of the great influence they exerted in both guiding and exonerating behavior, especially during the Middle Ages. The *Decretum* (c. 1140), the first enduring systematization of church law, specified that women were 'subject to their men' and needed to be corrected through castigation or punishment. This punishment was necessitated by women's supposed inferiority and susceptibility to the influence of devils. Jacob Sprenger's *Malleus Maleficarum* carried misogyny to the extreme, using susceptibility to diabolic influence as the rationalization for murdering women during the Middle Ages in order to suppress witchcraft. It is interesting to note that one basis for suspecting a woman of witchcraft was male impotence.

Modern concepts of personal responsibility for violent behavior were foreign to the medieval mind, where violence was either excused as part of a great cosmological scheme or justified as being in the best interests of the victim (e.g., to help her avoid the influence of devils). As we shall see in Chapter 3, this tendency to externalize the causes of violent behavior is

Figure 1.5

Trauma Symptom Checklist (Briere & Runtz 1989)

How often have you experienced each of the following in the last two months? Please circle the appropriate number.

0	1	2	3
never	occasionally	fairly often	very often

1. Insomnia (trouble getting to sleep)	0 1 2 3
2. Restless sleep	0 1 2 3
3. Nightmares	0 1 2 3
4. Waking up early in the morning and can't get back to sleep	0 1 2 3
5. Weight loss (without dieting)	0 1 2 3
6. Feeling isolated from others	0 1 2 3
7. Loneliness	0 1 2 3
8. Low sex drive	0 1 2 3
9. Sadness	0 1 2 3
10. 'Flashbacks' (sudden, vivid, distracting memories)	0 1 2 3
11. 'Spacing out' (going away in your mind)	0 1 2 3
12. Headaches	0 1 2 3
13. Stomach problems	0 1 2 3
14. Uncontrollable crying	0 1 2 3
15. Anxiety attacks	0 1 2 3
16. Trouble controlling temper	0 1 2 3
17. Trouble getting along with others	0 1 2 3
18. Dizziness	0 1 2 3
19. Passing out	0 1 2 3
20. Desire to physically hurt yourself	0 1 2 3
21. Desire to physically hurt others	0 1 2 3
22. Sexual problems	0 1 2 3
23. Sexual overactivity	0 1 2 3
24. Fear of men	0 1 2 3
25. Fear of women	0 1 2 3
26. Unnecessary or over-frequent washing	0 1 2 3
27. Feelings of inferiority	0 1 2 3
28. Feelings of guilt	0 1 2 3
29. Feelings that things are 'unreal'	0 1 2 3
30. Memory problems	0 1 2 3
31. Feelings that you are not always in your body	0 1 2 3
32. Feeling tense all the time	0 1 2 3
33. Having trouble breathing	0 1 2 3

still common in males who assault women, although cosmic influences have been replaced by alcohol. Victim-blaming is also still common, although female susceptibility to diabolic influence has been replaced by the concept of female masochism (Caplan 1984; Dutton 1983) and/or provocation (see Chapter 3).

Unfortunately, knowledge of medieval misogyny tells us little about the prevalence of wife assault during the Middle Ages. Davidson (1977) reports that in sixteenth-century France a group of carnival actors called *charivaris* (who existed in each community) staged pranks upon any members of the town whose actions deviated from the local norms. This dramaturgical social control focused on any husband who allowed his wife to beat him. The unfortunate male was dressed up, seated backwards on a donkey, draped with kitchen paraphernalia, and punched in the genitals. That no such derision descended upon battered women suggests to Davidson that wife beating was normative, since only counter-normative behavior was punished by the *charivaris*.

Davidson also cites the eighteenth-century Napoleonic Civil Code, which influenced French, Swiss, Italian, and German law, as vesting absolute family power in the male and recognizing violence as a grounds for divorce only when the courts decided that it constituted attempted murder. Hence the male had a legal right to use violence up to the point of attempted murder in order to protect his absolute power within the family.

This situation also apparently existed in England and, in 1869, prompted John Stuart Mill to write his famous essay, 'The Subjection of Women,' which Davidson cites as the first significant document to spark the raising of public consciousness about the plight of battered wives. In this essay, Mill decried 'bodily violence towards the wife,' which he viewed as arising from men's 'mean and savage natures' (Mill 1970:62). These natures were checked and resisted in public transactions but went unchecked at home because men's wives were viewed as chattels 'to be used at their pleasure' (p. 63).

Mill's essay helped spark controversy about family violence and an 1874 report to the British Parliament. At that time, British Common Law allowed a man to beat his wife with a rod no bigger than his thumb. This 'rule of thumb' was believed to be humane because it replaced an older law that allowed beating 'with any reasonable instrument.' Mill's argument is credited with accelerating the perceived need for legal policy on the control of wife assault, something that was a prominent issue in late nineteenth-century England.

A Brief History of Legal Policy

The history of the attempts of socio-legal policy to control family violence is eloquently described by Elizabeth Pleck in *Domestic Tyranny* (1987).

According to Pleck, such policy appears to have first been implemented by the Puritans (who had laws against wife beating and 'unnatural severity' towards children) in the colony of Massachusetts between 1640 and 1680. In non-Puritan society at that time, wife beating was punished informally; Pleck cites an example from Boston in 1707 in which nine men tore the clothes off a neighbour and flogged him for having beaten his wife. In the 1750s, the Regulators of Elizabethtown, New Jersey, painted their faces, dressed up like women, and whipped reputed wife beaters. More typically, the man, if he belonged to a church denomination, was brought to trial within the church community (p. 33).

Pleck argues that the history of the criminalization of family violence is contemporaneous with widespread social attitudes about the family. Historically, when the rights and privileges of the family (e.g., family privacy, freedom from government interference) are viewed as paramount, interest in criminalizing family violence wanes. However, when family violence is seen as threatening not only its victims but the social order, support for criminalization increases. Attitudes that develop during periods of disinterest in criminalizing family violence have to do with the idealization of the family and include the following beliefs: parents have the right to physically discipline children, a husband has the right to have sexual access to his wife, 'nagging' women or disobedient children often provoke the beatings they receive, wives and children need a male economic provider, and the law should not disrupt this traditional pattern of support except in extreme circumstances.

As the eighteenth century progressed, legal thinkers distinguished between public and private behavior. According to Blackstone's *Commentaries on the Laws of England* (1765-9) crimes were acts that produced mischief in civilized society, while private acts that produced moral disapproval were vices and were not considered the legitimate subject of law. Hence, the family came to be considered a private institution, beyond the purview of legislation designed to enforce morality (which had been the reason for the Puritan interest in legislating family violence).

In her review of nineteenth-century court decisions, Pleck (1989) concludes that courts decided to punish husbands when permanent injuries were inflicted but to treat other wife assaults as 'trifling cases,' refusing to interfere with family government.

A wave of interest in reform occurred between 1874 and 1890 in England, the US, and Canada. At this time societies for the prevention of cruelty to children were founded. As described above, in 1869 John Stuart Mill wrote 'The Subjection of Women,' sparking an 1874 report to the

British Parliament. At the same time, US judges and lawyers campaigned to have wife assaulters flogged. US president Theodore Roosevelt, in his annual message to Congress in 1904, decried 'brutality and cruelty towards the weak.' According to Roosevelt, 'The wifebeater ... is inadequately punished by imprisonment, for imprisonment may often mean nothing to him, while it may cause hunger and want to the wife and children who have been the victims of his brutality. Probably some form of corporal punishment would be the most adequate way of meeting this crime' (Pleck 1989:119). Also at this time, female advocates of temperance helped pass laws giving tort protection to the wives and children of drunkards. Since many of these men also abused their families, these laws often benefited victims of abuse.

Pleck attributes this revival of interest in criminal sanctions to an upswing in interest in the state's responsibility to enforce public morality. Family violence was taken seriously because it was believed to lead to other forms of crime. Pleck sees this generalized fear of crime as emanating from the chaos and increase in violent crimes that followed the American Civil War. As with most wars, intra-societal violence increased in the postwar era and was blamed, in this case, on the 'dangerous classes' (which included blacks, immigrants, and homeless men). Abused children were viewed as potential members of these dangerous classes.

By 1899 the US had hundreds of societies to protect children but only one to protect women. While Victorians believed that women were abused by drunken men, they also believed that women should sacrifice themselves for the sake of the family. Strong support existed, however, for the flogging of wife beaters in order to 'give them a taste of their own medicine.' Between 1854 and 1875, this idea was proposed four times (unsuccessfully) in the British Parliament. In the US, flogging bills were proposed in twelve states as well as in the District of Columbia. Most supporters were eminently respectable – mainly Republican male lawyers, district attorneys, and members of grand juries. They were supported by suffragist leaders. In 1906, the US Congress (and most state congresses that bothered to consider the matter) defeated whipping-post legislation on the grounds that it was cruel and barbaric (Pleck 1989). In states where the whipping post was used (e.g., Maryland, Delaware, and Oregon), it was used disproportionately against black males convicted of wife beating. (In Delaware, six whites and fifteen blacks were flogged for wife beating between 1901 and 1942.) Eventually, public opinion turned, and the whipping post began to be seen as cruel and unusual punishment even in the states that had enacted it.

As a result of the advocacy of both feminists and the Women's

Christian Temperance Union (WCTU), the last quarter of the nineteenth century also saw an increase in the use of tort protection for battered wives. The WCTU believed that men were morally inferior to women and more susceptible to alcohol, which was seen as the cause of wife beating. They succeeded in passing legislation in twenty states to expand tort protection for victims of violence so that saloonkeepers and/or saloon owners could be sued for damages caused from injury inflicted by an intoxicated person. Pleck points out that women usually won in court, although few could afford to sue.

During the first quarter of the twentieth century the perception of family violence as a serious crime began to diminish. With the creation of family courts and social casework, criminal justice system sanctions against family crime came to be viewed as inhumane and outmoded. There was an attitudinal shift towards rehabilitation and family privacy.

The 'rediscovery' of family violence in the 1970s is usually attributed to the pioneering work of Kempe, who first identified the *battered child syndrome* (Kempe, Silverman, Steele, Droegemuller, & Silver 1962). His description of x-ray evidence of young children with multiple fractures at various stages of healing cast doubt on parents who tried to argue that the former had sustained such injuries in single mishaps. At this time, laws were passed requiring professionals to report child abuse to police or social agencies, and now mandatory reporting laws exist in virtually all states and provinces (Gelles & Straus 1988). However, the social intervention of choice has been rehabilitation rather than punishment. Pleck (1989) argues that the domination of child assault reform by medical and social work professionals has resulted in the problem being defined as a psychological illness in the parent – an illness which requires social services and mental health treatment.

In contrast, wife assault reform advocates were mainly lawyers and feminists who saw social inequality and lack of proper law enforcement as major contributors to the problem. The battered women's movement viewed marital rape and wife assault as crimes and sponsored legislation to increase criminal penalties and to make the filing of criminal charges and the accessing of civil remedies easier for women.

By the end of the nineteenth century, wife assault, even by the 'rule of thumb,' had become illegal under British Common Law and in many US states (Goldman 1978). However, in practice, the criminal justice system in England, the US, and Canada routinely ignored family violence unless a murder occurred. In the 1970s, the women's movement pointed out this discrepancy between the law and legal policy. It identified wife assault as a social problem of considerable magnitude and incidence, and it brought attention to the criminal justice system's failure to deal with wife assaulters.

Chapter Summary and Conclusions

In this chapter we have reviewed the incidence of wife assault and have concluded that severe assaults occur in 8.7% to 12.1% of marriages and that about two-thirds of the assaulters re-offend. Repeat assaults may be preventable through outside intervention. The demand created by wife assault on both police and hospital emergency services is considerable; more effective intervention could reduce the substantial social costs incurred.

Social history reveals that wife assault was beginning to be recognized as a social problem in nineteenth-century England, and that this led to the beginning of legal reform. In practice, the criminal justice response throughout the first part of the twentieth century was inadequate. By the 1970s, women's groups began to lobby for more effective criminal justice action.

2
Explanations for Wife Assault: Psychiatry, Sociobiology, and Sociology

Single-Factor Explanations for Wife Assault

In the Psyche of the Assaulter

John Stuart Mill's attribution of wife assault to the 'mean and savage natures' of some men exemplifies nineteenth-century explanations of human behavior: actions were attributed to an inferred construct residing within the person – a construct referred to as human nature. Such reasoning was clearly circular: the construct was considered to be the cause of behavior, but the only proof for the former's existence was the latter. Considerable credence was given to a belief that human nature, be it savage or superior, was the product of breeding.

Early twentieth-century attempts to explain wife assault were based on case studies of men who had been incarcerated for the crime. Those cases were either exceptional in the extent of their violence (since nothing short of extreme assault or attempted murder led to conviction [Fields 1978]) or else were revealed during psychiatric treatment of individuals who were being tended for other psychological problems. These few exceptional case studies served as a basis for the overgeneralized conclusion that all men who assault their wives do so because of pathology or psychiatric disorder. Clinical syndrome explanations of wife assault attributed it to pathological dependency (Snell, Rosenwald, & Robey 1964; Faulk 1974), brain lesions such as temporal lobe epilepsy (Elliot 1977), or sadistic character (Pizzey 1974). Such explanations helped to reinforce the view of wife assault as rare and the men who committed it as unusual, atypical, and pathological.

The *Diagnostic and Statistical Manual of Mental Disorders* (*DSM-III*) (American Psychiatric Association 1981) contains a variety of disorders that share symptomatologies with descriptions of wife assaulters given by their victims (Rounsaville 1978; Rosenbaum & O'Leary 1981), by clinicians working with them (Ganley & Harris 1978), and/or by the men themselves (Gayford 1975). These include conjugal paranoia, with delusions of sexual infidelity by one's spouse; intermittent explosive disorders, including temporal lobe epilepsy (Elliot 1977), with intense acceleration of autonomic activity and post-episode amnesia; and borderline personality disorders, with intense mood swings, interpersonal disturbances, anger, and suicidal gestures. Also, Rounsaville (1978) and Gayford (1975) reported substance abuse syndromes in approximately half of an assaultive population, although Rounsaville reported that only 29% had been drinking at the time of the assault. Furthermore, Rounsaville found that only 6 of 31 wife assaulters had a history of psychiatric contact, and that 15 had no prior psychiatric contact at all.

The clinical explanation of wife assault was based on an overgeneralization from small clinical samples obtained under extremely selective circumstances. Faulk (1974), for example, discussed the 'psychiatric disturbance of men who assault their wives' based on a sample of twenty-three men 'remanded in custody for charges of seriously assaulting their wives.' The extremity of this sample is indicated by the fact that all the men had either murdered their wives (8), tried to murder them (9), or wounded or seriously injured them (6). Faulk reported that 16 of these 23 men had a 'psychiatric disorder,' but that, of these, 7 were suffering from anxiety or depression that might have been a consequence of their violence and ensuing incarceration.

Faulk's methodology exemplifies the problems associated with early clinical views of wife assaulters: the sample is small and non-representative. The extremity of the violence is not considered prior to generalizing to less violent wife assaulters. The empirical basis for the psychiatric diagnoses is not fully described but seems to be based on prison records, depositions, and interviews. What these early studies lacked was a large sample of wife assaulters drawn not just from prison populations but from typical non-incarcerated wife assaulters as well. Furthermore, consideration of whether several subpopulations of wife assaulters existed was lacking. Faulk had differentiated overcontrolled types of wife assaulters (whom he called passive-dependent) from those who were undercontrolled (whom he called violent and bullying), but the differentiation was rudimentary and unsystematic. Comparison with appropriate control groups was also lacking.

Recent psychiatric studies are more methodologically sound than were earlier studies, but they still suffer from some serious interpretative problems. For example, Bland and Orn (1986) presented data from an urban random sample (*n* = 1,200) of an adult population that used the *Diagnostic*

Interview Schedule (Robins, Helzer, Croughan, Williams, & Spitzer 1981), which asks 259 questions related to diagnostic criteria from the *DSM-III* and the use of violence. Only 20% of those contacted refused to participate (295/1,495). The authors reported only three diagnostic categories: anti-social personality disorder, major recurrent depression, and alcohol abuse/dependence. For respondents with any one of the above diagnoses there was a 54.5% chance of violent behavior (hitting or throwing things at their partners). For respondents with no diagnosis based on the *Diagnostic Interview Schedule,* the self-reported violence rate dropped to 15.5%. When alcoholism was combined with anti-social personality disorder and/or depression, the violence rate jumped from 80% to 93%. The study was largely descriptive and did not seek to causally disentangle family violence from other diagnoses. Hence, the reader does not know whether depression causes violence towards the spouse or whether both are produced by some unreported third factor.

Hamberger and Hastings (1986) report clinical assessments of 105 men attending a wife assault treatment program. Using the *Millon Clinical Multiaxial Inventory* to assess personality disorders (based on the *DSM-III*), Hamberger and Hastings factor-analyzed the protocols, identifying three orthogonal factors which they labelled as: (1) schizoidal/borderline, (2) narcissistic/anti-social, and (3) passive-dependent/compulsive. Their assaultive sample fell equally (10-16 men each) into these three categories, into four other categories that combined various aspects of the first three pure categories, and into one category that had no aspects of the clinical pathology indicated in categories (1) through (3).

Subsequent comparison of assaultive males with a non-assaultive population indicated that the former had greater difficulty than did the latter when attempting to modulate affective states and to feel comfortable in intimate relationships. As is relatively frequent in family violence research, the authors reported that subject-selection factors may have influenced their results. They did not explain in detail how particular personality disorders could lead to assaultive behavior or even what sense one could make of their subject-selection factors. Schizoids, for example, present a very different clinical picture from borderlines, yet the two are combined in one factor in the Hamberger and Hastings study. What common thread leads both groups to assault their wives? Despite the unanswered questions raised by this study, the implication that assaultive males tend to exhibit personality disorders not only suggests one way that they may differ from other men but also that, as personality disorders are notoriously difficult to change via short-term therapy, treatment programs may have limited success.

To illustrate more concretely what wife assaulters are like, throughout the remainder of this chapter we will describe some case studies of men who underwent treatment in the Assaultive Husbands Program, a court-mandated treatment program in Vancouver, BC. These cases show how wife assault can have widely different etiologies, and it provides concrete examples of the difficulty of using a single perspective to explain all cases of wife assault. Names and certain aspects of the men's lives have been changed to protect their identity. Psychiatric studies have one common epistemological problem: the association between clinical categories is too frequently used as a substitute for systematic explanation. By systematic explanation, we mean the examination and integration of both the causal origins of intimate rage (coupled with the cultural shaping of expectations about intimacy and the use of violence) and the immediate antecedents and consequences of adult assaultiveness. A systematic explanation might account for the co-occurrence of personality disorders, substance abuse, dysphoric moods, and the use of violence towards one's spouse. The psychiatric approach, as it was offered in these early studies, substituted the reference to a clinical category for an explanation. The appearance of a similarity between descriptions of assaulters and some *DSM-III* categories is not a substitute for a systematic analysis. In the next chapters we will begin to develop a systematic explanation for wife assault, presenting research evidence for a model of intimate assaultiveness.

In the Genes: Sociobiology and Wife Assault

Sociobiologists have extended Charles Darwin's (1871, 1872) notion that physical characteristics and behaviors of species develop over time through the process of natural selection. Characteristics and behaviors that enable a species to function in a specific environment are maintained and gradually evolve to enable the species to survive. In more recent years, the evolutionary point of view has been extended to account for the *social* behavior of animals (Wynne-Edwards 1962) and humans (Wilson 1975, 1978).

In extending evolutionary ideas to human social behavior, sociobiologists attempt to account for cooperation, competition, and aggression by arguing that each behavior has an evolutionary function; that is, it maximizes the likelihood that individuals who demonstrate it will survive and that their offspring will survive (Bigelow 1972), and that their contribution to the gene pool is maximized. In so doing, sociobiologists tend to focus on social behavior that is common to humankind across all cultures (rather than focusing on cultural variations, as do anthropologists). They regard these common types of social behavior as part of an evolutionary

Case Study
Robert

Robert was referred to our treatment group while his wife was still hospitalized for injuries sustained from his beating. He appeared tense and volatile, making other men in the group nervous. He would rock back and forth in his chair and clench and unclench his fists repeatedly; he looked to be on the verge of tears. Robert reported no feelings and was surprised to find out that other men viewed him as tense and angry.

The incident that led to his being in the group occurred at his wife's office party. About thirty people were drinking and chatting, when, according to Robert, his wife disappeared (i.e., he could not find her in a large, unfamiliar house). After ten to fifteen minutes he saw her and insisted that they leave the party. He recalled feeling nothing at this point. They drove home, she went to bed, and he began to watch television.

His next memory was of seeing her lying in a pool of blood and realizing that he had severely beaten her. He called relatives and the police.

During treatment, Robert revealed that he believed his wife was having an affair and that, when she disappeared at the party, she was having sex with a co-worker. (She was talking to two female co-workers on an outside balcony.) Two months into treatment Robert phoned me in a panic and said that he was 'about to kill [his] wife.' He had returned from an out-of-town business trip to find 'a key with a man's name on it.' (It was the name of the key manufacturer.) He again assumed his wife was having an affair and became enraged. It took him three days to completely calm down, despite my pointing out his erroneous assumption.

Subsequent therapy revealed that Robert had been put up for adoption at age two. Whenever he failed to comply with their wishes, his adoptive parents threatened 'to send him back.' He experienced strong arousal states at the prospect of abandonment. His delusional beliefs about his wife and his chronic anxiety mutually reinforced each other, spiralling upwards into an extreme state of arousal and panic. The outburst of rage temporarily reduced this aversive state. A psychiatric label for Robert would be conjugal paranoia.

Case Study
Dan

Dan came into treatment on a court order, having been convicted of assault. He was articulate and intelligent, if a little disorganized. The incident that led to his being in the group occurred when Dan was phoning a movie theatre to find out when a film started. His wife called to him from another room, and he somewhat curtly told her to be quiet because he couldn't hear the telephone announcement. His wife became enraged and began screaming, smashing furniture, striking Dan, and verbally berating him. The colour in her face turned to purple. Dan tried to leave, but his wife threatened to (1) follow him and publicly embarrass him and (2) to kill herself. After five hours of abuse, Dan lost control and struck his wife. She called the police.

Dan's wife had been sexually and physically abused by her stepfather and would fly into rage states when she felt dismissed or neglected. She promised to seek treatment after these episodes were over but subsequently reneged. Dan was strongly attached to her and felt powerless either to change her or to leave her.

heritage. So, for example, groups and individuals who developed aggression in early hunting cultures would be more likely to compete successfully for territory and mates, thus maximizing the survival of themselves and their offspring. Sociobiological theory comes under strong attack by most social scientists, who claim that it underestimates the impact of socio-cultural factors and overestimates the impact of biological factors on contemporary social behavior (Gould 1983). It is not necessary to get into the current controversy, however, in order to raise a question that is difficult for sociobiologists to answer: How does one explain domestic violence and, in particular, the killing of one's spouse? It seems a less-than-optimal way to increase one's contribution to the gene pool. In fact, it seems evolutionarily unsound; yet it has occurred with alarming frequency since the beginnings of recorded history (Davidson 1977; deReincourt 1974).

Wilson (1975, 1978), a sociobiologist, concedes that the evolution of aggression has been jointly guided by three forces:

(1) the genetic predisposition towards learning some form of aggression
(2) the necessities imposed by the environment in which a society finds itself

(3) the previous history of a group, which biases it towards adopting one cultural innovation over another.

Wilson views humans as disposed: (1) to respond with an unreasoning hatred to external threat and (2) to escalate hostility sufficiently to overwhelm the source of threat to such an extent that a wide margin of safety is ensured. If we apply this analysis to cases of sexual threat, it seems that sociobiologists would predict an inherited predisposition of aggression towards invading *males*, but there is nothing in the sociobiological argument to account for jealousy based on sexual threat resulting in violence towards the intimate partner. Simeons (1962), for example, argues that men have a genetic predisposition to react with rage to sexual threat. However, the stimuli that constitute sexual threat are often, as we shall see, socially determined; and the response to such stimuli, while most certainly a form of physiological arousal, is itself often labelled in ways that are also culturally shaped (e.g., rage, hurt, anxiety, etc.).

Finally, the behavior that follows from the emotion is again directed by what one's culture deems to be more or less acceptable. Indeed, most recent sociobiological writers (e.g., Symons 1980) addressing the evolution of human sexuality argue that molar behavior (with the exception of simple motor patterns) 'is too variable and too far from the genes' to accurately predict (Symons, personal communication, 1981). Indeed, Symons states, 'I imagine that many psychological systems are involved (in uxoricide) – emotional goals, cognitive abilities to appreciate the relations between various events (real and imagined), and goals, anger, and the like' (ibid.). Indeed, it would seem to be safer, from a sociobiological perspective, to aggress against perceived marauding males, than against an intimate female.

Hence, it is our argument that the strongest statement that can be made on sociobiological grounds is that men have an inherited tendency to secrete adrenalin when they *believe* themselves to be sexually threatened, and that they will experience this state as arousing. The label applied to this arousal, however, will be socially determined, as will the behavioral response and the choice of target.

The above arguments notwithstanding, one major empirical work on intimate violence has been produced from a sociobiological perspective – *Homicide* by Daly and Wilson (1988). In this book, the authors argue that intimate homicides follow patterns that cannot be interpreted without the aid of a sociobiological perspective. The book does provide an impressive array of statistics. For example, Daly and Wilson examine 212 homicides in Detroit categorized by motive (in 164 homicides a male killed a male, in 19 a male killed a female, in 18 a female killed a male, and in 11 a female killed a female). A sociobiological perspective argues, for example, that males are far more likely than are females to experience extreme sexual jealousy because they have no guarantee of paternity. Hence, jealousy as a motive for homicide should be more frequent with male perpetrators. The Detroit data found that 13.6% (25/183) of male homicides, as opposed to 31% (9/29) of female homicides, were jealousy driven. A comparable study in Canada found that 24% (195/812) of male and 7.6% (19/248) of female homicides were jealousy-driven.

Daly and Wilson view these data as supportive of their argument. To me, the data say something else. They say that the relationship between gender, jealousy, and homicide varies considerably when one introduces race and culture. The Detroit homicides are mainly black, the Canadian are mainly white. The jealousy-driven rate for female homicides in Detroit is 4.5 times that shown in the Canadian data, while the male rate for Detroit drops by almost half (the reason being a much larger number of homicides in Detroit falling into other categories). These data are not inconsistent with Darnell Hawkins's (1986) study, *Homicide Among Black Americans*.

For me, this exemplifies the inability of sociobiological explanations to account for cultural variability. In fact, Daly and Wilson don't even attempt to account for it. Instead, they talk about 'male proprietariness' and argue that cross-cultural studies show 'no exceptions to this dreary record of connubial coercion' (Daly and Wilson 1988:203), while their own reported data suggest the contrary.

From a sociobiological perspective, jealousy motives should influence the homicide rates of various age categories. For example, so-called May-December (younger woman-older man) relationships should be at risk because of greater jealousy. Daly and Wilson cite statistics that show that marriages with high age disparities have four times the risk for homicide that do marriages with a small (two-year) gap. At highest risk for homicide victimization are wives who are more than ten years younger than their husbands.

Daly and Wilson do admit that there are alternative interpretations for these data. However, one alternative to which they do not admit is this: In relationships identity issues are bound up with intimacy issues in a way that is naturally confounded with what sociobiologists call kinship – the closer the person, the more our personal identity is founded upon our relationship with them. Hence, if our identity is unstable and the relationship is troubled, there may be a greater risk for anger and violence.

It is our argument that no set of statistics provided by sociobiologists as evidence for their position prove what is claimed. It may not be kinship or zealous protection of the gene pool that drives rage, it may be that the threat of a loss of identity is heightened when intimacy is imperiled. Indeed, one's sense of identity is inextricable from one's intimate relationships. Among the cases of jealousy-precipitated homicides in Detroit (cited by Daly and Wilson as evidence for their sociobiological theories) are two cases of homosexuals killed by their partners for alleged infidelity. Can protection of genetic fitness be a motive for homosexual men? We think not.

In order to understand the influence of societal values more fully, we now turn our attention to North American macrocultural explanations of wife assault.

In the Culture: Patriarchy and Wife Assault

Sociological/feminist explanations for wife assault developed in the 1970s endeavoured to correct the impression created by psychiatric explanations that wife assault was a rare event that was committed only by men with diagnosable psychiatric disturbances. Rather, sociologists viewed wife assault as a common event, generated both by social rules that supported male dominance of women (Goode 1971; Dobash & Dobash 1978) and by the tacit approval of society (Straus 1976, 1977a, 1977b, 1977c).

Straus (1976) and Gelles (1974) revealed what psychiatrists had ignored: that wife assault was mainly normal violence committed not by madmen but by men who believed that patriarchy was their right, yet who lacked the resources to fulfil the role it demanded of them. As Straus (1977b) claimed, 'Our society actually has rules and values which make the marriage license also a hitting license' (p. 32). The sociological claim, therefore, was twofold: that society was patriarchal, and that it sanctioned the use of violence to maintain itself as such. As Dobash and Dobash (1979) put it, 'Men who assault their wives are actually living up to cultural prescriptions that are cherished in Western society – aggressiveness, male dominance and female subordination – and they are using physical force as a means to enforce that dominance' (p. 24).

As support for this claim, sociological writers cited evidence that included criminal justice system inaction and the protection husbands enjoy against civil actions brought by wives for damages resulting from assault. A survey by Stark and McEvoy (1970) found that 24% of men and 17% of women approved of a man slapping his wife 'under appropriate circumstances.'

This latter finding, however, hardly seems to prove a cultural norm for the use of violence against wives. First, only a minority of men or women approved of a man slapping his wife under *any* circumstances. Viewed

Table 2.1

Attitudes towards use of violence

	% agreeing with statement	
	Men	Women
Stark & McEvoy (1970):		
'could approve of a husband slapping his wife's face'	24	17
'could approve of a wife slapping her husband's face'	26	19
Straus (1980):		
'some justification in hitting a spouse'	31	25

from another perspective, the survey result tells us that the majority believe slapping is never appropriate. Second, the wording of the question was ambiguous. The phrase 'appropriate circumstances' is loaded, and we do not know what egregious transgressions which respondents may consider necessary before a slap is appropriate. Finally, the question tells us nothing about the degree of violence that is acceptable. While 24% of men may approve of slapping a wife, fewer may approve of punching or kicking a wife, and still fewer may approve of beating or battering a wife.

When we add the Stark and McEvoy survey of acceptance of wife assault to the incidence surveys reviewed above (which indicate that a small minority of men assault their wives), the case for wife assault being 'normative' is weakened. Also, as we shall see in Chapter 4, many men who have been convicted of wife assault do not feel that what they did was acceptable; instead, they feel guilty, minimize the violence, and try to exculpate themselves in the manner of those whose actions are unacceptable to themselves. The sociological view of violence as normal would lead us to expect the opposite: that, as the behavior would be considered normal, no guilt would follow it.

The reluctance of the criminal justice system to prosecute wife assault also fails to offer clear-cut evidence for its tolerance, as sociological writers would have us believe. As we shall see below, criminal justice inactivity over domestic disturbances may not be substantially less than it is for other crime. Furthermore, police reluctance to intervene in family trouble may have to do with emotional discomfort over witnessing strident conflict, beliefs about the inefficacy of the charges, beliefs about women dropping the charges, and informal professional socialization (Dutton 1981a; Levens & Dutton 1980). The claim that this indicates 'legitimation of husband-wife violence' (Straus 1976) is somewhat facile, given, as we shall see in Chapter 8, that the criminal justice system's response to wife assault does not differ appreciably from its response to other forms of assault which are defined as crimes by the victim and reported to police.

Shotland and Straw (1976) performed a bystander intervention study in which a man verbally abuses and physically threatens a woman in order to investigate both third-party perceptions of this event and the likelihood of third-party intervention. Shotland and Straw had one male and one female actor engage in a verbal altercation in an elevator, the door of which opened across the hall from where experimental subjects awaited another study. In one experimental condition the woman yelled, 'Get away from me, I don't know you!'; in another she yelled, 'Get away from me, I don't know why I married you!' In all other respects the conditions were the same, with moderately high levels of verbal abuse and low levels of physical conflict. Subjects who witnessed the fight between strangers took intervening actions 69% of the time, while those who believed the couple was married did so only 19% of the time.

Subsequent examination of the beliefs and perceptions of third-party witnesses to a film of a man-woman fight revealed that when the couple was believed to be married (as opposed to being strangers) onlookers believed the woman to be in less danger and less likely to want their help, while the man was perceived as more likely to stay and fight. In other words, an entire constellation of perceptions about the seriousness of the violence and the costs of personal intervention altered with the belief that the couple were married. Some of these perceptions may be erroneous (such as the belief that there is less violence if the couple is married), and some may be rationalizations of personal inaction. Nevertheless, the complex alteration of perception argues against the mere tacit approval of wife assault.

What is required to clarify this issue is a systematic extension of the Shotland and Straw study that varies the degree of violence and the social relationship between the third party and the couple in conflict. Complex issues affect intervention decisions, and when professional objectives (such as arrest and conviction for police officers) are added, it becomes difficult to deduce approval for wife assault from intervention decisions per se (see Chapter 8).

Finally, the sociological viewpoint has difficulty explaining several key empirical studies. One is a fascinating study of intimate assault in lesbian relationships. The prevalence of violence in homosexual relationships, which also appear to go through abuse cycles, is hard to explain in terms of men dominating women (see Bologna, Waterman, & Dawson 1987; Island & Letellier 1991; Lie & Gentlewarrior, in press). Bologna et al. (1987) surveyed 70 homosexual male and female college students about

Table 2.2

Types of abuse experienced by lesbian respondents in prior relationships with male and female partners

	By male partner	By female partner
Physical abuse	34.0%	45.0%
Sexual abuse	41.9	56.8
Verbal/emotional abuse	55.1	64.5
Overall abuse	65.4	73.4

Source: Lie, G., Schilit, R., Bush, J., Montagne, M., & Reyes, L. (1991), Lesbians in currently aggressive relationships: How frequently do they report aggressive past relationships? *Violence and Victims*, 6(2), 121-35

the incidence of violence in their most recent relationships. Lesbian relationships were significantly more violent than were gay relationships (56% versus 25%). Lie and Gentlewarrior (in press) surveyed 1,099 lesbians, finding that 52% claimed to have been a victim of violence by their female partners, 52% said they had used violence against their female partners, and 30% said they had used violence against non-violent female partners. Finally, Lie, Schilit, Bush, Montague, and Reyes (1991) reported, in a survey of 350 lesbians (who had both prior lesbian and heterosexual relationships), that reported rates of verbal, physical, and sexual abuse were all significantly higher in lesbian relationships than in heterosexual relationships (see Table 2.2).

Of this sample of women, 78.2% had been in prior relationships with men. Reports of violence committed by men were all lower than were reports of violence committed by women in prior relationships. This finding is difficult to accommodate from the perspective of patriarchy: why are violence rates so high in lesbian relationships and why are they higher for past relationships with women than they are for past relationships with men? Keep in mind that the women in this sample reported past abuse victimization rates for both lesbian and heterosexual relationships. Hence, because each woman served as her own control, issues about whether this is a representative sample are reduced in importance.

It might be argued that lesbians adopt the values of the dominant patriarchal culture and that a dominance-submissiveness relationship may exist in a lesbian relationship, whereby the functional male (i.e., the dominant member) is the abuser. The problem with this argument is that even in heterosexual relationships a variety of power relations exist. The functional male theory maps a stereotype onto lesbian relationships that has no data support. Homosexual battering seems more consistent with other views on intimate violence: that intimacy generates anger which is sometimes expressed violently.

The variety of power-sharing agreements in heterosexual relationships is demonstrated in a national (US) study of 2,143 couples by Coleman and Straus (1986). Respondents reported on their power-sharing arrangements in terms of who had the final say on family decisions in six major areas. Couples were classified as equalitarian, male-dominant, female-dominant, and divided power. For each couple, consensus about marital power arrangements was also assessed, as was the degree of conflict and violence. Table 2.3 shows the percentage of couples falling into each power category, the percentage in each category reporting high degrees of conflict, and the percentage agreeing about their power arrangements.

Table 2.3

Power structure, marital conflict, and minor violence rates

Power type	n	%	% high conflict	% consensus	% violent
Male dominant	200	9.4	39.0	22.0	27
Female dominant	160	7.5	33.1	26.3	31
Divided power	1,146	54.0	33.8	30.7	21
Equalitarian	616	29.0	20.5	47.7	11

Source: Coleman, D.H. & Straus, M.A. (1986), Marital power, conflict, and violence in a nationally representative sample of American couples, *Violence and Victims*, *1*(2), 141-57

Only 9.4% of couples qualified as male-dominant, and, of those, 22% exhibited consensus about this arrangement. The largest contributor to conflict was not the specific power arrangement but the level of agreement over the power-sharing (the Power Norm Consensus). Where consensus was low, conflict increased by a factor of 2.5 independent of power arrangement. But power arrangement only marginally increased conflict. Husband-to-wife minor violence rates were highest (31) in the female-dominant group, followed by male-dominant (26), divided power (21), and equalitarian (11).

The notion of a male-dominant marriage where both parties agree to that power-sharing arrangement may be reprehensible to some, but it is not a strong cause of violence. When we compare the survey results in the preceding section with the Coleman and Straus results above, we see that 90% of men are non-assaultive (using the criterion of *CTS* Severe Violence) and that only 9.4% are dominant. In other words, the large majority of men raised under patriarchal norms are non-assaultive and non-dominant. Clearly, some individual difference factor must operate to discriminate these men from non-assaultive men.

If sociological/feminist analysis is correct, we should expect greater violence directed towards women in more patriarchal cultures. However, this prediction is not always supported. Campbell (1992) reports that 'there is not a simple linear correlation between female status and rates of wife assault' (p. 19). Female status is not a single variable. For example, in Table 2.4 spousal violence rates are shown for Mexican and US white populations (Sorenson and Telles 1991). Although Mexican culture is more patriarchal than is US culture, spousal assault rates are lower in Mexico than they are in the US. The higher rates for US-born Hispanics may reflect both stress and acculturation, as they exceed the non-Hispanic US white rate. For example, US-born Hispanic males may be more concerned with maintaining the Mexican patriarchal approach to family than are US-born Hispanic females, and this may create more conflict within an intimate relationship.

Table 2.4

Responses to question: 'Did you ever hit or throw things at your spouse?'

Sample	Size	Rate
Mexican	705	12.8
Mexican American	538	30.9
Non-Hispanic American (White)	1,149	21.6

Source: Sorenson, S.B. & Telles, C.A. (1991), Self-reports of spousal violence in a Mexican-American and Non-Hispanic White Population, *Violence and Victims*, 6(1), 3-15

Levinson (1989) found family-related female status (economics, decisionmaking, and divorce restrictions) to be more predictive of wife beating than were societal level variables (control of premarital sexual behavior, place of residence, and property inheritance). The exception to this finding was female economic work groups, the presence of which correlated negatively with wife assault incidence.

Campbell (1992) also points out that sociological/feminist notions that male sexual jealousy is an expression of a cultural belief that women are male property is not supported by cross-cultural studies of jealousy and wife assault. Except in extreme cases, jealousy varies widely between cultures and appears unrelated to variations in wife assault incidence.

Direct Tests of Patriarchy

Some direct empirical tests of how patriarchal norms affect assaultiveness have been reported in the literature. Yllo and Straus (1990) attempted a quantitative analysis of the relationship between patriarchy and wife assault by assessing the latter with the *CTS* and the former with state-by-state economic, educational, political, and legal indicators of the structural inequality of women. A composite *Status of Women Index* was created, with Alaska having the highest status (70) and Louisiana and Alabama the lowest (28). An ideological component of patriarchy was also assessed: the degree to which state residents believed that husbands should dominate family decisionmaking (patriarchal norms).

A curvilinear (U-shaped) relationship was found between structural indicators and wife assault rates, with the lowest and highest status-of-women states having the highest rates of severe wife assault. Structural indicators and patriarchal norms had a correlation of near zero. Patriarchal norms were related to wife assault in that states with the most male-dominant norms had double the wife assault rate of those with more egalitarian norms.

Yllo and Straus explain their data by arguing that high violence rates in states where the status of women is highest are caused by a breakdown of patriarchal norms, which results in males resorting to violence in order to bolster their threatened masculinity. This explanation assumes that patriarchal norms lag behind structural changes, thus generating conflict. However, no independent evidence to support this temporal relationship is presented.

Another problem with this explanation is that low-status states also have high rates of wife assault. The authors explain this as due to 'greater force being necessary to keep women in their place and because women in these states have fewer alternatives to violent marriage' (p. 394). It is not clear why greater force is necessary in such states (since alternatives to marriage are few), although it could be explained by viewing the finding as having two interactive elements: the man feels he must, or is free to, maintain the status quo of low female status within the relationship; and the woman, having few alternatives, remains and continues to be abused.

The implication of this study is that in low-status states women are more likely to be trapped in abusive marriages than they are in high-status states, and that in high-status states women feel freer to leave abusive relationships than they do in low-status states, thus increasing their partners' sense of threat. Hence, the higher rates of abuse at both ends of the *Status of Women Index*. However, while trapping women in a marriage through lessened opportunity should produce higher violence frequency scores within violent couples, it should not necessarily produce higher incidence scores. In other words, it accounts for why women could not leave an abusive marriage, but it does not supply an empirically supported motive for male violence.

A final problem is that structural inequality and patriarchal norms are not associated in this study. This is potentially problematic for sociological/feminist analysis, since although the patriarchal structure is frequently implicated as a cause of assaultiveness, it still must operate through the ideology of individual men. The slippage between structural patriarchy and individual assaultiveness exemplifies what community psychologist Barbara Dohrenwend termed the *ecological fallacy* (Dooley & Catalano 1984). Broad macrosystem features cannot predict the thoughts or actions of individuals nested within the system. Some moderating variables from the exosystem (community), the microsystem (family), and the individual's own developmental history are necessary in order to complete the predictive picture.

Smith (1990) also conducted a test of patriarchy by asking each of 604 Toronto women to guess their respective male partners' responses to a series of questions about patriarchal beliefs. He then correlated the responses with socioeconomic factors and with the woman's responses to the *CTS* measure of wife assault. Smith claimed that this method of assessing patriarchal ideology, in combination with sociodemographic factors, could enable him to predict wife assault. However, the responses that these women supplied for their male partners described a very non-patriarchal group, with the majority disagreeing with the patriarchal statements of the measure in all cases save one, that 'sometimes it's important for a man to show his partner that he's the head of the house.'

One conclusion that could be drawn from these attitudinal data (as with the Yllo and Straus data) is that the patriarchal structure of North American society has a weak effect on the patriarchal ideology of most individual men. Smith does not draw this conclusion. As he puts it, 'When all the socioeconomic risk markers and indexes of patriarchal ideology were combined in a single model assessing the extent to which these variables predicted wife beating, the combination of husband's educational attainment, patriarchal beliefs, and patriarchal attitudes parsimoniously explained 20% of the variance in wife beating' (p. 268).

Control and Violence

Another tenet of sociological/feminist thought is that male violence is part of a wider repertoire of control tactics used by men to dominate women. In the literature on feminist therapy (e.g., Adams 1988) emphasis is placed on male control and domination. However, in one of the few studies to examine controlling behaviors and psychological abuse, Kasian and Painter (1992) found that females were more jealous, more verbally abusive, and more controlling than were males in a sample of 1,625 dating undergraduates. Use of controlling behaviors and verbal abuse appears to operate in both directions in intimate relationships. If feminist therapy seeks to reduce control tactics in men who are in a bi-directionally controlling relationship and who use violence to counter feelings of powerlessness, a positive therapeutic outcome may be contra-indicated.

Feminist analysts are acutely aware of the sociopolitical powerlessness of women and have taken important steps to help remedy this situation. However, what defines powerlessness for a politicized woman and what defines it for a non-politicized man are not the same. For a man, socio-political comparisons with women or with a woman are irrelevant. What is experienced, especially in intimate relationships, is the power advan-tage women appear to have in their ability to be introspective and to ana-lyze and to describe feelings. Transference from early relationships in which a female (mother) had apparently unlimited power still affects male assessments of power in adult relationships (Dutton & Ryan 1994). Hence, assaultive males report feeling powerless in relation to their inti-mate partners (Dutton & Strachan 1987a).

One is reminded of Eric Fromm's definition of sadism as the conversion of feelings of impotence to feelings of omnipotence. While batterers may appear powerful in terms of their physical or sociopolitical resources, they are distinctly impotent in terms of their psychic and emotional resources – even to the point of depending on their female partners to maintain their sense of identity (Dutton, 1994a).

Gender and the Use of Violence

One other empirical finding that is difficult for the sociological/feminist viewpoint to explain is the US national survey finding (Straus et al. 1980; Straus 1980) that the use of violence within marriage is approximately equal for males and females. If violence is a last resort used to defend a patriarchal status quo, we would expect to find males using violence much more often than we find females using violence. However, Straus (1980) reports that the annual incidence rate for use of violence by husbands was only slightly higher (12.1 per hundred husbands) than it was for wives (11.6 per hundred wives). Straus found that, contrary to the expectation that each spouse would tend to cover up his or her own use of violence, rates were slightly higher when the computation was based on data provided by respondents reporting on their own use of violence. Indeed, Dutton and Hemphill (1992) found that the reporting of violence rates was unaffected by social desirability. In fact, for respondents reporting victimization by violence, the correlation is virtually zero.

Straus also found that wives were slightly more likely than were husbands to use severe violence (11.8 versus 11.4 per hundred), and that when acts of severe violence are considered (kicking, biting, hitting with an object, beating up, attacking with a weapon), the proportion of acts in which the woman was the only one using violence increases. When less violent actions are considered (e.g., pushing, slapping, shoving), more mutual use of violence is reported. As Straus reports, 'Contrary to our original expectations, the wives in this sample maintain their rough equality with respect to violence, irrespective of whether one measures it by incidence rate, mutuality of violence, degree of severity of the violent act, or prevalence of violence at each level of severity' (pp. 685-6).

Straus attempts to explain this surprising result by differentiating self-defensive violence (where women used minor violence and their husbands used severe violence) from other violence (where the woman used severe violence and the husband used only minor violence). To support the defence-of-patriarchy view, one would have to assume that female violence was primarily self-defensive. According to Walker (1989), 'Women usually use violence as a reaction to men's violence against them' (p. 696). However, Stets and Straus (1990) compared couples whose violence pattern was male-severe/female-minor with those whose pattern was reversed. They found the female-severe/male-minor pattern to be significantly more prevalent. For dating couples, 12.5% reported the female-severe pattern and 4.8% reported the male-severe pattern; for cohabiting couples, 1.2% reported the male-severe pattern and 6.1% reported the female-severe pattern; and for married couples, 2.4% reported the male-severe pattern while 7.1% reported the female-severe pattern.

Furthermore, the Bland and Orn (1986) study referred to earlier in this chapter did include temporal sequence questions in its assessments of family violence incidence. Of those males in Bland and Orn's sample ($n = 355$) who reported hitting or throwing things at their wives (14.6%),

57.7% said they were the one to do so first. In a sample of 616 women, of the 22.6% who reported hitting or throwing things at their husbands, 73.4% said they were the one to do so first. These data suggest that the women were somewhat more likely than were the men to escalate arguments into the realm of physical acts.

These gender data raise three issues that are important to an understanding of family violence. The first issue is that the sociological explanation of family violence as caused by defence of patriarchy is not well supported. If we focus on the *use* of violence, it appears that, within marriages, men and women both use violence as a means of resolving conflict, with women often being the first to escalate a conflict into the physical and also frequently going to a level of severity of behavior beyond that of the male. Outside of marriage, men are overwhelmingly more likely than are women to use violence (Straus 1980) against both men and women.

A second issue arising from these data is that any explanation of human action must apply to both male and female action. Some sociological views of wife assault have implied that patriarchy fosters violence because men are naturally violent (Davidson 1978; Dobash & Dobash 1979). It follows from this view that women's violence, to the extent it happens at all, occurs in response to male-initiated violence, while male violence occurs automatically (e.g., in response to unwarranted jealousy or unrealistic expectations about a woman's housekeeping responsibilities). Our view is that both men and women will use violence if they are rewarded for doing so and if alternative actions are not available. If this is so, why is wife assault a more serious problem than husband assault?

The answer to this question brings us to our third issue. Straus's data are for use of violence, and social explanations focus on actions. However, whether an action constitutes a social problem depends on its *effects*. The effects of male violence are far more serious than are those of female violence.

Stets and Straus (1990) reported that, in a subsample of victims reporting severe violence used against them (using the *CTS* definition) 7.3% of the women, but only 1.0% of the men, needed medical attention. Berk, Berk, Loseke, and Rauma (1981) analyzed 262 domestic disturbance incidents reported to police, using a scale of effects that ranked the severity of injuries sustained by the victim. When assaultive incidents are classified by injurious effects rather than by use of violence, women are the victims 94% of the time and men are the victims 14% of the time (as with the Stets and Straus study, a seven to one ratio). Berk et al. also report that data from the National Crime Survey, collected from a nationally representative sample of households, indicated that when victimization occurs between spouses, 95% of the time it is the woman who suffers. This discrepancy between the mutual use of violence and the unilateral victimization of women may have a distinctly simple and nonsocial explanation: greater male strength and musculature creates greater capability to cause injury (Steinmetz 1977). It is not known if wife-to-husband rates of severe violence would be as high if women had that same capability. In other words, given the different outcomes, do the genders have similar motivations for their violent actions? In any event, husband assault is not a major social problem because few males are injured by female violence. Wife assault, on the other hand, does produce serious injuries and physical risk.

Focus
The Meaning of Violence

Can male intimate violence and female intimate violence even be equated through 'hit counts?' Psychologist Angela Browne (1992) argues that equating the two is like equating head-on collisions with fender benders. When a larger/stronger man uses violence against a woman that is potentially injurious, and performed to threaten or intimidate her, its function and consequences will be different than when a women uses violence against the man. From this perspective, counting hits in terms of gender aggregates makes little sense. We have argued that the explanation of violence focuses on acts and not consequences. However, if the perpetrator knows the potential consequences of the violence, these become part of his motivation in being violent – part of what is called the function of violence. But if those consequences are unforeseeable, or if the perpetrator is too aroused and/or dissociated to think about consequences, then they may not be part of his motivation.

Interactionist Explanations: A Nested Ecological Approach

One of the points of consensus that developed amongst family violence researchers by the late 1970s was the need for more sophisticated, multifactor theories that took into account both the intrapsychic features of the violent offender and the interpersonal context in which the violence occurred. Gelles and Straus (1979) reviewed fifteen theories of wife assault and described the contributions and limitations of each. Sociology, psychiatry, psychology, and sociobiology have all made theoretical contributions, and, as Gelles and Straus point out, their contributions tend to be complementary rather than competitive. Sociological/feminist theories focus more on attempting to explain rates or incidence of violence in target populations, while psychological, psychiatric, and sociobiological theories focus more on attempting to explain the violence of an individual or group of individuals with similar qualities. These theories further subdivide into those that seek to explain expressive violence (the use of force to cause pain or injury) and those which explain instrumental violence (use of force for control over another's behavior).

Since so many varied theories have been applied to family violence, attempts to disentangle them are necessarily cumbersome and lead the reader into the realm of metatheory and philosophy of science. Even single theoretical contributions, such as Straus's (1973) general systems cybernetic model, is so complex that, in the twelve years since he published it, it has not been possible to conduct adequate empirical testing either to confirm or to deny its validity (see Figure 2.1). Rather than attempt to disentangle this welter of theoretical perspectives, we shall instead describe our own criteria for a theory of wife assault and then go on to describe how it might be developed and tested.

Social-psychological theories concentrate on the individual as a unit of analysis. Hence, our interest will be in building a theory to explain the behavior, feelings, and beliefs of the individual wife assaulter. This will involve a focus both on internal, or intrapsychic, events and on those interpersonal, or social, relationships which influence his assaultive behavior.

Instead of analyzing social relationships in the top-down fashion of sociology, which begins with broad macrosystem analysis, social psychology first determines which social relationships are of relevance to the individual whose behavior is to be explained. Theories are then built from the bottom up (e.g., from the context of the lifespace of an individual [Lewin 1951]). This approach allows social-psychological analysis to be sensitive to the sociopolitical context that shapes behavior while accounting for individual differences in behavior. Rather than arguing that a norm exists that allows wife assault to occur (Straus 1977a, 1977b; Dobash & Dobash 1979), we are interested in:

(1) How much violence towards wives is considered acceptable by various social groups and under what circumstances?
(2) How does this vary from one social group to another?
(3) Does an assaultive man's behavior fall within this range of acceptability?

(4) If not, how does he justify his behavior to himself?

(5) How do broader social values shape individual experience?

By originating inquiry at the psychological level, some fine tuning of sociological perspectives is possible. Straus, Gelles, and Steinmetz (1980) state that predictive checklists based on economic, demographic, and family power measures make too many false-positive identifications: they predict that many males will assault their wives when, in fact, they will not (p. 219). Straus, Gelles, and Steinmetz point out the 'obvious need to include data on the psychological characteristics' (p. 220).

In selecting these psychological characteristics, care must be taken to avoid the reductionism of the psychiatric explanations of wife assault. Characteristics should be chosen that have prima facie relevance for male-female interaction (such as power motivation) in intimate relationships (e.g., intimacy anxiety). In Chapter 3, we will describe how our therapeutic program for men convicted of wife assault provided a list of characteristics which we empirically tested.

The theoretical structure into which these social and psychological characteristics are fitted is called a *nested ecological theory* (Belsky 1980; Dutton 1981b, 1985). Nested ecological theories were developed primarily by developmental psychologists and ethologists (e.g., Tinbergen 1951; Bronfenbrenner 1977; Garbarino 1977; Burgess 1978).

Belsky (1980) integrated Bronfenbrenner's (1979) analysis of the social context in which individual development takes place with Tinbergen's (1951) emphasis on individual development, which he called *ontogeny*. Bronfenbrenner divided this social context or ecological space into three levels: (1) the macrosystem, (2) the exosystem, and (3) the microsystem. The *macrosystem* refers to broad cultural values and belief systems that influence ontogenetic development and the exosystem and microsystem. For example, patriarchy, as a macrosystem value, might influence both the development of individual expectations about appropriate levels of authority in a male-female relationship and the nature of social interaction at the family level.

The *exosystem* refers to 'social structures both formal and informal that impinge upon the immediate settings in which that person is found and thereby influence, delimit or determine what goes on there' (Belsky 1980:321). Hence, work groups, friendship or support groups, or other groups which connect the family to the larger culture represent the exosystem. Work stress or the presence or absence of social support might increase or decrease the likelihood of wife assault.

The *microsystem* refers to the family unit or the immediate context in which wife assault occurs. The interaction pattern of the couple, the

Figure 2.1

The Straus (1973) general systems theory of family violence

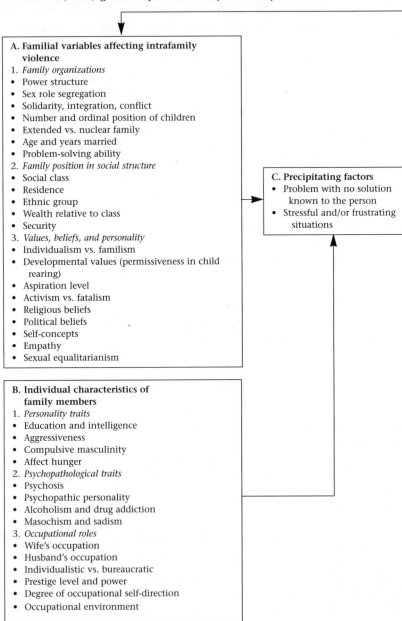

A. Familial variables affecting intrafamily violence
1. *Family organizations*
- Power structure
- Sex role segregation
- Solidarity, integration, conflict
- Number and ordinal position of children
- Extended vs. nuclear family
- Age and years married
- Problem-solving ability
2. *Family position in social structure*
- Social class
- Residence
- Ethnic group
- Wealth relative to class
- Security
3. *Values, beliefs, and personality*
- Individualism vs. familism
- Developmental values (permissiveness in child rearing)
- Aspiration level
- Activism vs. fatalism
- Religious beliefs
- Political beliefs
- Self-concepts
- Empathy
- Sexual equalitarianism

C. Precipitating factors
- Problem with no solution known to the person
- Stressful and/or frustrating situations

B. Individual characteristics of family members
1. *Personality traits*
- Education and intelligence
- Aggressiveness
- Compulsive masculinity
- Affect hunger
2. *Psychopathological traits*
- Psychosis
- Psychopathic personality
- Alcoholism and drug addiction
- Masochism and sadism
3. *Occupational roles*
- Wife's occupation
- Husband's occupation
- Individualistic vs. bureaucratic
- Prestige level and power
- Degree of occupational self-direction
- Occupational environment

Figure 2.1 (continued)

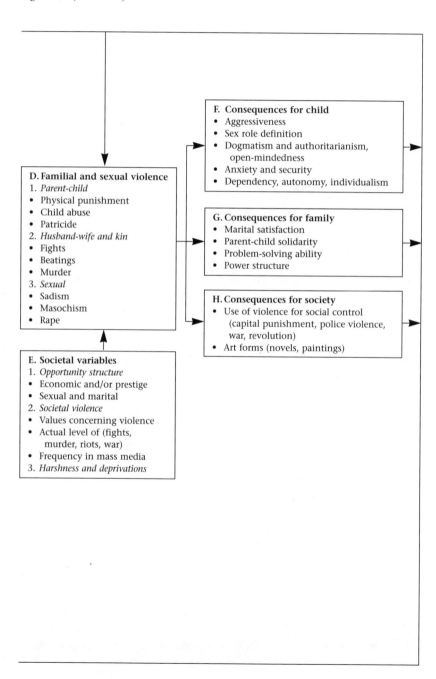

conflict issues that were salient to them, and the antecedents and the consequences of assault (how the man felt, how the woman acted after it was over) constitute the microsystem level of analysis.

The *ontogenetic level* refers to individual development and defines what a particular individual brings into this three-level social context as a result of his or her unique developmental history. By examining the interaction of ontogenetic characteristics with features of the social context, we can begin to make predictions about individual behavior patterns. Hence, two men may both have been raised with the same cultural beliefs, have similar work and support networks, and equal amounts of conflict in the home environment; yet one man may react with violence to this social context while the other does not. The basis of this differential reaction is sought in the different learning experiences of the two men: differential exposure to violent role models, different response repertoires for handling conflict, and different emotional reactions to male-female conflict.

Conversely, these individual characteristics are not viewed as existing in a vacuum; they require a particular social context in which to manifest themselves. Two hypothetically identical individuals (in terms of relevant behaviors) would behave differently with different micro-, exo-, or macrosystems. It is in this sense that the levels of explanation are said to be nested, one under the other. Table 2.5 demonstrates the types of variables associated with each level of analysis, the scales used in our own research, and the types of questions (re. causal variables affecting the likelihood of wife assault) these scales attempt to answer.

In predicting risk for assault, the profile of an assaultive male produced by a nested ecological theory borrows factors from all four levels. For example, wife assault would be viewed as likely when a male has strong needs to dominate women (ontogenetic), has exaggerated anxiety about intimate relationships (ontogenetic), has had violent role models (ontogenetic), has poorly developed conflict resolution skills (ontogenetic), is currently experiencing job stress or unemployment (exosystem), is isolated from support groups (exosystem), is experiencing relationship stress in terms of communication difficulties (microsystem) and power struggles (microsystem), and exists in a culture in which maleness is defined by one's ability to respond aggressively to conflict (macrosystem).

This hypothetical profile combines both sociodemographic and family interaction factors with psychological characteristics in the form of response repertoires, relevant motives, and anxieties. The combination produces a finely tuned profile of a hypothetical assaultive male while yet remaining sensitive to the social factors described by sociologists. One way of testing such a theory would be to investigate representative

Table 2.5

A nested ecological model for wife assault

Level of analysis	Variable	Scale	Question
Macrosystem	Attitudes Beliefs	Burt Attitude Scales	• Does man think women are enemies/adversaries? • Does man believe use of violence is acceptable?
Exosystem	Isolation Stress	Demographic Information Sheet	• Is man employed? • Is job stressful? • Does man use support group?
Microsystem	Couple conflict Communication pattern	Spanier Dyadic Adjustment Scale	• Is primary relationship rewarding, conflicted, etc.? • What is communication pattern?
Ontogentic level	Verbal skills Emotional response Conscience Empathy Learned habits	Assertiveness scales Test of emotional style Videotape analogue studies Studies of own explanation for own violence Childhood CTS Marlowe-Crowne	• Does man have communication skills? • Can he express affect? • Does he have exaggerated anger response to male-female conflict? • How does he excuse his violence to himself? • Did he witness use of violence in family of origin? • Is he telling the truth on the other scales?

samples of assaultive males with samples who were not assaultive but who shared a variety of common characteristics with the former (e.g., same demographics, similar degree of marital conflict). By so doing, the search for essential characteristics associated with assault could be more finely focused. The long-term goal is to ascertain which of the several ingredients suggested by a nested ecological approach plays the major role in determining wife assault. An ultimate objective is to produce a profile which, like a chemical formula, could tell us precisely what amounts or weights to give to each factor in assessing the likelihood of wife assault. Now, at each level, we consider some of the factors which might increase such a likelihood.

The Macrosystem

Broad sets of cultural beliefs and values relevant to wife assault constitute the macrosystem level of analysis, which has been the main focus of sociological investigation. Dobash and Dobash (1979), for example, focus on patriarchy and claim that 'the seeds of wife beating lie in the subordination of females and in their subjection to male authority and control' (p. 33). The ideology of patriarchy holds that male supremacy is natural and that control of women and strong reactions to their insubordination is vital. Dobash and Dobash trace the history of this ideology and show how it is buttressed by legal and religious dogma.

The impact of this macrosystem belief on the family unit was to increase the power of the husband and the Crown while disenfranchising large feudal households. At the same time, the belief that hierarchy was the natural order was encouraged. The patriarchal belief system presumably contributes to the incidence of wife assault both by creating in males the expectation that their wishes will not be opposed by their wives and by justifying the use of violence to enforce this expectation. Societies which regard women as chattels and maintain a strong double standard should, according to this view, demonstrate higher rates of wife assault (to the extent that male authority is occasionally resisted).

Macrosystem patriarchy refers to the broad-based structural features of a culture's ideology towards women. Other things being equal, it is generally assumed that cultures with structural patriarchy will have a greater percentage of individual males who hold patriarchal attitudes or beliefs than other cultures. It is not known whether the cognitive and behavioral aspects of patriarchal ideology occur concomitantly. Bugenthal, Kahn, Andrews, and Head (1972) report that a majority of North American males approve of the use of violence to achieve political ends; however, as discussed earlier, Stark and McEvoy (1970) reported that only a minority

(24% of North American males) approved of slapping a wife under 'appropriate circumstances.'

One relatively unexplored consequence of hierarchical systems is their influence on subjective emotional states. When someone who believes that he or she should be in a position of authority is challenged, might this challenge produce an enhanced arousal/anger reaction? Would the same conflict generate less anger if that person did not define himself or herself as an authority? We are suggesting (and will explore in greater detail below) that one psychological mechanism that may connect patriarchy to wife assault is that the male emotional response, as opposed to the female emotional response, to male-female conflict is likely to be experienced as anger. Anger does not lead inextricably to violence, but it may increase the probability of violent behavior (Rule & Nesdale 1976).

One final note on structural patriarchy: remember from our discussion of cross-cultural studies that, as Campbell (1992) reported, 'There is not a simple linear correlation between female status and rates of wife assault' (p. 19). Clearly, macrosystem level variables such as structural patriarchy must interact with variables nested under the macrosystem to fully account for the incidence of wife assault.

The Exosystem

Exosystem factors that could contribute to wife assault include job stress, unemployment, and the presence or absence of social support systems. Straus, Gelles, and Steinmetz (1980) reported that wife abuse rates increased with the number of stressful events a family experienced (as measured by a modified version of the Holmes and Rahe [1967] stress scale). However, as the authors concluded, 'Counting stressful events and relating the tally to percentages of violent families does support the theory [that stress increases wife assault] but it does not convey the reasons for the relationship' (p. 184).

Similarly, low income, unemployment, and part-time employment were also related to violence amongst spouses. The mechanisms that connect unemployment to wife assault include increased contact, greater likelihood of conflict over financial matters (Parke & Collmer 1975), lowered self-esteem in the unemployed male (Gelles 1976), and redirected aggression whereby frustration that accumulates from an unsatisfying work situation is taken out on the wife (Gelles 1976). These exosystem factors alone would lead to the prediction that economic downturns would be followed by increases in wife assault. An alternative view, which we will consider in Chapter 4, is that exosystem factors interact with microsystem and ontogenetic factors so that increases in unemployment would produce violence only in families with dysfunctional interaction patterns or in men with learned dispositions to react to stress with violence.

Dooley and Catalano (1984) point out the difficulty in testing the relationship between economic factors and pathological behaviors. Tests founded on aggregate measures of unemployment and pathological behaviors (such as wife assault) commit what they term the *ecological fallacy*: they attribute individual symptoms to individual economic circumstances based on aggregate data. Dooley and Catalano avoided this methodological problem by taking both economic and psychological measures on individuals as well as aggregate economic measures. Via this type of analysis they discovered that unemployment had a significant relationship to symptoms of psychological problems, but that the relationship was much stronger when the unemployment rate was considered in combination with a person's being in the workforce (as opposed to retired or a student) and with her/his education level. Unemployment rates do not affect everyone equally; they have the greatest impact on middle-status groups in the workforce (low-status groups already have high rates of undesirable individual economic events). Hence, these authors caution against interpreting behavior through a simplistic application of exosystem instigators.

Unemployment and job stress represent exosystem instigators that increase the likelihood of wife assault. Informal support groups, on the other hand, represent a potential ameliorative variable within the exosystem. By providing emotional support, corrective feedback, and so forth, friendship groups could prevent individuals from acting out their worst excesses. Isolation has been found to be associated with child abuse (Belsky 1980), which leads Belsky to point out 'the crucial assistance that members of one's social network can contribute in times of stress' (p. 328). Such an analysis, however, assumes people to be motivated to make use of support systems when under duress. An alternative possibility is that people with available social support systems fail to utilize them out of either a belief that they should be able to handle their problems on their own or the failure to perceive that they have a problem. An exosystem view of wife assault would predict wife assaulters to be either more isolated or less capable of using available support groups under duress (or both) than is the average person.

The Microsystem
The microsystem refers to the interaction pattern that exists in the family itself and/or to the structural elements of that family. Straus, Gelles, and Steinmetz (1980), for example, refer to structural elements like marital

power as being related to incidence of abuse. Straus et al. used the Blood and Wolfe (1960) power index, which measures who has final authority in six common household decisions (e.g., buying a car, having children, money spent on food, and so on) and relates this measure of marital power to marital violence. They found that acts of violence towards wives were most common in husband-dominant households, second most common in wife-dominant households, and least common in democratic households. The explanation they provide for this relationship is that violence is used by the man to either legitimize his dominant position or as an attempt to gain dominance.

Psychological studies of the microsystem have tended to focus on the interaction process as a contributor to eventual assault. Some of this research has focused on verbal and nonverbal communication patterns in conflicted versus nonconflicted couples (Notarius & Johnson 1982; Levenson & Gottman 1983). Gottman's intriguing work on interpersonal psychophysiology indicates that marital satisfaction is closely related to 'physiological linkage' during discussion of problem areas in the marriage. Specifically, conflicted couples communicate negative affect, reciprocate this negative affect, and produce parallel patterning of physiological responses between the spouses. Gottman sees this process as the basis for the subjective state of being trapped or locked into a destructive, self-sustaining interaction pattern.

More recently, Babcock, Waltz, Jacobson, and Gottman (1993) examined marital power as a microsystem variable. They examined three power domains: discrepancies in economic status, decisionmaking power, and communication patterns. The latter was assessed through using a behavioral observation coding scheme to observe couple interactions. The authors argued that dyadic, or interactive, power-communication deficits moderated other power sources. In other words, power bases (education, income, and so forth) and power outcomes (decisionmaking power) are moderated by power process (demands and withdrawals). All three forms of power were assessed in their study.

They examined couples who were domestically violent, maritally distressed/non-violent, and maritally happy/non-violent. Domestically violent couples were more likely than were the other two groups to engage in husband demand/wife withdrawal interaction patterns. This specific communication pattern was significantly correlated with wives' (*CTS*) reports of their husbands' use of both physical and psychological abuse. Husbands who had less power were more abusive to their wives. The authors viewed this as a compensation for the husband's lack of power in other arenas of marriage.

Another aspect of the interactive patterns of violent couples is that they seem to get locked into negative interaction cycles. Margolin (1984) has reported findings comparing physically abusive couples with verbally abusive, withdrawn, and nonconflicted couples. Margolin tentatively reports that physically abusive and withdrawn couples are quite similar in certain communication styles, such as low assertiveness and conflict avoidance.

In more recent studies, Burman, Margolin, and John (1993) discovered that physically aggressive couples showed strong, long-lasting patterns of reciprocal hostility and rigid behavior patterns, literally appearing to be locked into a type of coercion trap similar to those found in studies of parent-child interaction (Patterson 1981; Reid, Patterson, & Loeber 1981; Wahler 1980).

Patterson and his colleagues at the Oregon Social Learning Center have concentrated on reducing children's aggressive behaviors (tantrums, disobedience, acting out, and so forth) by altering parent-child interaction patterns. Specifically, Patterson focuses on interaction as a communication process in which expectations for behavior (and rewards or punishments for fulfilling those expectations) are communicated either well or poorly. One conclusion from Patterson's work is that violent intrafamily behavior has its roots in the mismanagement of banal daily routine (Patterson 1979).

A coercion trap develops when a child demands an act of compliance from a parent through engaging in behavior aversive to the parent (e.g., by whining or screaming). The parent provides punishment (by doing something that is aversive to the child), and the child (in response to the punishment) either stops its demands or acts defiantly by repeating the original aversive demand. When these three-part interchanges become a characteristic feature of the parent-child relationship, both parties are trapped into frequently using coercive interchanges in their daily interaction (Patterson 1981).

Some parents respond to the child's aversive demands with their own set of aversive behaviors, intermittently accompanied by a positive reinforcer. This periodic positive/negative reinforcement and punishment keeps the coercion trap functioning. Eventually, the reinforcement value of each person's actions begins to diminish (Wahler 1980), and a form of social insularity develops. Wahler reports that coercive interaction patterns generalize for some parents, so that they become multiply entrapped.

The main point of Patterson's and Wahler's work is that it represents the advances that have been made in interaction analysis and shows how aggressive behavior can be produced by dysfunctional interaction. Margolin's work applies such analysis to wife assault. Non-distressed couples in the Burman et al. (1993) study showed the same negative behavior patterns as did physically abusive couples, but they were able to exit this pattern much sooner than were the latter.

The research of Margolin, Jacobson, Gottman, and Patterson presents the possibility that assaultive behavior is a joint function of microsystem processes, ontogenetically learned traits, and hierarchies of responses to conflict. While microsystem process may produce conflict and anger, the individual's behavioral response to this anger (withdrawal, depression, aggression, etc.) may be ontogenetically learned.

Giles-Sims (1983) has also developed an interactive approach to understanding wife assault. Her model accepts that predispositional factors exist but views repeated violence as being a system product (i.e., a product of the interaction of two individuals). Giles-Sims views family process as evolving in stages. Stage one requires analysis of the following questions: How do patterns established in other social systems affect the family system? How does the commitment that establishes family boundaries evolve? What rules concerning power relationships and the use of violence are part of the family system in the initial stage?

Stage two begins with the first incident of violence and focuses on questions such as how the couple's interaction at the time of the first violent incident affected the possibility of future incidents. For example, to what extent were the goals of the violent person satisfied? How did the victim respond? Giles-Sims found that, of the 31 battered women she studied, 86% felt angry after the first incident but did not respond in an angry, retaliatory, or rejecting way; and she found that 64% sought no intervention and did not leave the house. Giles-Sims then goes on to analyze how this victim response feeds back to the batterer, stabilizing an interactive pattern that includes rewards for violence and, hence, intermittent violence.

The Ontogenetic Level

Ontogenetic-level factors focus on features of the individual's developmental experience that shape responses to microsystem or exosystem stressors. From an interactive perspective, both the cognitive appraisal of what is stressful and the emotional and behavioral reactions to the stressor are learned predispositions shaped by the unique experience of the individual. Hence, one obvious area of interest has been the wife assaulter's own developmental experience with violence in his family of origin. Straus, Gelles, and Steinmetz (1980) correlated *CTS* reports of violence by wife assaulters with reports of parental violence. They reported that 'men who had seen parents physically attack each other were almost

---

Case Study
Jack

Jack came into the group at age forty-one, having lived most of his life in small towns and working as a fisher. His early upbringing was dominated by one event: his mother shot and killed herself in front of him when he was three years old. He received no counselling and little in the way of explanation. (His father later told him that she couldn't handle the financially hard times that had beset them.) At age thirty, on an LSD trip, Jack saw blood on his arm, which he related to his mother's death. As an adult, Jack developed a bad drinking problem while working in the wilderness and sought treatment for it, winding up in Alcoholics Anonymous. When he started treatment for his assaultiveness, he insisted that drinking was the cause of his violence. We pointed out to him that many men got drunk without becoming violent, and we further pointed out that there were times when he was violent without being drunk.

Jack's girlfriend, Lisa, had been living with him for two years. She liked to drink too. In fact, it seemed that their favourite pastime was to get drunk on a Friday night. The problem was, when they got drunk, they started to argue. (Typically, they couldn't remember what the issue was; sometimes it was an event that had occurred years before they met, at other times it was Jack accusing her of being a slut.) When they argued they got loud and, eventually, violent. Lisa volunteered that she 'wasn't afraid of that son of a bitch' and had a bit of a drinking problem and a bad temper herself. She described Jack as 'going through phases: calm, tension build-up, alcohol, explosion, back to calm again.' She said she had the police remove him from the house about six times and had left him three times before he started treatment.

Jack made an effort to stop drinking and being violent but eventually relapsed. Lisa was still drinking heavily on Fridays and Jack couldn't resist. Finally, he decided that, if he was going to straighten up, he was going to have to leave the relationship with Lisa. He moved away two weeks before his treatment was to be completed.

---

three times more likely to have hit their own wives during the year of the study' (p. 100). Straus et al. are careful to point out, however, that many wife assaulters had not experienced violence in their family of origin (also, many men who witness father-mother assault are not violent themselves). The experience of violence used as a conflict tactic in the family of origin was one modelling source for learning violence. Similarly, being a victim of parental violence increased the likelihood of wife assault: males who were physically punished as teenagers had a rate of severe violence towards their wives that was four times greater than was that of those whose parents did not hit them. We will discuss this intergenerational transmission of violence in Chapter 4.

Finally, Straus et al. report the double-whammy effect: the men who both observed and experienced violence were five to nine times more likely to be violent (depending on the specific violence measure) than were those who did not. What the Straus et al. survey did not reveal was exactly how this modelling mechanism operates: Do sons in violent families learn to define potential conflict issues as more serious than do sons in non-violent families (i.e., do they perceive more causes for anger)? Do they react to conflicts with more anger than do those from non-violent families? Do they automatically use violence as a means of dealing with conflict? The answers to these questions await comparison studies matching violent and non-violent men with their experiences of violence in their respective families of origin.

The Straus et al. survey reported that people fought most frequently over 'money, housekeeping, social activities, sex and children' (1980:173). Assaultive males frequently reveal the emotional meaning of such conflict sources in the course of therapy. Money, housekeeping, and child-raising issues often involve beliefs and expectations about power and authority in the household. These beliefs may be shaped partly by macrosystem notions about family and patriarchy; but they also indicate a variety of expectations shaped partly by experience in the family of origin and partly by individual needs for power and control over family process.

Issues arising from social activities and sex often involve anxieties about too little or too much intimacy with one's spouse. Power and intimacy needs represent another constellation of perceptions and affective responses learned in the family of origin and, hence, represent another ontogenetic feature that could interact with stress and conflict at micro- or exosystem levels. A conflict event, such as a wife's desire for increased independence from her husband, could trigger vastly different reactions in men with different power and intimacy needs. In Chapter 3, we will examine the role of power and intimacy in shaping reactions to couple conflict; in Chapter 5, we will argue that ontogenetic factors can help to shape an abusive personality.

Explanations of Wife Assault and Their Policy Implications

What is done about wife assault depends, in part, on how it is explained; that is, on how it is seen to be caused. Hence, Elliot (1977), who views explosive rage as stemming from an 'episodic dyscontrol' syndrome, recommends pharmacological and psychiatric treatment. Shainess (1977), who sees wife battering as a personality problem, recommends counselling and self-esteem building for wives. Straus (1977a, 1977b, 1977c), who views wife assault as being supported by cultural norms which condone 'normal' violence, suggests a radical restructuring of society.

Caplan and Nelson (1973) distinguish between person blame and system blame. *Person blame* views the problem as caused by individual characteristics (ontogenetic factors), while *system blame* views the problem as caused by social system characteristics (macro- or exosystem factors). Person blame explanations lead to inherently conservative solutions: change the individuals who cause the problem. An example of person blame-oriented policy would be the practice of tertiary intervention into wife assault, whereby identified offenders (typically men convicted by the courts) are ordered into cognitive-behavior modification programs as a condition of their probation (see Chapter 9).

System blame explanations are more consistent with radical solutions, requiring a basic restructuring of societal institutions (such as the patriarchal family). Hence Straus (1977a, 1977b) calls for the elimination of the husband as head of the family in law, religion, and administrative procedure. This policy is described as primary prevention and is aimed at lowering the incidence of wife assault in the general population by removing one of its societal/structural causes.

Tift (1993) expands on what the magnitude of a macrosystem change would look like: the legitimacy of controlling others is repudiated and gender stratification and gender inequality are ended (and replaced by egalitarian social values), as are 'objectification, indignity and violence' (phenomena which produce anger and fear in intimate relationships) in the work setting (p. 161).

A mid-range policy between those of Straus and Tift is secondary prevention, involving programs that seek to identify high-risk groups through improved diagnosis and treatment. Since treatment typically still involves the alteration of individuals as opposed to the alteration of social structures, secondary prevention is philosophically closer to tertiary prevention.

If one were to establish an intervention strategy on purely pragmatic rather than on political grounds, then prevention would be based on: (1) an assessment of the major contributors to wife assault across all levels (individuals, family, societal) and (2) an appraisal of the ease with which any of those levels could be changed. A nested ecological approach lends itself particularly well to the first of these criteria, in that it does not decide a priori whether the phenomenon is inherently a person or system problem. If social-structural factors accounted for most of the statistical variance in measures of wife assault, then they would be its likely cause; if considerable variance were unaccounted for after relevant societal factors had been assessed, then psychological-individual factors should be considered; finally, if the inclusion of these psychological factors accounted for a significant amount of the variation in incidence of wife assault, then tertiary intervention solutions should be considered.[1]

If neither societal nor individual factors adequately accounted for variance, alone or in interaction, then social science analysis is not yet prepared to suggest policy. From our reading of the current literature, we suggest that the jury is still out on what constitute the major causes of wife assault, although we are getting closer. The Smith (1990) study cited above found that when all measures of patriarchal beliefs were assessed, about 20% of the variance of wife assault was explained. A study by Dutton and Starzomski (1993) cited in Chapter 5 found that about 20% of assaultive acts could be accounted for by a test of psychological factors. We are at a stage where we have the analytic capability and methodology to answer questions about wife assault; what is needed is the political will to invest in a solution to this problem.

Since wife assault is a topic that arouses passions and political opinions, a dispassionate analysis of the causes of wife assault is not easy. Early psychiatric explanations of wife assault occasionally blamed the victim for triggering the assault (Snell, Rosenwald, & Robey 1964). As a reaction to this type of explanation, feminist analyses balked at any line of research that attributed some responsibility to the assaulted female (Hilberman 1980). Consequently, examination of dysfunctional interaction patterns was discouraged because such an examination would attribute at least some responsibility to females.

Some females are responsible for contributing to some conflict patterns, but the use of violence to deal with the conflict is a response of, and hence a responsibility of, the assaultive male. Reid, Patterson, and Loeber (1981) describe some abused children as instigators in that they provide a high number of aversive behaviors that make parents irritable and that they are inept at terminating. Reid et al. found significant correlations between the rate of aversive/oppositional acts and the likelihood of the child getting hit. Reid et al. conclude that 'most children are at serious risk of instigating their own abuse at some time during their development' (p. 52). An instigation means any act or statement by a person that increases the likelihood of him/her being hit. Judgments of blame can be independent of instigation: we wouldn't blame a woman who refuses to run an errand for her husband, although such refusal can constitute an instigation. Our own judgments about what constitutes acceptable behavior enter into such determinations.

As the case studies we have presented show, highly varied causal patterns can produce wife assault. Stereotypes of assaultive males as pathological bullies are as incomplete as are the early psychiatric theories based on incarcerated samples of wife assaulters. Social scientists attempt to find common threads that link wife assaulters and differentiate them from other males. Therapists working with wife assaulters are impressed with the variety and idiosyncrasy of each client's background and use of violence. As a therapist trained as a social scientist, I have attempted to reconcile these two opposing views. The result has been the adoption of a theoretical framework that allows for individual differences in the client population, while at the same time seeking a common set of background causes. In the next chapter we will review this theory, and in Chapter 5 we will examine some initial attempts to devise a comprehensive new theory of wife assault.

Chapter Summary and Conclusions

Explanations for wife assault began by attributing it to a single factor (pathology in the male, biologically inherited dispositions to aggress when sexually threatened, and/or patriarchal norms), although accumulating empirical evidence now suggests multiple-factor or interactionist causal models. For example, a nested ecological model seeks to account for wife assault through the interaction of factors at the individual, microsystem, exosystem, and macrosystem levels. The most effective policy for diminishing the incidence of wife assault should be guided by an informed and systematic assessment of the relative weights of causes at each of these four levels.

3
The Social Psychology of the Wife Assaulter: The Theory

The core of sadism, common to all its manifestations, is the passion to have absolute and unrestricted control over a living being ... It is transformation of impotence into omnipotence.

– E. Fromm, *The Anatomy of Human Destructiveness*

Power and Intimacy in Male-Female Conflict

Against the backdrop of demographic descriptors provided by sociologists, psychological perspectives focus on the individual who uses violence against his wife. In the language of the nested ecological theory described in the last chapter, the psychological focus is on the ontogenetic level (where individual habits of aggression are acquired) and on the interaction of these individual habits with the microsystem or family unit. Clearly, not all men who assault their wives have the same etiology. In the next chapter we will examine some of the subcategories of assaultive males. In this chapter, however, we will concentrate on the development of a general psychological theory of wife assault. The requirements for such a theory are as follows:

(1) It must account for the use of violence in the majority of wife assaulters and show how, as a group, wife assaulters differ from non-assaultive males.

(2) It must originate with the individual and attempt to develop theoretical constructs from his lifespace.

(3) It must account for the development of wife assault as a habitual behavioral response and must indicate how the habit is sustained (and, by implication, how it could be changed).

(4) It must make predictions that can be subjected to experimental testing.

(5) It must be non-reductionistic; that is, it must explain behavior at the psychological, not the neurological, level.

(6) It must attend to the social context in which wife assault occurs.

Accordingly, to develop such a theory we began with the collection of some clinical hunches, or working hypotheses, about assaultive males that were developed in the course of providing treatment groups for men convicted of wife assault (see Chapter 5). These clinical hunches were not subjected to empirical testing right away but, rather, were compared to clinical descriptions compiled by therapists who worked with nonincarcerated populations of wife assaulters (e.g., Ganley & Harris 1978; Ganley 1981; Sonkin, Martin, & Walker 1985) as well as to victims' descriptions of batterers (e.g., Gelles 1975; Martin 1977; Rounsaville 1978; Walker 1979a).

Our objective at this point was merely to select explanatory variables that had some validity based on our clinical observations and some consensus support from the observations of other therapists. These subjective clinical hunches would then be subjected to empirical testing. Based on this approach, two potential explanatory variables were selected that met the following criteria: they occurred frequently in the therapeutic revelations of batterers and they were described in the clinical literature on batterers. These variables were power motivation and intimacy anxiety. In the remainder of this chapter, we will develop our theoretical rationale for studying power and intimacy issues and then show how they can be integrated into a social-learning analysis of wife assault.

Men in treatment groups indicated power issues through frequent mention of: [their need to control or dominate the female, their belief that female independence meant loss of male control, and their attempt to persuade or coerce the female into adopting their definition of how the relationship should be structured and how it should function.] Intimacy issues included sudden increases in the wife's demands for greater affection, attention, and emotional support; at the other end of the intimacy continuum were the wife's increased demands for greater independence from the male. Gelles (1975) and Rounsaville (1978) reported that for 40% of repeatedly assaulted wives, the onset of assault coincided with a sudden transition in intimacy, such as marriage or pregnancy. Correspondingly, Daly, Wilson, and Weghorst (1982) describe sexual jealousy, which might be viewed as a reaction to perceived relationship loss, as an instigator of wife assault.

Changes in socioemotional distance between the man and his wife can serve as instigators of wife assault. The unifying concept of socioemotional distance can serve to link instances of wife assault which apparently occurred as responses to ostensibly opposite instigators, such as increases and decreases in intimacy. An understanding of the interplay of power dynamics and how this relates to issues of intimacy and/or socioemotional distance can provide an explanatory framework which may enable us to deepen our understanding of men who are only assaultive in their primary relationship.

Power Issues

Although the consequences of the need for control and perception of control have been broadly researched (see, for example, Adler 1966; Bandura 1977; Baum & Singer 1980; Langer 1983; Perlmuter & Monty 1979; Seligman 1975), the need for control in primary relationships is not so thoroughly developed in the psychological literature.

McClelland's (1975) Type III power orientation describes men who satisfy their need for power (*n*-power) through having an impact on, or control over, another person. McClelland views power orientations as analogous to Freudian stages of psychosexual development and, accordingly, views the Type III-male as phallically fixated. Winter (1973) applied McClelland's Type III to males who compulsively seduce and abandon women. The Don Juan syndrome, as Winter described it, originated from twin motives to sexually conquer (or have an impact on), and to flee from, women. In such a transaction, a male purposely increases intimacy with a female up to the point of sexual seduction and then decreases intimacy immediately after. Sexual and power motives are intertwined, and ambivalence about intimacy produces a repeated approach-avoidance pattern on a continuum of socioemotional distance between the male and the objectified female.

Dutton (1985) extended Winter's analysis to males in monogamous relationships, arguing that the same combination of strong power motivation and ambivalence would operate to create strong needs to control socioemotional distance in order to move alternatively closer (through courtship, conquest, and impact) and further away (through emotional withdrawal, verbal criticism, or extramarital affairs). The specific behaviors involved in these control attempts may vary from one individual to the next as a function of idiosyncratic reward histories. Margolin (1984), for example, reported similarities in intermittently assaultive and intermittently withdrawn couples.

Stewart and Rubin (1976) obtained data consistent with this analysis, finding that college-age males who scored high on *Thematic Apperception Test* (*TAT*) measures of *n*-power were more likely to dissolve premarital monogamous relationships than were males scoring low on *n*-power. This dissolution was created by high *n*-power males in two ways: first, through threatening the primary relationship by forming other romantic attachments (which fulfilled the need for new conquests) and, second, through the generation of extreme control attempts in the primary relationship. These control attempts took the form of generating conflict through criticism of the female, and constant attempts to modify her attitudes and behavior, in order to have a renewed, discernable impact on her. Perceived change in her behavior was tangible evidence of such an impact.

High scores on n-power correlate significantly with frequency of arguments (McClelland 1975) and with a variety of behavioral indicators of aggression, such as destroying furniture or glassware (Winter 1973). In addition, high scorers write stories with themes reflecting adversarial sexual beliefs that portray women as exploitive and destructive (Slavin 1972). Whether these beliefs are a cause or a consequence of their adversarial behavioral tendencies towards women is not currently known.

As we shall report in Chapter 4, however, men in our own research who react with the greatest anger to scenes of husband-wife conflict tend to be men who report high degrees of verbal and physical abuse from their mothers (but not from their fathers). Winter (1973) had proposed that men who developed the conquest-abandonment Don Juan syndrome did so in response to mixed communications or double-bind communications (Bateson 1972) from mothers whose nurturance was mixed with hostility. This occurred, Winter speculates, in patriarchal societies – where women were repressed and reacted with anger towards the only safe male target: their sons. The ambivalence from the mother created ambivalence towards women in the son. In a study we report in Chapter 4, self-reports of feelings of both anger and humiliation (in response to watching videotaped husband-wife conflicts) were significantly correlated to both verbal and physical abuse from the mother.

Furthermore, as we shall see in Chapter 5, men with ambivalent attachment styles are also at risk for wife assault. Attachment style is believed by some (e.g., Ainsworth, Blehar, Waters, & Wall 1978; Bowlby 1969, 1977; Hazan & Shaver 1987) to be a lifelong pattern of intimate personality formed through interactions with caregivers during the individual's early years. Could attachment style explain the approach-avoidance process of the Don Juan?

If a certain amount of transference occurs from the opposite-sex parent to one's spouse, then we might expect sons who were verbally or physically abused by their mothers to feel quite powerless in adult relationships. Male sex-role socialization, however, teaches men that powerlessness and vulnerability are unacceptable feelings and behaviors (Pleck 1981). As a consequence, we might expect exaggerated power concerns in such men, along with mistrust of females and anxiety about intimacy with a female (except when he feels he is able to increase or decrease it as he pleases). Any perceived threats to male control over the amount of intimacy should produce exaggerated arousal, anxiety, and anger in such males. In Chapter 4, we will report a test of this prediction that uses videotaped couple-conflict scenes to present subjects with socioemotional threats.

Intimacy Anxiety

Pollack and Gilligan (1982) reported images of violence in *TAT* stories written by men in response to situations of affiliation. They suggest that while fear of success scores demonstrate reliable gender differences (with women scoring higher than men), fear of intimacy is a predominantly male anxiety. The working hypothesis we have adopted is that intimacy anxiety may have both trait (permanent) and state (short-term) properties. State properties involve increases in anxiety in response to sudden uncontrollable changes in the socioemotional distance between spouses. This distance we assume to be negotiated by both parties to a point that represents an optimal zone. An *optimal zone* for each person is that degree of emotional closeness or distance between themselves and their partners with which they feel comfortable at any given time. This comfort zone may be similar to optimal zones for interpersonal spacing (cf. Patterson 1976) in that, as with interpersonal spacing zones, invasions (too much intimacy) or evasions (too little) may produce physiological arousal. Clinical reports (e.g., Ganley 1981; Gondolf 1985a) suggest that assaultive males tend to label such arousal as anger.

Invasions by the woman (from the man's perspective) we term *engulfments*; evasions are called *abandonments*. Fear of engulfment can be produced in three main ways: first, by the woman moving emotionally towards the man through increased demands for closeness, attention, and affection; second, by the woman remaining static and the male developing an increased need for greater distance than is currently provided; and third, by shifts in formal role demands such as marriage or fatherhood. Ehrenreich (1983) has incisively described the sociological ramifications of the male breadwinner role and of male attempts to flee from its responsibilities and ensuing engulfment. Affective reactions to engulfment may vary but probably carry an admixture of anxiety and resentment along with a sense of guilt. When coupled with a lack of verbal assertiveness as a way to extricate oneself from engulfment, the probability of verbal or physical abuse may increase.

From the male's perspective, abandonment anxiety involves perceived uncontrollable increases in socioemotional distance. Abandonment anxiety could be produced by: (1) sexual threat or any other instance of the female moving emotionally further away (or re-investing her energy outside the primary relationship) or (2) the male developing an increasing need for intimacy but not successfully expressing it, so that a stationary female stays at what was previously an optimal distance but which is now too far. The consensus of clinical reports (Ganley & Harris 1978; Walker 1979a) is that, for battering males, acute anxiety accompanies perceived rapid changes in socioemotional distance (or intimacy) within relationships. Given the typical emotional isolation of such men and their exaggerated dependence on the female (accompanied by often traditional sex-role attitudes that tend to make them view their wives as possessions [Dutton & Browning 1988]), this disguised panic reaction may be viewed as similar to an anxiety-based aggression in response to the rapid depletion of any resource that is perceived to be both necessary and scarce. For assaultive males, the psychological and behavioral result of the perceived loss of the female produces panic and hysterical aggression. Formal redefinitions of the marital role can also produce shifts in intimacy. For example, motherhood redirects female attention towards the child (while simultaneously increasing male responsibility).

Many clinical reports indicate that males exacerbate abandonment anxieties by behaving in ways which maximize the likelihood of abandonment by females. Walker (1979a) describes the battering cycle, a process whereby assaultive males, having gone through an acute battering phase, experience guilt, remorse, and anxiety that their wives will leave. If the latter move to new lodgings, the men put them under surveillance, call them repeatedly, try to convince them to return, and promise they will never be violent again. Men in therapeutic groups who are in an abandonment panic idealize their partners and obsess over them and their mistreatment of them. Such men reveal the exaggerated dependency they have on their partners – a dependency which was previously masked by their attempts to make the latter dependent on them or by the exaggerated control of their partner's behavior through physical assaults and threats.

Sexual jealousy, especially to the extent that it involves delusions or distortions, may represent a form of chronic abandonment anxiety. Jealousy is mentioned frequently by battered women as an issue that incited violence (Rounsaville 1978; Roy 1977; Daly, Wilson, & Weghorst 1982; Whitehurst 1971). Recent studies (Clanton & Smith 1977; Murstein 1978; White 1980) have viewed jealousy as a mediating construct, produced by anticipated relationship loss. Jealousy produces a range of behavioral responses (including aggression and increased vigilance) and affective reactions (including rage and depression).

In many relationships, the degree of intimacy or socioemotional distance is a key structural variable that has a dramatic impact on the individuals in the relationship. Power and control over the degree of intimacy is especially important to the extent that (1) intimacy with one's spouse satisfies emotional needs unique to the primary relationship, (2) intimacy represents a major structural variable defining the form of the dyad, and (3) ontogenetically learned anxieties about intimacy transfer onto the spousal relationship. Perceived inability to homeostatically maintain the degree of intimacy within the optimal zone should produce arousal in assaultive males.

Finally, the question arises about individual differences with respect to the ability to tolerate abandonment. Put somewhat differently, are there some men who are more prone to abandonment anxiety than others? If so, is this tendency related to assaultiveness? How might this tendency have originated? Questions relating to individual differences will be addressed in Chapter 5.

Arousal

While arousal may be clinically viewed as a component of a state of anxiety, a variety of mechanisms operate to induce males to experience it as anger (Dutton, Fehr, & McEwan 1982; Novaco 1976). Male sex-role socialization is more compatible with expressions of anger than with expressions of fear (Fasteau 1974; Pleck 1981; Gondolf 1985). Feelings of agency, potency, expressiveness, and determination accompany the expression of anger (but not of fear) (Novaco 1976). Dutton and Aron (1989) found that males viewing interpersonal conflict scenarios demonstrated significant positive correlations between self-reports of arousal and anger. Females demonstrated significant positive correlations between arousal and anxiety. This finding is consistent with clinical reports that assaultive males tend to label many forms of emotional arousal as anger (Ganley 1980; Gondolf 1985a).

Males experiencing anger as a result of perceived loss of control over intimacy could behave in a variety of ways which do not involve the use of violence, including verbal expression, self-abasement, or discussion with friends. Behavioral aggression may be more likely for males who: (1) have poor repertoires of verbal-expressive skills and (2) who believe they should be in a position of coercive power vis-à-vis their wives. Hence, one way that macrosystem norms may influence violence towards women is through shaping the interpretation of arousal states produced in males by loss of control over intimacy with their wives. Our current research is testing the notion that arousal produced by witnessing intimate conflict may be experienced differently as a function of gender; males may be more likely to experience such arousal as anger, while females may be more likely to experience it as anxiety.

Some researchers have also suggested that aggressive or violent behavior may arise because of a need to seek stimulation in order to raise arousal levels. Berlyne (1967), Fiske and Maddi (1961), and Leuba (1955) have shown that a person will attempt to increase or decrease his or her level of stimulation depending on the prevailing level of input. Some findings consistent with this position can be taken from the research conducted with psychopaths. These are individuals who appear to be highly impulsive, who don't seem to learn from past experience, and who can't delay gratification. In a number of studies, Hare (1965a, 1965b, 1968) has supported the notion that psychopaths have less autonomic reactivity than do non-psychopaths.

Since low stimulation states appear to be unpleasant, violent behavior could occasionally arise from lack of stimulation (see also Fromm 1973). In other words, assuming that violent or aggressive people adapt more rapidly to stimulation than do psychopaths, they may have a need for stimulation variation to occur rapidly and with great intensity. They therefore may create situations of conflict, novelty, or surprise in their personal relationships in order to raise arousal levels that they find positively reinforcing. Viewed in this light, aggressive behavior could be motivated by a need to increase, rather than to decrease, stimulation.

On the other hand, some individuals engaging in violent acts of homicide and wife assault appear to be suffering from the effects of overarousal. Easterbrook (1959) has suggested that when arousal is low, selectivity is low, irrelevant cues are accepted uncritically, and performance is poor for all but the simplest tasks. As arousal increases, selectivity also increases, and performance improves because attention focuses on relevant cues while irrelevant cues are more likely to be rejected. However, as the individual becomes further aroused, the range of usable cues is correspondingly restricted, so that even relevant cues are ignored. The consequence of raising arousal levels beyond the optimal point, then, is an increase in the number of input sources competing for the individual's dwindling attentional capacity.

These input sources range from situational cues (such as recognition of a victim's distress signals), to cognitive processes (such as a consideration of alternative behavioral strategies), to physiological signs (i.e., the biological indicators of heightened arousal, such as increased heart rate and galvanic skin response). More important, there is a tendency for individuals to resort to stereotypic behavior under conditions of high arousal, stress, or threat. It is possible that these stereotypic behaviors represent those that the person has seen a role model perform. Below we shall see how witnessing parental violence increases the likelihood of wife assault.

Finally, Mandler (1975) has suggested that during heightened arousal there is an overall reduction in processing efficiency, resulting from competition for limited cognitive resources. Given that these attention deficits are created by high arousal, theory and treatment programs that emphasize behavioral choice may need to be augmented with stress reduction techniques, since a person in a state of high arousal cannot examine the alternatives or consequences of his/her behavior. Surprisingly, very few of the voluminous studies on decisionmaking have directly varied the decisionmaker's state of arousal (Abelson & Levi 1985). The implications of this notion for anger-management therapy – with its emphasis on choice and personal responsibility for violence – needs future consideration.

Our research emphasis on the psychological role of power, intimacy, and arousal can be integrated into a well-established theory of aggression. Social learning theory focuses on ontogenetic and microsystem factors which sustain habits of aggression. We turn now to the application of this theory to wife assault.

A Social Learning Theory of Wife Assault

Bandura (1979) has developed a comprehensive theory of aggression which posits that aggressive responses are shaped through the individual's learning history. His theory is relevant to the specific form of aggression called wife assault, although it was developed in other aggressive contexts. In this section, we will apply Bandura's social learning theory analysis to wife assault and then relate it to the concepts of power motivation and intimacy anxiety described in the last section.

Bandura's analysis focuses on three major determinants of aggression: (1) the origins of aggression, (2) the instigators of aggression, and (3) the regulators of aggression (see Table 3.1).

The Origins of Aggression

Social learning theory views biological factors, observational learning, and reinforced performance as the main origins of aggressive behavior. *Biological factors* such as activity level, physical stature, and musculature 'set limits on the type of aggressive responses that can be developed, influence the rate at which learning progresses,' and 'predispose individuals to perceive and learn critical features of their immediate environment' (Bandura 1979:201). People are endowed with inherited physical properties that enable them to behave aggressively, but the activation of these

Table 3.1

Social learning analysis of behavior

Origins of aggression	Instigators of aggression	Regulators of aggression
Observational learning	Modelling influences disinhibitory facilitative	External reinforcement tangible rewards social and status rewards
Reinforced performance	arousing stimulus-enhancing	expressions of injury alleviations of aversive treatment
Structural determinants	Aversive treatment physical assaults verbal threats adverse reductions in reinforcement thwarting	Punishment inhibitory informative
	Incentive inducements	Vicarious reinforcement observed reward observed punishment
	Instructional control	Self-reinforcement self-reward
	Bizarre symbolic control	self-punishment neutralization of self-punishment moral justification palliative comparison euphemistic labelling displacement of responsibility diffusion of responsibility dehumanization of victims attribution of blame to victims misrepresentation of consequences

Source: Bandura, A. (1979), The social learning perspective: Mechanisms of aggression, in H. Toch (ed.), *Psychology of crime and criminal justice* (New York: Holt, Rinehart, & Winston)

mechanisms depends on appropriate stimulation (i.e., instigators) and is subject to cognitive control (i.e., regulators or feedback from cognitive belief systems).

From a social learning point of view, males may be biologically predisposed to act aggressively, since they inherit greater musculature than do females. This musculature increases the probability that physically aggressive responses will produce their intended effect, thereby generating reward for the performer of the response.

Observational learning constitutes a major determinant of the acquisition of behaviors, allowing the individual to develop a conception of how a behavior is performed through attending to the modelled behavior, coding it into permanent symbolic modes, and integrating it through motor reproduction. Studies that indicate a higher likelihood of wife assault in a male population who witnessed their mothers being assaulted by their fathers provide data consistent with an observational acquisition of this behavior. Straus, Gelles, and Steinmetz (1980), for example, found that males who had observed parents attack each other were three times more likely to have assaulted their wives than were those who had not witnessed such attacks (35% of men who had seen their parents attack each other had hit their wives in the year of the study, compared to 10.7% of men who had not witnessed such an attack). As Straus et al. conclude, 'the scale of violence towards spouses seems to rise fairly steadily with the violence these people observed as children between their own parents' (p. 101).

Kalmuss (1984) found that such modelling was not sex-specific. Exposure to fathers hitting mothers increases the likelihood of both husband-wife and wife-husband aggression, and both sons and daughters who are so exposed are more likely to be both victims as well as perpetrators of violence against their respective spouses. Kalmuss suggests that exposure to father-mother violence communicates the general acceptability of marital aggression rather than particular rules about which sex parent is an appropriate perpetrator or victim.

Widom (1989) pointed out that support for the *intergenerational transmission* of violence hypothesis was limited by methodological problems. She specifically mentioned the problems of relying exclusively on uncorroborated retrospective accounts. To circumvent this problem, she performed a prospective study in which a large sample of validated child abuse victims (physical and sexual abuse) was traced for years to determine whether abuse increased the likelihood of later violence (Widom 1989). She found that the abused group had a significantly higher frequency of adult arrests for violence than did the non-abused group. This was especially true for male abuse victims.

The question remains, however, whether this is a modelling effect. No evidence exists that demonstrates that adult violence is of the same form as is the violence experienced in childhood. An alternative view is that early abuse victimization affects personality development and increases the risk for a variety of adult pathologies, including violence.

Focus

The Problem of Retrospective Accounts

Almost by definition, research on wife assault relies on retrospective accounts by both perpetrators and victims. With respect to identified problem populations such as assaultive men, who may seek to exonerate themselves for their violence by hyperbolizing the severity of their upbringing, these accounts could be self-serving. However, Dutton and Starzomski (1994) found that men court-mandated for wife assault tended to idealize their upbringing rather than paint their parents as being abusive.

Another problem with retrospective accounts is simply that people's memories are not accurate, especially if they are reporting events that allegedly occurred years before (Widom 1989; Yarrow, Campbell, & Burton 1970). However, from a therapeutic perspective, perceptions of experiences have more significance than the 'reality' of those experiences.

Finally, special problems arise when people are being asked to recall emotionally charged material such as childhood victimization. Although some reject the notion that repressed memories are real (Ofshe 1989; Loftus 1993), other memory researchers describe the concept of repressed memory as the foundation of psychoanalysis (Bower 1990). This latter issue raises the question of whether memories that occur during psychotherapy are of real or imagined events.

Social learning theory does not assume that any behavior observed will be practised. For an acquired response pattern to be enacted by an individual, it must have functional value and be either rewarded or at least not punished. The enactment of an acquired behavior such as wife assault depends, then, on: (1) appropriate inducements, (2) functional value, and (3) reward for or absence of punishment for performance (Bandura 1979). An appropriate inducement for wife assault, from the perspective of the assaulter, might be a statement or action by his wife that challenges his authority. The functional value would be the utility and meaning that an individual ascribes to using violence to restore that authority. Reward might include termination of an aversive stimulus (i.e., his wife's insubordinate statements or actions). Punishments could include anything from police intervention, to his wife leaving him, to feelings of guilt for his violence. If these punishments are absent, re-enactment becomes more likely.

Bandura (1979) suggested three major sources for observational learning: the family of origin (see Straus et al. 1980), the subculture or microsystem in which the family resides (see Short 1968; Wolfgang & Ferracuti 1967), and televised violence (Leyens, Camino, Parke, & Berkowitz 1975; Hendrick 1977). The mechanisms involved in each case have to do with: (1) explicit demonstration of an aggressive style of conflict resolution, (2) a decrease in the normal restraints over aggressive behavior, (3) desensitization and habituation to violence, and (4) a shaping of expectations.

Social learning theory also emphasizes symbolic modelling as an important source of response acquisition. Hence, any new behaviors introduced by salient examples (e.g., television portrayals of the macho use of violence, use of stereotyped responses to conflict situations) would contribute to a generalized, adopted role that integrated such responses.

Finally, social learning theory describes how aggressive behaviors can be acquired through direct experience and shaped through trial and error. Although modelling sources for aggression are universally present, successful enactments of aggression can rapidly entrench an aggressive habit. Patterson, Littman, and Brickner (1967) reported how passive children could be shaped into aggressors through a process of victimization and successful counteraggression. Passive children who were repeatedly victimized but who occasionally succeeded in halting attacks by counteraggression not only increased their defensive fighting over time but began to initiate attacks of their own. By comparison, passive children who were seldom maltreated because they avoided others, or whose counteraggression proved unsuccessful, remained submissive.

Wife assaulters could also learn to use physical aggression in an autodidactic fashion. The behaviors involved (e.g., punching, shoving) are not complex and, as Bandura points out, have been universally modelled. If a male uses these behaviors against his wife and is rewarded through (1) regaining control or dominance, (2) feeling expressive or agentic (i.e., acting out on the environment and taking charge in a male sex-role consonant fashion [Novaco 1976]), or (3) terminating an aversive state of arousal or upset, and if, further to this, he is not punished for using violence, then the likelihood increases of his reoffending in a similar conflict situation.

Although the likelihood of wife assault increases with witnessing interparental violence, the majority of wife assaulters never witnessed this. This suggests learning may not have occurred solely from their own experience in the family of origin but from another source. Kalmuss and Seltzer (1986) concluded from a transrelationship study of the use of violence that violence repertoires appeared to be learned in the first adult romantic relationship and tended to persist in new relationships.

Instigators of Wife Assault

Social learning theory holds that acquired behaviors will not be demonstrated unless an appropriate stimulus or instigator exists in the contemporary environment. Some of these instigators apply more frequently to acts of group aggression, such as *modelling instigators* (where one person performs the aggressive acts, thus serving to direct and disinhibit the aggressive actions of others) or *instructional instigators* (where a directive to act aggressively is received from, for example, a formal authority).

Focus
Football Games as Instigators of Assault

Part of the folklore of wife assault is that assault rates go up dramatically after football games. Some folk theories claim that when a team loses, its male fans take out their frustrations on wives and girlfriends. Others claim that when a team wins, the contagion of power feelings translates into increases in wife assault. Only one published systematic study of this question has come to light. White, Katz, and Scarborough (1992) examined all emergency-room admissions in northern Virginia over a two-year period. Admissions were counted for both male and female victims of gunshot wounds, stabbings, assaults, falls, hits by objects, and lacerations. The largest football-related significant increase (.52 or about 52% above normal) was for male admissions on the day when the local NFL team (the Washington Redskins) lost. The second largest increase (.38) was for female admissions the day after the team won. Of all effects on admission rates, the largest was for female admissions on New Years' Day (2.4), followed by male admissions on Thanksgiving Day (1.5). An attempt to replicate these results in Norfolk, Virginia, was not successful. No significant relationships were found between football and emergency-room admissions in these data. The authors claim that the second set of data were contaminated by the presence near the hospital of a large number of military men with affiliations to a variety of football teams.

For wife assault in particular, three types of instigation mechanisms seem typically to apply. These are aversive instigators, incentive instigators, and delusional instigators. In social learning terms, the motivation to act aggressively comes either from an aversive stimulus – which, by definition, is something we would work to remove – or from an incentive inducement: an anticipated payoff for aggressive action.

Aversive stimulation (see Figure 3.1) produces a general state of emotional arousal that can activate or facilitate a variety of learned responses, including aggression, achievement, problem-solving, withdrawal, dependency, psychosomatic illness, and blunting (i.e., self-anaesthetization with drugs or alcohol). Which response occurs will depend on two factors. The first factor is the individual's acquired cognitive appraisal of the arousal source – specifically, whether or not he can control the response. The active responses to an aversive stimulus – achievement, problem-solving, and aggression – follow from an appraisal of the source being controllable, according to this analysis. Note that aggression is viewed here as an active response, like achievement. In other words, it attempts to directly modify the aversive stimulus. If the aversive stimulus is viewed as uncontrollable, then the person tries to *blunt* it – to turn it down in volume – thereby reducing its aversiveness. For example, a teenager who spaces out or dissociates whenever a tyrannical father starts yelling is using blunting techniques. When blunting proves impossible, individuals attempt *withdrawal* (e.g., teenage runaways). When this last-ditch action is impossible, many lapse into drug abuse, depression, and learned helplessness (Seligman 1974; see also Chapter 6).

Figure 3.1

Relationship of aversive events to agression

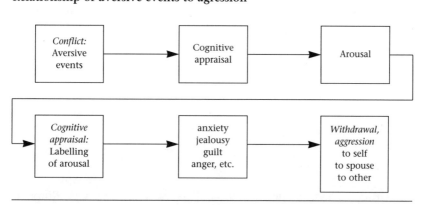

The second factor which determines an individual's response to aversive stimulation is his or her unique reinforcement history with respect to using aggression (or observing it used), including the rewards or punishments that accompanied such use throughout his or her personal development. Both the mode of appraisal and the mode of action are acquired by the individual's unique reinforcement history; they are predispositions that individuals have acquired and utilize under appropriate conditions.

The arousal generated by aversive stimulation has both a physiological and an experiential component to it; that is, when exposed to an aversive stimulus subjects: (1) demonstrate arousal via conventional physiological indices (such as heart rate, galvanic skin response, or pulse transit time) and (2) feel aroused and tense. In Chapter 4 we will investigate the resulting feelings of arousal and anger in assaultive males when they view male-female conflict scenarios on video.

The emotional consequence of such arousal depends on a cognitive appraisal of the instigator and on the situation (Hunt, Cole, & Reis 1958; Schachter & Singer 1962; Mandler 1975). Social learning theory has not placed great emphasis on the role of affect or emotion. Hence, anger is viewed as a by-product of aversive arousal that is not necessary for aggression, although it does increase its likelihood (Rule & Nesdale 1976).

Konecni (1975) postulated that anger and aggression had a bidirectional relationship, in which each could influence the level of the other. The emphasis of social learning has been on the appraisal of aversive events and consequent aggressive behavior. The relationship between these concepts is depicted in Figure 3.1. Several of the relationships operative in this model have empirically demonstrated relevance for the onset of aggression:

(1) When people are disposed to behave aggressively, nearly any source of emotional arousal can heighten aggression (Rule & Nesdale 1976; Tannenbaum & Zillman 1975).

(2) Aggression can be self-generated by ruminating on anger-provoking incidents (Bandura 1973).

(3) Aggression can increase anger (Konecni 1975).

(4) Anger can increase aggression (Konecni 1975).

(5) Aggression is increased by perceiving the actions of the other person as intentionally aggressive (Taylor & Epstein 1967), as threatening to one's self-esteem (Rosenbaum & deCharms 1960), or as causing one's own aversive arousal (Geen, Rakosky, & Pigg 1972).

(6) By varying the anticipated consequences, the same aggressive acts can either increase or decrease arousal (Hokanson, Willers, & Koropsak 1968).

Other relationships are implied by the model in Figure 3.1. Aggression, for example, is controlled by the perception of its immediate consequences, by prior anger, and by generalized arousal. However, any one of these factors is sufficient for aggression to occur. The other factors play a facilitating role. Therapists working with wife assaulters describe them as engaging in cognitive processes that are consistent with this aggression model. Ganley (1981), for example, describes wife assaulters as personalizing disagreements with their wives so that the conflicts are viewed as intentional (i.e., as intentional personal attacks on them). Ganley also describes the tendency wife assaulters have of expressing a wide range of emotions as anger, so that emotional states other than anger can lead to assault. Gondolf (1985) describes the *male emotional funnel system*, whereby a wide range of arousal-producing emotions are experienced as anger (see Figure 3.2). Novaco (1976) sees anger as serving a defensive function in that it overrides other, less acceptable, emotions such as guilt or humiliation, replacing them with a renewed sense of agency and control. All these perspectives view this affective narrowing as being caused, in part, by male sex-role socialization.

Figure 3.2

The male emotional funnel system (Gondolf 1985)

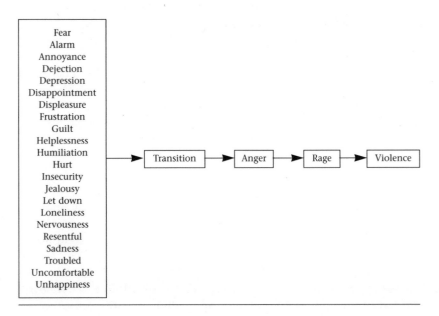

Social learning theory views anger arousal (see point 6 above) as facilitative to, rather than as necessary for, the occurrence of aggression. The arousal itself is cognitively based in the individual's appraisal of the situation. Its relationship to aggression also has a cognitive component based, in part, on the anticipated consequences of aggressive behavior. Novaco (1976) describes how the expression of anger has several built-in reward functions: it can be energizing, expressive, and lead to feelings of potency and determination. It can short-cut feelings of vulnerability and generate a sense of personal control. Many of these functions are shaped by male sex-role expectations of agency (i.e., taking action).

In primary relationships, these sex-role expectations may also define limits of acceptable male-female behavior by determining expectations of power, dominance, and the mode of conflict expression. Female behavior that exceeds those limits may be viewed as aversive. Hence, both perceived aversiveness and consequent anger expression may be shaped by sex-role expectations.

Social learning theory has examined physical assaults, verbal threats and insults, and adverse reductions in the conditions of life as three types of stimuli that produce aversive arousal. Its major contribution has been to generate evidence to refute simplistic notions that aggression in response to pain is merely unlearned reflexive behavior. Bandura describes how avoidance and flight are prepotent responses to pain when environmental constraints to flight are removed. Correspondingly, Toch (1969) found that counterattacks were evoked more by humiliating affronts or threats to reputation and 'manly' status than by physical pain.

Clinical reports of wife assaulters rarely cite physical attack by a woman as an instigator for assault, although a verbal threat that challenges authority and feelings of humiliation are frequent instigators. As with the population of assault-prone individuals studied by Toch (1969), high sensitivity to perceived devaluation and deficient verbal skills for dispute resolution (and for the restoration of self-esteem) may characterize wife assaulters.

Intimacy Anxiety Recast
We have proposed that intimacy anxiety is a by-product of male socialization that, in combination with other traits, could predispose males to wife assault. From this perspective, a man's sudden and uncontrollable changes in relationship intimacy with his wife could produce aversive arousal. In other words, if a man perceived his wife to be increasing or decreasing socioemotional distance beyond an optimal zone, and if he did not have the verbal skills to restore equilibrium, aversive arousal would

Focus
Anger and Humiliation

The *humiliating affronts* described above by Toch (1969) bring to mind the special relationship between anger and humiliation. We have described how anger serves an override function (Novaco 1976) to prevent less palatable emotions from remaining in conscious experience. Some researchers have noticed that humiliation is an emotion that seems to lead to extreme displays of anger. In his 1988 book, *Seductions of Crime*, criminologist Jack Katz argues that humiliation is an experience that makes us feel as though our identity is about to be lost. It carries with it a sense of profound impotence or powerlessness. Humiliation is 'a holistic feeling ... that takes over ... the whole body. The humiliated body is unbearable alive' (p. 25). 'Humiliation drives you down ... in contrast, rage proceeds in an upward direction. It may start in the pit of your stomach and soon threaten to burst out of your head. "Don't blow your top" and "keep your lid on," we counsel the angry' (p. 27).

Implicit in Katz's analysis is the notion that rage is a desperate attempt to preserve the self – that one's very identity feels at risk. This is an idea that we shall explore in more detail in Chapter 5. For present purposes, suffice it to say that the notion that an assault, verbal or otherwise, may threaten our very notion of selfhood and, thus, humiliate us, is beyond social learning theory.

ensue. Male sex-role socialization would increase the probability of that arousal being felt as anger (Pleck 1976; Gondolf 1985). With men who had developed verbal modes of expression for anger, that expression would serve to reduce anxiety and to enhance feelings of power. However, with men in whom this repertoire is not developed, or with men whose violent aggression has been rewarded in the past, violence is the most likely response to aversive arousal.

If violence resulted in reestablishing male dominance (at least temporarily), ending female verbal demands, and creating a feeling of male control, its use would be more likely in similar future situations. Negative consequences of the use of violence could include the woman leaving the relationship or threatening to leave, feelings of guilt and remorse, and criminal justice intervention (arrest and a court appearance).

Even if aggression only intermittently produces expected rewards, it will be a difficult habit to extinguish (Turner, Fenn, & Cole 1981). In Chapter 4 we will discuss some empirical studies that examined the relationship between power, intimacy change, and anger in a population of males who had been convicted of wife assault.

Adverse Reductions in the Conditions of Life

Relative deprivation refers to the negative conclusion reached through the comparison of one's present economic circumstances with one's past, with one's expectations, or with the circumstances of a relevant reference group (Turner et al. 1981). Relative deprivation is itself an aversive instigator that produces aggression in people who are so predisposed (Bandura 1973). Social learning theory would predict that discontent would lead to attempts to increase control in people with a history of personal success or efficacy. These people believe themselves capable of regaining control over aversive circumstances. People who lack feelings of self-efficacy respond to aversive stimuli with avoidance or withdrawal. They are prone to use passive responses to aversive stimuli, including substance abuse or television addiction. Recall Margolin's (1984) study (referred to in Chapter 2), which described certain similarities between physically abusive and withdrawn couples (in terms of communication problems). Hence, aggregate reductions in economic conditions (resulting in relative deprivation) would produce increases in violent behavior only in violence-prone individuals, not in those who had learned other habits in response to stress. As we shall see in Chapter 10, Dooley and Catalano (1984) found that economic downturns only adversely affected economically marginal groups. In these marginal groups, symptomatology occurred most frequently in those with passive habits (psychosomatic illness, depression, withdrawal). Only a subcategory of the marginal group indicated increases in intrafamilial assault. Taken from the perspective of this latter subgroup, however, wife assault increases with the degree of stress (Straus et al. 1980), as measured by the *Holmes and Rahe Scale* (1967).

Delusional Instigators

Social learning theory acknowledges that the perception of an instigator is highly subjective. Bandura cites a study by Weisz and Taylor (1970) that shows that presidential assassins are typically either delusional or have a bizarre belief system.

Some wife assaulters also have bizarre belief systems. One such system is called *conjugal paranoia* (*DSM III*) and is described as persecutory delusions and delusional jealousy that convinces an individual, without due cause, that his mate is unfaithful. The case study of Robert in Chapter 2 is an example of this sort of belief. However, determining what constitutes bizarre beliefs in longstanding interactions is very difficult and requires more than merely dichotomizing males into deluded and non-deluded categories.

Beliefs about sex-role appropriate behavior, power, and legitimate use of violence exist on continua. In some cases, the bases of conflict arise in differing male and female views on relationship rules. A man may have a traditional view of gender relations that his wife does not share, and, in this context, his expectations of her and his perceptions of her behavior may be a source of conflict (recall the study by Coleman and Straus [1986] described in Chapter 2). The instigators of aggression may exist on a continuum between consensually defined instigators (such as threats or attacks) and delusional instigators. This becomes obvious when we treat intimacy change as an aversive stimulus. What constitutes appropriate behavior in this domain? When is perception of threat real? When is it delusional?

Furthermore, the social learning focus on the immediate instigator prior to violence overlooks the potential forcing function of the aggressor's behavior in producing similar behaviors in his victim, whom he subsequently punishes. Kelley and Stahelski (1970) showed how in interactive games some people act in a consistently competitive fashion. These conflict-generators attribute more competitiveness to their opponents and view them as the cause of their own competitiveness, even though they themselves have produced their opponents' competitive reactions.

Therapists working with batterers (e.g., Ganley 1980) describe the batterer's tendency to project anger onto others. Clearly, batterers also produce extreme anger in their victims, which is frequently indirectly expressed (i.e., through emotional withdrawal or irritability), since direct expression carries a threat of physical retaliation. Unexpressed reactions to less extreme forms of abuse can accumulate over time, generating behaviors in the female victim that are then perceived as aversive instigators. It is important to stress that describing the wife as producing aversive instigators is in no way a form of blaming the victim. There may be extremely valid reasons, from her perspective, as to why such behaviors were produced. The term *aversive* refers to the perspective of the assaultive male. So, for example, if a man finds it aversive that his wife talks to any other man, this does not suggest that his wife is behaving inappropriately.

The social learning focus on the immediate instigator of an aggressive act and the categorizing of that instigator as delusional, aversive, or incentive, assumes a world of discrete stimuli and responses. However, in a long-term marital interaction, each person's response becomes his or her partner's stimulus in a continual shaping and reshaping of each other's behavior. Under these circumstances the simple, discrete categories of social learning sometimes fail. Determining whether one member of a couple is deluded or not may entail an elaborate analysis of the behavior of his or her partner and its meaning to him or her.

One other problem exists with the social learning view of wife assault: it treats all aversive stimuli as exogenous. In other words, it assumes that stimuli always originate outside the aggressor. In Chapter 4 we will see that wives' descriptions of assaultive males suggest that the latter may be reacting to *internal* stimuli in the form of accumulating tensions that become aversive and that generate a variety of such behaviors as alcoholic binge drinking and abusiveness. There is no provision in the social learning model for these internally generated states.

Regulators of Assaultive Behavior

As we saw in Chapter 1, about two-thirds of males who once commit wife assault repeat within a year. Straus (1977a) reported that, within a victim survey sample reporting wife assault, the mean frequency of serious assault was eight times a year. Keep in mind that about 2.5% of all men are committing these frequent serious assaults in any given year (see Table 1.1). It is these repeatedly assaultive males who constitute the most serious risk to their wives.

Bandura (1979) describes a variety of regulators or maintaining mechanisms that sustain aggression. These include intermittent reinforcement (Walters & Brown 1963) that functions to make aggression especially persistent. In the case of wife assault, when aggression serves to allow the male to regain control of a male-female conflict, thereby reducing aversive arousal, reinforcement occurs.

Patterson's (1979) analysis of hyperaggressive children documented the role of intermittent negative reinforcement in promoting aggressive behavior. In such families, children are inadvertently trained to use coercive behavior as a means of commanding parental attention or terminating social demands. The children's antagonistic behavior rapidly accelerates parental counteraggression in an escalating power struggle. By escalating reciprocal aggression, each member provides aversive instigation for the other, and each is intermittently reinforced for behaving coercively by overpowering the other. Patterson found that mutual coercion was a locked-in interaction pattern in families referred to his clinic for problem children (Reid & Patterson 1976).

Berk, Berk, Loseke, and Rauma (1981) dismissed the mutual combat myth based on injuries sustained by women from the violence of men.

However, mutual combat simply suggests that both men and women use violent conflict tactics, perhaps in the reciprocally aversive fashion described by Patterson. Straus's (1980) data support the notion that use of conflict tactics does not differ greatly by gender. However, even if the conflict tactics used were essentially verbal, if it were physical tactics that put a stop to the dispute (in the male's favour), then it is the use of the latter that would be reinforced.

Social learning theory argues that when this outcome (favourable to the male) occurs intermittently, strong reinforcers for using violence will exist. However, even if this outcome does not occur, the feelings of agency associated with the expression of anger would still have reinforcement value. Hence, from a social learning perspective, wife assault would tend to be repeated because of the variety of rewards associated with it. Only expectations of punishment would serve to stop the habit once it were initiated.

The Expression of Pain by the Victim

Two points of view exist on whether expressions of injury by a victim increase or decrease the likelihood of future assault. One perspective argues that because the purpose of aggression is the infliction of pain, aggression is reinforced by signs of the victim suffering (Sears, Maccoby, & Levin 1957; Feshback 1970).

Another point of view argues that signs of suffering function as inhibitors of aggression. This latter perspective argues that most social groups establish strong prohibitions against cruel and destructive acts (except under special circumstances) because of the dangers of intragroup violence. As a result of such socialization, most people adopt self-evaluation standards that adjudge ruthless aggression as morally reprehensible. Consequently, aggression that produces evident suffering in others elicits both fear of punishment and self-censure, both of which inhibit further injurious attacks. Empirical support for this position derives from studies of the effects of pain expression on assaultive behavior (Geen 1970).

Aggressors behave less punitively when their victims express anguished cries than when they do not see or hear their victims suffer (Baron 1971a, 1971b; Sanders & Baron 1977). Pain cues from a victim reduce aggression regardless of whether assailants are angered or not (Geen 1970; Rule & Leger 1976). When an aggressor *sees* his or her victim suffering, aggression is reduced even further than it is when he/she *hears* him or her suffering (Milgram 1974).

Hence, laboratory studies of aggression seem to indicate that expression of pain should inhibit further aggression. To what extent could such studies be generalized to wife assault situations? The degree of arousal and anger generated in the lab does not match that generated in genuine husband-wife conflict. And, as Bandura (1979) points out, when one party injures another whom they perceive to be an oppressor, pain cues from the injured party may signal the alleviation of aversive treatment. However, in cases of wife assault, expressions of pain by the female victim may not inhibit aggression when the man perceives her to be an oppressor or the man's arousal is so high that his focus of attention is shifted away from her (Dutton, Fehr, & McEwen 1982; Zimbardo 1969). In our section on deindividuated violence, we will examine a situation in which the expression of pain has no inhibitory effect on the assaulter.

Punishing Consequences

A fundamental tenet of social learning theory is that behavior is regulated by its consequences. So far we have examined the gains or rewards that might attend the use of violence against one's wife. We have also reviewed one consequence: expressions of pain in the victim, whose ability to regulate behavior is ambiguous. At this point we examine two sources of punishment, one external or social, the other internal or personal, which should function to limit aggressive actions.

External Punishment

Much has been written about the inability or unwillingness of the criminal justice system to punish men for wife assault (US Commission on Civil Rights 1978; Fields 1978). In Chapter 8, we will examine these claims to see whether or not stronger criminal justice action would deter wife assault (Dutton 1986a). For present purposes, our focus is on the effectiveness of external punishment in controlling aggressive behavior.

Bandura (1979) reviews the empirical literature on this issue and concludes that for external punishment to be effective, a variety of factors must be considered. These include:

• the benefits derived from aggression
• the availability of alternative means for obtaining these benefits
• the likelihood of punishment
• the nature, severity, timing, and duration of punishment.

Bandura concludes that, when alternative means are available and the risk of punishment is high, aggression decreases rapidly. However, when aggression is rewarded, and when alternative means of obtaining these rewards are not available, punishment must be forceful and consistent in order to suppress aggression. Even when this is so, control is only temporary. Functional aggression (i.e., aggression that obtains rewards) recurs when threats are removed and is readily performed when the probability of punishment is low.

These results have implications for the regulation of wife assault where external punishment for assault, in theory, could be applied by the wife-victim, by a friendship or kinship group, or by the criminal justice system. In practice, however, the wife-victim may not have sufficient power or resources to punish the aggressor; informal kin groups may or may not have knowledge of the assault and, even if they do, may be unwilling to interfere; and criminal justice punishment for wife assault is rare (Dutton 1987a). In any event, Bandura's conclusions suggest that in order for the occurrence of future assaults to diminish, alternative means of obtaining the goal that the oppressor normally obtains via assault must be developed. Attaining such alternative means are typically one objective of treatment groups for wife assaulters. Such groups seek: (1) to alter unrealistic male expectations about their wives, (2) to improve assertive communications as a means of non-violent conflict resolution, and (3) to improve the male's empathy for his victim and to instil in him processes of self-punishment for aggression.

Conscience and Reprehensible Behavior: Self-Punishment
Self-regulatory mechanisms such as self-punishment imply that people respond not only to the external consequences of their behavior but to internal reactions as well. Through intuition and modelling, people adopt certain standards of behavior and respond to their own actions in self-punishing (or self-rewarding) ways. These standards of behavior are the by-product of social norms and mores, subgroup influences, and personal experiences.

With regard to wife assault, tremendous variation in self-regulation exists. Walker (1979a) describes a cycle of violence in which assaultive males go through a phase of guilt and contrition about their violence – a phase which they indicate by responding to their wives in an exaggeratedly positive way. Dobash and Dobash (1984), however, dispute Walker's theory, claiming that for the majority of Scottish men, wife assault is followed by total denial of the event. Therapy with wife assaulters reflects this variation: some men who are court-mandated to treatment believe their conviction was unjust and their violence justified, others enter treatment filled with self-recrimination.

In Chapter 4, we report an empirical study of wife assaulters' personal explanations for their violence. This study confirms that a variety of explanations/rationalizations exist in an assaultive population. While wife assaulters have various beliefs about the propriety of assaultive behavior,

Bandura's theory makes the point that wife assault could stem from two generally different etiologies. First, it could occur because some men simply view it as acceptable behavior, are rewarded by it, and feel personal pride about their use of it. Sociological theories which suggest that wife assault has normative support would favour this etiology (e.g., Dobash & Dobash 1979). Second, it could occur because some men, even though they have socialized constraints against the use of violence towards their wives, violate their own self-constraints because of high arousal, anxiety about relinquishing control to their wives, and the perceived seriousness of the conflict issues. As Bandura (1979) puts it, moral (i.e., normally socialized) people perform culpable acts through processes that disengage evaluative self-reactions from such conduct rather than through defects in the development or the structure of their superegos.

Neutralization of Self-Punishment
When people violate their own self-standards, a variety of cognitive processes may result to keep negative self-evaluation (and consequent guilt) from becoming overwhelming. Self-deterring consequences are activated most strongly when the connection between conduct and the detrimental effects it produces are clear (Bandura 1979). To dissociate consequences from behavior, one can: (1) cognitively restructure one's behavior through euphemistic labelling, palliative comparison, or moral justification; (2) cognitively restructure the relationship between one's behavior and its effects on one's victim by displacing responsibility; (3) cognitively restructure the detrimental effects of one's behavior by minimizing or ignoring the consequences for one's victim; or (4) cognitively restructure one's perceptions of one's victim through blaming the latter for one's violence.

In the case of wife assault, some form of all these cognitive restructurings appears to occur for assaultive males (as we will see in Chapter 4). Treatment manuals (Ganley 1981; Sonkin & Durphy 1982) provide explicit directions for therapists to confront their clients' use of each of the forms of neutralization of self-punishment described above. Men in treatment for wife assault will frequently cognitively restructure their behavior so that it appears to be less violent than it actually was.

Browning and Dutton (1986) obtained Straus *CTS* ratings from thirty couples in which the husband had been convicted of wife assault. Husbands reported less than half the frequency/severity of violence that their wives reported. Men's recall and reporting of their own violence was frequently at odds with police and hospital emergency room reports of women's injuries. *Euphemistic labelling* occurs when a serious assault

Figure 3.3

Mechanisms through which behavior is disengaged from self-evaluative consequences at different points in the behavior process (Bandura 1979)

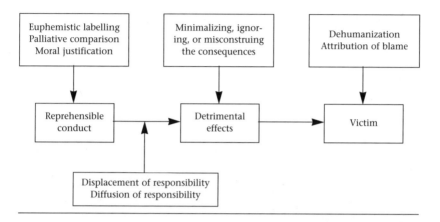

is described in non-serious terms (i.e., 'The night we had our little problem,' 'You know, when I pushed her'). *Palliative comparison* in treatment groups is also frequent. Some convicted wife assaulters will volunteer the observation that all men beat their wives and that only they themselves had the misfortune to get caught. *Moral justification* takes the form that the nagging, infidelity, or other supposedly unacceptable behavior of their wives needed to be brought into line. Recall the medieval emphasis on the 'need' women had to be punished (see Chapter 1).

For wife assaulters, the connection between their own actions and the injurious consequences to their victims is obscured by displacing responsibility. Some therapists feel that assaultive men sometimes get drunk in order to get violent. Alcohol is involved in 30% to 56% of domestic dispute calls attended by police, but in only 10% of these cases did the complainants allege that their spouses were drunk (Bard & Zacker 1974). The role of alcohol in wife assault is not completely clear; although it is a disinhibitor and, thus, can be viewed as having a pharmacological effect that contributes to violence, it is also *known* to be a disinhibitor and, hence, can be chosen by men who want to act out or to be violent. Marlatt and Rohsenow (1980) have shown that expectations about the disinhibiting effect of alcohol usage are as powerful as is the pharmacological effect of the drug itself. Also, both alcohol abuse and wife assault may be correlated symptoms of a type of personality disorder that generates intermittent dysphoric states (or, in social learning terms, internal aversive stimuli).

Focus
Neutralizing Self-Statements

(1) *Moral justification*: 'The Bible (Koran, etc.) says I am the head of the household and she must submit.'
(2) *Palliative comparison*: 'I'm not a real batterer because I never used a weapon.'
(3) *Displacement of responsibility*: 'I was so drunk, I didn't know what I was doing.'
(4) *Diffusion of responsibility*: 'It happens in every marriage.' 'It's no big deal in my culture.'
(5) *Dehumanizing the victim*: 'My old lady deserves everything I dish out.'
(6) *Attribution of blame to the victim*: 'She drove me to it.' 'If she didn't keep nagging me, none of this would have happened.'
(7) *Minimization/selective memory*: 'I got mad at her only once.'

Source: Ganley (1989)

The seriousness of injuries and psychological trauma to their victims are frequently overlooked by assaulters; that is, assaulters often restructure the consequences of their assaults. The assaulter's action is rendered less reprehensible by his denying to himself that it caused pain and distress to his victim. Finally, the victim is frequently said to have caused the man's violence through her own actions. Ganley and Harris (1978), Walker (1979a, 1979b), and Dutton and Painter (1980) all report the excessive minimizing of personal responsibility that goes on during the first month of therapy with assaultive males. Often, this is accompanied by fixating on some real or imagined aspect of the wife's behavior that is described by the batterer as having caused his violence.

As we shall see in Chapter 9, part of the traditional therapeutic approach to anger management with respect to battering males (Novaco 1975; Ganley & Harris 1978) is to demonstrate to them that, even if their wives do the things that they claim make them violent, it is *their* choice to so interpret their wives' behavior, *their* choice to label the resulting arousal as anger, and *their* decision to express this anger by the use of violence. In short, the therapy seeks to establish and to strengthen a sense of personal responsibility that has been diminished by rationalization and lack of awareness. A major objective of treatment is to confront and to alter the neutralization of self-punishment.

Severe Wife Assault and Deindividuated Violence[1]

Particularly severe forms of violence sometimes appear to violate the reward-and-punishment rules that typically control our behavior in the fashion described above. Normal constraints, such as pleas from the victim, do not operate to reduce aggression, and the aggressor launches into a self-reinforced series of progressively more destructive actions that are extremely difficult to terminate. These episodes, termed *deindividuated violence* by social psychologist Phillip Zimbardo (1969), appear to occur in the most extreme cases of wife assault (often termed *battering*).

These most severe cases of wife assault generally involve, on the part of the batterer, an inability to recall the actual assaultive incident, even after shame and embarrassment about reporting it have subsided. Reconstruction of the assaultive incident from interviews with the wife and from police and medical testimony depict the male as being in a highly aroused state of rage, unresponsive to begging or pleading, and, in some cases, beating her until he was too exhausted to continue. The men usually remember the events leading up to the actual battering as well as its aftermath (some were shocked and sickened by what they had done) but not the intervening battering. Several therapists working with assaultive husbands have reported this phenomenon (Ganley 1980; Walker 1979; Martin 1977).

Walker (1978) described the batterer's uncontrollable destructiveness and lack of responsiveness to cues from the victim. Ganley (1980) has confirmed the tendency of women victims to have comprehensive recall of the battering incident (since their lives depended on being able to defend themselves) and of the male batterers to blank out on it.

The descriptions of acute battering incidents provided by Walker and Ganley's interviews with victims as well as by our own (Dutton & Painter 1980, 1981) appears to fit Zimbardo's (1969) analysis of deindividuated aggression. Certain key features of such violence stand out in both descriptions: (1) escalating violence that increases to a point of frenzy, that (2) cannot be terminated by the victim, and that (3) ends only when the aggressor is exhausted. Furthermore, several of the antecedent conditions that Zimbardo postulates as increasing the likelihood of deindividuated violence are present in severe wife battering: anonymity from public purview, diminished personal responsibility, generalized arousal, and altered states of consciousness.

The memory lapse on the part of the batterer might be explicable by another feature of deindividuated aggression: the shift in control over the batterer's behaviour from external, environmental stimuli to internal, proprioceptive (physical) stimuli. With the exception of being able to locate and direct violence towards the victim, an individual in a deindividuated state is attuned to and registering only stimuli from within. What has not been stored in memory cannot be retrieved, hence the persistent inability to remember external details of the battering incident.

Zimbardo (1969) depicts both sexual and aggressive behavior as being stringently controlled by social norms that have evolved to regulate behavior that could affect the size and longevity of social groups. For individuals living in such groups, both external normative control and internal control constitute the essentials of what we commonly refer to as socialization. Hence, we learn to inhibit inappropriate sexual and aggressive behavior due to our fear of receiving negative responses from a group that satisfies our social needs. The impulses to be sexual or aggressive, however, do not disappear, and their expression can be facilitated by any psychological states or social circumstances that temporarily minimize social controls.

Zimbardo's position is that proscribed emotional, sexual, and aggressive behavioral expressions are inherently pleasurable (Zimbardo 1969). Such expressions are 'self-reinforcing; therefore, once initiated, they should be self-maintaining and perpetuating until a marked change occurs in the state of the organism (e.g., exhaustion, emotional breakdown) or in environmental conditions (e.g., a weapon breaks)' (Zimbardo 1969:252). Zimbardo's innovative combination of psychoanalytic assumptions, social learning behavioral analysis, and social psychology produced a perspective for linking antecedent conditions with subsequent impulsive behavior; although, as we shall see below, the evidence for the assumption that the expression of violence is inherently pleasurable is questionable.

As a social psychologist, Zimbardo has been primarily concerned with those social conditions that might decrease social controls over proscribed behavior. One of these social conditions is group size. People in crowds, or who are disguised, masked, or indistinguishable from others, are more likely to perform impulsive expressions of proscribed behaviors than are individuals who are identifiable. Citing riots and mob violence as examples, Zimbardo speculates that crowds provide anonymity, action models, and a reduced sense of personal responsibility for ensuing behavior. Subsequent research on deindividuation has tended to focus on such group variables and their effect on aggression (Diener 1976; Jorgenson & Dukes 1976; Maslach 1974; Watson 1973).

At first glance, wife battering appears to depart from the group-induced violence that Zimbardo describes, yet the intrapsychic input variables that increase the likelihood of deindividuated violence are all present in wife battering situations. The effect of anonymity is to reduce social control simply because an anonymous individual cannot be identified for reprisal or sanction. Immersion in a group is not, of course, the only way to produce anonymity. Anything that severs our connection to the everyday trappings of our social role (such as travelling in a foreign country), feelings of alienation from one's self and others, or any other circumstances that make one feel unidentifiable could produce anonymity.

While wife battering usually occurs in the home, where, in one sense, the batterer should feel most connected to symbols of his identity, this is also the place where he is most free of public scrutiny and surveillance. In many jurisdictions, policy, attitudes, and beliefs make police less than eager to respond to family dispute calls (see Chapter 8) (Levens & Dutton 1977; Dutton 1977; Loving & Farmer 1980). Furthermore, public attitudes about the privacy of the family (see, for example, Steiner 1981) as well as the victim's own shame (which often prevents her from reporting the assault [Dutton & Painter 1980, 1981]) may contribute to a wife assaulter's feeling of anonymity. Belsky (1980) reports that family isolation (i.e., absence of informal support networks) is associated with the incidence of assault. Isolation also contributes to anonymity, since, by definition, it connotes an absence of others – others who might make norms salient and who might judge and individuate the batterer. Hence, one could argue that anonymity, as a central input variable for deindividuated violence, is present in most cases of wife battering.

The action model supplied by the group or crowd can often be supplanted for wife batterers by role modelling in their families of origin. As stated previously, studies profiling batterers report increased likelihood of wife assault for men who have witnessed father-mother violence (Straus, Gelles, & Steinmetz 1980; Kalmuss 1984).

As we have argued, only a minimal opportunity for learning proscribed behaviors is required in order to facilitate their expression. If the expression of sexual or aggressive behavior is self-rewarding, such behavior will in all likelihood be repeated and amplified. Indeed, evidence suggests that violence tends to escalate from initial discrete incidents until it becomes serious enough to warrant outside intervention (Wilt & Breedlove 1977; Dutton & Painter 1980; Jaffe 1982). This occurs because of self-rewarding mechanisms, such as feelings of power, agency, and catharsis (Novaco 1975, 1976), that may augment proprioceptive feedback conducive to the expression of accelerated aggression.

Are some individuals more prone to deindividuated violence states than are others? In Chapter 5, we will examine the notion that men with cyclical or phasic personalities build up tension and intermittently explode in a type of deindividuated rage, typically in response to internal aversive cues.

Personal Responsibility

The reduced sense of personal responsibility for the consequences of proscribed violence, although aided by immersion in a group, also can occur intrapsychically either through externalizing the violence to the use of alcohol or by blaming the victim. Zimbardo suggests that any drug that alters consciousness will tend to increase the likelihood of deindividuated behavior by diminishing cognitive control. Alcohol, therefore, may serve to diminish personal responsibility in acts of wife assault, as the aggressor often blames his violence on drunkenness despite incidents of being violent while sober (Dutton & Painter 1980; Rounsaville 1978). The criminal justice system often inadvertently reinforces this excuse by placing undue emphasis on alcohol usage per se (see Bard & Zacker 1974; Levens & Dutton 1980). Diminished responsibility is also brought about by blaming the victim of the assault, as we described in the last section.

Interestingly, Diener (1976) posits that lessened self-awareness may be the crucial psychological construct that produces deindividuated behavior. While group or crowd situations may contribute to lessened self-awareness, they are certainly not essential to producing it. The cognitive mechanisms that neutralize self-punishment can also operate to diminish self-awareness.

Arousal and Deindividuated Violence

A final major antecedent variable posited by Zimbardo is arousal that 'increases the likelihood that gross "agitated" behavior will be released, and that cues in the situation which might inhibit responding will not be noticed' (Zimbardo 1969:257). Again, Zimbardo cites social bases for the generation of extreme arousal, while our own research investigates arousal generated within intimate relationships as a function of perceived uncontrollable intimacy change. Hence, we would argue that the expression of extreme anger in intimate relationships is supported by a variety of mechanisms in addition to those posited by Zimbardo. Furthermore, as we have discussed, high arousal states tend to narrowly focus attention and to simplify behavioral repertoires.

Alternative Sources of Reinforcement for Deindividuated Battering

Zimbardo sees the deindividuated expression of violence as originating when some crucial conjunction of anonymity, arousal, and diminished responsibility occurs and, presumably, when some instigating stimulus is perceived. According to Zimbardo, once normative control is lost, the aggressor focuses on pleasurable proprioceptive feedback from his own body, which results in 'a self-reinforcing amplification process [being] generated. Once begun, each subsequent response should have progressively shorter latencies, coupled with greater vigour' (Zimbardo 1969:259). Blows, stabs, trigger pulls, or other acts of violence accelerate, coming faster and faster and with greater vigour up to the point of exhaustion. Of course, if this is true, we should expect to see this pattern occur most frequently with actions that provide the most proprioceptive feedback (e.g., hitting a pillow from an overhead position provides greater proprioceptive feedback than does pulling a trigger). If, on the other hand, the environmental result of such behavior is more important than Zimbardo speculates, then actions that produce disproportionate reactions (rather than actions which have the greatest proprioceptive feedback) should produce the self-accelerating pattern (e.g., pulling a trigger to shoot out plate-glass windows should be more rewarding than smashing a pillow [see, for example, Allen & Greenberger 1978]). Zimbardo's own empirical test of portions of his theory provided little opportunity for proprioceptive feedback, as subjects merely pushed a shock button. However, later demonstrations of deindividuated vandalism led him to conclude that ideal conditions are those in which the physical act is energized and expressive, thus producing considerable noncognitive feedback. It is pleasurable to behave at a purely sensual, physical, unthinking level – whether one is making love or making war (Zimbardo 1969).

This may indeed be the case. However, it is our contention that, in addition to proprioceptive feedback, there are many other reinforcers for the expression of aggression. Batterers in therapeutic groups report feelings of power, even sexual arousal, following battering incidents, bringing to mind Eric Fromm's statement that sadism (physical control of another) is an attempt to convert feelings of impotence into a temporary feeling of omnipotence (Fromm 1973).

Novaco (1976) has outlined a variety of reinforcers which are built into anger expression (e.g., feelings of energy, expressiveness, and potentiation), all of which are consonant with the romanticizing of violence and with traditional male sex-role values. In addition, anger serves the defensive function of short-circuiting anxious feelings of vulnerability. Thus, proprioceptive feedback is hardly the only explanation for what might cause and/or determine accelerating aggression.

As is often the case when new phenomena are applied to theory, the latter provides new insights into the former and vice versa. Zimbardo's notion of deindividuated aggression makes a valuable contribution towards the understanding of extreme wife assault, but the notion of deindividuation itself seems to require refinement, particularly in view of the reinforcers which operate in the expression of such assault. Our own research has investigated the role of arousal (produced by rapid, uncontrollable changes in intimacy) as an instigator of aggression. In the next section we report these studies.

Chapter Summary and Conclusions

In this chapter we have attempted to apply social learning theory to the phenomenon of wife assault. As was seen in the nested ecological perspective developed in Chapter 2, the emphasis of social learning theory is, primarily, on ontogenetic development and, secondarily, on the interaction of ontogenetic with microcosmic factors. Considerable basic research on aggression, which has tested predictions based on a social learning model, were reported. Although this research provided a rich perspective on the etiology of wife assault, very little of it was focused on the specific context of intimate violence. While social learning analyses have been used in developing treatment programs for wife assaulters (Ganley 1981), they have not as yet generated substantial empirical studies. In the next chapter, we report in detail on what is being done to rectify this: intimacy and power are systematically studied as constituting elements of aversive stimuli, and the consequences for anger responses in assaultive males are compared to a non-assaultive control group. Also, the cognitive machinations that constitute the neutralization of self-punishment are examined in order to ascertain how repeat wife assaulters sustain a habit of violence.

4
The Social Psychology of the Wife Assaulter: The Research Studies

Sit down before fact like a little child, and be prepared to give up every pre-conceived notion.

– Thomas Henry Huxley, quoted in Aldous Huxley,
The Human Situation

In Chapters 2 and 3 we examined several theoretical explanations for wife assault. In Chapter 2 we established a framework for a nested ecological theory of wife assault that concentrated on the interaction of individually acquired dispositions with social-contextual features of the family, the subculture, and the broader culture. Using this framework, we established a hypothetical profile of an assaultive male that incorporated individually acquired factors such as: (1) the desire to have control over or dominate women, (2) exaggerated anxiety about control over the amount of intimacy in a relationship, (3) violent role models for conflict resolution, and (4) poor verbal conflict resolution skills. To this profile were added contextual factors from the microsystem (coercive interactions), the exosystem (unemployment, job stress, and social isolation), and the macrosystem (beliefs in patriarchal rights, double standards, etc.).

In Chapter 3 we developed a social learning analysis of the individual assaulter and examined the acquisition and maintenance mechanisms of the habit of assault. We suggested that for men who assault their wives, but who are not generally assaultive, some special categories of aversive stimuli or instigators to assault may exist. These categories include (1) the man's perception that his wife wishes to change the degree of intimacy with him and (2) his perception that he is powerless to stop her.

In this chapter we will describe some experiments conducted with wife assaulters and control subjects in order to test hypotheses generated by the aforementioned theoretical notions. Our objective in doing this research has been to examine general instigators to aggression specific to wife assaulters, and one particular regulator of aggression: the neutralization of self-punishment.

The first experiment tests the notion that power and intimacy issues produce exaggerated anger in assaultive males; the results of this experiment are then set in the broader context of the social milieu of the assaultive population. Power and intimacy issues were tested by presenting videotapes of male-female conflict to our subjects and measuring their reactions. The contextual factors were measured through the use of an elaborate set of questionnaires. As you will see, these studies showed that power and intimacy issues differentiated wife assaulters from control subjects. From a social learning perspective, intimacy change that is beyond their power to control produces strong anger responses in assaultive men. We turn now to a description of this research.

What Differentiates Wife Assaulters from Other Males?

Our interest was in comparing a group of men who had histories of repeated wife assault with appropriate control groups on the dimensions described above. We hypothesized, for example, that wife assaulters (WA) might have higher scores on tests measuring the need for power and dominance, might react with greater anger to scenes depicting male-female conflict over intimacy issues, and might have had a greater exposure to violent role models than did our control subjects.[1]

We selected three groups of control subjects: (1) men who were demographically similar to our assaultive population but who were *happily married* (HM), (2) men who were demographically similar to our assaultive population and were *maritally conflicted* but not violent with their wives (MC), and (3) men who had assaulted their wives but who were *generally assaultive* as well (GA).

In contrast to the members of the generally assaultive group, the members of our *wife assaultive* group did not engage in violence outside their primary relationships. The inclusion of each of these groups allowed us to make specific comparisons: the happily married group presented some baseline information on frequency of conflict and types of conflict resolution, and the maritally conflicted group allowed us to separate frequency of conflict from other factors as a cause of assault. The members of the maritally conflicted group reported as much conflict with their wives as did the wife assaulters but did not use physical aggression to resolve it. Finally, the members of the generally assaultive group used physical aggression both inside and outside their primary relationships. Hence, we hypothesized that they might not react to the same specific aversive instigators as did men whose violence was wife-specific.

The wife assaulters group and generally assaultive group were made up of men who had been referred to the Assaultive Husbands Program, a treatment program run in conjunction with the Vancouver Family Court. The members of these two assaultive groups participated voluntarily in order to obtain some feedback on their conflict-resolution techniques. The maritally conflicted group was comprised of men attending counselling groups for marital conflict, and the happily married group was comprised of men who were solicited through ads in local newspapers; these two groups were paid to participate in the research. All subjects first attended an assessment session, where, amongst other questionnaires to be described below, they were administered the Straus CTS (see Chapter 1). In addition, so that we did not need to rely exclusively on the men's self-reports, an added requirement for participation was that they currently be in a relationship and that their partners fill out the CTS as well.

Men's and women's scores were averaged to establish criterion scores.[2] Criteria for selection were as follows: wife assaulters (at least three incidents of serious assault against their wives in the prior year [corroborated by their wives] and no assault outside their relationships); generally assaultive (three incidents of serious wife assault in the prior year [corroborated by their wives] and three or more incidents of serious assault outside their relationships); maritally conflicted (80th percentile or above for previous year's scores on the Verbal Aggression Subscale of the CTS and no physical violence [corroborated by their wives]); happily married (65th percentile or below on the Verbal Aggression Subscale and no physical violence [corroborated by their wives]). Table 4.1 demonstrates their scores.

Men in both assaultive groups were predominantly in blue-collar professions or unemployed, and their average age was thirty-two. In order to ensure a socioeconomic and demographic match, men who most fit this profile were selected for participation in the maritally conflicted and happily married groups. Men who did not fit these profiles, or whose scores on any subscale of the CTS fell outside the criterion range, were rejected. Table 4.2 demonstrates some demographic properties of these groups.

Participants were required to attend two individual testing sessions, each lasting approximately two hours. The first session involved a prolonged rationale for the study, with an emphasis on the necessity for honesty and completion of all items. Assaultive males were told that an accurate assessment of their anger and conflict-resolution problems necessitated their answering all items honestly. Since these men had volunteered for this research and were also in treatment for anger problems, there is some reason to believe they were motivated to answer honestly.

Table 4.1

CTS scores for experimental groups during prior year

	Wife assaulters	Generally assaultive	Maritally conflicted	Happily married
$n =$	45	18	45	45
Husband's ratings (of own behavior)				
Reasoning	7.6	7.8	9.60	7.0
Verbal aggression	18.9	16.6	15.70	3.8
Physical aggression				
with wife	10.9	2.3	0.67	0.2
outside marriage	0.8	8.9		
Wife's ratings (of husband's behavior)				
Reasoning	7.4	7.2	7.70	7.5
Verbal aggression	21.2	12.2	13.80	5.7
Physical aggression	17.2	16.8	0.90	0.3

Reasoning subscale   = 0-18
Verbal aggression subscale   = 0-36
Physical aggression subscale = 0-48

The 95th and 99th percentile scores for the general population are as follows: verbal aggression, 19 and 30; physical aggression, 4 and 14 (Straus 1979).

The men completed a battery of questionnaires bearing on experimental hypotheses. After these were completed, *CTS* scoring determined whether or not each man met the selection criteria. If he did, a second session, which involved his being tested on the videotape analogue of the research, was arranged. All men were provided with feedback based on their responses to session one. This feedback appeared to be a prime motivation for participation.

The Questionnaire Study

We wished to assess features of each subject's: (1) work and friendship network (exosystem); (2) beliefs and attitudes about women, acceptance of violence, and so forth; (3) assertiveness and communication skills; and (4) power motivation. The rationale and test used for each of these is described below:

(1) *Demographic Information Sheet.* This sheet assessed the following

Table 4.2

Demographic characteristics of experimental groups

	Wife assaulters	Generally assaultive	Maritally conflicted	Happily married
n =	45	18	45	45
Age	32.2	32.8	32.9	31.9
Education:				
Some high school	40%	50%	35%	35%
High school grad	40%	35%	40%	40%
Some college	15%	15%	20%	20%
College grad	5%	0%	5%	5%
Occupation				
Blue collar	85%	88%	82%	83%
White collar/prof. 15%	15%	12%	18%	17%
Unemployment	45%	45%	25%	30%
Years married	6.8	6.9	8.6	9.1
Number of children	1.5	1.7	1.5	1.4
Number of drinks/week	12.8	13.2	5.4	5.8

exosystem factors: (a) employment situation – whether the man was employed or unemployed and how stressful his life was according to the Holmes and Rahe (1967) stress scale and (b) the frequency and quality of his contacts with friends or support groups (for this, we used a modified version of the *Fischer Scale* [1982]).

(2) *Power motivation: The Thematic Apperception Test of n-power.* In Chapter 3 we described McClelland's (1975) and Winter's (1973) work on the power motive. Men with a Type III power motivation were described by Winter as having an exaggerated need to persuade and to generate compliance. Such men appeared to generate conflict in primary relationships (Stewart & Rubin 1976). If this tendency to generate conflict was combined with poor conflict-resolution skills and an exaggerated anger reaction to certain forms of perceived conflict, potential for assaultive

behavior could increase. Hence, we wanted to test our assaultive populations against other populations on a measure of power (*n*-power). Winter (1973) developed a scoring system for *n*-power that has been widely used to test power motivation in male populations (e.g., McClelland 1975; Stewart & Rubin 1976; Winter 1973). Winter's test measures a power motive described as having an impact on the behavior or emotions of another person, and it was empirically derived from experiments designed to arouse such a motive in subjects. The scoring system allows power imagery to be scored from a *Thematic Apperception Test* story that includes references to: (1) strong assertive actions, (2) actions that induce strong emotions in others, and (3) concern about the reputation of the actor.

Participants write stories in response to five pictures selected by Winter on the basis of their being able to elicit power imagery.[3] The pictures represented a variety of gender relationships (two were male-male, two were male-female, and one was female-female). Participants look at the pictures one at a time and write short stories that answer the following questions: What is happening? Who are the people? What has led up to this situation? What is being thought? What is wanted? By whom? What will happen? What will be done? Trained raters scored these stories.[4] Our hypothesis was that assaultive males would demonstrate comparatively high scores of power imagery, suggesting a high need for power.

(3) *The perceived quality of the marriage: The Spanier Dyadic Adjustment Scale.* The *Dyadic Adjustment Scale (DAS)* (Spanier 1976) is a 32-item scale that measures marital adjustment, and it has four subscales: consensus, satisfaction, cohesion, and expression of affect. *DAS* was used in this study to provide a standardized estimate of marital adjustment.

(4) *Measures of assertiveness and communication style.* Two measures of assertiveness were obtained for all subjects: The *Rathus Assertiveness Schedule* (Rathus 1973), which is a 30-item inventory covering a wide range of assertive behavior, and the *Spouse-Specific Assertiveness Scale* (Rosenbaum & O'Leary 1981), a 29-item scale that measures assertiveness and aggression within the primary relationship.

In addition, the *Test of Emotional Style (TES)* (Allen & Hamnsher 1974) was used. *TES* contains three subscales assessing responsiveness (the covert experience of emotion), orientation (one's attitude towards emotional expressiveness), and expressiveness (the frequency and intensity of overt emotional expression). The expressiveness subscale contains reference to four basic emotions: anger, fear, sadness, and joy.

The purpose of the above scales is to assess whether communication deficits, which may combine with other factors to increase the likelihood of physical violence as a means of conflict resolution, are characteristic of wife assaulters.

(5) *Marlowe-Crowne Social Desirability Scale.* The MC (Crowne & Marlowe 1960) is a 33-item scale designed to assess the need to respond in a culturally acceptable manner. While all subjects were told that feedback on their conflict-resolution problems required honest responses on all questionnaires, the SDS allowed us to assess for differential image management by group.

(6) *Burt Attitude Scales.* Burt's (1980) scales assess sex-role stereotyping (nine items [e.g., 'A woman may have a career but her marriage and family should come first']); adversarial sexual beliefs (ten items [e.g., 'A woman will only respect a man who will lay down the law to her']); and acceptance of interpersonal violence towards women (five items [e.g., 'A man is never justified in hitting his wife']). Burt (1980) has argued that these attitudes serve to target and release violent assault, and he has demonstrated a strong relationship between having these scale scores and holding the myth that females enjoy being raped. The inclusion of these beliefs in the present study has a twofold objective: (a) to establish whether wife assaulters have a generalized mistrust of women (i.e., adversarial sexual beliefs) and (b) to establish whether assaultive males place a positive value on the use of violence. As described above, social learning theory would indicate widely differing etiologies for men who believe that the use of violence against their wives is acceptable and for those who do not so believe but who act violently anyway.

(7) *Straus Conflict Tactics scales: Childhood Exposure to Violence.* In addition to the husband-wife CTS (Straus 1979), a CTS that assessed childhood exposure to violence was used. Straus, Gelles, and Steinmetz (1980) had reported higher than normal rates of physical abuse in the childhoods of males who subsequently used violence.

Results of Questionnaire Assessment
As a general strategy of data analysis, given the large number of variables examined in this study (and consequent concern for holding down the false positive error rate), we first analyzed items in which no differences were anticipated. The remaining variables were then grouped and subjected to multivariate analysis of variance (MANOVA) (Marascuilo & Levin 1983). If significant differences were found, the MANOVAs were followed up by univariate analyses of variance (ANOVA)[5] in order to assess specific differences. Newman-Keuls multiple-comparisons were performed on pairs of means as a follow-up to significant ANOVAs.

We used the *Dyadic Adjustment Scale* (Spanier 1976) to assess degree of marital dissatisfaction. We had hoped for similar scores for the WA, GA, and MC groups in order to rule out degree of conflict and marital quality as confounds. This is what we found: there were no significant differences between these groups, but, using Newman-Keuls pairwise comparisons, all differed significantly from the HM group (*p* < *.01*). Similarly, we had hoped that no one group would demonstrate exaggerated scores on the *Marlowe-Crowne SDS*. A one-way ANOVA on the *MC* did not reveal any significant differences on this scale. The HM group had the highest scores (i.e., the most socially desirable), but they were not significantly higher than were those of the other groups.

With respect to the remaining questionnaire items, we expected group differences to show up. Accordingly, they were combined and analyzed via one-way multivariate analysis of variance as follows: (1) attitudes towards women, (2) *n*-power, (3) assertiveness, (4) emotional expressiveness, and (5) exposure to childhood violence.

Do Wife Assaulters Have More Negative Attitudes Towards Women than Do Other Men? Our analysis revealed no differences between the wife assault group and other groups on the *Burt Attitude Scales*. Wife assaulters, as a group, were not more stereotyping of females, more mistrustful of females, or more accepting of the use of violence against females than were the members of other groups. Using the Spence and Helmreich (1978) *Attitudes Towards Women Scale*, Neidig, Friedman, and Collins (1986) also failed to find differences between wife assaulters and control group males with respect to attitudes towards women.

One obvious possibility for these failures is that too many demand characteristics (Orne 1969) exist in research that measures attitudes. *Demand characteristics* are those cues available to subjects from the experimental setting and from instructions; they tell them what an appropriate or correct response might be to the experimenter's questions. Men who are selected for research on the basis of their having been violent may try to answer attitudinal questions in a self-exonerative manner, which can diminish any possible differences between groups of subjects. Since the correct answer (in terms of exoneration) is usually obvious on attitude measures, real differences between groups of men tend to be obscured.

An alternative explanation for the failure to find between-group differences is that assaultive males may simply not hold particularly negative or adversarial attitudes towards women in general (i.e., any more so than control-group males) but simply act with a learned pattern of violence. We will return to this question towards the end of this chapter, when we examine studies of the conscience of the wife assaulter.

Do Wife Assaulters Have a Stronger Motive to Control or Dominate Women than Do Other Men? General scores on power motivation did not differ significantly across our four treatment groups. However, we did find a significant difference in need for power between our wife assault group and the happily married group when the stimulus materials used were male-female scenes.[6] The wife assaulters did not differ significantly from those in the maritally conflicted control group. (Generally assaultive men were not tested using this particular measure.) This suggests that wife assaulters have a stronger need to dominate in a male-female context than do men who are happily married. *TAT* stories are not so obviously related to violence against women as are direct attitudinal measures. Consequently, they are more difficult for subjects to answer in a socially desirable fashion.

Dutton and Strachan (1987a) have argued, for this reason, that *TATs* may be more revealing of broader motives related to dominance and control of women than are attitudinal questionnaires. Dutton and Strachan cite work by Pollack and Gilligan (1982), who scored men's and women's *TAT* stories for violent imagery in response to scenes cued for affiliation, achievement, and power motivation. Sex differences were found not only in frequency of violent imagery but also in terms of which stimuli cued that imagery. Men wrote stories with a greater incidence of violent imagery overall, but the sex differences were most pronounced in response to scenes of men and women together (which the authors refer to as affiliation scenes). Women demonstrated the greatest frequency of violence themes in response to pictures of people in work situations (which Pollack and Gilligan refer to as achievement scenes.)

Pollack and Gilligan interpreted violence themes as indicating perceptions of danger and concluded that men perceived danger in intimate relationships, while women perceived danger in work-related social situations. Pollack and Gilligan suggest that this sex difference in the perception of relationship danger is one basis for male-female conflict in intimate relationships. They speculate that males may develop exaggerated needs to control what they perceive to be danger situations; namely, their relationships with women.

The need for power demonstrated by wife assaulters manifests itself only in male-female scenes. Browning (1983) found no significant between-group differences when a variety of gender relationships were depicted in the stimulus materials. There are, of course, many ways that a male could be high in power motivation vis-à-vis women and not be assaultive; he may, for example, attempt to establish control or dominance through verbal means. However, if a man with a strong motive to dominate is low in verbal skills, a certain amount of chronic frustration might develop, increasing the likelihood of violence.

Are Wife Assaulters Less Assertive than Other Men? One measure of verbal competence is assertiveness. We measured both general and spouse-specific assertiveness in our subject groups and found qualified support for the expectation of low assertiveness in wife assaulters. Wife assaulters obtained the lowest scores of all four groups on general assertiveness, although these scores did not differ significantly overall. However, on spouse-specific assertiveness the scores of wife assaulters were significantly lower than were those of the other three groups (Browning 1983; Dutton & Strachan 1987a), replicating a finding obtained by Rosenbaum and O'Leary. So far, our data provides a profile of wife assaulters as scoring high in their need for control and influence over their wives but low in spouse-specific assertiveness (which is required in order to manifest such influence). This deficit differentiates the wife assaulters from the members of the maritally conflicted but non-violent control group. Tests of emotional expressiveness revealed no group differences.

Where Is the Violence Learned? The combination of the need for power over one's wife with poor verbal assertiveness skills might combine to produce a chronic frustration level in wife assaulters. If these men have learned to express frustration as anger and violence, then the power motive and verbal deficits, in combination with the reinforced learning of violence, will interact to produce wife assault.

One source of learning how to express frustration and marital conflict as violence is the family of origin. A variety of published results indicate that observation of father-mother violence increases the likelihood of wife assault (Straus, Gelles, & Steinmetz 1980; Kalmuss 1984). Results of our research confirmed these earlier findings: wife assaulters had higher scores than did all other groups for both observation of interparental violence and for being victims of violence from their parents. As we have described, however, another way in which violence is learned occurs when assaultive males use it to satisfy their personal needs for power and dominance and escape punishment. These reinforced learning experiences increase the probability of the repetition of violent acts.

The Instigators of Wife Assault: The Videotape Studies
The questionnaire assessment reported above gave a general profile of the background factors that described our subjects. Against this backdrop, the videotape studies were designed to test specific arousal and anger

responses to vivid depictions of male-female marital conflict. We were especially interested in intimacy and dominance issues, as described in Chapter 3. The general strategy was to present the subject with a series of videotaped scenes depicting verbal conflict between a man and a woman, to encourage him to identify with the man, and to obtain measures of physiological arousal and reported affect.[7]

This analogue format was derived somewhat from our observations in therapy groups that wife assaulters' anger was frequently experienced during guided fantasies of conflict situations with their wives. The use of videotapes allowed us to present a consistent (as opposed to imagined), yet vivid, stimulus to subjects. Conflict scenarios varied between the dimensions of power and intimacy. The power/dominance dimension was meant to represent two levels of verbal control of a conflict situation (one level indicative of male control, the other of female control). The videotape scenario was meant to represent a conflict event (i.e., something that happened or might happen in a male-female relationship) and, to that extent, an aversive stimulus occurring in the microcosm of husband-wife interaction.

Clearly, however, the *perception* of that event by our subject population is important and may be affected by such predispositional factors as *n*-power. For example, a man high in *n*-power may perceive a moderate level of female control as female dominance. Similarly, a man with extreme anxiety about being rejected or abandoned may perceive moderate moves towards independence by his wife as abandonment. This delusional state is called *conjugal paranoia* (see the case of Robert in Chapter 2). Hence, careful checks on the manipulation of both variables were instituted.

General Procedure

(1) *Design.* The videotape component employed a factorial design with four levels of subjects (WA, GA, MC, HM), two levels of power (male-dominant, female-dominant), and three levels of attempted intimacy change (abandonment, engulfment, neutral). Power and intimacy change were manipulated by varying the videotaped scene. Therefore, there were six different videotaped scenes, one for each power x intimacy combination. The power variable was varied between subjects, while the intimacy variable was a within-subjects variable.[8] Specifically, the participants in each group were randomly assigned to viewing either male-dominant scenes or female-dominant scenes. Each participant then viewed three videotapes, each of which depicted a different intimacy condition.

(2) *Videotaped Scenes.* The scenes were between 5.5 and 7.5 minutes in

duration. They all involved the same man and woman arguing heatedly over an issue. The subjects were told that the man and woman were a couple who had been involved in an in-depth study of marriage at the university and who had allowed a camera crew access to their home over a period of several months. In fact, the couple were professional actors.

Relative power was manipulated by having either the man or the woman in the scene dominate the argument verbally. Family interaction researchers (see Mishler & Waxler 1968; Jacob 1975) have specified a number of discrete behaviors that seem to constitute verbal dominance. These were employed here to manipulate relative power. Specifically, the powerful person was instructed to have a greater total talking time, interrupt his or her partner (successfully) more often, and to finally get his or her way. In the male-dominant scenes, the man displayed this verbal prowess while the woman appeared cowed and submissive. In the female-dominant scenes, the roles were reversed.

Attempted movement towards intimacy was manipulated by varying the issue discussed during the conflict. There were three issues: abandonment (woman attempting to move away from the man), engulfment (woman attempting to move closer to the man), and neutral (no attempted movement). It was decided to have the woman instigate this movement because the dynamic of interest was the man's attempt to control the former's behavior, not the other way around.

The specifics of the enactment of the abandonment and engulfment issues were selected on the basis of clinical experience as well as descriptions of actions by battered women that appear to anger their husbands. The abandonment issue involved the woman stating that she wished to become more independent, to spend more time with her friends (i.e., go away for a weekend with them), and to join a women's group. The engulfment issue involved an argument in which the woman complained that the man didn't spend enough time communicating his thoughts and feelings to her. Finally, the neutral scene involved an issue that is common to most couples but did not involve a change in intimacy. The couple argued over whether they would spend their vacation camping (the man) or in the city (the woman). All the tapes were constructed so that the severity of conflict increased over the first part of the tape, peaking around the middle, trailing off towards the end, and, finally, resulting in acquiescence by the non-dominant person. The conflict was purely verbal; there was no physical contact between the man and woman in the scenes.

The videotapes were pre-tested on twelve men in their late twenties who were currently involved in an intimate relationship with a woman. The pre-test was conducted in order to fine-tune the physiological measurement procedure and to obtain some preliminary ratings on the tapes in terms of the manipulations. Six men viewed the female-dominant tapes and another six viewed the male-dominant tapes. Essentially, the pre-test indicated that the tapes were seen as highly realistic and conflictual; the twelve men reported that they produced a moderate degree of anger and anxiety. The men's ratings on the power and intimacy dimensions indicated that the tapes were perceived as was expected. One exception to this was that the abandonment tapes (particularly the male-dominant abandonment tape) were not seen as significantly different from the neutral tapes. However, it was reasoned that assaultive men who had been seen in clinical settings would be hypersensitive to abandonment cues and, therefore, would perceive a greater reduction of intimacy in these tapes. Since no assaultive men were available for pre-testing, it was decided to proceed with the experiment proper using the six pre-tested tapes.

(3) *Dependent Measures.* Self-report measures of perceived affect were obtained immediately after each videotape scene. While a number of standardized measures of affective state are available (e.g., Zuckerman, Lubin, Vogel, & Valerius 1964; Izard, Dougherty, Bloxom, & Kotsche 1974), these instruments were considered too lengthy or too broad-based for the present purposes. Therefore, we utilized two scales used by Russell and Mehrabian (1974) to measure anger and anxiety. Each scale consisted of three adjectives that tap feelings of anger (angry, hostile, aggressive) and anxiety (tense, nervous, anxious). The scales had the advantage of being short while yet providing some breadth in the coverage of the two emotional states. The anger scale provided the primary test of the notion that assaultive men would respond differentially to intimacy issues with an emotion that increases the likelihood of aggression. A list of fourteen other adjectives describing affective states were selected from an extensive list compiled by Russell and Mehrabian (1974) and were included in the form given to the men following each scene. These items were included primarily as a background for the anger and anxiety items.

The adjective list was presented to the men using a nine-point semantic differential format. Each man completed the checklist twice after each scene. The first administration requested a rating of his feelings while watching the scene, and the second administration requested an estimate of his feelings had he actually been involved in the situation. Scores on the first administration likely reflect some combination of the relevance of the scene's stimulus characteristics for the man plus his ability to get into the scene and experience emotion.

In addition to their ratings of affect, the men also rated each scene on a nine-point scale for realism and severity of conflict and on a seven-point scale for dominance and attempted intimacy movement. The latter two ratings provided manipulation checks for the power and intimacy factors. The dominance manipulation generally worked as anticipated, with male-dominant tapes differing from female-dominant tapes over combined intimacy conditions and also at each individual level of the intimacy factor. The ratings of attempted intimacy movement confirm that the intimacy manipulation was generally successful.

(4) *Videotape Analogue Data*. The approach to analyzing the dependent measures in this portion of the research closely followed that outlined above for the questionnaire data. Repeated MANOVAs were performed on logically combined groups of variables, followed by Bonferroni-adjusted univariate ANOVAs and Newman-Keuls post-hoc comparisons (given statistical significance in the preceding analyses).[9]

Self-Reports of Anger
Self-report measures of anger ('while watching the scene' and 'had you actually been in the situation in real life') in response to the tapes were analyzed using a MANOVA. Means and standard deviations for these measures and pre-rating scores are presented in Table 4.3 (the range of possible scores is 0 to 27). Two-way ANOVAs were performed on the two pre-rating scores. Analyses of pre-ratings revealed that there were no group differences or differences distinguishable by dominance condition (or interaction effects) on pre-rated anger.

A MANOVA of anger ratings in response to the scenes yielded a significant overall difference amongst groups[10] – a difference that remained significant when the anger ratings were corrected for initial levels of anger by using pre-ratings (taken prior to showing the scenes) as a covariate. Observation of the means suggests a linear relationship, with the WA group rating the most anger and the HM group the least. Furthermore, specific comparisons indicated that the WA group reported significantly more anger to the abandonment scene than did the other three groups ($p < .01$). No main effect was found for male versus female dominance; the F score approached but did not attain the conventional (.05) level of significance. A similar analysis on anxiety ratings indicated no significant between-group differences.

Men were also asked to indicate their most likely response had they been the man in the conflict scene (see Novaco 1976). These behavioral likelihood scales yielded consistent between-group differences, with the WA group reporting the least amount of constructive reasoning,[11] the most verbal aggression,[12] and the most physical aggression.[13] Post-hoc

Table 4.3

Means and standard deviations for anger ratings (scale range = 1-9)

Group	Dominance	Pre-rating	Abandonment	Engulfment	Neutral
				Intimacy condition	
Wife assaulters	Male	6.05 (4.61)	18.64 (6.10)	9.80 (5.90)	12.60 (6.70)
	Female	5.36 (3.05)	16.90 (5.90)	10.60 (6.10)	12.10 (6.20)
Generally assaultive	Male	6.00 (4.61)	13.00 (6.10)	10.33 (5.90)	13.44 (6.70)
	Female	5.22 (3.05)	15.22 (5.90)	11.00 (6.10)	12.67 (6.20)
Maritally conflicted	Male	8.22 (4.61)	15.78 (6.10)	13.11 (5.90)	14.78 (6.70)
	Female	5.11 (3.05)	14.78 (5.90)	12.67 (6.10)	11.78 (6.20)
Happily married	Male	5.78 (4.61)	12.22 (6.10)	11.11 (5.90)	10.67 (6.70)
	Female	3.78 (3.05)	8.33 (5.90)	6.11 (6.10)	6.67 (6.20)

comparisons revealed the WA group to be significantly different from each of the other three groups on these measures. This was especially true for the abandonment scenes. Finally, the men were asked what relevance the issues portrayed had to their own relationships. The percentages generated by this question are contained in Table 4.4. An overall chi square performed on these data was significant ($X^2 = 38.3$, $df = 6$, and $p < .001$). It would appear from observation of the cell frequencies that the abandonment issue was the most relevant for the WA group and the least relevant for the other groups.

To generate directions for future research, some 'data snooping' techniques were performed. Specifically, an internal analysis that correlated all anger ratings, collapsed across both subjects and videotapes, was performed. Composite self-report anger ratings correlated most highly with composite anxiety ratings (+.86, $p < .001$) and humiliation ratings (+.60, $p < .001$). The emergence of humiliation as a key descriptor of affective reactions poses potential heuristic value. Recall from Chapter 3 Katz's focus on humiliation and rage. Self-reports of humiliation while watching the conflict scenarios correlated +.40, $p = .001$ with reports of being verbally abused by the mother. Correlations of humiliation with reports of verbal and physical abuse by the father, however, were not significant. This finding suggests support for Winter's notion of maternal mixed messages contributing to strong ambivalence about intimacy for wife assaulters and is, in our opinion, deserving of further study.

Conscience and the Rationalization of Wife Assault

So far we have examined the exaggerated tendency of wife assaulters to become aroused and angry in response to certain aversive stimuli. Although anger is obviously not the same as aggression, it has been found to increase the likelihood of the latter (Konecni 1975). We have argued in Chapters 2 and 3 that this is especially true when the angered person has no alternative resource (i.e., verbal skills) for expressing anger and removing the aversive stimulus. Once a habit of aggression is established as a primary means of controlling an aversive stimulus, a normally socialized aggressor has to develop ways of perceiving his aggression as justified and its consequences as not serious. If he does not, his behavior will clearly violate standards of self-conduct.

In this section we examine the excuses that wife assaulters use to justify their behavior, render it less reprehensible, and thereby maintain their habit of aggression. Recall that in Chapter 1 we estimated (based on the Schulman [1979] and Straus, Gelles, & Steinmetz [1980] surveys) that if a man once abuses his wife, there is a 63% chance that he will do so again.

Table 4.4

Relevance of intimacy issue portrayed to own relationship

	Condition		
Group	Abandonment	Engulfment	Neutral
Wife assaulters	78%	58%	42%
Generally assaultive	54	66	40
Maritally conflicted	39	72	56
Happily married	29	56	0

$x^2 = 38.3$, $df = 6$, $p < .001$

Repeat wife assaulters must find ways to rationalize their habit if they are to sustain it.

When normally socialized men commit behavior that violates their own self-standards, a variety of cognitive mechanisms become operative to neutralize self-punishment for reprehensible behavior. Clinical reports suggest that some of the cognitive restructuring tendencies described by Bandura are used frequently by wife assaulters. Both Ganley (1981) and Sonkin, Martin, and Walker (1985) describe this population as minimizing both their violent behavior and its consequences by victim-blaming. In fact, a primary means of altering habitual assault is through the therapeutic confrontation of these forms of neutralization of self-punishment in order to have the assaulter assume personal responsibility for his violence (Sonkin, Martin, & Walker 1985).

Despite the clinical emphasis on the cognitive restructuring tendencies of wife assaulters, little in the way of empirical research has been reported. Shields and Hanneke (1983) compared the wife assaulters' attributions of assault with those of their wives. They found that the husbands tended to externalize the cause of their assault by attributing it to their wives' behavior (45%) or to alcohol (23%), while the wives attributed the assault to a locus internal to the husband (e.g., his anger, personality, or intoxication). The finding that criminal actions tend to be externalized by the perpetrator was consistent with previous studies (Saulnier & Perlman 1981; Felson & Ribner 1981).

Felson and Ribner (1981) analyzed perpetrators' accounts of criminal violence, distinguishing between excuses (accepting that the act was wrong but denying personal responsibility) and justifications (accepting personal responsibility but denying that the act was wrong). For most criminal acts, justifications were more frequent than were excuses (50%

vs. 18.7%). However, when the victim was female, excuses became more prevalent.

Henderson and Hewstone (1984) replicated this finding with a maximum security prison population serving time for murder, attempted murder, manslaughter, wounding, grievous bodily harm, and/or assault. Free responses were coded into locus of attribution categories (victim, self, situation) and excuses versus justifications. Again, justifications were more frequent than were excuses (70% vs. 30%). When the victim was an intimate and no third party was present, 50% of the actions were attributed to the victim.

Unfortunately, Henderson and Hewstone did not specify the gender of the victim nor the victim's specific relationship to the perpetrator. Their method of assessing both attributions and excuses/justifications, however, provides a technique for generating a more complex analysis of a perpetrator's explanation for his own violent actions (see Fincham & Jaspars 1980). These explanations could provide an insight into the means by which potentially negative self-evaluations are neutralized by wife assaulters.

As reported below, Dutton (1986a) extended Felson and Ribner's analysis to the explanations given by males for their having assaulted their wives. Neither Felson and Ribner (1981) nor Henderson and Hewstone (1984) focused on wife assault per se, although the latter study did include violent crimes committed on intimates in private situations.

General Procedure

Two groups of men who had assaulted their wives took part in this study. Self-referred men ($n = 25$) were men who had contacted the Assaultive Husbands' Project directly,[14] or via a community mental health clinic or social worker, seeking treatment for an acknowledged problem. Typically, their motivation for seeking treatment was to prevent their wives from leaving them. Court-referred men ($n = 50$) had been convicted of wife assault and were referred to the Assaultive Husbands' Project as a condition of their probation. The two groups were matched demographically, in terms of average length of marriage, time since first wife assault, and number and severity of wife assaults.

To assess frequency and severity of wife assault, subjects and their wives filled out the Straus (1979) *CTS* (Form N). The men in our two groups generated the following self-report scores of physical aggression: self-referred = 14.8; court-referred = 14.2. Their wives generated the following scores for their husbands' use of physical aggression: self-referred = 22.1; court-referred = 21.8. Hence, both groups of men are in the top 1% of the population for frequency of use of physical aggression against their wives, both by their own ratings and by their wives' ratings. *CTS* scores by both the men and their wives in the self-referred and court-referred groups did not differ significantly from the referral source, nor did length of time married or duration of assaultive behavior.

All subjects were interviewed about their history of assaultive behavior, use of violence outside their marriage, and history of arrests, and were asked to describe their most recent assaultive action in detail. If not mentioned spontaneously, the following aspects were probed in the interview:

(1) *Victim*: Her age, relationship to the offender (married, common-law), years together.

(2) *Situation*: Time of day when incident occurred, location, whether others were present, whether police were called.

(3) *Precipitating events*: Type of interchange with victim, circumstances leading up to first blow, victim's behavior, alcohol use, prior history of violence between offender and victim.

(4) *Details of incident*: Whether a weapon was used, what part of the victim's body was attacked, injuries to victim, injuries to offender.

(5) *Attitude*: The offender was asked to relate his feelings at the time, whether he perceived he had control over his own aggression, whether victim deserved the attack, his own motivation.

(6) *Explanation*: The offender was asked why the violence occurred.

Interviews were recorded verbatim where possible, lasted forty-five to seventy minutes, and were carried out by four therapists with experience in treating wife assault. Following the coding procedure developed by Henderson and Hewstone (1984), the following coding scheme was used for responses to item (6).

(1) *Locus of attribution:*

(a) *Victim*: Explanation for violence is attributed to the behavior or characteristics of the victim. This category includes reference to victim provocation or to perceived acts of aggression by the victim, victim denigration of the perpetrator's significant others, or verbal abuse by the victim.

(b) *Self*: Explanation for violence involves own characteristics or behavior (temper, arousal, chronic alcohol problem, upholding reputation, or pride).

(c) *Situation*: Explanation in terms of non-personal situational factors (e.g., acute stress or drunkenness where the interviewee has not described a chronic alcohol problem).

(2) *Excuses vs. justification:*

(a) *Excuses*: A denial of personal responsibility for the act. This category includes drink, drugs, accidents, uncontrollable arousal, and other situational factors.

(b) *Justifications*: An acceptance of personal responsibility but also an attempt to justify the act in terms of valid reasons or norms. This category includes egregious (from the perpetrator's perspective) victim provocation, acting according to subgroup norms, self-defence, and so on.

(3) *Minimizing:*

(a) *Of act*: Comparison was made between the offender's description of the specifics of his assault and a composite description from the victim, social worker, probation officer, police, and court records. *High Severity-Minimizers* were defined as men who described their most severe acts against their wives in the past year as two levels less severe than those described by their wives on the CTS. For example, if a wife reported beating (item Q) as her husband's most severe act, and the man reported kicking, biting, or hitting with a fist (item O), the man was classified as high in severity-minimizing. For a description of within-couple discrepancies in reports of husband's violence, see Browning and Dutton (1986).

High Incidence-Minimizers were defined as men who reported less than half the total incidents of violence that their wives reported them to have committed on the Severe Physical Aggression subscale of the Straus CTS. If the man reported six acts, for example, and his wife reported thirteen, he was classified as high in incidence-minimizing. The 50% criterion was based on the finding by Browning and Dutton (1986) that a sample of (mainly self-referred) wife assaulters reported about 50% the incidence of violence that their wives reported. It is not known whether the wives' reports reflect incidence accurately. For a discussion of the veridicality of wives' reports see Browning and Dutton (1986).

(b) *Of effects*: Comparison was made of the offenders' descriptions of their victims' injuries with the latter's reports and with hospital and police reports. Berk, Berk, Loseke, and Rauma (1981) developed an eight-point scale for severity of effects of wife assault. High minimizers of effects were defined as men who described their wives' injuries as one level or more (on the Berk et al. scale) less severe did than police and hospital reports.

Results

Although it was theoretically possible for men to neither excuse nor justify their actions, none of the men in this study fell into either of these categories. As in the Henderson and Hewstone (1984) study, justifications were far more prevalent than were excuses (n = 59, 16, respectively). These data are for both court-referred and self-referred men. Men who excuse their assaults are most likely to attribute them to situational circumstances, whereas men who justify their assaults tend to attribute them to their victims.[15] Self-referred men are more likely than are court-referred men to attribute assaults to themselves,[16] and court-referred men are likely to attribute assaults to situational circumstances (44%) or to the victim (42%).

Locus of blame had no differential effect on the type of minimization pattern used by the men.[17] Men who minimized severity tended to also minimize frequency and effects independently of how they viewed the cause of the assault. One-third of the men (25/75) used no minimization pattern. This proportion was not affected by referral type. Thirty per cent of the men (22/75) used all three types of minimization.

Locus of cause for assault had a strong effect on minimization.[18] Men who attributed cause for assault to the victims were more likely to fall into the high minimizing category (using all three kinds of minimization), whereas men who attributed cause to themselves were more likely to fall into the no minimization category.[19] Men who attributed cause to the situation fell overwhelmingly into the moderate-minimization category (27/28).

Patterns of Neutralization of Self-Punishment
One-third of the men in this study attributed their assault to actions or provocations from their victims. Our court-referred sample of wife assaulters gave justifications 79% of the time and excuses 21% of the time. Hence, the general pattern of excuses versus justifications for assault found by Henderson and Hewstone (1984) appears to have been replicated for a population of wife assaulters. Indeed, this current group responds similarly to the group (which committed violent crime on intimates in private) in the Henderson and Hewstone study.

From the perspective of treating assaultive males, it is useful to know that self- and court-referred men evince different trends in attribution for assault. In one sense, the court-referred men present an additional treatment problem: that of getting them to realize their causal role, since only 14% attribute the cause for violence to themselves. The self-referred men appear to have already come to this realization. They appear to compensate for acknowledging personal responsibility, however, by minimizing the incidence, severity, and effects of their actions. Fifty-two per cent of self-referred men were high minimizers, compared to only 18% of court-referred men.

Wife assaulters do appear to cluster into various patterns in their neutralization of self-punishment. Although most minimize the frequency, severity, and effects of their violence, some attribute it to themselves and others attribute it to their wives or to some situational feature (e.g., being drunk). Therapy includes a direct confrontation of these beliefs in order to stop the neutralization of self-punishment.

Conscience and Social Desirability

Dutton and Hemphill (1992) further explored the conscience of the wife assaulter by establishing the strength of the association between various self-reports to measures of socially desirable responding. Dutton and Hemphill argued that the strength of these associations signalled a sense of shame, guilt, or outright self-deception. Hence, the correlation of these reports with scores on image management or social desirability scales gives us some insight into those aspects of the assaulter's actions which he views as reprehensible. Specifically, those acts which he experiences as unacceptable should show report rates that correlate negatively with scales measuring a tendency to respond in a socially desirable fashion.

The results of this study are presented in Table 4.5. Social desirability scores correlated significantly and negatively with self-reports of verbal abuse, emotional abuse, and anger. Hence, the higher the need to present a favourable image (as assessed by the *MC* [Crowne & Marlowe 1960]), the lower the reports of these forms of abuse and of anger. Physical abuse reports were also negatively, but not significantly, correlated with the *MC*. This lack of significance may be due to the relatively restricted range of scores on the *CTS*. It is interesting that anger itself was under-reported as social desirability increased, reflecting the unacceptability of this feeling to men who do not know how to express it constructively and who confuse it with abusiveness.

Female victims of assault have no significant correlations between their *MC* scores and reports of their own or their partners' violence frequency, suggesting that, in aggregate, victims' reports may be more accurate than perpetrators' reports. Clearly, the perpetrators of intimate violence find their own abusiveness and their own anger unacceptable. On the other hand, victims' reports of abuse on the *CTS* surveys may be fairly accurate.

Chapter Summary and Conclusions

What do we know about the psychology of the wife assaulter as a result of this research? We know that he tends to have pronounced needs for interpersonal control vis-à-vis his wife but poor verbal skills with which to

Table 4.5

Correlations of perpetrators' self-report measures with the *Marlowe-Crowne Social Desirability Scale* (from Dutton & Hemphill 1992)

	Marlowe-Crowne Social Desirability Scale	
	Perpetrators	Victims
CTS: verbal aggression	-.38[a]	.01
CTS: physical aggression	-.20	-.09
MAI	-.44[a]	n/a
PMWI (emotional abuse)	-.50[a]	-.05
PMWI (dominance/isolation)	-.57[a]	-.08

[a] $p < .01$
MC: *Marlowe-Crowne Social Desirability Scale* (Crowne & Marlowe 1960)
CTS: *Conflict Tactics Scale* (Straus 1979)
MAI: *Multidimensional Anger Inventory* (Siegel 1986)
PMWI: *Psychological Maltreatment of Women Inventory* (Tolman 1989)

generate this control. We know that he reacts with exaggerated arousal and anger to scenes of male-female conflict. His anger is greatest when his wife has verbal power and appears to be abandoning him. Feelings of humiliation correlate highly with his feelings of anger.

Is there a common source for the need for control, the exaggerated anger and humiliation? We found that a background of verbal abuse by the mother correlated significantly with anger and humiliation responses to the conflict scenes. Psychoanalysts might argue that if a man experiences feelings of powerlessness and humiliation due to his relationship with a verbally abusive mother, then these feelings will be transferred into his marriage and an exaggerated anger response will result. Recall from Chapter 3 Winter's analysis of male reactions to maternal mixed communications: the male is both vulnerable to maternal nurturance and humiliated by maternal anger-rejection. Winter suggested that these mixed communications were the result of a patriarchal system that frustrated women and led to their ambivalent reactions to their sons.

We have noticed considerable suspicion amongst assaultive males about female motives. Although not all assaultive males would qualify as conjugally paranoid, exaggerated perceptions of malevolent intent behind female actions are common. We know that wife assaulters subdivide roughly into thirds (actually 25, 20, 30) in terms of whether they blame their wives, themselves, or their situations for their violence. We also know that victim-blamers are most likely to minimize their violence (its severity, incidence, and effects), and that self-blamers subdivide into two groups: one in which members minimize their violence and one in which members seem relatively honest about both the extent of, and their causal role in, their violence.

It is becoming clearer that all wife assaulters do not have similar etiologies. Instead, they differ both in terms of what aversive stimuli trigger their violence and how they rationalize it. What we have not yet addressed is whether subcategories of wife assaulters exist and whether some men become assaultive not in reaction to an external aversive stimulus but in reaction to an internal aversive state.

5
The Abusive Personality

The foregoing research located men who assault their wives in a social learning paradigm and began to formulate some general differences between those individuals and men who do not assault their wives. It may be misleading, however, to view all men who assault their wives as psychologically similar, as they do not all have the same patterns of violence.

As we saw in Chapter 1, some men engage in violence as part of a bidirectional exchange; others are generally violent; and still others engage in violence only in intimate relationships. This latter group in many ways represents a pure form of intimate violence. Unlike generally assaultive men, these men appear to have psychological issues that manifest themselves only in intimate relationships (as demonstrated by the exaggerated anger they showed to the abandonment scenarios).

Subcategories of Wife Assaulter

Subdividing wife assaulters into a variety of identifiable groups was first reported by Elbow (1977), who described four sets of clinical categories. She called them the *controller*, who views his wife as an object of control; the *defender*, who overprotects his wife; the *approval-seeker*, who makes excessive demands for approval from his wife to compensate for his poor self-esteem; and the *incorporator*, who needs his wife in order to validate and define himself.

Snyder and Fruchtman (1981) developed a typology based largely on battering behaviors described by women in shelters. The most frequent and severe violence was reported for men whose wives also described them as alcoholic and who saw their violence as alcohol-related. The authors did not attempt to relate the patterns of abuse to the mens' psychological characteristics.

Shields and Hannecke (1983) differentiated men who were violent only towards their wives, men who were generally violent, and men who were violent only outside the family. The wife assaulters were distinguishable from the other two groups in terms of social structural variables. Shields, McCall, and Hannecke (1988) also compared three such groups of men, finding that the men in the *family-only* violent group tended to be more law-abiding, of higher occupational status, less likely to have substance abuse problems, and more likely to have been victims of parental abuse than were the men in the other groups.

Hamberger and Hastings (1986) have taken a more traditional clinical approach to ascertaining whether subcategories of wife assaulters exist. They report assessments of 105 men attending a wife assault treatment program. Through factor analysis of self-reports on the *Millon Clinical Multiaxial Inventory* (*MCMI*) (Millon 1992) the authors identified three orthogonal factors: schizoidal/borderline, narcissistic/anti-social, and passive-dependent/compulsive. Their assaultive sample fell approximately equally into these three categories, four mixed categories, and one category that had no aspects of the pathology described in the others.

Subsequent comparison of the assaultive men with a non-assaultive population indicated that the former had greater difficulty modulating affective states and feeling comfortable in intimate relationships. The authors indicated that subject selection factors precluded generalization of these results to non-identified batterers, but they emphasized that their results had clinical relevance for batterers in treatment. Clearly, this is the case. If the majority of men entering treatment for wife assault are personality disordered the prognosis for effective treatment is lessened, as characterological disorders are unlikely to respond to short-term therapy.

Caesar (1986) administered the *MMPI* (Hathaway & McKinley 1967), the *Michigan Alcohol Screening Test* (Selzer 1971), and a two-hour clinical interview to twenty-six wife assaulters and to eighteen non-violent men in therapy. While the *MMPI* scores failed to discriminate between these two groups, the clinical interview did ascertain differences. From a content analysis of the clinical interviews, Caesar developed extensive descriptions of four subgroups of wife assaulters: the *tyrant*, the *exposed rescuer*, the *non-exposed altruist*, and the *psychotic wife assaulter*.

The *tyrant* subgroup was described as self-centred, hostile, paranoid, and less likely to be arrested than those in other wife assaulter subgroups. This particular description matches those of wife assaulters given by victims in shelters. The *exposed rescuers* were described as having hysterical personalities and alternating between sociability and hostility. This description is also similar to that given by battered women in shelters, according to Walker's 1979 study. The *non-exposed altruists* were unassertive and

constantly trying to please their wives, consequently feeling unappreci-
ated and victimized. The small sample size precluded clear distinctions
between groups.

Gondolf (1987) presented a typology of wife assaulters based on a cluster analysis of intake interviews with battered women in Texas shelters.
He labelled his subgroups *sociopathic, anti-social, chronic,* and *sporadic.*
Sociopathic wife assaulters were the most violent, both inside and outside
the home. They were also the most likely to indicate substance abuse. The
other subcategories seem to represent decreasing severity of abuse and are
described by Gondolf in a manner that implies ordinal severity of violence. A factor these subcategories have in common, according to
Gondolf, is that they all appear to compensate for their failure to live up
to the prescriptions for masculinity stipulated by their sex-role stereotypes.

The approach of Caesar, Elbow, and Gondolf runs the risk of generating
subjective categories that are not empirically and independently validated. The relationship of empirical scores to labels is unclear. In the
Caesar study the labels were largely subjective and the empirical aspect
of the research failed to generate clear subgroups. In the Gondolf study
two groups have labels that are virtually identical: sociopathic and anti-
social.

A better fit between data and label was provided by Saunders (1992),
who assessed 182 wife assaulters referred for treatment for the severity
and generalizability of their violence (using a modified form of the *CTS*),
sex-role stereotyping (using the *Attitudes Toward Women Scale* [Spence &
Helmreich 1978]), decisionmaking power (using the Blood and Wolfe
[1960] scale), level of conflict (*Marital Conflict Index*), anger (*Novaco Anger
Index* [Novaco 1976]), jealousy (White 1977), depression (*Beck Depression
Inventory* [Beck 1967]), and alcohol use (*Michigan Alcohol Screening Test*
[Selzer 1971]). Saunders began an elaborate clustering analysis that was
designed to assess whether distinct clusters, or subgroups, of batterers
existed. Initial analysis of scores indicated that the variables showing the
presence of subgroups were alcohol use (trimodal), sex-role stereotyping
(normal but bimodal distribution), and anger at partner (trimodal).

By combining variables Saunders made a preliminary case for three
types of wife assaulters (see Figure 5.1). The most severely violent is a man
who is assaultive both inside and outside the home and who abuses alcohol; such a man is likely to have been severely abused in his family of
origin and has current problems with impulse control. This description
is similar to that of Shields and Hannecke's *generally violent* type and
Gondolf's *sociopathic* type. A second group had the highest scores on

depression, jealousy, and anger. Saunders describes these men as *emotionally volatile*, most afraid of losing their partners, and suicidal. A third group could be described as *overcontrolled*: men who cannot express feelings (including anger) and who, presumably, let conflicts build to the explosive stage.

Figure 5.1

Saunders's (1992) categories of wife assaulter

Saunders's category	Descriptors	Psychological classification
1. Generally violent	• anti-social • impulsive • generally violent	psychopathic
2. Emotionally volatile	• angry, jealous, depressed • only violent with wife • cyclical tension	borderline
3. Overcontrolled	• unassertive, pleasing • tries to escape conflict • only violent with wife	avoidant

An obvious future step, pending the outcome of Saunders's present cross-validation work, would be to relate his subcategories to standardized clinical assessments. Of particular interest is the subcategory Saunders describes as *emotionally volatile*. These men manifest the strongest anger in intimate relationships (like the men in the Dutton and Browning [1988] videotape study) and sound similar to the descriptions given by transition house women in Walker's (1979a) study of batterers.

In Walker's study, wives of assaultive men often reported the man becoming moody and irritable in the absence of any change in his external environment. They described a tension-building phase of what came to be known as the abuse cycle. The observation of the tension-building phase suggested an internal build-up of tension that occurred independently of events in the social environment. If this is true, a subgroup of assaultive men may exist for whom the *aversive stimulus* (in the social learning terminology of Chapter 3) is internal. These men may have a personality structure that is distinct from other men and even from other wife assaulters. Part of that personality structure may include repeated internally generated dysphoric states that cause them to become moody, irritable, and abusive. These states could be the basis of the abuse cycle. Our next set of studies, called the Borderline Personality Organization (BPO) studies, represent an attempt to discover the nature of this abusive personality.

The Cycle of Violence and the Cyclical Personality

In her seminal study of 120 battered women, Lenore Walker (1979a) described what she termed the *cycle of violence*, whereby relationships go through a cycle of three stages: tension-building, acute battering, and contrition (see Figure 5.2).

Figure 5.2

Walker's (1979) cycle of violence

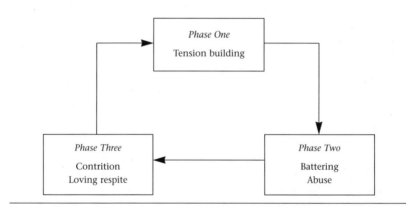

The first phase is characterized by escalating anger and outbursts on the part of the man, accompanied by a recognition that his behavior is wrong (but feeling it is out of his control), fear of the woman leaving, and a manifestation of greater oppression, jealousy, and possessiveness in an attempt to keep her captive. Phase two 'is characterized by the uncontrollable discharge of tensions that have built up during phase one' (p. 59). The trigger for moving into phase two, as reported by Walker's respondents, was either 'an external event or the *internal state of the man*' (p. 60). This uncontrollable rage generates acute battering until the batterer becomes 'exhausted and emotionally depleted' (p. 61), typically after from two to twenty-four hours. Victims report the battering occurring in response to anything they do (e.g., both staying quiet and answering back escalate anger). Upon exhaustion, phase three begins. It is characterized by contrition, confession, promises of reform and help-seeking behaviors, and by attempts to convince the victim and others that the abuse will not recur. Walker's respondents depicted these three phases as predictable and described pre-emptive strikes in which they would act to hasten the inevitable abuse phase.

Until recently, little attention has been paid to the dynamics generating cyclical abuse by men. In this section we review potential explanations for intermittent anger in intimate relationships from the perspective of personality, and we suggest what might be the origins of these particular personality types. Our focus is on the man who is an intermittent, predatory batterer in intimate relationships.

Cyclical (Phasic) Personality Types

In a description of homicidal perpetrators, Revitch and Schlesinger (1981) describe a *catathymic personality* which undergoes three stages: incubation, violent act, and relief. The primary affect during incubation is depression, accompanied by a constant sense of tension build-up. When the violent act is homicide, it appears to be preceded by a period of brooding. Retrospective accounts of this incubation period indicate that the perpetrator viewed the tension build-up as being caused by the victim, whom he perceived to be acting in a malevolent and persecutory manner towards him. The relief experienced after catathymic violence comes from a release of stored up affect: specifically, depressive and anxious symptoms and muscular tension. Although Revitch and Schlesinger's analysis was meant to be applied to intimate homicides, it appears, prima facie, to also describe the abuse cycle. Meloy (1988) notes that chronic catathymic violence necessitates a borderline personality organization in the perpetrator.

Kernberg (1977) had identified borderline personality organization as one of the three major forms of character pathology, bounded by psychotic and neurotic personality organization, and estimated its prevalence in the general population at about 11% to 15%. The more severe borderline personality disorder was estimated as less prevalent. Borderline personality was earlier called *cyclothymia* and *la folie circulaire*, terms that captured the cyclical nature of its behavioral and mood manifestations (Akiskal 1992; Millon 1981).

Gunderson (1984) described a three-phase defence structure of borderline personality (BP) that produced sudden shifts in the individual's phenomenology, affect, and behavior. This defence structure could produce the kinds of behavior depicted by Walker's (1979a) abuse cycle description of some wife assaulters. Gunderson describes the BP as existing in a *dysphoric stalemate* in relationships, in which intimacy needs are unmet and the requisite motivation and skills to assert those needs are non-existent. This first stage resembles the tension-building phase of Walker's abuse cycle (and Revitch and Schlesinger's incubation phase). Stage two, according to Gunderson, expresses itself as anger, devaluation of the significant other, and/or open rage. This would correspond to Walker's battering stage of the abuse cycle. Stage three occurs when the relationship with the significant other appears to be lost. At this point, the BP engages in behaviors designed to ward off the subjective experience of aloneness, such as the exaggerated appeasement behaviors that assaultive husbands engage in after the abusive episode.

If the Revitch and Schlesinger analysis applies to wife assaulters, then relief from stored negative affect would contribute to the man's subjective capacity to express positive emotions at this juncture in the abuse cycle – a point realized by Walker, who claimed that 'the tension built up in phase two and released in phase three is gone' (1979a: 65).

The essential characteristics (in order of importance) of the borderline personality are described in the Focus section below. Dutton (1994a, 1994b) viewed borderline personality organization as a continuum of personality problems characterized by identity difficulties that become salient in intimate relationships. This continuum is reflected by scores on the *BPO* scale (described below) and relates to a variety of abuse behaviors and emotions.

Focus
Essential Characteristics of the Borderline Personality

(1) A proclivity for intense, unstable interpersonal relationships characterized by intermittent undermining of the significant other, manipulation, and masked dependency.
(2) An unstable sense of self with intolerance of being alone and abandonment anxiety.
(3) Intense anger, demandingness, and impulsivity, usually tied to substance abuse or promiscuity.

Source: Gunderson (1984)

The Borderline Personality Organization Studies

In order to test the notion that borderline personality organization may constitute a personality explanation for cyclical, predatory abusiveness,

Dutton and his colleagues conducted a series of studies designed to esti-mate the strength of its relationship (as assessed by a self-report instru-ment) to the man's reports of the frequency and severity of his physical violence. Further tests validated the initial test by relating the man's *BPO* scores to his partner's reports of his abusiveness, including psychological maltreatment.

Self-report scales were administered to 140 men in treatment for wife assault as part of their general assessment. All men were assessed either prior to or during the first three weeks of a sixteen-week treatment pro-gram in order to minimize the latter's effects on test results. A demo-graphically matched control group was obtained by paying subject fees for questionnaires completed by members of a local blue-collar union. The measures are described below.

Essentially, we assessed differential patterns of emotional expression and violence and the presence of current trauma symptoms and substance abuse. A full report on the technical aspects of the design and analysis of this study is available in Dutton (1994a) and Dutton and Starzomski (1993, 1994).

Measures

Testing and assessment included:

(1) *Conflict.* As described in Chapter 1, the *Conflict Tactics Scale* (*CTS*) (Straus 1979) is a standardized scale designed to measure the frequency and intensity of nineteen tactics used in dyads to resolve conflict. The scale includes rational tactics, withdrawal, and a variety of verbally and physically abusive strategies. Respondents report both their own use of these tactics and that of an interactant. This allows independent assess-ment of both making use of, and being a recipient of, various conflict tac-tics in a specific relationship. Straus, Gelles, and Steinmetz (1980) have published population norms for usage of each tactic in a variety of inti-mate relationships.

(2) *Borderline Personality Organization.* The *Self-Report Instrument for Border-line Personality Organization* (*BPO*) (Oldham, Clarkin, Appelbaum, Carr, Kernberg, Lotterman, & Haas 1985) is a 30-item instrument derived through factor analysis of a 130-item questionnaire designed by the authors (see Figure 5.3). The 30-item scale retains components with the strongest factor loadings for each of three subscales: identity diffusion, primitive defences, and reality testing.[1]

Identity diffusion measures a poorly integrated sense of self or of signifi-cant others. It may be reflected in a subjective experience of chronic emptiness, or in contradictory perceptions of the self, contradictory

Figure 5.3

Borderline Personality Organizational Scale (Oldham et al. 1985)

For each of the statements below, please indicate how true it is about you by *circling* the most appropriate number beside each statement.

1	2	3	4	5
never true	seldom true	sometimes true	often true	always true

1. I feel like a fake or an impostor, that others see me as quite different at times. 1 2 3 4 5
2. I feel almost as if I'm someone else like a friend or relative or even someone I don't know. 1 2 3 4 5
3. It is hard for me to trust people because they so often turn against me or betray me. 1 2 3 4 5
4. People tend to respond to me by either overwhelming me with love or abandoning me. 1 2 3 4 5
5. I see myself in totally different ways at different times. 1 2 3 4 5
6. I act in ways that strike others as unpredictable and erratic. 1 2 3 4 5
7. I find I do things which get other people upset and I don't know why such things upset them. 1 2 3 4 5
8. Uncontrollable events are the cause of my difficulties. 1 2 3 4 5
9. I hear things that other people claim are not really there. 1 2 3 4 5
10. I feel empty inside. 1 2 3 4 5
11. I tend to feel things in a somewhat extreme way, experiencing either great joy or intense despair. 1 2 3 4 5
12. It is hard for me to be sure about what others think of me, even people who have known me very well. 1 2 3 4 5
13. I'm afraid of losing myself when I get sexually involved. 1 2 3 4 5
14. I feel that certain episodes in my life do not count and are better erased from my mind. 1 2 3 4 5
15. I find it hard to describe myself. 1 2 3 4 5
16. I've had relationships in which I couldn't feel whether I or the other person was thinking or feeling something. 1 2 3 4 5
17. I don't feel like myself unless exciting things are going on around me. 1 2 3 4 5
18. I feel people don't give me the respect I deserve unless I put pressure on them. 1 2 3 4 5
19. People see me as rude or inconsiderate and I don't know why. 1 2 3 4 5
20. I can't tell whether certain physical sensations I'm having are real, or whether I am imagining them. 1 2 3 4 5
21. Some of my friends would be surprised if they knew how differently I behave in different situations. 1 2 3 4 5

(continued on next page)

Figure 5.3 (continued)

Borderline Personality Organizational Scale (Oldham et al. 1985)

22. I find myself doing things which feel okay while I am doing them but which I later find hard to believe I did.	1 2 3 4 5
23. I believe that things will happen simply by thinking about them.	1 2 3 4 5
24. When I want something from someone else, I can't ask for it directly.	1 2 3 4 5
25. I feel I'm a different person at home as compared to how I am at work or at school.	1 2 3 4 5
26. I am not sure whether a voice I have heard, or something that I have seen, is my imagination or not.	1 2 3 4 5
27. I have heard or seen things when there is no apparent reason for it.	1 2 3 4 5
28. I feel I don't get what I want.	1 2 3 4 5
29. I need to admire people in order to feel secure.	1 2 3 4 5
30. Somehow, I never know quite how to conduct myself with people.	1 2 3 4 5

Average score for control group males = 60.0
Average score for diagnosed borderlines = 75.0
Average score for wife assaulters = 71.0

behavior that cannot be integrated in an emotionally meaningful way, and impoverished perceptions of others. Identity diffusion is assessed by ascertaining difficulties in describing one's own personality or the personalities of others, uncertainty about career or goals, contradictory behaviors, and instability in intimate relationships.

Primitive defences include splitting, idealization, devaluation, omnipotence, denial, projection, and projective identification. All these defences are theoretically understood to protect the ego by dissociating contradictory experiences of the self and of significant others. They are called 'primitive' because they are believed to develop very early (around age 2-3).

Reality testing items cover external versus internal origins of perceptions, evaluation of one's own behavior in terms of social criteria for reality, differentiation of self from non-self, internal reality testing, and the cognitive process of reality testing. The assumption the subscale makes is that men suffering from borderline personality organization have transient psychotic episodes. The *BPO* self-report instrument does not assess abusiveness or aggression. Hence, any associations with other scales reported below are not attributable to item overlap.

(3) *Anger.* The *Multidimensional Anger Inventory* (*MAI*) (Siegel 1986) (see

Figure 5.4) is a 38-item self-report scale assessing the following dimensions of anger response: frequency, duration, magnitude, mode of expression, hostile outlook, and range of anger-eliciting situations.[2]

(4) *Jealousy*. The *Interpersonal Jealousy Scale* (*IJS*) (Mathes & Severa 1981; Mathes, Philips, Skowran, & Dick III 1982) is a 28-item scale that measures romantic jealousy. Tests of the construct validity of this measure have shown it to be correlated with dependency. This scale has a high internal reliability and a low correlation with social desirability response bias.

(5) *Trauma Symptoms*. The *Trauma Symptom Checklist* (*TSC-33*) (Briere & Runtz 1989) is a brief (33-item), reliable instrument that has been shown to discriminate female victims of childhood sexual abuse from non-victimized women (see Figure 1.5). The *TSC-33* contains five subscales: dissociation, anxiety, depression, post-sexual abuse trauma-hypothesized (PSAT), and sleep disturbance. The PSAT-hypothesized includes those symptoms thought to be most characteristic of sexual abuse experiences but which may also occur as a result of other types of trauma.[3]

(6) *Psychological Maltreatment*. The *Psychological Maltreatment of Women Inventory* (*PMWI*) (Tolman 1989) was used to provide a more comprehensive assessment of abuse, since psychological abuse is more common than is physical abuse (Straus, Gelles, & Steinmetz 1980). It was completed by women who reported their male partners' abusiveness. The *PMWI* contains 58 items (rated from 0 'never' to 4 'very frequently'), which comprise forms of emotional/verbal abuse and dominance/isolation (see Figure 1.4). Dominance/isolation includes items related to rigid observance of traditional sex roles, demands for subservience, and isolation from resources. In contrast, emotional/verbal abuse includes withholding emotional resources, verbal attacks, and behavior that degrades women.[4]

Results

The overall *BPO* scale score obtained by assaultive men was 71; the mean score reported for a group of men diagnosed with borderline personality was 75 (Oldham et al. 1985). The mean score obtained by our non-assaultive control group was 60.0; the mean score reported for Oldham et al.'s non-borderline group was 61. At first glance, the scores of assaultive men are similar to diagnosed borderlines.

To assess the relationship between the *BPO* scale and other scales two techniques were used: first, correlations were computed (see Table 5.1); second, the top ($n = 29$) and bottom ($n = 30$) quartile scorers on the *BPO* scale were compared. All reported results are significant at .05 or beyond. Specific statistical information is available in the published reports.

Figure 5.4

Multidimensional Anger Inventory (Siegel 1986)

Everybody gets angry from time to time. A number of statements that people have used to describe the times they get angry are included below. Read each statement and circle the number to the right of the statement that best describes how it applies to you, from 1 (completely *undescriptive* of you) to 5 (completely *descriptive* of you). There are no right or wrong answers.

1	2	3	4	5
completely undescriptive of you	mostly undescriptive of you	partly descriptive and partly undescriptive	mostly descriptive of you	completely descriptive of you

1. I tend to get angry more frequently than most people.	1 2 3 4 5
2. Other people tend to get angrier than I do in similar circumstances.	1 2 3 4 5
3. I harbor grudges that I don't tell anyone about.	1 2 3 4 5
4. I try to get even when I'm angry with someone.	1 2 3 4 5
5. I am secretly quite critical of others.	1 2 3 4 5
6. It is easy to make me angry.	1 2 3 4 5
7. When I am angry with someone, I let that person know..	1 2 3 4 5
8. I have met many people who are supposed to be experts who are no better than I.	1 2 3 4 5
9. Something makes me angry almost every day.	1 2 3 4 5
10. I often feel angrier than I think I should.	1 2 3 4 5
11. I feel guilty about expressing my anger.	1 2 3 4 5
12. When I am angry with someone, I take it out on whoever is around.	1 2 3 4 5
13. Some of my friends have habits that annoy and bother me very much.	1 2 3 4 5
14. I am surprised at how often I feel angry.	1 2 3 4 5
15. Once I let people know that I am angry, I can put it out of my mind.	1 2 3 4 5
16. People talk about me behind my back.	1 2 3 4 5
17. At times, I feel angry for no specific reason.	1 2 3 4 5
18. I can make myself angry about something in the past just by thinking about it.	1 2 3 4 5
19. Even after I have expressed my anger, I have trouble forgetting about it.	1 2 3 4 5
20. When I hide my anger from others, I think about it for a long time.	1 2 3 4 5
21. People can bother me just by being around.	1 2 3 4 5
22. When I get angry, I stay angry for hours.	1 2 3 4 5
23. When I hide my anger from others, I forget about it pretty quickly.	1 2 3 4 5

(continued on next page)

Figure 5.4 (continued)

24. I try to talk over problems with people without letting them know I'm angry.	1 2 3 4 5
25. When I get angry, I calm down faster than most people.	1 2 3 4 5
26. I get so angry, I feel that I might lose control.	1 2 3 4 5
27. If I let people see the way I feel, I'd be considered a hard person to get along with.	1 2 3 4 5
28. I am on my guard with people who are friendlier than I expected.	1 2 3 4 5
29. It's difficult for me to let people know I'm angry.	1 2 3 4 5
30. I get angry when:	
a. someone lets me down	1 2 3 4 5
b. people are unfair	1 2 3 4 5
c. something blocks my plans	1 2 3 4 5
d. I am delayed	1 2 3 4 5
e. someone embarrasses me	1 2 3 4 5
f. I have to take orders from someone less capable than I	1 2 3 4 5
g. I have to work with incompetent people	1 2 3 4 5
h. I do something stupid	1 2 3 4 5
i. I am not given credit for something I have done	1 2 3 4 5

For anger, the high *BPO* (top quartile) scorers reported significantly higher scores on the *MAI* than did the low *BPO* scorers (the high *BPO* mean was 99.2, compared with a low *BPO* mean of 76.7). High *BPO* scorers reported significantly greater ($p < .001$) scores on all subscales of the *MAI*. High *BPO* scorers also reported significantly higher jealousy scores than did low scorers.

As can be seen from Table 5.1, the total and all subscales on the *BPO* measure correlated significantly with self-reported anger and with verbal/symbolic and physical aggression. To further examine the relationship of BPO to the use of verbal and physical aggression, high and low quartile scores on the *BPO* scale were compared for verbal and physical abuse scores. High *BPO* scorers reported significantly more verbal and physical abuse than did low BPO scorers.

All *BPO* scores (total and subscales) correlated significantly with all scores on the *TSC-33* (total and subscales). To further examine the relationship of *BPO* to trauma symptoms, top and bottom quartile *BPO* scorers were compared on their total *TSC-33* scores. High quartile *BPO* scorers had significantly higher totals on every subscale of the *TSC-33*. High *BPO*

Table 5.1

Correlation of *Borderline Personality Organization Scale* total and subscale scores with other scales

		BPO Subscales		
	BPO total	Reality testing	Primitive defences	Identity diffusion
CTS:				
Verbal/symbolic aggression	.32[b]	.28[b]	.33[b]	.29[b]
Physical aggression	.24[a]	.22[a]	.26[a]	.24[a]
MAI (anger)	.62[c]	.62[c]	.48[c]	.60[c]
TSC-33 (trauma symptoms)	.67[c]	.63[c]	.65[c]	.68[c]

[a] $p < .05$
[b] $p < .01$
[c] $p < .001$

scorers had a mean *TSC-33* score of 44.6, compared to 17.4 for bottom quartile *BPO*.

Finally, a discriminant function analysis was performed to ascertain which concurrent variables discriminated low from high *BPO* scorers. Overall, three variables (trauma symptoms, anger, and jealousy) correctly classified 88% of high and low scorers.

To validate the apparently powerful correlations between *BPO* and abuse, Dutton and Starzomski (1993) correlated men's *BPO* scores with their partners' reports of the former's abusiveness. These data are reported in Table 5.2.

Table 5.2

Correlations of borderline personality organization and anger scales with victims' reports of psychological and physical abuse

	PMWI		CTS
	Dominance/isolation	Emotional abuse	Total physical abuse
BPO total	.58[c]	.55[c]	.29[b]
Anger total	.48[c]	.42[c]	.18[a]

[a] $p < .05$
[b] $p < .01$
[c] $p < .001$

We attempted to predict the variability in the women's reports of abuse victimization by entering scores on the *BPO* and *MAI* scales into a multiple regression on the women's *PMWI* scores. The results can be seen in Table 5.3. As can be seen, the combination of the men's *BPO* and *MAI* scales is a major factor in predicting women's reports of maltreatment. They accounted for 50% of the variance in women's scores of dominance/isolation and 35% of their scores for emotional abuse.

The Centrality of *BPO*

The results of these studies suggest that *BPO* is a useful unifying construct with which to examine a wide inventory of abuse-related emotions and behaviors. The *BPO* scale scores correlated significantly with anger, jealousy, experienced trauma symptoms, and frequency of use of both verbal and physical aggression. The version of the *CTS* used in this study had a format that compressed *CTS* scores, resulting in a smaller range than that obtained with other formats (Browning & Dutton 1986; Dutton & Hemphill 1992). Hence, the correlations of *BPO* with *CTS* scores may be higher than the present study suggests.

Clearly, a variety of conflict issues can lead to assaultiveness, including those that are not directly intimacy-related (such as finances); further, as discussed in Chapter 2, an individual becomes assaultive within the context of familial, communal, and cultural environments – all of which play a role in the development of his or her perceptions and behaviors. However, men with high BPO tend to respond to intimacy issues with more anger and aggression than do other men and may, in fact, be angered by the very experience of intimacy.

The high levels of jealousy and anger reported by the men with high *BPO* scores, compared to those with low *BPO* scores, helps cast some light on the potential etiology of these emotions. As described earlier, assaulted women in the Walker (1984) and Rounsaville (1978) samples reported extreme possessiveness, mood shifts, and anger in their husbands, all of which escalated out of all proportion to the triggering event.

With our current sample, two subscales (comprised of only sixteen items) from the *MAI* and the *BPO* scales account for 18% of the variance in women's reports of physical abuse – a fairly significant amount for prediction purposes. However, as reported above, the *MAI* and the *BPO* scales account for an impressive amount of the variance found in psychological abuse measures (50% of dominance/isolation and 35% of emotional abuse). Interestingly, this predictive power was maintained for psychological abuse in the control group (where physical abuse was rare), implying that *BPO* scores and anger may define an abuse profile that manifests

Table 5.3

Multiple regression of the *Psychological Maltreatment of Women Inventory (PMWI)*

Domination-isolation subscale

Variable	Beta	Corr	Mult R	R square	Adj R square
Anger magnitude	.63	.63	.63	.40	.39
Anger-in	.31	.58	.68	.46	.44
BPO: reality	.23	.56	.70	.49	.47
Anger: hostility	-.22	.20	.73	.53	.50

Emotional abuse subscale

Variable	Beta	Corr	Mult R	R square	Adj R square
Anger magnitude	.56	.56	.56	.31	.30
BPO: identity	.29	.52	.61	.37	.35

Adjusted R^2 = the amount of variance on the PMWI accounted for by a variable or combination of variables.

Figure 5.5

The centrality of borderline personality organization to abusiveness

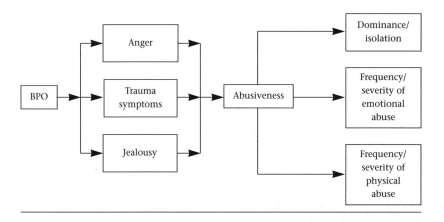

differently in different groups of men, possibly as a function of abuse styles learned in the family of origin. Thus, we are currently examining the *CTS* data for these men's families of origin.

The notion that borderline personality organization constitutes a central feature of an abusive profile is consistent with previous research demonstrating a psychopathological aspect to wife assault causation (Beasley & Stoltenberg 1992; Hamberger & Hastings 1986, 1991; Hart, Dutton, & Newlove 1993; Hastings & Hamberger 1988). In these studies, rates of psychopathology in wife assaulter samples have been very high – in the 80% to 90% range. Although Pagelow (1993) has argued that these rates may not generalize to non-clinical samples, Dutton and Starzomski (1994) found high rates of psychopathology to be true for self-referred wife assaulters as well as for court-referred wife assaulters. Furthermore, they found *BPO* scores to be significantly higher for self-referred than for court-referred men. Maiuro, Cahn, Vitaliano, and Zegree (1986) found elevated anger and hostility scores, as well as elevated depression scores, in domestically violent men. Dutton and Starzomski (1994) replicated this and found pronounced anger and depression to be even stronger for self-referred assaultive men than for court-referred men. Hence, an accumulating body of evidence points towards the presence of personality disorders and strong dysfunctional negative affect in assaultive men.

Our focus on borderline personality organization argues for a trait component to abusiveness that may interact with early modelling and culturally learned cues to direct the form of abusiveness in intimate relationships. Curiously, given the clinical feature of intense anger described by Gunderson (1984), the *BPO* does not directly assess for anger. For this reason, the addition of an anger measure (*MAI*) strongly assists in abuse prediction.

Why do these men get so angry in intimate relationships? The answer may lie in part in what intimacy means to them. For men high in borderline personality organization, intimate relationships serve the unenviable task of maintaining their ego integrity. With an unstable sense of self (as measured by the identity diffusion subscale) and an inability to tolerate aloneness (Gunderson 1984), these men depend on their relationships with their women partners to prevent their fragile selfhoods from disintegrating. Yet those very relationships are fraught with dysphoric stalemates – the men's inability to communicate intimacy needs coupled with their being extremely demanding. The intimate partner of the high *BPO* scorer is asked to do the impossible, and when she fails, or appears in his eyes to fail, extreme anger results because his very sense of self is threatened and because his use of projection as a defence (as measured by the primitive defences subscale) results in externalizing blame to his partner. He views her, at that phase of the relationship, as all bad. If that impasse resolves, he then tends to view her as all good and himself as all bad and enters the contrition phase of the abuse cycle (see Walker 1979a).

It may be that the wife assaulters' self-reports of extreme anger in response to videos depicting uncontrollable intimacy change (Dutton and Browning [1988]) have this same basis: an unstable sense of selfhood in a subgroup of wife assaulters that depends on the woman partner for stability while denying and masking such dependency. Clinicians such as Ganley (1981) and Sonkin (1987) have described this dependency. The jealousy that also characterizes such men can be viewed as a subset of this dependency and the consequent anxieties about relationship loss.

In my opinion, much of the literature on causative factors in wife assault has overlooked the issue of intimacy anxiety, focusing instead on patriarchy and the use of abusive tactics by men to reinforce male dominance (Dobash & Dobash 1979; Straus 1976). While it is important to acknowledge how societal inequalities contribute to the victimization of women, power does not appear to have a strong effect on the frequency of abuse (Coleman & Straus 1986) and sociopolitical profiles of abusers do not accurately discriminate them from non-abusers (Hotaling & Sugarman 1986). Indeed, the majority of men living under patriarchal norms remain non-violent towards intimate partners for the duration of their marriage (Straus et al. 1980; Straus & Gelles 1986). Hence, it appears that some other factor, in addition to patriarchy, must operate to determine whether a man will become abusive in an intimate relationship. I contend that this other factor is a personality component that relates a man's selfhood to intimacy, as is the case with borderline personality organization. Depending on another to maintain one's sense of selfhood is a powerless role which many men attempt to mask with the trappings of sociopolitical power. Analyses of wife assault that focus solely on sociopolitical factors may mistake such trappings for a subjective sense of control (see also Adler 1966; Ng 1980).

Sociological/feminist criticism which argues that perspectives treating assaultiveness as a product of individual pathology overlook broader forces that support violence towards women makes an important point. We attempt to address it here by viewing borderline personality organization as a continuum rather than as a discrete pathological category. If early experience contributes to a propensity for assaultiveness, it may be that elements of borderline personality organization are strongly attuned to aspects of the culture that direct and justify abuse. The primitive defences of the borderline personality, which involve splitting 'good objects' from 'bad objects,' and, hence, as seeing a woman or women in black-and-white categories, are reinforced by cultural judgements about women's sexuality. Cultures that divide women into 'madonnas' and 'whores' provide a sanctioned reinforcement of this splitting of objects in the assaultive borderline man. Cultures that socialize men to expect women to be responsible for relationship outcomes provide a rationale for men to expect that their intimate female partners should maintain their ego integrity. Any dysphoric stalemates that occur are then viewed as the woman's fault and contribute to her devaluation. From this perspective, the borderline personality pattern contains emotional demands that are directed and justified through the ambient culture.

The Origin of the Abusive Personality

How does the abusive personality originate? Are there factors in the family of origin that increase the likelihood of abusive sons? Although Chapter 3 reviewed some evidence on modelling of abusive responses, the development of an entire personality constellation seems too comprehensive to simply be a result of such modelling. Our research has developed some promising leads based on retrospective reports of assaultive men. We turn now to these studies.

Wife Assault and Early Trauma

In a review of empirical studies, Hotaling and Sugarman (1986) found that husband-to-wife violence was associated with childhood witnessing of interparental assault in 88% of studies and with direct childhood experience with violence in 69% of studies. Straus et al. (1980) and Kalmuss (1984) found rates of having been physically abused and witnessing interparental abuse that were three times the population average in groups of men who used physical violence against their wives.

Clinical and research descriptions of wife assaulters clearly share many of the characteristics attributed to trauma victims. Wife assaulters have been described as poor monitors of affect (Ganley 1981; Gondolf 1985a) and as suffering from problems with impulse control and exaggerated dependency (Ganley 1981; Dutton & Browning 1988). Trauma victims have exaggerated separation anxiety, problems with regulation of affect and impulse control, an intense dependency on primary interpersonal relationships, and an inability to tolerate being alone. All of these clinical characteristics are similar to those of persons diagnosed as having borderline personality organization.

The literature we have reviewed suggests that there is a similar clinical profile for men who were victims of childhood abuse, men who assault their wives, and men exhibiting borderline personality organization. While van der Kolk (1987) reports evidence linking trauma to borderline personality organization, this connection has never before been studied in a population of wife assaulters. The strong relationship we found between borderline personality organization and trauma symptoms may indicate that the two have a common origin. It is our hypothesis that there is a correlation amongst childhood trauma, frequency/severity of wife assault, and borderline personality organization in a group of wife assaulters. In order to investigate this question, Dutton and Ryan (1994) had assaultive men fill out assessments of parental treatment during childhood as well as the *BPO* scale. The sample used was, once again, men seeking treatment for wife assault.

Measures

(1) *Conflict in the Family of Origin.* As described above, the *CTS* (Straus 1979) is a standardized scale designed to measure the frequency and intensity of nineteen tactics used in dyads to resolve conflict. For assessment of conflict tactics in the family of origin, dyadic pairs, such as father-mother, father-you, and mother-you, are presented. Straus et al. (1980) have published population norms for usage of each tactic in a variety of intimate relationships.

(2) *Recollections of Early Parenting.* In addition, the *Egna Minnen Betraffande Uppfostran* (*EMBU*) scale (Perris, Jacobsson, Lindstrom, von

Knorring, & Perris 1980) was used to provide a quantitative measure of the respondents' memories of their upbringing. The *EMBU* (English version) is an 80-item scale with a number of subscales scored separately for mother and father. For purposes of the present study, just forty-three items were used: the subscales assessing recollections of maternal warmth and rejection and those assessing paternal warmth and rejection.

(3) *Early Sexual Experiences.* A scale to assess early sexual experiences was created as follows: Respondents were asked, 'Before the age of sixteen did you experience any of the following activities with an adult non-relative much older than you, or a child your age whom you felt forced or pressured you?' A list of eight sexual activities followed. This question was repeated specifically for family members. If any activities were acknowledged, follow-up questions on the relationship to the other person, frequency of the acts, age at onset, and so on, were asked.

Table 5.4

Current *BPO* scores and experiences of abuse in the family of origin

BPO scores	Verbal abuse		Physical abuse	
	By father	By mother	By father	By mother
Primitive defences	.00	.30[b]	.44[c]	.36[b]
Identity diffusion	-.12	.17	.32[b]	.25[a]
Reality testing	-.17	.29	.25[a]	.24[a]
Total	-.10	.20[a]	.37[b]	.32[b]

[a] $p < .05$
[b] $p < .01$
[c] $p < .001$

Results

Borderline personality organization was found to be significantly associated with reports of parental abuse during childhood on the *CTS*. These findings are reported in Table 5.4.

The results for the *EMBU* reports of parental warmth and rejection are reported in Table 5.5.

Scores for sexual abuse were not significant.

To estimate the impact of all early abuse factors on the formation of the borderline personality organization pattern in assaultive men, a discriminant function analysis was performed on high versus low *BPO* scores, using all early treatment self-report data. The results of this analysis can be seen in Table 5.6.

Table 5.5

Correlations of *BPO* scale with reports of parental warmth and rejection (*EMBU*)

	Warmth		Rejection	
BPO scores	By father	By mother	By father	By mother
Primitive defences	-.28[b]	-.24[b]	.39[c]	.34[b]
Identity diffusion	-.42[c]	.36[c]	.50[c]	.30[b]
Reality testing	-.35[b]	-.23[a]	.39[c]	.16[a]
Total	-.39[c]	-.31[b]	.49[c]	.30[b]

[a] $p < .05$
[b] $p < .01$
[c] $p < .001$

Table 5.6

Correlations between discriminating variables and canonical discriminant function for abusiveness

Variable	Function 1
Paternal rejection	.87
Paternal physical abuse	.64
Paternal warmth	-.63
Maternal warmth	-.37
Maternal rejection	.35
Maternal physical abuse	.30

In this analysis we found that paternal rejection (as assessed by the *EMBU*) was the strongest contributor to *BPO* scores, followed by physical abuse by the father. Cold, rejecting, and abusive fathers may do more than model abusive behaviors; they may contribute to the formation of a personality pattern that is associated with adult abusiveness, anger, depression, and mood cycles.

Linear comparisons of men in the top quartile of the *BPO* scale with men in the bottom quartile revealed significant differences in parental rejection ratings, especially for rejection by the father (58.5 for high *BPO*, 39.6 for low *BPO*). The results indicate, in other words, that early parenting has strong effects with respect to abusiveness. The effects of having a cold, rejecting father are especially strong.

Attachment and Abusiveness

All intimate relationships contain the accumulated baggage of previous intimate attachments. In our first intimate attachment we are exceptionally open and vulnerable to the actions of those who care for us. As we shall see below, when this care is withheld or given sporadically, hurt and fear can ensue, feelings that are eventually converted into angry behaviors. These behaviors then become part of the individual's repertoire in later relationships.

When a wife assaulter is asked why he acted as he did, most often he will either say he doesn't know or he will blame his behavior on some trivial action of the woman. The anger often seems inexplicable even to himself. One is left with the sense that a residual pool of anger exists in these individuals that, in some crucial way, is related to intimacy and the vulnerability that it generates. This intimacy developed very early in the man's existence and is largely unconscious.

Attachment theorists analyze the development of emotional and behavioral responses to intimate relationships. Originating in the theoretical work of British psychoanalyst John Bowlby and the empirical studies of American psychologist Mary Ainsworth, in the past two decades attachment theory has amassed a huge corpus of empirical studies.

Early Attachment

John Bowlby (1969, 1973, 1980), in a landmark series of books entitled *Attachment and Loss*, developed the notion that attachment was of paramount importance for human emotional growth, serving a vital biological function and indispensable for the survival of the infant. In his view, the human need for secure attachment is the result of an evolutionary development that rivals feeding and mating in importance. In our search for early developmental factors related to adult abusiveness it occurred to us that attachment, or, more precisely, *insecure* attachment, could be a candidate.

Bowlby (1969, 1973) and Ainsworth (Ainsworth, Blehar, Waters, & Wall 1978) identify three important principles that drive infant attachment behavior. First, alarm of any kind, stemming from any source, activates an *attachment behavioral system* in the infant. Second, when this system is intensely active, only physical contact with the attachment figure will serve to terminate it. Third, when the *attachment behavioral system* is activated for a long time without reaching termination, angry behavior results. Hence, a fundamental principle of attachment research is that *anger follows unmet attachment needs*.

Bowlby defined attachment as a bond developed with 'some other differentiated and preferred individual *who is conceived as stronger and/or wiser'* (1977:203). Proportional to this sense of the other having absolute and unrestricted power over the infant, threats or separations to that secure attachment should produce emotional responses that are extremely strong, such as terror, grief, and rage. The reader is reminded that in men these fundamental and primitive emotions are initially connected to the opposite sex.

Bowlby emphasized the importance of the relationship between the infant and the primary caretaker for the development of the self and of later social behavior. During the first six months the infant develops many behaviors (e.g., smiling, crying upon the caretaker leaving) that function to create closer proximity and interaction with that person. In the second six months, proximity and interaction promoting behaviors are integrated into a coherent system organized around a particular figure. At nine months, the goal of proximity/security regulation includes loco-motion towards attachment figures and away from strangers. All of the behaviors that serve to generate proximity to the caregiver during times of threat form the general attachment system.

Bowlby reported observations of the reactions of children (aged fifteen to thirty months) in nurseries who were separated from their parents for the first time. This reaction can be broken into three distinct phases: protest, despair, and detachment. It is instructive to read Bowlby's own description of these reactions:

> [In] the initial phase [Protest], the young child appears acutely distressed at having lost his mother and seeks to recapture her by the full exercise of his limited resources. He will often cry loudly, shake his cot, throw him-self about, and look eagerly towards any sight or sound which might prove to be his missing mother. All his behavior suggests strong expecta-tion that she will return ... During the phase of despair, ... his behavior suggests increasing hopelessness. The active physical movements dimin-ish or come to an end, and he may cry monotonously or intermittently. He is withdrawn and inactive ... and appears to be in a state of deep mourning ... [In] the phase of detachment, when his mother visits it can be seen that all is not well, for there is a striking absence of the behavior characteristic of strong attachment normal at this age. So far from greet-ing his mother, he may hardly seem to know her; so far from clinging to her, he may seem remote and apathetic; instead of tears there is a listless turning away. (Bowlby 1969:27-8)

In other words, the actions associated with the first phase of the separa-tion cycle can be construed as angry. They all involve actions generated agentically (outwards on the world) in order to produce a result (in this case the return of the mother). Loud crying and shaking of the cot are prototypical forms of aggressive acts. By adulthood the man has learned and reshaped these actions so that crying is replaced by shouting, shaking the cot by throwing or smashing objects. But the form of trying to magically regain control through physical actions remains the same. With the infant, it is only after prolonged failure to have agentic actions lead to a successful recreation of the caregiver's presence that the subsequent emotions of depression (mourning) and eventual detachment appear. With adult men, it is not until full realization that a wife or lover is leaving or has left that deep depression and suicidal ideation occur, replacing the anger and violence that were used to control the woman's emotional proximity (although threats and/or actions can continue well past the time a securely attached person might see them as being futile as a way to regain proximity).

In the process of developing a relationship with primary caregivers through repeated transactions in which the consistency and adequacy of the former's responses are crucial, infants form internal representations of the self and others which are 'a set of conscious or unconscious rules for the organization of information relevant to attachment, attachment-related experiences, feelings, and ideations (Main, Kaplan, & Cassidy 1985:66-7). These internal representations direct feelings and behavior related to attachment as well as memory, attention, and cognition. They contain a model of the self as worthy or unworthy of care and love, generate unconscious expectations about the consequences of attachment, and provide a context for later social relationships. Although these models can be restructured, it is difficult to do so. Once they are organized they tend to operate outside conscious awareness and to resist dramatic change.

Bowlby (1969) pointed out that attachment patterns (secure, avoidant, and resistant) correlated 'with the patterns of social and play behavior with adults other than mother.' This maintained 'during both the second and subsequent years of life' (p. 361), although research evidence available at the time of his writing already indicated continuity into the five- to six-year-old range. As we shall see below, attachment has now been related to behavioral problems in three- to six-year-olds (Belsky & Nezworski 1988) as well as to adult romantic attachment styles (Collins & Read 1990; Hazan & Shaver 1987).

Empirical Tests of Attachment in Infants
Ainsworth developed the first empirical test of attachment, called the

Strange Situation. In this test researchers first use naturalistic observation of the mother's parenting style in the home during the initial year of the infant's life. Then the mother and infant go to a psychology lab where the latter's reaction to separation from the former is observed. On the basis of these observations, infants are assigned to one of three categories.

The first category, or style, is called *secure* (B Category). These infants tend to greet their mothers with pleasure when they return, stretching out their arms and moulding to their bodies. They are relatively easy to console and are distinguished from other groups by the frequency with which they seek emotional sharing with their caregivers and by their ability to seek comfort from, and to be calmed by, them when distressed. It is estimated that about 62% to 75% of North American middle-class infants fit this category. They have caregivers who readily perceive, accurately interpret, and promptly and appropriately respond to their needs. These caregivers (predominantly mothers) provide a predictable and controllable environment that promotes the infant's regulation of arousal and sense of efficacy (Ainsworth et al. 1978). Haft and Slade (1989) refer to this maternal responsiveness as attunement, the essential feature of which is that the parent matches, through expression, the affective state expressed by the infant. They found vast differences in mothers' abilities to do this.

A second attachment style, described by Ainsworth as *anxious-avoidant* or *dismissing* (A Category), gives the impression of independence. The infants explore a new environment without using their mothers as a base, and they don't turn around to be certain of their mothers' presence (as do the securely attached). When separations occur, anxious-avoidant infants do not seem affected, and when mothers return they are snubbed or avoided. A later study by Grossmann (1988) found that infants who exhibited an avoidant attachment style communicated with their caregivers only when they were feeling well. When distressed, these infants tended not to signal their primary caregivers or to seek bodily contact. At six years of age, many of these behaviors were still evident. Main, Kaplan, and Cassidy (1985) found that anxious-avoidant children directed attention away from their mothers upon reunion, moved away from their mothers physically, seemed ill at ease discussing separation, and turned away from family photographs.

This set of responses, then, defines the anxious-avoidant style: minimal displays of affect or distress in the presence of the caregiver, avoidance of the attachment figure under conditions that usually (i.e., with the securely attached) elicit proximity seeking and interaction, and an attendance to the environment while actively directing attention away from the parent. Robert Karen (1990) describes this group as follows:

The avoidant child [20% to 25% of children] takes the opposite tack [to that of the ambivalent child (see below)]. He becomes angry and distant (even though he becomes no less attached). His pleas for attention have been painfully rejected, and reaching out seems impossible. The child seems to say, 'Who needs you – I can do it on my own.' Often in conjunction with this attitude, grandiose ideas about the self develop: I am great, I don't need anybody ... Bowlby believes that avoidant attachment lies at the heart of narcissistic personality traits, one of the predominant psychiatric concerns of our time. (p. 50)

About 32% of Ainsworth's sample fit this category. Mothers of anxious-avoidant children tend to be insensitive, unresponsive, understimulating, and have an aversion to physical contact (Ainsworth et al. 1978). Haft and Slade (1989) found *dismissing* mothers to be rejecting of the babies' bids for comfort and reassurance, using comments to override the babies' affect. If this didn't succeed in quelling the babies' emotional display, it was followed by *sadistic misattunement* (i.e., the expression of misaligned feelings). Such mothers tend to be either unable to remember details of their own childhoods or to have idealized their relationships with their parents, even though they may have memories of rejection (Main et al. 1985).

Bartholemew (1990) has observed that although avoidant children's behavior could be interpreted as reflecting a lack of need or desire for contact, there is compelling evidence to the contrary. Bartholomew makes a strong case for anger being central to the anxious/avoidant attachment style. Its description makes one wonder whether this particular pattern represents the emotional origin of later withdrawal styles in which anger is suppressed. Margolin (1984), for example, found similarities between the communication styles of physically abusive and withdrawn couples. Both were characterized by low assertiveness and conflict avoidance.

The infants in a third attachment group, called *anxious-ambivalent* or *preoccupied* (C Category), tend to cling to their mothers and to resist exploring rooms on their own. They become extremely agitated on separation, often crying profusely. The members of this group typically seek contact with their mothers when they return but *simultaneously arch angrily away from them and resist all efforts to be soothed*. The implication is that these infants somehow incorporate anger into their terror at being abandoned by their mothers. The mothers of these infants tended to be inconsistent and lacking in confidence regarding their ability to perform early caregiving tasks (Spieker & Booth 1988). They were preoccupied with meeting their own strong dependency needs vis-à-vis their own parents. Haft and Slade (1989) described a preoccupied group of mothers who either totally ignored their babies' expressions of exuberance and initiative or else misattuned them.

Karen (1990) describes this group's resulting behavioral style as follows:

> The ambivalent child [ambivalent children represent about 10% of children from middle-class US homes] is desperately trying to influence her. He is hooked by the fact that she does come through on occasion. He picks up that she will respond – sometimes out of guilt – if he pleads and makes a big enough fuss. And so he is constantly trying to hold onto her or to punish her for being unavailable. He is wildly addicted to her and to his efforts to make her change. (p. 50)

The behaviors accompanying the anxious/ambivalent attachment style sound similar to wives' descriptions of physically abusive husbands (Walker 1984). The intensity of the infants' emotions and their need to have an impact on their mothers are reminiscent of borderline personality organization in assaultive males (see Dutton 1994a).

Adult Attachment
What evidence suggests that attachment patterns formed in infancy can affect adult relationships? Weiss (1982) points out how adult attachment differs from infant attachment. One essential difference, according to Weiss, is that

> attachment in adults is not nearly so capable of overwhelming other behavioral systems as it is in infancy. Infants often seem unable to give energy or attention to other matters when attachment bonds are imperiled. Adults, in contrast, can attend to other relationships and other concerns despite threats to attachment. (They, may however, experience difficulties of concentration when such threats impinge on their attention). (p. 173)

While it may be true that adult attachments are less encompassing than are infant attachments, we are still left with the question of whether the pattern established in infancy carries over into the style of attachment experienced as an adult.

One intriguing bit of evidence for the longevity of attachment longings is the research reported by Silverman and Weinberger (1985). Claiming that there are powerful unconscious wishes for a state of oneness with 'the good mother of early childhood' and that gratification of these wishes can enhance adaptation, Silverman and a variety of colleagues have presented subliminal stimuli (four milliseconds in duration) that read MOMMY AND I ARE ONE. These presentations have produced ameliorative effects on a variety of problem behaviors, ranging from schizophrenia to smoking. Silverman refers to this as 'activating symbiotic-like [oneness] fantasies in which representations of self and other are fused and merged' (pp. 1296-7). These representations are believed to originate when the mother is experienced very early in life as comforting, protective, and nurturing (Mahler, Pine, & Bergman 1975).

Gender differences were found in this research, with men showing the ameliorative effect more than women. Silverman has speculated that this may be because daughters have less of a basis for differentiating themselves from their mothers than do sons. Studies using DADDY AND I ARE ONE or MY LOVER AND I ARE ONE subliminal stimuli produced ameliorative effects on schizophrenia and anxiety in women subjects.

Silverman speculates that the activation of oneness fantasies alleviates anxiety and gratifies dependency-related needs as well as providing empirical results to support these notions. Although Silverman and Weinberger report studies on forty groups of subjects with a variety of adult problems, they do not report tests that vary attachment style. Given that insecurely attached infants experienced less of the ideal nurturing mother than did securely attached adults, one might expect a difference in the ameliorative effect of the subliminal stimulation in these two groups.

Bowlby (1973) postulated some premises of attachment theory that suggested early attachment styles would carry over into adulthood. As he put it:

When an individual is confident that an attachment figure will be available to him whenever he desires it, that person will be much less prone to either intense or chronic fear than will an individual who for any reason has no such confidence. The second proposition concerns the sensitive period during which such confidence develops. It postulates that confidence in the availability of attachment figures, or lack of it, is built up slowly during the years of immaturity-infancy, childhood, adolescence – *and that whatever expectations are developed during those years tend to persist relatively unchanged throughout the rest of life.* (p. 235)

These expectations (sometimes called *working models* or *internal representations*) of self and relationship partners are central components of personality.

Hazan and Shaver (1987) and Shaver, Hazan, and Bradshaw (1988) argued that adult romantic love has attachment properties which may derive from its infantile forms. As they put it:

> Personal continuity, in fact, is primarily due to the persistence of mental models, which are themselves sustained by a fairly stable family setting ... We are ready to suggest more explicitly that all important love relationships – especially the ones with parents and later ones with lovers and spouses – are attachments in Bowlby's sense ... For every documented feature of attachment there is a parallel feature of love, and for most documented features of love there is either a documented or a plausible feature of attachment. (p. 73)

In a study of more than 700 adults (in which subjects chose items descriptive of their own attachment style), the authors found that attachment styles fell into approximately the same proportions as did Ainsworth's infant populations: 56% self-described as securely attached, 25% as avoidant, and 20% as anxious/ambivalent. The anxious/ambivalent subjects experienced love as involving obsession, desire for reciprocation and union, emotional highs and lows, and extreme sexual attraction and jealousy. These features also figure prominently in profiles of persons with borderline personality organization and of at least one subcategory of wife assaulter. Anxious/ambivalent respondents claimed that it was easy to fall in love and said that they frequently feel themselves beginning to do so, although they rarely find what they would call 'real' love. They had more self doubts and felt more misunderstood than did others.

Attachment history was assessed by asking respondents to describe how each of their parents had generally behaved towards them (and towards each other) during childhood. Anxious/ambivalent respondents described their mothers as more intrusive and unfair than did secure respondents, and they described their fathers as unfair and threatening. The main term used by Ainsworth in describing mothers of anxious/ambivalent infants was *intrusive*. However, anxious/ambivalent respondents' descriptions of their mothers also paralleled Ainsworth's characterization of *avoidant* infants' mothers.

Hazan and Shaver's research was an important first step in relating early attachment to adult relationship functioning. Some further empirical studies have followed their lead. Using Hazan and Shaver's scale, Pistole (1989) assessed a variety of measures of adult relationship function in 137 subjects. Compared to either anxious/ambivalent or avoidant subjects, securely attached subjects reported higher relationship satisfaction and were more likely to use non-adversarial conflict resolution strategies.

Figure 5.6

**The dynamics of infant-mother attachment and adult romantic love
(Shaver, Hazan & Bradshaw 1988)**

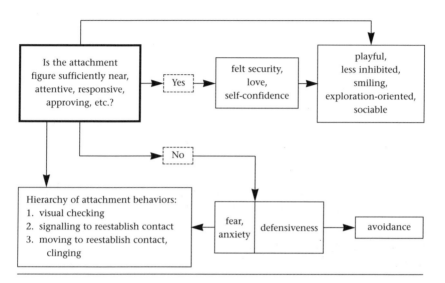

Kobak and Sceery (1988) found that peers rated college students who self-described as dismissing/detached (anxious/avoidant) as high on hostility. The authors interpreted this hostility as displacement of anger arising from frustrated attachment needs.

Collins and Read (1990) elaborated on an 18-item scale, taken from the Hazan and Shaver, which they factor analyzed. Their analysis revealed three factors: comfort with closeness, feelings that others are dependable, and anxiety about abandonment. The authors found evidence that attachment style related to a constellation of beliefs about social relationships. Anxious/ambivalent subjects had the lowest self-esteem, lowest trust in human motives, least belief in the dependability of people, and least belief in the altruism of others. They were most likely to hold an obsessive/dependent *love style* (set of attitudes about love).

Attachment and Choice of Partner
Collins and Read (1990) found that people chose partners who matched the caregiving style they had received from their opposite-sex parent. They concluded that the opposite-sex parent may be used as a model for what heterosexual relationships are like, or should be like, and what a person should expect in a romantic partner.

Sroufe and Fleeson (1986) suggested that the similarity of lovers' attachment styles to that of their parents was an unconscious attempt to maintain consistency and coherence within the self by choosing to be with those who will maintain a familiar style. Weiss (1982) argued that people may seek partners for whom their attachment system is prepared to respond – a type of self-fulfilling prophecy established by choosing someone whose attachment style fulfils our expectations.

Interestingly, in the Collins and Read study men who described their mothers as cold and inconsistent were more likely to be dating women whose attachment style was anxious. (Female attachment anxiety was the key predictor of male relationship dissatisfaction.) Anxious women tend to be less trusting and more jealous, which can result in men perceiving their mates as restricting their freedom. If so, this presents another scenario for chronic male anger in relationships: *primary anger* with the mother for coldness/inconsistency and *secondary anger* with the behavior of an anxious/jealous mate.

The Bartholomew Attachment Model

Building on Hazan and Shaver's (1987) work, Bartholomew developed a four-category (secure, dismissing, preoccupied, and fearful) model of adult attachment that defines attachment patterns in terms of the intersection of positive or negative representations of two dimensions: the self and the other (Bartholomew 1990; Bartholomew & Horowitz 1991). The *self-model* dimension indicates the degree to which individuals have internalized a sense of their own self-worth; thus, a negative self-model is associated with excessive anxiety and dependency in close relationships. The *other-model* dimension indicates the degree to which individuals expect significant others to be supportive and trustworthy and, thus, is associated with the tendency to seek out or to avoid intimacy in relationships (Griffin & Bartholomew, in press).

A *secure* attachment pattern is defined in terms of a positive self-model and positive other-model; secure individuals are both confident and comfortable with intimacy in their close relationships. Therefore, this pattern is expected to be negatively associated with emotional reactivity and abuse in intimate relationships.

A *dismissing* attachment pattern is defined in terms of a positive self-model and a negative other-model. Dismissing individuals maintain a positive self-image by defensively downplaying the importance of attachment needs and maintaining emotional distance in their relationships. Although the frustration of attachment needs associated with this style may give rise to anger (Kobak & Sceery 1988), the dismissing are not

prone to insecurity in close relationships (presumably due to the deactiva-
tion of the attachment system), and, therefore, they should not be especially prone to angry protest in intimate relationships.

Figure 5.7

Bartholomew's (1990) model of attachment

Model of Self
(Dependence)

		Positive (Low)	Negative (High)
	Positive (Low)	*Secure* Comfortable with intimacy and autonomy	*Preoccupied* Preoccupied (Main) Ambivalent (Hazan) Overly dependent
Model of Other (Avoidance)	Negative (High)	*Dismissing* Denial of attachment Dismissing (Main) Counter-dependent	*Fearful* Fear of attachment Avoidant (Hazan) Socially avoidant

In contrast, individuals showing the two attachment patterns defined
in terms of a negative self-model (*preoccupied* and *fearful*) are chronically
anxious about rejection and abandonment in their close relationships. As
a result, these anxious attachment patterns are expected to be associated
with high levels of negative affect, including anger, in intimate relationships. *Preoccupied* individuals (negative self-model and positive other-
model) actively seek to gain their attachment figures' approval in order to
validate their tenuous sense of self-worth. Their feelings of unworthiness
and strong approach orientation are expected to be associated with high
levels of intimacy-anger.

However, the *fearful* attachment pattern (negative self-model and negative other-model) may be most strongly associated with intimacy-anger.
Fearful individuals desire social contact and intimacy but experience pervasive interpersonal distrust and fear of rejection (Bartholomew 1990). This
style manifests in hypersensitivity to rejection and active avoidance of close
relationships (where vulnerability to rejection exists). While the fearful
attached share anxiety over abandonment with the preoccupied, their
avoidance orientation may lead to more chronic frustration of attachment needs. Bartholomew (1990) argues that strong and unresolvable

approach/avoidance may underlie the behavior of chronically fearful (anxious/avoidant) people. In other words, perceived threats of abandonment lead to tendencies to approach the attachment figure who rejects physical contact, thus generating withdrawal accompanied by an even stronger need for attachment. A self-perpetuating feedback loop ensues that leads to chronic avoidance, frustration of attachment needs, and anger. Hence, intimacy-anger may be central to the fearful attachment style.

In sum, individuals with fearful and preoccupied attachment patterns are prone to experience abandonment anxiety in their intimate relationships, and, therefore, these patterns are expected to be positively related to anger, jealousy, and affective instability. Dutton (1994a) and Dutton and Starzomski (1993) found that anger, jealousy, and affective instability were all strongly and significantly related to frequency of verbal and physical abuse in intimate relationships. Hence, there appears to be a link between anxious attachment patterns and a propensity for abusiveness. We argue that attachment-anger (intimacy-anger) and affective instability are produced by chronically frustrated attachment needs and are risk factors for increased abusiveness in intimate relationships.

Attachment and Wife Assault

Male violence towards women frequently occurs in the context of intimate relationships (Straus, Gelles, & Steinmetz 1980; Straus & Gelles 1990). With the exception of serial killers, almost all cases of men killing women occur in the context of an ongoing intimate relationship (Daly & Wilson 1988; Crawford & Gartner 1992), and much male intimate violence occurs in the process of real or perceived relationship dissolution (Dutton & Browning 1988; Daly & Wilson 1988; Crawford & Gartner 1992).

Prior research indicates that men who assault their wives have high chronic anger scores (Dutton 1994a), and that their anger is frequently triggered by attachment change which they perceive as uncontrollable. Dutton (1988) describes these changes as abandonments and engulfments, and he has found that these kind of changes produce the greatest anger reactions in male subjects watching couple-conflict videotapes (Dutton & Browning 1988). In their study of 551 femicides, Crawford and Gartner (1992) concluded 'the offender's anger or rage over the actual or impending estrangement from his partner typified 45% of the cases where a motive could be established' (p. 44). In another 15% of cases, the motive was the offender's suspicions about his partner's relationship with another man. It appears, in other words, that intimacy or attachment issues generate strong reactions that include anger and violence towards intimate others.

The thesis of the study to be described below (Dutton, Saunders, Starzomski, & Bartholomew 1994) was that men who have anxious attachment styles will be more likely to report chronic anger, associated features of wife abuse (such as jealousy and trauma symtoms), and abusive actions. In particular, we focused on the attachment styles Bartholomew (1990) described as *fearful* (anxious-avoidant) and *preoccupied* (ambivalent). As described above, both styles involve negative self-models and intimacy-anxiety and are characterized by frustrated attachment needs, subjective distress, and hypersensitivity. Both styles should contain high levels of intimacy-anger.

Measures
In addition to using measures described earlier (the *BPO* scale, *MAI*, *TSC-33*, and *PMWI*), we administered the *Relationship Style Questionnaire* (RSQ) (Griffin & Bartholomew 1994). The *RSQ* is a 30-item self-report scale measuring the four attachment patterns (secure, fearful, preoccupied, dismissing) identified by Bartholomew and Horowitz (1991). Measures of each of the attachment patterns were created by summing four or five items from the corresponding prototypic descriptions. Each subject receives a continuous rating for each attachment pattern.[6]

Results
Table 5.7 shows the relationship of attachment styles to scores for borderline personality organization (*BPO*), anger (*MAI*), trauma symptoms (*TSC-33*) and psychological abuse (*PMWI*).

Significant differences were found between attachment groups on all measures. The fearful group appears to generate the highest degree of anger and abusiveness.

In order to examine the specific strengths of the associations between attachment and other measures, simple linear correlations were conducted.

Fearfully attached men experience high degrees of both chronic anxiety (as measured by the *TSC-33*) and anger (as measured by the *MAI*). In addition, both trauma scores in general, and dissociation scores in particular, were highest for the fearful group. Alexander (1992) speculated that fearful adults 'would be expected to exhibit the most severe disorders of affect regulation, including PTSD [post-traumatic stress disorder] and dissociation' (p. 190).

Since anxiety and anger are both strongly associated with fearful attachment, one could argue that an emotional template of intimacy-anxiety/anger is the central affective feature of the fearful attachment pattern. These high correlations were maintained in the non-assaultive

Table 5.7

Means and differences for attachment groups on dependent measures

	Secure (n = 32) (1)	Fearful (n = 32) (2)	Preoccupied (n = 54) (3)	Dismissing (n = 42) (4)	Significance (p < .05)
Anger	71.7 (12.6)	96.4 (13.7)	86.7 (18.0)	83.8 (11.6)	2 vs. 1,4
Trauma	15.1 (9.7)	36.9 (11.1)	26.1 (14.9)	18.8 (10.5)	2 vs. 1,4
Jealousy	-6.4 (30.6)	33.7 (32.9)	5.7 (39.5)	-2.4 (40.6)	2 vs. 1,4
BPO	61.9 (16.0)	84.4 (9.3)	76.5 (14.9)	63.4 (11.7)	2 vs. 1,4
Dominance	62.2 (14.9)	109.5 (20.1)	106.3 (19.8)	86.0 (17.6)	1 vs. 2,3
Emotional abuse	29.4 (11.6)	43.9 (18.8)	39.8 (17.7)	37.7 (16.9)	1 vs. 2

Table 5.8

Correlations of *Relationship Style Questionnaire* with total scores on other measures for entire sample (*n* = 160)

	Secure	Fearful	Preoccupied	Dismissing
BPO	-.35[c]	.58[c]	.42[c]	-.04
Trauma symptoms	-.28[c]	.50[c]	.34[c]	-.03
Anger	-.36[c]	.49[c]	.20	.02
Jealousy	-.16[a]	.34[c]	.18[a]	-.015
Psychological abuse (*PMWI*):				
Domination/isolation	-.30[a]	.46[b]	.27[a]	.06
Emotional abuse	-.09	.52[c]	.26[a]	-.20

[a] *p* < .05
[b] *p* < .01
[c] *p* < .001

control sample, suggesting that this emotional template does not only reside within physically abusive men.

As has been discussed earlier, a prominent feature of borderline personality organization is intimacy-anger (Gunderson 1984; Dutton 1994a). The correlation of fearful attachment to borderline personality organization is so strong that one could argue that the latter is a representation of this particular attachment style (see also Mahler 1971). With the fearfully attached man, anger is an aspect of attachment independent of what transpires interpersonally, and when that anger is experienced it is both blamed and projected onto the attachment object, resulting in chronic anger towards the latter.

Scores on fearful attachment also correlated significantly with the *BPO* subscale for primitive defences, which assesses the tendency to split women into ideal and devalued objects and to project angry impulses onto the devalued woman-object. This affective template sets the stage for intimate conflict and increases the risk for intimate violence.

Intimacy-Anger and Wife Assault: A Developmental Perspective

Although the focus of recent attachment research has been on anxiety, much of the early focus of Bowlby and Ainsworth was on what could be called *attachment-anger* or *attachment-rage*. As has been discussed, when an infant's attachment needs are activated for a long time without being satisfied, angry behavior is regularly observed (Bowlby 1969, 1973; Ainsworth et al. 1978).

Avoidant children tend to have experienced rejecting parenting and are characterized by their avoidance of caretakers after separation in a controlled laboratory setting (Ainsworth et al. 1978). Some time afterwards, however, avoidant children direct considerable anger towards their mothers at home. Main and Weston (1982) also noted unpredictable outbursts of aggression by the members of this group towards their mothers when they were at home. And the greater the avoidance upon reunion with their mothers, the greater the display of anger and dependent behavior towards them over the ensuing weeks. Main and Weston (1982) suggest that in response to separation, avoidant infants feel angry with their mothers, but their expression of anger in this situation risks decreased proximity; so chronically rejected infants only express anger in circumstances that do not risk decreased proximity from their caregivers.

In contrast, Main and Weston report that members of an anxious-ambivalent group became extremely agitated on separation from their mothers, often crying profusely. The members of this group typically sought contact with their mothers when they returned but simultaneously arched away from them angrily and resisted all efforts to be soothed. The implication is that these infants somehow incorporate anger into their terror at being abandoned by their mothers. The simultaneous seeking of contact and arching away represents the prototypical physical manifestation of ambivalence. At present, it is not yet clear whether our fearful group resembled avoidant or anxious-ambivalent children. My personal hunch is that anxious-ambivalent children grow up to be fearfully attached.

In our own studies of adult males, both dominance/isolation and emotional/verbal abuse (as measured by the *PMWI*) were significantly related to fearful and preoccupied attachment. One could speculate that emotional abuse is a product of attachment-rage. The anxiously attached man, unaware that his dysphoria is related to his issues around intimacy, attributes it to the real or perceived actions of his partner and retaliates with abusiveness. The dominance/isolation factor can be viewed as an overgeneralized attempt to diminish anxiety about abandonment. The yoked dysphoric modes – anger and anxiety – thus may have a common origin in insecure attachment and may operate to generate both abusing and controlling behaviors.

Anger increases the probability of aggression (Konecni 1975), and assaultive men with high anger scores report a greater frequency of physical assault than do other men (Dutton 1994a). Men with early attachment problems may be more likely than others to experience anxiety and anger about intimacy regulation. These feelings may originate in a felt anxiety about their childhood attachment figures and, *ceteris paribus*, increase the probability of aggression towards their intimate partner. Figure 5.8 demonstrates the relationship of attachment to borderline personality organization and the centrality of the latter to abuse and abuse-related phenomena (such as anger and trauma symptoms).

Figure 5.8

The centrality of borderline personality organization in a group of assaultive males

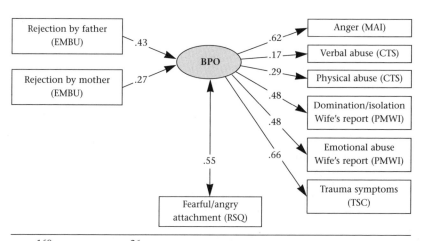

n = 160	r > .26
p < .00001	p < .05
r > .52	r > .15
p < .01	

Chapter Summary and Conclusions

The research reported above has identified a subgroup of wife assaulters whose violence seems to occur in reaction to internal aversive states which recur cyclically. This type, which scores high on borderline personality organization and trauma symptoms, is characterized by *intimacy anger*, an affective state that occurs as a by-product of attachment.

This subgroup can also be described in terms of attachment theory, showing a fearful pattern, or style, of attachment. This personality type appears to be formed, in part, by cold, rejecting parenting, possibly accompanied by instances of physical abuse. Figure 5.9 represents the relationship of family of origin variables (*EMBU, CTS*) to abusive personality (*BPO, MAI, TSC-33*, fearful attachment) and behavior (*PMWI, CTS*).

A tentative conclusion of this research is that early experiences in the

Figure 5.9

Family of origin effects on abusive personality and behavior

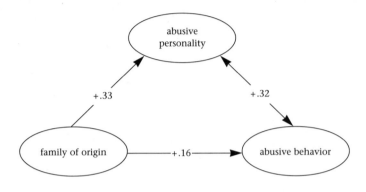

all correlations *p* < .01

family of origin influence not only behavior (through a modelling process) but an entire constellation of reactions that, taken together, might be called the abusive personality.

It may appear discomfiting that anxious attachment patterns could be a risk factor for abuse. Contemporary abuse treatment models focus on discrete cognitions or controlling behaviors (Saunders 1989; Ganley 1989; Dutton & McGregor 1991). The foregoing analysis has two potential treatment applications. First, it appears therapeutically important for the client to separate dysphoria produced by anxious attachment from negative attributions to the person with whom he is currently attached. Second, attachment anxiety can potentially provide a better understanding of control issues by providing insight into the origins of intimacy fear. What is controlled in intimate relationships is that which is most feared – namely, the degree of intimacy or emotional distance from the object of attachment. Learning to negotiate emotional distance with greater awareness would seem therapeutically beneficial. Finally, better skills at managing cyclical tension states would seem helpful in reducing abusiveness.

An informed social policy for wife assault will require better information about the psychology of the offender than currently exists. It will also require better information on the psychological effects of abuse on its victims. We will examine how societies detect and control wife assault in a later chapter. We turn now to an examination of the social-psychological circumstances of the victims of wife assault.

6
Effects on the Victim

Never again will you be capable of ordinary human feeling. Everything
will be dead inside of you. Never again will you be capable of love, or
friendship, or joy of living, or laughter, or curiosity, or courage, or
integrity. You will be hollow. We shall squeeze you empty, and then we
shall fill you with ourselves.

– George Orwell, *1984*

Over the last decade a considerable literature has developed on the psychological effects of victimhood, describing reactions to being a victim of
rape (Schram 1978; Burgess 1983; Meyer & Taylor 1986), hostage-takings
(Strentz 1977; Flynn 1986; Terr 1991), assault (Sales, Baum, & Shore 1984;
Ochberg 1988; Herman 1992), sexual assault (Scheppele & Bart 1983),
incest (Silver, Boon, & Stones 1983; Eth & Pynoos 1985), and technological disaster (Baum, Fleming, & Singer 1983). Out of this victimization literature researchers have developed some understanding of the cognitive
means victims use to regain feelings of self-control (Janoff-Bulman &
Lang-Gunn 1985; Wortman 1976) and the models that attempt to
account for successful victim recovery (Sales, Baum, & Shore 1984). In this
section, we will examine this general literature on victim reactions with a
view to how it might apply to assaulted women.

Victim Reactions to Traumatic Events
Studies on victim reactions have focused on aftermath effects, both emotional and cognitive, and on post-trauma decisions such as reporting the
attack to police, proceeding with charges, and staying with or leaving the
abuser. Fattah (1981) reviewed these studies and concluded that, as far as
post-victimization reactions were concerned, generalizations were difficult
to make. Victim reactions appeared to depend on a variety of factors, such

as the nature of the experience and the circumstances surrounding it, the characteristics of the victims themselves, and the degree of violence employed. Variability in both short- and long-term reactions were reported by victims of violence.

Post-traumatic stress disorder (PTSD), for example, varies with the severity of the stressor, the circumstances of its experience, and the victim's characteristics (Rubonis & Bickman 1991). In the general US population, about 13% of women and 5% of males show signs of PTSD (Helzer, Robins, & McEvoy 1987). For men, the major causes of PTSD are combat (47%) or seeing someone hurt or die (32%); for women, the causes are threats (45%), seeing someone hurt or die (41%), and physical attacks (31%). Below, we will consider another set of trauma consequences called the *battered woman syndrome*. A question that is raised in this area of study is whether battered woman syndrome is a form of PTSD.

The Stockholm Syndrome

As early studies in victim reactions began to develop, two highly publicized hostage-taking events occurred that focused public awareness on the occasionally paradoxical reactions of hostage victims. The first was the kidnapping of Patty Hearst, granddaughter of newspaper magnate William Randolph Hearst, by the Symbionese Liberation Army (SLA) in California in 1974. Hearst was imprisoned in a closet and subjected to intermittent bouts of violence and to sexual and psychological abuse. Subsequently, she denounced her parents, joined the SLA, and assisted it in bank robberies. When finally captured she took the Fifth Amendment to the American Constitution (a total of forty-two times) to avoid self-incrimination. A debate ensued over whether Patty Hearst was acting voluntarily or had been brainwashed by the SLA.

At about the same time, reports began to surface about something called the Stockholm Syndrome, a constellation of unexpected positive feelings developed by captives for their captors. The syndrome was named after an event in Stockholm, Sweden, where four bank employees were held hostage in the bank's vault for 131 hours by two escaped prisoners. The hostages in this event feared the police more than their captors and, when finally freed, expressed gratitude towards the latter for sparing their lives (Strentz 1979).

Early explanations for this phenomenon were psychoanalytic in orientation. Strentz (1979) cited Anna Freud's concept of identification with the aggressor, whereby, in a life-and-death situation with a powerful authority figure, the ego identifies with the aggressor-authority to avoid punishment and anxiety. Bruno Bettleheim (1943) described a particularly

Focus
Post-Traumatic Stress Disorder (PTSD)

The *DSM-III* (American Psychiatric Association 1987) defines *Post-Traumatic Stress Disorder* as a type of anxiety disorder caused by a traumatic event 'outside the range of usual human experience.' However, as we learn more about the frequency of extreme abusiveness, this definition may have to be reformulated. It may be that most humans experience some type of traumatic experience during their lifetime.

The diagnostic criteria for PTSD are as follows:

(1) The existence of a *recognizable stressor* that would evoke significant symptoms of distress in almost everyone.

(2) *Re-experiencing* of the trauma as evidenced by at least one of the following:

(a) Recurrent or intrusive recollections of the event.

(b) Recurrent dreams of the event.

(c) Sudden acting or feeling as if the traumatic event were recurring because some stimulus triggers an association (includes a sense of reliving the experience, illusions, hallucinations, and dissociative [flashback] experiences).

(d) Intense psychological distress at exposure to events that resemble or symbolize the traumatic event.

(3) *Numbing* of responsiveness to, or reduced involvement with, the external world beginning some time after the trauma, as shown by at least one of the following:

(a) Markedly diminished interest in one or more significant activities.

(b) Feelings of detachment or estrangement from others.

(c) Constricted affect.

(4) Persistent symptoms of increased arousal that were not present before the trauma:

(a) Hypervigilance.

(b) Sleep disturbance.

(c) Memory impairment or trouble concentrating.

(d) Irritability or outbursts of anger.

(e) Exaggerated startle response.

(f) Intensification of symptoms (and physiological reactivity) by exposure to events that symbolize or resemble the traumatic event.

(5) Duration of these symptoms of at least one month.

vivid instance of identification with the aggressor: Jewish prisoners in Nazi prison camps emulated their captors to the extent of sewing scraps together to imitate SS uniforms and taking over punitive rule-enforcement functions vis-à-vis new prisoners.

Flynn (1986) reviewed the literature on victim reactions to being held hostage and noted that the Stockholm Syndrome was most likely to develop when no serious physical abuse had occurred. But even victims who are injured when initially captured eventually identify with the offenders and their cause during later phases of their captivity. The Stockholm Syndrome seems not to develop if prisoners have a strong ideology that sustains them through captivity. One of the more fascinating literatures is that composed of the collection of reports on coping under the extreme duress of captivity and harassment (Timmerman 1981; Fallaci 1981). The individuals who seem capable of sustaining such resistance, however, constitute a very small minority.

Stages of Victimization

More typical responses to severe victimization are a sense of helplessness, powerlessness, and *idiocide* (Flynn 1986), which describes the total loss of the social self. Symonds (1980) describes the acute response to victimization as having four stages. The symptoms of the first stage are shock, disbelief, denial, and delusion. Only when the victim perceives the reality of the situation does the second stage begin. This is a terror-induced pseudo-calm that Symonds calls frozen fright, where feelings of isolation and powerlessness are so intense that a victim separates his/her consciousness from his/her body. This dissociation is occasionally reported by assaulted women (Walker 1979a). This acute phase gives way to a delayed coping response of rumination and busywork that frequently includes a review and reflection of one's past life with vows to change for the better if given another chance (Strentz 1979). The final stage is described as traumatic psychological infantilism, where individuals lose their ability to function as adults and regress to behaviors first learned in early childhood: compliance, submission, and ingratiation. If this final stage continues, attitude shifts that we have described above as identification with the aggressor occur. Symonds calls this attitude shift *pathological transference*.

Since the initial descriptions of this syndrome in the victim literature (Symonds 1975:1980), we have become more aware of its effects on victims of hostage-takings and sudden, unpredictable traumas. A second line of reports suggests, however, that the compliant, submissive stage can be reached in more prolonged, less traumatic situations.

Conway and Siegleman (1978), Sage (1976), and others have described how the infantilism produced in cults can be so extreme that parents occasionally attempt to kidnap and deprogram their children. The literature on cult members describes a form of idiocide and infantilism that is reached gradually through isolation from normal social contacts and through being rewarded for behavior consistent with their new role. Schein (1971) described these factors as essential ingredients of what has come to be termed *brainwashing*.

As we shall see below, assaulted women also demonstrate some of the affective and cognitive reactions of these other victims. They frequently are unexpectedly positive about their abusers and may blame themselves for their abuse (Walker 1979a). They sometimes seem passive and inert about taking steps to leave their situations, even though visible impediments do not exist. Hence, some outside observers, for reasons we shall describe below, tend to view their staying in abusive relationships as indicative of masochistic predispositions.

Differential Victim Reactions
As research on victims grew more sophisticated, studies began to emerge that attempted to account for differential victim reactions. Sales, Baum, and Shore (1984), for example, interviewed 127 rape victims to obtain retrospective reports of pre-rape symptoms, immediate post-assault symptoms, and follow-up symptoms. They found a complex picture of post-assault recovery that included immediate post-assault increases in symptoms (anxiety and depression) that were followed by an apparent return to normalcy, with symptoms diminishing over a six-month period. However, a reactivation of symptoms occurred after six months and did not return to pre-assault levels over a three-year period. The Sales et al. study is important for two reasons: first, it demonstrated that a different pattern of results was obtained with long-term follow-up; second, it began to examine factors that explained differential victim reactions.

Predictive Factors
Sales et al. divided their predictive factors into three categories: (1) pre-assault factors – demographic and psychosocial aspects of the victim herself, including pre-rape psychological problems, chronic life stressors, and quality of relationships; (2) assault factors – degree of violence and relationship to perpetrator; and (3) post-assault factors – criminal justice involvement and reactions of the victim's informal support system.

Demographic variables were not strongly predictive of post-assault reactions; however, some relationship did exist between the latter and personality characteristics. In both their own data and the studies of others, Sales

Case Study
Elly

I met Elly under unusual circumstances. She had been charged with a variety of offences that involved an evening when she was intoxicated and driving wildly through city streets with a man clinging to the hood of the car. The man, it turned out, had several prior convictions for assaulting her.

Elly described how she met him when she was twenty-five. At first, she said, he seemed very nice, but their relationship 'evolved to the point where he was always there.' She described him as going through 'Jekyll-and-Hyde mood swings' and claimed that he became verbally abusive out of the blue. This turned into physical abuse and accusations that she was having sex with other men. The accusations became so oppressive that she began to cringe whenever a man phoned her at home for any reason (usually work-related). As I was interviewing her, my phone rang and she startled.

Elly tried to leave several times, but her partner always found out where she was. He would bring her back, promising good behavior and simultaneously threatening to have his biker friends beat up her family if she left again.

The night of the charges, her abusive partner was drunk and had already been in a physical fight with another man (his brother). He threatened Elly that she was next, that he was going to kill her. She tried to flee by jumping into the car and driving off, but, as she did so, her partner jumped onto the hood and hung on. She tried to shake him but he wouldn't let go. Eventually, she crashed. Her partner's legs were crushed, and she was charged with drunk driving causing bodily harm. He assaulted her again, despite being a paraplegic, and was convicted.

et al. found post-assault functioning to be affected by prior biosocial problems (psychosis, drug use, alcoholism, etc.). Coping ability was also reduced by prior life stressors such as finances and absence of social support. Degree of violence strongly predicted symptom severity; threats of death had a particularly strong impact on symptoms. Acquaintanceship with the aggressor had no effect on reported symptoms, nor did the reactions of the victim's informal support network after the assault.

One particularly interesting result was that victims who proceeded with charges showed fewer post-assault symptoms (immediate and at six months) than did victims who did not. However, further progress towards trial exacerbates such symptoms. Victims whose cases were tried showed more heightened symptoms than did those not pursuing their cases. Sales et al. interpret this as suggesting that the legal process may inflict additional stress on victims and/or keep a victim from returning to normal functioning.

The Sales et al. study represents an example of the sophisticated, multivariate studies of victim reaction beginning to emerge in the victim literature. It suggests a conceptual model for analyzing reactions of battered women that subdivides predictive factors into pre-assault circumstances, post-assault circumstances, and the severity of the assault itself. Furthermore, it raises an issue that we will return to when we consider criminal justice policy for wife assault: if proceeding to trial exacerbates victim symptoms, what interest is served by doing so?

Perceptions of Assaulted Women: The 'Fundamental Attribution Error' and the 'Just World' Belief

In Chapter 1 we examined victim surveys and concluded that serious repeated wife assault occurred in about 6.8% of all marriages. The women who are repeatedly assaulted by their husbands in these marriages perplex and exasperate outside observers. The obvious question that arises for police, social workers, or transition house personnel who observe the aftermath of the assault and the woman's subsequent return to the marriage is, simply, why doesn't she leave?

Casual discussion with police or other professionals typically generates an account of a woman who needed police intervention to save her life, who agreed to charge her husband, and who was given shelter in a transition home. After a few weeks, despite the support of transition house staff and in the absence of face-to-face contact with her husband, she decides abruptly to return to the marriage and drop the charges. The state is left without its key witness if it proceeds to trial, the police mutter knowingly about 'these women always dropping the charges,' and inexperienced transition-home workers wonder what they did wrong. Jaffe and Burris (1982) found that women who charged their husbands with assault had been previously assaulted an average of thirty-five times.

Rosenbaum and O'Leary (1981) report that, whereas nearly 70% of their sample of 52 battered women had experienced abuse from their spouses by the end of the first year of marriage (and, of these, 15% experienced abuse even prior to the marriage), the women continued to live with their husbands for an average of over 12 years before they presented themselves at a clinic for problems related to marital violence. Rounsaville (1978), discussing the strength of the emotional bonds in his sample of thirty-one battered women, notes:

> The most striking phenomenon that arose in the interviews and in treatment with battered women was the tenacity of both partners to the relationship in the face of severe abuse sustained by many of the women. Even those who had divorced or separated from the partner stayed in contact with the partner beyond ordinary activities such as visitation of children. In all cases, this continued to lead to abuse such that only three of the women had been free from abuse for more than three weeks at the time of the interview, despite 10 of the women having been separated or divorced from their partners. (pp. 20-1)

The Masochism Explanation

Although economic factors (children, no job, etc.) exist for many women who return to an abusive relationship, they do not seem to be a major consideration for many others. Outside observers who witness repeated returns to the marriage begin to draw conclusions about the kind of women who return. Typically, these women are viewed as returning because they enjoy the violence or because the initial report of violence was hysterical and exaggerated. The action of returning is attributed to a predisposition in the victim, such as masochism or pathological dependence. (For critical reviews of the professional literature drawing this conclusion see Dutton [1983], Caplan [1984], and Shainess [1977].)

Unfortunately, the very agencies and resources to which the battered woman might turn for assistance often reflect such beliefs. Medical professionals frequently attempt to deal with the battered woman by treating her symptoms (e.g., her depression or anxiety) rather than by recognizing the origin of such responses to an injurious or life-threatening situation (Davidson 1978; MacLeod 1980). Researchers (e.g., Dutton 1981a; Hogarth 1979) have found that the courts are often mired in mythology about the victims of family violence and are thus unprepared to deal effectively with a woman's attempts to protect herself through the legal system. Social service agencies are likely to provide counselling that stresses the responsibility of the woman to adjust to the situation in which she finds herself rather than to assist her in leaving that situation (MacLeod 1980). In short, those who encounter a woman who has been beaten and who returns to her partner do not always respond sympathetically; to the contrary, they frequently blame her for her plight.

Masochism Defined

A variety of definitions of the term *masochism* exist in psychology. At the broadest level, Fromm (1973) uses the term to describe a giving up of personal control to another in order to satisfy existential needs for connection and freedom from existential anxiety. Deutsch (1944) uses the term to apply specifically to women who are willing to accept pain paired with pleasure as part of life. She suggests that this 'normal' masochism differs from *neurotic masochism*, where pain becomes a condition of pleasure. Unfortunately, derivative reports from Deutsch's work do not always make this distinction.

In addressing the concept of masochism as it may apply to battered women who remain with their tormentors, we refer to Freud's narrow definition of masochism as 'gratification ... connected with suffering or physical or mental pain at the hands of the sexual object' (Freud 1938:569). This definition presumes that battered women remain in abusive relationships because they derive gratification from being abused.

Fundamental Attribution Error

While it is not beyond the realm of possibility that some women may be masochistic, a much more commonplace set of factors operate to keep most battered women in relationships. When a battered woman endures intermittent abuse or returns to an abusive relationship, outside observers are likely to attribute her behavior to her predisposition or to an indigenous character trait. While this has been described by some as blaming the victim (Ryan 1971) or as the need to believe in a just world (Lerner 1977), it can also be explained by current research in social cognition (Nisbett & Ross 1980), attribution (Jones & Nisbett 1971), and human judgment (Kahneman & Tversky 1973).

A woman returning to an abusive relationship represents a salient example of what, to common sense, is unusual or counternormative behavior. In other words, outside observers, be they male or female, believe that they and others would act differently than does the assaulted woman. Furthermore, from their perspective, there do not appear to be tangible impediments to her leaving: she is not physically confined, imprisoned, or under constant surveillance. When we observe behavior that appears unusual and is not externally determined, we tend to attribute it to a trait indigenous to the person who performs the behavior (Jones & Nisbett 1971; Nisbett & Ross 1980) and overlook the impact of subtle situational forces on his/her behavior. In social cognition research this tendency is termed the *fundamental attribution error*. Hence, in the

Case Study
Janet

Janet came to see me as a private client. She was in an abusive relationship with a man fifteen years younger than herself and wanted help to leave. She was a lawyer and had used her knowledge of law to get charges against her partner dropped or reduced on prior occasions. She claimed that she wanted him out but couldn't get rid of him as he had a key. I told her to change her locks, but she said that wouldn't work as he would just break in.

The next time I saw her, her tone, memory, and attitude towards the relationship had changed. She was considering getting back with her partner. 'Why shouldn't I?' she asked. I went over, in detail, the descriptions of his abusiveness that she had reported to me in the prior session: choking her, insulting her, threatening her life, putting a gun to her head and pulling the trigger (the barrel was empty). She agreed, but I could see the emotional undercurrent pulling her back. She missed her next appointment. One month later she came to see me again but was dishevelled and barely sober. She seemed in a dissociative state. She told me she was back with her partner but it was all right. I again reminded her of his abuse potential.

Three months later I found out that the police had been called back to her residence twenty-three times but that she either refused to charge her partner whenever they arrived or else dropped the charges the next day. And when the police said they would insist on taking him to court, she told them she would show up in court and say she made the whole thing up. Eventually, the police stopped responding.

case of assaulted women, outside observers may attribute their behavior to masochism.

The 'Just World' Hypothesis
The tendency to attribute her behavior to a predisposition is further strengthened when professionals believe, rightly or wrongly, that the criminal justice system cannot protect the assaulted woman. Lerner (1977) discovered a cognitive bias in subjects which he described as a need to believe in a just world. People have this need, according to Lerner, because they need to believe that the universe is orderly and that

their good actions will be rewarded. It both justifies one's behavior in the past and promises rewards for good behavior in the future. Good behavior simply means doing the type of thing that society has taught one to do.

When someone is victimized or suffers a tragedy, people look for a way to restore justice to that person – to right the wrong. When justice cannot be restored, that person's fate threatens our belief in a just world. In order to protect these beliefs, we find a way to view the victim as deserving his or her fate. In the case of the assaulted woman, viewing her as provoking or enjoying the violence or as being psychologically flawed are all ways of restoring a belief in a just world. She is getting, in effect, what she deserves. One could argue that world-weary police officers should be the last people to believe in a just world, but Lerner's notion of justice goes beyond a narrow legal concept of justice. Even with criminal justice professionals, Lerner would argue, a tendency exists to blame the victim in order to avoid the conclusion that the universe is chaotic and that consequences do not necessarily follow from actions.

The 'just world' hypothesis would predict that, to the extent the criminal justice system or other social agencies fail to provide early and effective assistance for an assaulted woman (and, therefore, fail to assist her to break away from a repeatedly assaultive relationship), the professionals who work in those systems may adopt the view that the woman herself was partially to blame for the violence because she remained in the relationship. This belief serves three functions: (1) it protects the professional from recognizing that their particular system is not functioning efficiently, (2) it maintains the belief that the world is 'just', that is, that people get what they deserve, and (3) it precludes the necessity of working for system change. It is ironic that these attitudes, when held by professionals within the medical, social, and justice systems, help to create the very social and legal climate that contributes to the battered woman's inability to get out of the battering relationship, thus resulting in a self-fulfilling prophecy.

Psychological Hostages

The attribution of masochism to an assaulted woman depends on the outside observer overlooking any situational factors that impede her from leaving her assaultive husband. Clearly, however, a variety of situational inducements to remain might exist, ranging from broad macrosystem pressures (such as economic deprivation or socialized beliefs that a woman must be loyal to her husband) to the use of threats of violence and intermittent surveillance by her husband. Furthermore, short-term reinforcers could occur after the assault that might operate to prevent the woman from leaving.

The Macrosystem

The macrosystem (or cultural) explanations for the difficulty associated with leaving a violent relationship have focused on the socialization of women to feel responsible for marriage outcomes, to rescue males from their problems, and to demonstrate loyalty to their marriages in the face of adversity (Maccoby & Jacklin 1974; Greenglass 1982). Martin (1977) discusses how the fact that females are socialized to be responsible for marital success leads to a sense of shame if the marriage fails and to attempts to save face, such as covering up bruises received in assaults by their husbands. Martin and others show that to many women self-worth becomes equated with marital success.

Similarly, a culturally developed nurturer role leads women to rationalize their husbands' outbursts as signs that they need them. As Martin points out, this rationalization forms a tight circle of logic: the worse the man behaves, the more he appears to be sick and, therefore, to need the woman. Interestingly, while feminist writers (e.g., Caplan 1984) have decried the explanation of the loyalty of battered wives as due to masochism, the explanation of other feminist writers (e.g., Martin 1977) sounds like a form of socialized masochism. Becker (1973) and Fromm (1973), for example, describe masochism as a character form whereby someone else's existence takes precedence over one's own. As Becker puts it, 'We may prefer to deflate ourselves in order to keep the relationship, even though we glimpse the impossibility of it and the slavishness to which it reduces us' (1973:167).

We shall return to this consideration below. For now, however, the macrosystem explanation of the behavior of battered women suffers from the same problem as do cultural explanations of assaultive husbands: it fails to account for individual differences. If the socialization of women to be loyal to abusive husbands was so compelling, the surprise, chagrin, and lack of comprehension of female observers raised with the same socialization would be hard to explain. Again, macrosystem factors may direct or set parameters on the responses of battered women, but an interaction with factors from other levels seems required in order to understand fully the unusual loyalty of battered women.

The Exosystem: Access to Social/Economic Resources

It has been suggested that assaulted women fail to escape the battering relationship because of the many social and economic obstacles in their way (e.g., MacLeod 1980; Strube & Barbour 1983, 1984). These include economic dependence on husbands due to inequitable pay (women traditionally earn about 60% of men's salaries) and/or unequal employment opportunities for men and women; inadequate resources (e.g., no alternative accommodation, no transition houses, no nearby family and friends); and lack of adequate protection from the criminal justice system (e.g., poor police response, unenforced peace bonds, etc.).

Gelles (1976) interviewed a sample of women who had sought police intervention, social service assistance, or who had begun divorce proceedings because of their husbands' physical violence. He found that those women who were entrapped (by a lack of formal education or job skills, unemployment, or young children) were less likely to seek a divorce or outside assistance after being beaten. While such system inequities *do* exist as barriers to a woman leaving the battering relationship, and should be corrected, they still do not provide a sufficient explanation for the fact that women often stay in violent relationships.

Rounsaville (1978) found that the availability of outside resources (fewer children to care for, better jobs, better social adjustment, higher social class) did not differentiate those who left their partners from those who did not. Leaving the relationship seemed to be more a function of the internal dynamics of the relationship (e.g., severity of abuse, fear of being killed by the husband, having called police and/or having discovered that the husband was also abusing the children). As Rounsaville pointed out, 'When these circumstances prevailed, it did not seem to matter whether there were adequate resources or not. Given sufficient motivation, women even with few resources found a way to leave' (p. 17).

Gelles (1976) also found that severity and frequency of abuse were the best predictors of a woman's decision to seek help or to leave the relationship. Below, we will review recent empirical studies on the economic and psychological determinants of leaving/staying. In these studies, economic variables, taken by themselves, rarely account for more than 15% of the variance in decisions to leave or to stay.

The Microsystem: Dynamics of the Relationship

Several writers have suggested that the relationship of the battering couple is characterized by unmet dependency needs on the part of either or both partners (Kardiner & Fuller 1970; Lion 1977; Rounsaville 1978; Shainess 1977). The constant round of doomed attempts to satisfy one another's unrealistic needs fuels the arguments that lead to violence and keeps the couple locked in battle. For example, a high percentage of battered women report that their partners are jealous and possessive in the extreme, often to the point of obsession (Rounsaville 1978; Walker 1979a), and that arguments about their outside activities or imagined affairs are a frequent cause of violent episodes. The man attempts to restrict his partner's independent existence, which is a constant threat to his security. The woman, in the hope of avoiding arguments and reducing their accompanying violence, begins to organize her life completely around her partner and his demands.

The woman's compliance legitimizes his demands while systematically eliminating opportunities for her to build up a supportive network that could eventually assist her in leaving the relationship. Her compliance also builds up a store of repressed anger and frustration on her part. Compliance deepens the woman's dependence upon her partner, as she devotes herself completely to fulfilling his needs. In time, the woman's self-esteem may become wrapped up with her attempts to placate her partner and to fulfil her 'wifely duties' by keeping the relationship together. As Walker (1979a) notes, 'Since most battered women adhere to traditional values about the permanency of love and marriage, they are easy prey for the guilt attendant on breaking up a home, even if it is not a very happy one' (p. 67). Thus, the battered woman becomes trapped in the relationship by both her own and her partner's expectations of her behavior and responsibilities.

There has been some research on how the battered woman's behavior can affect the perpetrator's behavior. For example, Follingstad, Hause, Rutledge, and Polek (1992) interviewed 234 women with a history of physical abuse. Subjects were divided into two groups: short-term (*ST*) abuse (44.4% of the sample), those who experienced abuse for less than six months from the time of the first incident; and long-term (*LT*) abuse (55.6% of the sample), those who experienced persistent abuse (at least once a month) beyond a six-month time period. For this latter group, abuse increased for eighteen months and then levelled off.

A stepwise regression procedure was used to select the variables that best predicted *ST* from *LT* battered women. The authors report the best predictor to be frequency of abuse in the first six months (higher for *LT*), which accounted for 26.6% of the variance, followed by the battered women believing that violence in relationships is inevitable (3.3% of the variance). *ST* women were more likely to form a plan after the first incident (3.3% of the variance), and *LT* women experienced more threats of abuse as a form of emotional abuse (1.5% of the variance). The total variance accounted for was 34.8%.

My reading of this study's results is that the longevity of abuse has much more to do with the perpetrator than with the victim. Differences in victims' beliefs about the inevitability of violence in relationships could simply reflect post-hoc differences between a group of women for whom the violence stopped and another for whom it continued. I do not think this variable should be interpreted as reflecting a pre-violence belief. The only remaining victim factor from Follingstad et al.'s list is the formation of a plan after the first incident, and this accounts for only 3.3% of the variance. Two perpetrator factors (frequency of abuse and threats) account for 28.1% of the variance. This suggests that, if the man is abusive, there is little the woman can do to stop his abusiveness except leave (or perhaps call the police right away).

Ontogenetic Factors

Family History, Parental Role Models, and Role Expectation
As we described in Chapter 3, parents who behave violently towards, or in the presence of, their children are providing role models of behavior that the latter readily learn. As with assaultive males, the women who are victims of wife battering are also likely to have witnessed domestic violence. A study by the National Organization of Women (NOW) in Ann Arbor, Michigan, found that one-third of battered women had seen violence between their parents (Fleming 1979). There is also evidence that being the victim of abuse as a child is related to becoming involved in a violent relationship as an adult. In a large-scale study of family violence, Straus found that the more frequently a woman had been struck by her parents, the more likely she was to be in a domestically violent relationship (Straus 1977a).[1] Gelles (1972) found that those who had been hit frequently as a child were more likely to fight physically with their spouses. Hilberman and Munson (1977-8) found that the sixty battered women in their study had often been both witnesses to and victims of violence in their families of origin.

Children who witness violence not only learn specific, aggressive behaviors, but they are also likely to acquire the belief that violence is a legitimate way to solve personal problems. They are therefore likely to expect that they will be involved in violence as a part of their adult relationships. Furthermore, children who witness violence between adults may develop attitudes and sex-role orientations that predispose them to become involved in violent relationships as adults. Men who saw their mothers being beaten may develop the attitude that women are second-class citizens and deserve to be ill-treated. In the normal development process of adopting the female sex-role, girls come to identify with their mothers as the victims of aggression (Fleming 1979). They may begin to see themselves as powerless and deserving of scorn, and they may come to see the world as a place where they have no control over what happens to them.

Being predisposed to enter an adult relationship where they will be treated in the same way in which they saw their mothers treated, these women may believe that violence is simply an expected part of married life and accept it just as did their mothers. Consequently, they are not inclined to believe that they deserve better, or that they would be able to survive in the world alone. They are therefore unlikely to leave their relationships and, if they do, usually return to their husbands to resume the kind of marriage that was modelled for them by their own parents.

Personality Characteristics
As described above, one of the traditional and most persistent explanations for why battered women remain in an abusive relationship centres around the notion that they are masochistic and, thus, consciously or unconsciously invite and encourage abuse (e.g., Snell, Rosenwald, & Robey 1964). If it were the case that battered women invited or encouraged abuse, one would expect to find that these women have a history of battering relationships in adulthood or other forms of self-destructiveness apart from the present battering relationship. The assessment of indirect self-destructive behavior as prima facie evidence for masochism (Farberow 1980) has not, however, been connected to the problem of battered women. Since much of the battering occurs later on in a relationship and involves, as we will argue below, situational forces that diminish the control and volition of the battered woman, we would argue that battering does not constitute a form of indirect self-destructive behavior.

Furthermore, one researcher who has investigated this issue has found that the majority of battered women do not fit a pattern of being abused in other relationships. In a sample of thirty-one battered women interviewed in hospital emergency rooms and a mental health facility, Rounsaville (1978) found that only four (13%) had been physically abused in previous relationships. Although Rounsaville notes that some of the women in his sample reported that they sometimes deliberately escalated arguments that they thought might lead to violence, he rejects the notion that battered women are masochistic and, therefore, stay in battering relationships in order to suffer. An occasionally deliberate escalation of conflict by a woman was an attempt on her part to hasten the inevitable and 'get it over with.'

Psychological State
A second type of explanation often advanced for the fact that battered women stay in abusive relationships is that they are in a state of *learned helplessness*. Seligman's theory of learned helplessness (1975) states that

when an individual learns through experience that he or she has no control over an unpleasant environment – that is, that certain outcomes are independent of his or her own behavior – he or she loses the motivation to change that environment or situation. Walker (1979a) has applied the concept of learned helplessness to the battered woman's position. She proposed that women come to expect battering as a way of life because they have learned that they cannot influence its occurrence. The experiences recounted by battered women certainly support this notion, with personal recountings of being awakened and dragged out of bed in the middle of the night and beaten by their enraged partners.

A corollary of the learned helplessness theory is that the feelings of helplessness learned in the primary situation generalize to other situations. Thus, the abused woman may come to believe that none of her behavior in any sphere will be effective, and her resulting sense of futility regarding alternative courses of action will preclude the possibility of her leaving the assaultive relationship. Furthermore, Frieze (1979) has suggested that when the assaulted woman internalizes the blame for the abuse (e.g., blaming herself for being a poor wife), her self-esteem is additionally lowered, which leads to even greater feelings of depression and helplessness. The situation may come to constitute a particularly vicious cycle if the woman blames herself for her failure to stop the abuse or to control the behavior of the batterer. The very occurrence of abuse is then further evidence of how helpless and incompetent she is, contributing to lower self-esteem and to the further unlikelihood that she will free herself from the relationship.

The concept of learned helplessness has been criticized in recent years. Many battered women show resilience and initiative and perhaps should be thought of as having survival skills rather than as being helpless (Gondolf 1988). Bowker (1983), for example, found that battered women had persistently sought a wide range of help. The more prolonged the abuse, the more varied were the victims' help-seeking activities. In his sample of battered women, Gondolf (1988) found that, on average, they had contacted five potential sources of help; over half had contacted the police and 20% had sought legal advice. This, of course, is the opposite of what one would predict from a learned helplessness model.

Pre-abuse psychosocial functioning can be inferred from women's medical histories. Stark, Flitcraft, and Frazier (1979) examined the medical records of 481 women who sought treatment at an urban hospital emergency room. The pre-assault medical records for assaulted women were remarkably similar to the medical records of non-assaulted women. The two groups did not differ significantly on number of suicide attempts, drug abuse, or the frequency of use of psychiatric emergency services, the community mental health centre, and the state mental hospital – although assaulted women had a higher pre-assault incidence of alcohol abuse. Post-assault comparisons revealed significant differences on all measures, suggesting that deficits in psychosocial functioning are more a result than a cause of assault.

Rounsaville, indeed, found a high level of depression in a sample group of assaulted women (80% reported symptoms of depression). However, this may be the inevitable consequence of feeling trapped by violence rather than an indication that assaulted women are in a state of learned helplessness. These women were not found to have generalized their feelings of helplessness and ineffectiveness to other areas of their lives.

Rounsaville and his colleagues found that the assaulted women in their study reported themselves to be competent in their work outside the home, in their relationships with their families of origin, and in their relationships with their children (Rounsaville, Lifton, & Bieber 1978). Reports of impaired functioning were specific to the spouse relationship and to leisure-time activities. These data suggest that if a syndrome of learned helplessness exists at all, it may be a contributing factor to these women's inability to leave the battering relationship. It is not, however, an exhaustive explanation of the situation in which assaulted women find themselves.

Battered Women's Causal Attributions for Violence

In 1983, one of my graduate students, Carol Porter, interviewed fifty women in a shelter in San José, California, in order to ascertain how they explained their husbands' violence towards them. She was interested in the role these explanations might play in the long-term ability of these women to cope with the crises of being assaulted, separated from their husbands, and forced to consider traumatically imposed life changes. Shelter counsellors made individual, independent ratings of each woman's emotional state and her ability to cope with her respective situation.

Self-Blame

Porter made a surprising and counter-intuitive prediction in this study (which constituted her doctoral dissertation). She correctly predicted that women who blamed themselves for the violence directed towards them would cope better, and be less likely to return to an abusive relationship, than would women who did not. What makes this prediction so surprising is the conventional wisdom of therapists that self-blame acts to keep battered women in abusive relationships.

In a related study, Frieze (1979) interviewed assaulted and non-assaulted women about actual and hypothetical cases of wife abuse. For the hypo- thetical cases, 81% of assaulted and 79% of non-assaulted women attrib- uted causality to the men – only a small minority (16%, 20%) attributed it to the women. However, when assaulted women were asked about actual assaults they had experienced, 50% attributed them to something *they* had done. Frieze (1979) found that the greater the frequency of assault, the greater the tendency to attribute causality to the self. When assault was relatively rare, only 12% of women attributed it to themselves; when it occurred frequently, 40% did so. Frieze (1979) suggested that when bat- tered women internalize blame for abuse, their self-esteem is lowered and greater depression and helplessness ensue.

Porter, however, was using an elaborate notion of the function of self- blame – a notion that had been developed in social psychological research on attribution. Wortman (1976) speculated that self-blame could be linked to the need for perceived control. In other words, victims may accept blame for their victimization because, if they are to blame for the occurrence of violence, then they must have some control over it and, hence, should be able to control its future occurrence. In order to be cer- tain that we can control our future, we must accept responsibility for the past. For example, Bulman and Wortman (1977) found that there was a positive correlation between the degree of self-blame accepted by para- plegic victims of accidents and independent assessments of how well they were coping with their injuries.

Porter distinguished between various types of self-blame, following a distinction made by Janoff-Bulman (1979). One level of self-blame is behavioral; that is, certain specific aspects of our behavior are seen as hav- ing caused the violence. The second kind is characterological and views the violence as caused by a permanent, nonmodifiable aspect of our char- acter. Janoff-Bulman found that depression following a traumatic event was related to characterological self-blame. The rape victims which she interviewed reported behavioral but not characterological self-blame. They blamed themselves for walking home alone at night but didn't feel that they were raped because of the kind of people they were.

Porter suggested that behavioral self-blame might constitute an effective coping strategy for battered women, as it would allow them to feel that future violence could be modified. Assuming that they do not immedi- ately return to an abusive relationship in which they cannot modify the violence, behavioral self-blame could constitute a temporarily effective cognitive coping strategy by regenerating a belief in personal control. Characterological self-blame, on the other hand, leads to the belief that some unmodifiable aspect of oneself would continue to recreate similar future victimization. The benefits from this coping strategy depend on the woman being out of the relationship. Furthermore, behavioral self-blame might be a functional transitional stage that could later be supplanted by a more interactive view of the cause of violence.

Self-Blame, Partner-Blame, and Contingency

Porter found that the more women blamed their partners, the less likely they were to describe themselves as calm, happy, or optimistic. Women who were rated by shelter staff as good copers were more likely to acknowledge a relationship between their own behavior or personality and their partners' violence. This finding, however, speaks more to a sense of contingency than to a sense of blame. In other words, the women saw their husbands' violence as contingent upon something they did, but not on something for which they blamed themselves (see also Campbell 1987). Furthermore, women who perceived this contingency between aspects of themselves and their partners' abuse were likely to perceive the latter as unavoidable and were less likely to return to the relationship then were other women.

In fact, perception of avoidability was the second strongest predictor of staying out of the relationship (the only stronger one being the duration of the abuse). Women who blamed their partners for the occurrence of violence were *more* likely to return to abusive relationships than were those who did not. One possible explanation for this blame-return relationship is that partner-blaming is a by-product of anger – and anger connotes a strong, continuing emotional bond to the partner.

There is a strong distinction between contingency and blame. For example, the women in this sample, while recognizing that their husbands' violence was contingent upon something they did, did not blame themselves for doing it – quite the opposite. Thus, although a number of subjects reported that they felt their independence or tendency to be outspoken was related to the abusive behavior of their partners, they also felt that they were entitled to these aspects of themselves.

Porter did not find strong support for the characterological-behavioral self-blame distinction she had made, presumably because this distinction is blurred for chronic or repeated events. The prior literature (e.g., Janoff-Bulman 1979) had concentrated on single victimizations. Porter concluded that even distinguishing characterological from behavioral self-blame is too imprecise. Battered women can blame themselves for a variety of reasons: for causing the abuse, for being unable to modify it, or for tolerating it and not leaving sooner. With self-blame having so many different meanings to different women, it is easy to see why it did not have a strong relationship to subsequent coping. On the other hand, the ability to perceive a contingency between one's behavior and one's abuse might have facilitated coping because, unlike blame, perceived contingency might be saliently linked to a woman's self-concept. A woman who viewed her partner's abuse as contingent upon positively valued aspects of herself was more likely to think well of herself and to describe her partner as insecure, jealous, or threatened.

Consistent with this speculation of Porter's is a study by Cohn and Giles-Sims (1979). The authors elicited attributions for cause of violence from thirty-one battered women when they first entered a shelter. Follow-up interviews at six months revealed that women who viewed assault as contingent on some aspect of their behavior were more likely to have left their husbands in the interim. Surprisingly, women who viewed the assault as caused by an aspect of their husbands' character were more likely to return.

The authors could offer no strong explanation for this latter finding. If replicated it certainly would contradict attribution theory assumptions, since it suggests a pattern of irrational behavior (returning to a situation where violence is likely and uncontrollable). Traumatic bonding theory (to be discussed in Chapter 7), on the other hand, would have no difficulty in accounting for the members of this group of women returning to their husbands: Since power imbalances, periodicity of abuse, and incremental increases in abuse were arranged so as to maximize the strength of traumatically established affective bonds, these would override the effects of rational attributions.

Campbell's (1987) study of ninety-seven battered women and ninety-six non-battered women with serious relationship problems also found that perception of interactive blame resulted in less troubled individuals, whether battered or not. Despite the tendency to believe that abused women usually concentrate blame on themselves, only 21.6% of the women in this study did so (which was not significantly different from what was found with the control group). Although self-blaming battered women were more likely to be depressed and to have low self-esteem than were external-blaming women, the interaction of perceived stability of the relationship and self-blame with self-esteem suggests the following: self-blame when women perceive the situation as unchanging may be healthier for them than would be external blame when they perceive the situation as changeable. Campbell's qualitative data suggest that, regardless of attribution of blame, accepting that the relationship was not going to change precipitated actions such as leaving or seeking an abuse injunction, with a resultant lessening of depression and an increase in self-esteem.

Finally, Porter speculated that battered women's assessments of blame might change over time. Many of her subjects had reported that they blamed themselves for their abuse until they finally reached the point at which they truly believed they were doing nothing wrong. Many women reached this point through counselling or through learning that many others had had similar experiences. This information reduced pluralistic ignorance (the belief that one's problem is particular to oneself), thus reducing self-blame.

An alternative view on the effects of blame and perception of contingency on returning to an abusive relationship is that blame connotes an emotional reaction while contingency connotes a letting go of this reaction. When we are angry (and still strongly emotionally involved), we tend to blame someone for relationship failure. Our blame reactions may be highly unstable, especially when the relationship failure is recent and emotions are quite strong. At this point, anger (blaming the other) and guilt (blaming the self) may alternate. Both, however, connote that a strong affective connection still remains. Hence, Porter's finding that women who blamed their partners were more likely to return is not so paradoxical.

With time and effective counselling, the emotional attachment to the partner may weaken, and, as it does, blaming (and emotional reaction) may be supplanted by a less emotional appraisal of the causes of relationship problems. In the case of battered women, this would include perceptions of the contingency between aspects of their behavior (which they positively value) and their partners' violence. Porter's finding that self-blame altered over time might have masked a more general finding that all forms of blame diminish with time. Research in this area needs to pay close attention to the precise amount of time between relationship dissolution and data collection in order to clarify these blame/contingency distinctions.

Social Traps: The Incremental Character of Wife Assault

A social trap, according to Platt (1973), is a situation in which behavior produces short-term pay offs and long-term costs. The latter are obscured by the former, leading the person to perform behavior that is not in his or her long-term self-interest. From this perspective, an assaulted woman's beliefs and perceptions about the causes of her husband's violence are important because they help to shape her private payoff matrix. For example, if she views the violence as originating in her husband and being out of her control, she may be less likely to attempt to modify her own behavior. A high percentage of initial wife assaults occur during the first year of marriage (Dutton & Painter 1980; Rosenbaum & O'Leary 1981) – a time when the woman is still experiencing the novelty and optimism of the new relationship. At this point, the violence appears to be an anomaly, out of keeping with the husband's character. Retrospective accounts indicate that at the time of the first assault, a majority of women blamed themselves (Dutton & Painter 1980). This, combined with the relative lack of severity that usually characterizes the first violent incident (Wilt & Breedlove 1977), the husband's post-assault contrition, and his attempts to make amends and promises that it will not happen again, serve to reinforce both the belief that the violence is an isolated incident and the affective bonding processes described above. Hence, the traumatically established emotional bonds are strengthened *before* the victim realizes that the violence is not an anomaly.

Repeated incidents of increasing severity tend to shift the woman's cognitions from the belief that the violence will never happen again to the belief that it may recur unless she alters *her* behavior (Frieze 1979; Walker 1979a). With repeated incidents of violence and subsequent good behavior, the emotional bond is further strengthened. At the same time the woman still views the violence as avoidable. Only when she views it as unavoidable will she be strongly motivated to leave (Rounsaville 1978; Porter 1983). As the emotional bond strengthens and the duration of the relationship increases, the woman also comes to feel that she has more invested in the relationship than does the man and, consequently, has more to lose if she leaves. These feelings and beliefs serve to preserve homeostasis and to keep the woman in the relationship.

Furthermore, negative feelings of self-worth develop as a result of continuous assault (Rounsaville 1978; Porter 1983). These feelings, along with post-assault depression (Rounsaville 1978), lead the woman to believe that she could not make it on her own and/or would not be attractive to other men. This results in inertia.

In addition to all of the above, many women fear that if they try to leave, their husbands will find them and become even more violent. From this perspective, the entrapping features of intermittent abuse become evident. It is for this reason that personality profiles do not predict who will become an assaulted woman. The dynamics of the social forces at work override personality features. When assaulted women finally do leave an abusive relationship, it is because the severity of abuse has become so great that they fear for their lives or for the safety of their children (Rounsaville 1978).

Psychological and Economic Determinants of Returning to Abusive Relationships

Economic factors that could contribute to battered women returning to abusive relationships include an entire constellation of factors contributing to their economic dependence on their husbands. These range from macrosystem features such as male-female wage differentials to the woman's own job skills, employability, or number of dependents. Both psychological and economic explanations counter the notion that battered women remain in abusive relationships because of some disposition such as masochism. Instead, psychological and economic explanations determine which situational forces operate to trap women in abusive relationships; they differ, however, in the type of situational forces they see as entrapping.

Economic explanations view these forces as objective economic factors that are directly measurable: a low salary, poor employability, or number of dependents. Psychological theories focus more on the woman's subjective perception of her life alternatives both inside and outside the relationship. Since these factors are subjective, their measurement requires a careful examination of the woman's perceptions, beliefs, attitudes, and anxieties. Some studies have examined directly why women remain in violent marriages, and we will review them here with a view towards comparing the relative weights of psychological or economic factors in a woman's decision to leave.

Rounsaville (1978) administered open-ended and structured interviews to 31 battered women (17 from a hospital emergency room and 14 from a mental health centre). He compared the women in this sample who left their partners with those who stayed and found that they were not differentiated by lack of resources (social class, social functioning, employment, and number of children). Rounsaville concluded that women who stayed in abusive relationships had resources that they either overlooked or did not use.

In 1976, Kalmuss and Straus (1982) measured wives' objective dependency (employment, children five years old or younger, whether husbands earned 75% of the family income) and subjective dependency (whether they perceived that they or their husbands would be most hurt if their marriages were to break up) in a nationally representative sample of 1,183 intake marriages. They found a correlation of .147 between these two measures of dependency. Abuse was defined by items on the Straus *CTS* which measured the husband's behavior and whether the abuse carried a high risk of serious injury. Kalmuss and Straus reported that 'knowledge of a wife's level of objective dependency on her marriage appears to be a better predictor of whether her husband severely abuses her than is knowledge of her subjective dependency' (p. 283).

Strube and Barbour (1983) assessed objective and subjective economic dependence as well as objective and subjective commitment to a marriage in a sample of ninety-eight physically abused women who had contacted a counselling unit associated with a county attorney's office. Counsellors made an initial assessment of dependence and commitment factors, and a follow-up was conducted when the case was closed (one to eighteen months later). The woman's status (in or out of the relationship) at this time constituted the study's dependent variable.

Objective economic dependence was defined as the presence or absence of a job; *subjective economic dependence* was defined as the woman's stating during the initial intake interview that economic hardship was one of her reason's for staying in the relationship; *objective commitment* was defined as the length of time the woman had been in the relationship; and *subjective commitment* was defined as the woman's stating during the initial interview that she still loved her partner as a reason for staying in the relationship. Sixty-two per cent of the women in this sample had left their partners at follow-up (cf. the 40% reported by Snyder & Fruchtman 1981). Objective measures accounted for 11.6% of the variance in relationship decisions, while subjective measures accounted for 26.6% of the variance. The authors suggest that entrapment principles that involve subjective estimates of what has already been invested in a relationship be further studied.

A later study by Strube and Barbour (1984) obtained more elaborate objective demographic records from a sample of 251 abused women. In addition, social support availability and subjective reasons for remaining in their relationships were recorded. At the time of this initial assessment, all women were still in their relationships. Follow-up contact was made two to three months later, at which point 70.5% of the women had left their abusive partners. Strube and Barbour reduced their intercorrelated predictor variables to a set of eight via multiple regression. The variables with the greatest predictive power weights were employment ($\beta = .28$), economic hardship ($\beta = -.22$), love ($\beta = -.21$), and length of relationship ($\beta = -.16$). All eight combined variables, however, only accounted for 25% of the variance in decisions to stay or to leave.

Smith and Chalmers (1984) interviewed 100 women in a Saskatchewan transition house in order to find out what conditions made it possible for women to leave an abusive relationship. They differentiated women who had left home many times (multiple leavers) from those who stayed away permanently after their first departure (single leavers). The single leavers had as their aim in leaving their homes a re-evaluation of their relationships or a desire to establish their own residences. The multiple leavers, however, had as their primary purpose escape from fear of their partners and effectively ending the violence. Typically, the departure of these women was effective in this regard for a short-term period. They usually returned when their partners promised to change their violent behavior and/or to stop drinking. Smith and Chalmers pointed out that the woman's own hopes for her partner's change also influenced the decision to return.

This study suggests that homeostasis in some abusive relationships may accommodate successive leavings by one partner, even though she/he lacks a sustained intent to remain out of the relationship. This being the case, these women do not really change their minds when they return. Smith and Chalmers found that one-third of their sample permanently established their own residences.

Aquirre (1984) had interviewers assess 312 women in Texas shelters. All women were married and residing with their husbands immediately prior to entering the shelter. Aquirre's outcome measure was whether respondents reported at the time they exited shelters that they were returning to their husbands. Aquirre examined the impact eight predictor variables had on this outcome, including the respondents' previous experiences with violence, the number of injuries they had sustained, issues they had experienced during their batterings, economic dependence on their husbands, and four variables assessing their experiences in the shelter. The only statistically significant predictor was the respondent's economic dependence (based on the respondent's own income level). However, Aquirre did not assess for psychological or relationship features. Thus, as with the studies reviewed above, his study does not constitute a test of economic versus psychological explanations for staying or returning to an abusive relationship. Furthermore, Aquirre's outcome measure is a measure of intent, not of actual staying or leaving.

Effectiveness of Current Studies

In a critical review of these studies, Painter (1985) pointed out that the samples of women are typically from one source and may not generalize to women from other sources. Strube and Barbour (1983, 1984) and Gelles (1976) used women from counselling programs. Rounsaville (1978) drew his sample from a hospital emergency room and a mental health centre. Other researchers (Aquirre 1984; Okun 1984; Porter 1983; Snyder & Scheer 1981) contacted women in shelters. Painter thinks that these populations of women may differ in important ways. For example, women in shelters may lack economic resources and may come from more violent relationships than do other women.

Painter also pointed out the retrospective and static nature of the above studies. Women typically have already made a decision to leave or to stay and are categorized according to that decision, even though the decision process itself is fluid and dynamic. Painter suggested that a longitudinal study, despite its logistical difficulty, might be essential in order to avoid the retrospective 'snapshot' nature of current designs.

Finally, Painter criticized current studies for being merely descriptive rather than explanatory in so far as relationship dynamics were concerned. These studies told us the length of time the couple has been married, how soon in the relationship the violence began, and so forth; but they did not effectively assess relationship features such as interpersonal power, commitment (absolute and relative levels for each partner), or intermittency of abuse. In reviewing these studies, Painter reports that rates of women returning vary from 22% (Gelles 1976) to 78% (Nielsen, Eberle, Thoennes, & Walker 1979) in short-term follow-ups.

While the studies reported above present a mixed result in terms of evaluating economic versus psychological factors that entrap battered women, the range and depth of psychological factors has not been adequately measured. When one reads the psychological literature on the victim experience and then turns to the empirical literature, which uses simple bivariate reports (i.e., of who loses the most if a marriage breaks up or of whether or not the woman still loves her abuser), this inadequacy is clear.

Such questions do not begin to tap the depth or complexity of the victim experience for a repeatedly assaulted woman. This experience produces strong emotional bonds that the woman herself may not understand or be able to verbalize. Transition-house workers report the guilt and confusion of women who feel themselves being pulled back to relationships that they know will be negative. The empirical studies to date have not assessed, in any but a superficial manner, the network of negative beliefs about the self and the implications of these beliefs for forecasting a life of independence, strong positive associations with the abusive partner, and/or the preoccupation with, and obsessive ruminating on, the person who has been a salient force in one's life. Nor have they assessed the emotional consequences of terminating the relationship: anxiety, depression, and guilt about leaving. In the next chapter we will attempt to rectify this problem.

Some conclusions can be drawn from the few replicated results that arise from these studies: first, most studies indicate that economic independence contributes to the likelihood of women leaving abusive relationships; second, the longer the duration of the relationship at the time of the woman being interviewed, the greater the likelihood of her returning to her abuser (whether this indicates commitment, investment, or something else is not clear); and third, neither abuse in childhood nor severity of violence in the current relationship are reliable predictors of relationship breakup. At the time of writing, all of these conclusions must be considered tentative.

Chapter Summary and Conclusions

In this chapter we examined the psychological effects of victimhood, considering the similarities between the reactions of battered women and victims of such other forms of trauma as kidnapping. We reviewed a number of explanations that are used to understand why some women remain in, or return to, abusive relationships. Some of these studies blame the victims, thus providing a simplistic explanation for a complex problem. We favour a different approach – one that views these women through a nested ecological perspective which considers factors at the macrosystem, exosystem, microsystem, and ontogenetic levels. At this time, however, my conclusions are, at best, tentative.

Clearly, the ideal research design has not yet been implemented. However, such a study would be longitudinal in nature, drawing women from a variety of sources, and would include a systematic assessment of relationship dynamics (such as relative power, periodicity, time of onset of abuse, the woman's affective state [depression, strength of attachment to husband, or preoccupation with her mate], alternative support systems, and economic situation). These measures should be related to the woman's current life goals and the subjective probability of her achieving those goals in or out of her relationship.

Careful comparisons should be made to the difficulties of non-abused women in leaving relationships (see Kitson 1982), and it should not be assumed that returning to a previously abusive relationship constitutes a failure. Some women may successfully implement strategies that stop their husbands from using violence. Finally, a thorough assessment of the woman's beliefs about the causes of violence, her control over it, and its likelihood of stopping should be made. In the next chapter we review the literature which deals with some of the beliefs, emotions, and attachments that come together to form a syndrome for the victim of abuse.

7
Traumatic Bonding

We may prefer to deflate ourselves in order to keep the relationship, even though we glimpse the impossibility of it and the slavishness to which it reduces us.

– Ernest Becker, *The Denial of Death*

Traumatic Bonding as a Theoretical Framework

Each of the explanations for women staying with, or returning to, their assaulters presented in Chapter 6 receive qualified empirical support. Yet taken individually or together, they do not adequately account for the sudden about-face that often characterizes the return of an assaulted woman to a relationship that has a high prognosis of future violence. Most of the above explanations, in fact, either address the woman's initial choice of a relationship or else present a picture of an amotivational woman who has lost interest in attempting to change her situation.

While ambivalence may manifest itself behaviorally in the assaulted woman, most professionals support the view that such a woman experiences very strong post-traumatic emotional states and that these serve either to push her out of, or to pull her back into, the battering relationship. My colleague, Susan Painter, and I have developed a theory based on the social psychological research on power and social traps and on the developmental research on the formation of emotional bonds. This theory links the tenacity and loyalty of assaulted women to special features of the abusive relationship rather than to inferred aspects of her own personality or to the socioeconomic milieu in which she finds herself.

The formation of strong emotional attachments under conditions of intermittent maltreatment is not specific to assaulted women but has been reported in a variety of studies, both experimental and observational, with both human and animal subjects. For example, as described in Chapter 6, people taken hostage may subsequently show positive regard for their captors (Bettleheim 1943; Strentz 1979), abused children have been found to have strong attachments to their abusing parents (e.g., Kempe & Kempe 1978), and cult members are sometimes amazingly loyal to malevolent cult leaders. The relationship between assaulted women and their partners, then, may not be an isolated phenomenon. Rather, it might be seen as one example of what we have termed *traumatic bonding* – the development of strong emotional ties between two persons, with one person intermittently harassing, beating, threatening, abusing, or intimidating the other.

There are two common features in the social structures of such apparently diverse relationships as battered spouse/battering spouse, hostage/-captor, abused child/abusing parent, cult follower/cult leader, and prisoner/guard. The first is the existence of a power imbalance, wherein the maltreated person perceives himself or herself to be subjugated to or dominated by the other; the second is the intermittent nature of the abuse.

Power Imbalance
Attachment to a person or group larger or stronger than one's self increases feelings of personal power (Becker 1973; Fromm 1941; Lion 1977; McClelland 1975). Social psychologists have found that unequal power relationships can become increasingly unbalanced over time, to the point where the power dynamic itself produces pathology in individuals (Ng 1982). For example, Zimbardo, Haney, and Banks (1972) reported anxiety and depression in volunteer subjects playing the role of prisoners who were relegated to powerlessness in a simulated prison situation. Lewin, Lippitt, and White (1947) reported increased redirected aggression in powerless members of autocratic groups. As mentioned before, Bettleheim (1943) reported compulsive copying by Jewish prisoners of the behavior and expressed attitudes of their Nazi prison guards.

Recasting Anna Freud's (1942) concept of identification with the aggressor from its psychoanalytic, life-and-death mode, this concept would predict that, in situations of extreme power imbalance in which a person of high power is occasionally punitive, persons of low power would adopt the aggressor's assumed perspective of themselves, internalize aggression, and/or redirect it towards others similar to themselves.

As the power imbalance magnifies, the person of low power feels more negative in her/his self-appraisal, more incapable of fending for her/himself, and, thus, more in need of the high-power person, whether or not high dependency existed in the former prior to the present imbalanced relationship. This cycle of dependency and lowered self-esteem repeats itself over and over and comes eventually to create a strong affective bond to the high-power person. Concomitantly, the person in the high-power position will develop an overgeneralized sense of his/her own power (just as the low-power person develops an inflated sense of his/her own powerlessness), which masks the extent to which he/she is dependent on the low-power person to maintain his/her self-image. This sense of power, however, is predicated on his/her ability to maintain absolute control in the dyadic relationship. If the symbiotic roles that maintain this sense of power are disturbed, the masked dependency of the high-power person on the low-power person is suddenly made obvious.

One example of this sudden reversal of the power dynamic is the desperate control attempts on the part of the abandoned battering husband to bring his wife back to him through surveillance or intimidation. In romantic relationships as well as in cults, power imbalances magnify so that each person's sense of power or powerlessness feeds on itself. What may have been initially benign, even attractive, becomes ultimately destructive to positive self-regard. In the process, both persons (or groups) become welded together to maintain the psychological subsystem which fulfils the needs created, in part, by the power dynamic itself.

Periodicity of Abuse
The second feature of traumatic bonding situations is the intermittency of abuse. In other words, the dominant party intermittently and periodically maltreats the submissive party by threats and verbal and/or physical abuse. The time between bouts of abuse is likely to be characterized by more normal and acceptable social behavior. Thus, the victim is subject to alternating periods of aversive or negative arousal and the relief and release associated with its removal. The situation of alternating aversive and pleasant conditions is an experimental paradigm within learning theory known as *partial or intermittent reinforcement*. It is highly effective in producing persistent patterns of behavior that are difficult to extinguish (Amsel 1958). Such intermittent maltreatment patterns have been found to produce strong emotional bonding effects in both animals and humans.

Intermittent Reinforcement and Traumatic Bonding
There is considerable evidence from both naturalistic and laboratory-based studies with animals that severe arousal, even when caused by an attachment object, and especially when it is intermittently increased and reduced, provides a basis for strong emotional attachment. Scott (1963) reviewed the literature on critical periods for emotional attachment in animals and concluded that the evidence 'indicates that any sort of strong

emotion, whether hunger, fear, pain, or loneliness will speed up the process of socialization.' Scott further states:

> The surprising thing is that emotions which we normally consider aversive should produce the same effect as those which appear to be rewarding ... An animal (and perhaps a person) of any age, exposed to certain individuals or physical surroundings for any length of time will inevitably become attached to them, the rapidity of the process being governed by the degree of emotional arousal associated with them ... If this conclusion should apply to our species as well as other animals ... it provides an explanation of certain well known clinical observations such as the development by neglected children of strong affection for cruel and abusive parents, and the various peculiar affectional relationships that develop between prisoners and jailers, slaves and masters, and so on. (p. 189)

More recently, Rajecki, Lamb, and Obsmascher (1978) have written a comprehensive critical review of emotional bonding in infants, in which they assess the major theories of infantile attachment, including those on both human and animal attachments (e.g., Bowlby 1969; Lorenz 1937). One criterion for the comparative evaluation of these theories was their relative ability to explain maltreatment effects. In reviewing the literature on maltreatment effects, Rajecki et al. found conclusive evidence for enhanced infant attachment under conditions of maltreatment in birds, dogs, and monkeys. Attempts to inhibit infants' bonding to abusive attachment objects were found inevitably to fail unless (1) they were persistent and consistently punitive and (2) an alternative attachment object existed.

Harlow and Harlow (1971) reviewed the research they carried out with infant monkeys, in which 'evil surrogate mothers' were used as potential attachment objects. These surrogates would exude noxious air blasts, extrude brass spikes, hurl the infant to the floor, or vibrate so violently that it made the infant's teeth chatter. None of the above disrupted the bonding behavior of the infant monkeys. The authors concluded that, 'Instead of producing experimental neurosis we have achieved a technique for enhancing maternal attachment' (p. 206). Similarly, Seay, Alexander, and Harlow (1964) note, 'A surprising phenomenon was the universally persisting attempts by the infants to attach to the mother's body regardless of neglect or physical punishment' (p. 353).

When the physical punishment is administered at intermittent intervals, and when it is interspersed with permissive and friendly contact, the phenomenon of traumatic bonding seems most powerful. Fischer (1955) attempted to inhibit the social responses of young dogs. One group was indulged (thirty minutes of friendly and permissive contact with the experimenter each day), another punished (handled roughly or beaten for any approach response), a third intermittently indulged and punished, and a fourth kept in isolation. Using measures of human orientation to indicate the degree of bonding shown by the dogs at twelve to thirteen weeks of age, Fisher found that the indulged-punished group showed 231% of the human orientation of the indulged group. At sixteen weeks the indulged-punished group still showed the greatest amount of bonding of all four groups. As Rajecki and his colleagues conclude, 'The data show that inconsistent treatment (i.e., maltreatment by and affection from the same source) yield an accentuation of attempts to gain proximity to the attachment object' (Rajecki et al. 1978:425).

Intermittent Reinforcement Patterns in Domestic Violence
To what extent are findings based on animal studies applicable to humans? Rajecki et al. found no conclusive studies in the child-abuse literature, but it consisted mainly of descriptive case studies (none of it had been designed to test hypotheses regarding the nature of emotional bonds). However, prima facie evidence suggests that a process similar to that found in animals may be the mechanism that maintains the strong bond formed by battered women for their batterers. Rounsaville (1978) speculates that 'One feature that may weigh in favor of staying is the intermittent nature of the abuse ... Many [battered women] described highly pleasant periods of reconciliation between episodes ... This pattern was conducive to ignoring the problem or thinking of it as an aberrant, exceptional part of the relationship' (p. 17).

As outlined in Chapter 5, on the basis of over 120 detailed interviews with battered women, Lenore Walker (1979a) describes a cyclical pattern of domestic violence found in abusive spouse relationships that approximates the intermittent punishment-indulgence pattern used in animal research. Tension gradually builds (*phase one*), an explosive battering incident occurs (*phase two*), and a calm, loving respite follows (*phase three*). The battered woman's psychological reactions in each of the three phases, and the repetition of these phase-related responses, serves to 'bind a battered woman to her batterer just as strongly as "miracle glues" bind inanimate substances' (p. xvi). The immediate reaction of the battered woman during the battering incident is 'dissociation coupled with a sense of disbelief that the incident is really happening' (p. 62). This is followed by an emotional collapse indicative of extreme, aversive, prolonged arousal similar to that experienced by disaster victims or victims of hostage-takings (Flynn 1986). The collapse is accompanied by inactivity, depression, anxiety, self-blame, and feelings of helplessness.

In all, the exaggerated arousal and subsequent feelings make the battered woman extremely vulnerable and dependent for some time after the battering incident. The emotional aftermath of a battering incident for the batterer, usually guilt and contrition, leads him to attempt to make amends via exceptionally loving treatment towards his partner. Thus, he becomes, temporarily, the fulfilment of her hoped-for fantasy husband. At the same time, his improved behavior serves to reduce the aversive arousal he himself has created, while also providing reinforcement for his partner to stay in the relationship.

Arousal theory in psychology (e.g., Berlyne 1967; Zuckerman 1979) postulates that organisms are most content at mid-levels of arousal. Overload or underload triggers homeostatic behaviors that attempt to return the organism to a mid-level of arousal. Stimuli associated with an increase in arousal that is too low or with a decrease in arousal that is too high (or aversive) tend to become conditioned reinforcers. For example, Kendrick and Cialdini (1977) hypothesize that the reduction of aversive arousal builds attachments to people through the mechanism of negative reinforcement; that is, interpersonal or emotional associations are made stronger by the removal or cessation of an unpleasant stimulus, such as excessive arousal. In cases of battering, this mechanism of reinforcement could be especially strong due to the extremity of the aversive arousal caused by the battering incident and the subsequent reduction of that arousal in the form of pleasant contact during phase three of the cycle. When such negative reinforcement occurs intermittently over time, the reinforced response (i.e., the woman remaining with the batterer) is strengthened.

Hence, two powerful sources of reinforcement exist in intermittently abusive relationships: the excitement associated with an increase in arousal prior to violence and the relative tranquillity associated with postviolence calm. Both are homeostatic in that they might operate to produce an optimal state of arousal; both occur intermittently, creating a powerful reinforcement schedule. Thus, the more the cycle repeats itself, the less likely it is that the woman will leave the relationship (see also Solomon 1980).

Walker has noted the profound effect this series of events and behavior can have on the battered woman:

> As they progressed from the end of phase two into phase three of the battering cycle, the change in those women I visited daily in the hospital

was dramatic. Within a few days they went from being lonely, angry, frightened, and hurt to being happy, confident and loving ... These women were thoroughly convinced of their desire to stop being victims, until the batterer arrived. I always knew when a woman's husband had made contact with her by the profusion of flowers, candy, cards, and other gifts in her hospital room. (Walker 1979a:66)

During the third phase of the battering cycle, the batterer throws himself on his victim's mercy, reversing the power relationship between them dramatically. He places his fate in her hands; he will be destroyed – lost – if she doesn't rescue him by returning to the relationship. His behavior towards her, his pleas and his promises, are likely to relieve her fears and make her believe that she has control, that he will change his ways, that the violence will not recur. In other words, he reduces her aversive arousal, which had been caused by the build-up and battering phases of the cycle. As noted above, the psychological consequence of the power dynamics during the battering cycle serves to create and strengthen trauma-based emotional bonds between the man and woman, thus making long-lasting separation either difficult or impossible to achieve.

Traumatic bonding theory (Dutton & Painter 1981) postulates that when a woman finally leaves an abusive relationship, her immediate fears may begin to subside and her hidden attachment to her abuser will begin to manifest itself. At this particular point in time, the woman is emotionally drained and vulnerable. At these times in the past the husband has been present, contrite, and (temporarily) loving and affectionate. As the fear subsides and the needs fulfilled by her husband increase, an equilibrium point is reached and she suddenly and impulsively decides to return.

For an empirical test of this theory, several factors would need to be assessed: (1) the strength of the woman's emotional attachment to her husband, (2) the intermittent nature of previous abuse, (3) post-abuse positive reinforcement, and (4) the incrementally developed power imbalance that produces the attachment. According to traumatic bonding theory, the strength of the woman's attachment to her abuser should be predictable from knowledge of how much abuse she suffered from him and from the intermittent nature of this abuse. *Intermittency* would be assessed by measuring the extremity of the abuser's negative and positive behaviors towards her. Furthermore, emotional attachments of this nature should produce a constellation of beliefs about the causes of violence and its avoidability in the future – beliefs which are irrational (i.e., not based on past evidence) and which contribute to the woman returning to her abuser. Some assessment of these beliefs would also be required.

The Empirical Tests

To empirically test the theoretical notions of traumatic bonding theory, Dutton and Painter (1993a, 1993b) studied fifty women who had just left physically and emotionally abusive relationships and a control group of twenty-five women who has just left relationships that were primarily emotionally abusive.

To qualify for research participation, a woman had to have left her relationship within the past six months. Physically abused women were defined as those experiencing two or more incidents of severe physical abuse (on the *CTS* [Straus 1979]). They were recruited from two sources: transition houses and shelters in the Greater Vancouver region of British Columbia (n = 38), and the Assaultive Husbands Program, a treatment program for abusive men (n = 12).

A control sample of women who had been emotionally abused only was sought through newspaper advertisements. Some of the respondents had, in fact, been assaulted. The criteria for inclusion in the emotionally abused group were less than two incidents of physical violence and no incidents of severe physical violence (as defined by the *CTS*) during the relationship. Since our analyses were to be correlational, we were not concerned that some violence had occurred in this group. It is difficult to find women who have just left non-violent relationships.

Women completed two test batteries (as described below), the first upon initial contact and the second approximately six months later. In addition, structured interviews were conducted at Time 1. All subjects were paid for participation, and all interviews were audiotaped with the subjects' permission.

The mean age of subjects was 31.4, mean time in the relationship was 11.5 years (range 6 months to 44 years), and mean time separated was 20.5 weeks. On average, these women had initiated 2.1 prior separations. In this sample, 22 women were childless and half had experienced some form of abuse in their previous relationships. The women in the total sample reported very high degrees of verbal aggression directed towards them in their prior relationships. For example, the mean report of verbal aggression was 55.2 on the *CTS*, which places this sample beyond the 99th percentiles for population norms published by Straus, Gelles, and Steinmetz (1980). Women in the physically assaulted group also reported total physical aggression scores of 44.1 (SD = 16.0) and a severe physical aggression score of 13.4 (SD = 18.2), again beyond the 99th percentile for population norms. Women in the emotionally abused group reported total physical aggression scores of 1.2 (SD = 2.0) and severe physical aggression scores of 0.

Measures

Predictive Measures

Our relationship variables (factors that potentially affect a woman's ability to remain separated from an abusive partner) were as follows:

(1) *Measures of Abuse in the Prior Relationship.* The *CTS* and the *PMWI* (both described in Chapter 5) were used to assess physical and emotional abuse experienced by the women in our two samples. These measures were taken at Time 1 (when the woman had just left the relationship).

(2) *Intermittency of Abuse.* We created a measure of the *intermittency of abuse* to directly assess one of the key aspects of traumatic bonding. It was designed to assess the juxtaposition of extremely positive and negative behaviors. Respondents were asked to describe the first, last, and worst incident of abuse in detail (for non-battered women these were incidents of conflict and emotional abuse). For each incident, a variety of behaviors was listed, including threats and verbal and physical abuse. Post-abuse behavior was also assessed, including negative behaviors (e.g., threats) and positive contrition behaviors (see Walker 1979a).

An objective measure of intermittency was created by adding negative behaviors during abuse to positive behaviors after abuse, summed across the three incidents. Subjective measures of intermittency were created by having the respondent, after she had read the objective scale items, rate on a scale of -5 (very negative) to +5 (very positive) her partner's behavior before, during, and after each incident of abuse. The subjective intermittency scale was the sum of the three positive scores minus the three negative scores. Hence, the scale had a theoretical range of 0 to 30.

(3) *Power Dynamic.* Three measures of the respondent's rating of her own and her partner's *power* were taken. First, the *Decision Power Index* (Blood & Wolfe 1960), which assesses who has the final say on six issues (buying a car, having children, what apartment to take, what job either partner should take, whether a partner should work or not, and how much money to spend each week on food) was used. Second, because all so-called objective power measures have conceptual problems (see Huston 1983), a subjective measure of power, called *power differential*, was used. This simply asked the respondent to indicate on a ten-point scale how much power both she and her partner had (1) before the violence/abuse started, (2) after the violence/abuse started but before she left, and (3) now that she had left. The definition of power in this question was deliberately left unspecified. Third, a variable called *power shift* was calculated to assess the change in power differentials before and after battering on a ten-point scale.

Figure 7.1

Intermittency of abuse scale (Dutton & Painter 1993)

Intermittency Graph

We would like to see how your partner acted towards you, and how you felt about him, in the periods between three violent incidents. The incidents are numbered 1 through 3, with 3 being the last occurrence.

Please put a check mark beside the number of incident which was the worst.

Your Partner's Treatment of You

Please place an 'x' in the appropriate column to indicate how positively or negatively your partner treated you immediately before the incident, during the incident, immediately after, halfway between incidents, just before the next occurrence, and so on.

Your partner's treatment of you

	Very negative						Very positive				
	-5	-4	-3	-2	-1	0	+1	+2	+3	+4	+5
Before incident											
Incident #1											
After incident											
Halfway before next											
Before incident											
Incident #2											
After incident											
Halfway before next											
Before incident											
Incident #3											
After incident											
Halfway before next											

Feelings about Your Partner

Please place an 'x' in the appropriate column to indicate how positively or negatively you felt about your partner immediately before the incident, during the incident, immediately after, halfway between incidents, just before the next occurrence, and so on.

Feelings about your partner

	Very negative						Very positive				
	-5	-4	-3	-2	-1	0	+1	+2	+3	+4	+5
Before incident											

(continued on next page)

Figure 7.1 (continued)

Intermittency of abuse scale (Dutton & Painter 1993)

	Very negative	Very positive
	-5 -4 -3 -2 -1 0 +1 +2 +3 +4 +5	
Incident #1		
After incident		
Halfway before next		
Before incident		
Incident #2		
After incident		
Halfway before next		
Before incident		
Incident #3		
After incident		
Halfway before next		

(4) *Relationship Investment.* Another relationship feature described in earlier studies by Strube and Barbour (1983, 1984) was assessed. The *investment* in the relationship assessment was comprised of the length of time together and the number of prior separations.

(5) *Other Abusive Relationships.* Assessments were made of violence in each respondent's *family of origin* using the *CTS* (see Chapter 5). We also measured the presence of prior abusive relationships.

(6) *Financial Status.* Assessment of the woman's financial status (another relevant factor in determining her inability to remain out of an abusive relationship [Strube and Barbour 1983, 1984]) included family income before separation, her current (post-separation) income, percentage of child support paid by her partner, likelihood of these payments being interrupted, and financial outlook.

Dependent Measures

The effects of abuse and leaving a relationship were tested by three dependent measures which were collected at Time 1 and again at Time 2, six months later.

(1) *Attachment.* To assess attachment in this study we used a scale of attachment developed by Kitson (1982), supplemented with some items from a scale by NiCarthy (1982). The Kitson scale, which was used to assess attachment during divorce, measures the bereavement aspect of

separation and contains items such as 'I frequently find myself wondering what he is doing' and 'I spend a lot of time still thinking about him.'[1]

To supplement the assessment of attachment, ten items from an idealization measure developed by NiCarthy (1982) were used. These include items such as 'no one could ever understand him the way I do,' 'without him I have nothing to live for,' and 'I love him so much, I can't think of being with anyone else.' The NiCarthy scale added an element of continuing obsession with the partner that was not included in the Kitson scale.[2]

(2) *Self-Esteem*. Since self-esteem is frequently mentioned in the literature on effects of battering, we included it here. We used the ten-item self-report Rosenberg (1965) *Self-Esteem Scale*. Responses range from 'strongly disagree' to 'strongly agree' on a four-point scale; the higher the score, the greater the self-esteem.[3]

(3) *Trauma Symptoms*. The TSC-33 (Briere & Runtz 1989) assesses dissociation, anxiety, depression, PSAT-hypothesized, and sleep disturbance. Please see Chapter 5 for a full description of this scale

Results

The results of this research were reported in two articles that focused on different aspects of the problem. The first of these (Dutton & Painter 1993a) was a direct examination of whether traumatic bonding theory accurately predicted post-relationship effects. The second (Dutton & Painter 1993b) focused on whether or not the sequelae of battering comprised a syndrome. The *battered woman syndrome* (Walker 1979a, 1984) refers to a constellation of emotional and cognitive effects derived from repeated physical abuse. We will describe this concept in more detail below. First, however, we turn to the question of whether traumatic bonding theory accounted for the emotional consequences of leaving an abusive relationship.

Study 1: Traumatic Bonding and Post-relationship Emotions

The theoretical range of scores on the *PMWI* is from 0 to 232. The Battered (B) group's mean scores were: domination/isolation 79.1 (SD 25.9) and emotional abuse 95.5 (SD 15.9), indicating that frequent psychological abuse accompanied physical abuse. The Emotionally Abused (EA) group reported as follows: domination/isolation 43.1 (SD 27.5) and emotional abuse 69.4 (SD 20.1), indicating that psychological abuse occurred for this group as well (although it was significantly less severe than it was for (B). Social desirability measures (*MC*) did not correlate significantly with reports of partners' physical or emotional abuse, leading to

Figure 7.2

Attachment Scale (combined questions from Kitson [1982] and NiCarthy [1982])

Please respond to the following statements by circling the appropriate number.

| 0 | 1 | 2 | 3 | 4 |

not at all   very much
my feelings   my feelings

1. Everything I do seems like an effort.   0 1 2 3 4
2. I find myself spending a lot of time thinking about my husband/partner.   0 1 2 3 4
3. I'm feeling myself again.   0 1 2 3 4
4. Sometimes I can't believe we are breaking up.   0 1 2 3 4
5. I find myself wondering what my husband/partner is doing.   0 1 2 3 4
6. I have no interest in anything.   0 1 2 3 4
7. I'm angry at my husband/partner.   0 1 2 3 4
8. I feel I will never get over the break-up.   0 1 2 3 4
9. I could never find another man to love the way I loved him.   0 1 2 3 4
10. Without him, I have nothing to live for.   0 1 2 3 4
11. No one could ever understand him the way I do.   0 1 2 3 4
12. I suppose I should be interested in other people and activities, but I just want to be with him.   0 1 2 3 4
13. The idea of making love to another man is unthinkable.   0 1 2 3 4
14. I love him so much, I can't stand the thought of his being with anyone else.   0 1 2 3 4
15. When I try to imagine never seeing him again, I feel empty. 0 1 2 3 4
16. It's hard to separate from my partner because we share so many interests and friends in common.   0 1 2 3 4
17. It's hard for me to separate from my partner because of the children.   0 1 2 3 4
18. I feel strongly attached to my partner.   0 1 2 3 4
19. I am looking forward to establishing a relationship with another man.   0 1 2 3 4
20. I am looking forward to establishing an independent life. 0 1 2 3 4

the conclusion that these reports were uncontaminated by impression management concerns.

Three major sets of dependent measures were taken at Time 1: the *TSC-33*, the *Attachment Scale*, and the *Self-Esteem Inventory*. The average scores on these scales for the entire sample of 75 at Time 1 are as follows: (1)

TSC-33 (theoretical range 0 to 224) 44.9 (SD 20.7), (2) *Attachment Scale* (theoretical range 0 to 80) 28.5 (SD 18.0), and (3) *Self-Esteem Inventory* (theoretical range 0-40) 27.3 (SD 5.6). A total of 66 (44/50 B and 22/25 EA) of the original 75 respondents were contacted at Time 2 and completed the second assessment package.

At Time 2, 51% of the women had weekly contact with their partners and 14% had monthly contact. The most common reason for contact was their children. Seventeen per cent of the B group and 8% of the EA group still had sexual contact with their former partners. Of the B group, 35/44 partners had attempted reconciliation and 10/44 battered women had attempted reconciliation. However, only 4 women had actually returned to living with their partners. None of the EA group had returned. Only 13/44 B women and 6/22 EA women had absolutely no contact with their former partners. Just 3 of the 66 respondents rated themselves as less content than they had been six months previously.

Overall self-esteem scores at Time 2 showed no significant improvement, and attachment scores at Time 2 were 73% as strong as they were at Time 1. In other words, although attachment had begun to decrease, women at Time 2 still showed a moderate attachment to their ex-partners (21.2 out of a possible score of 80) when assessed using the attachment scale. Trauma symptoms had also diminished with time; they had decreased from their Time 1 level by 57%. The drop was equal across all subscales of the *TSC-33*.

Relationship of Predictor to Dependent Variables. The strongest association between individual predictor variables (i.e., *CTS*, *PMWI*, intermittency of abuse, power measures, relationship investment, prior abusive relationships, financial state) and dependent variables (i.e., attachment, self-esteem, trauma symptoms) was found between subjective intermittency of abuse and attachment. Significant relationships between predictor and dependent variables are presented in Table 7.1.

It is interesting to note that overall *CTS* scores for physical violence had a significant negative correlation with self-esteem at Time 1 but not at Time 2. The length of the relationship correlated negatively with trauma symptoms at both times. While the dominance/isolation subscale on the *PMWI* correlated significantly and positively with trauma symptoms at both Time 1 and Time 2, the emotional abuse subscale significantly correlated with trauma symptoms only at Time 1 (and in a negative direction).

To better estimate the overall effect of relationship, financial, and family of origin variables on post-relationship measures, composite measures of all three were constructed and entered into a multiple regression on the

Table 7.1

Relationship of predictor to dependent variables

		Attachment	Self-esteem	Trauma symptoms
Intermittency	Time 1	.62		
	Time 2	.60		
Power differential	Time 1	.27		
	Time 2	.31		
CTS (physical violence)	Time 1		-.58	
Length of relationship	Time 1		-.33	-.25
	Time 2			-.23
PMWI: dominance/ isolation	Time 1	-.33		+.20
	Time 2		-.27	+.44
PMWI: emotional abuse	Time 1			+.29

various dependent measures of the study. Only variables comprising the composite measure were entered into the stepwise regression. Relationship variables included intermittency, power shift, total physical abuse, dominance, emotional abuse, and length of relationship.

Table 7.2 shows the relationship of these composite variables to the post-relationship measures by indicating the amount of variance in each dependent variable accounted for by each composite variable. The percentages exceed 100% because the regressions were done independently.

In this analysis, *family of origin* variables affected only trauma symptoms, accounting for 23% of the trauma symptom variance at Time 1 and 9% of such variance at Time 2. The family of origin variables were: (1) total physical abuse by father to mother (beta = -.64) and (2) total physical abuse by father to daughter (beta = .87). Other family of origin variables entered into a regression had no additional effect on trauma symptom variance.

Relationship variables accounted for more of the post-relationship variance on the dependent measures. At Time 1, 41% of attachment scores were accounted for by a composite relationship variable comprised of

Table 7.2

Proportion of dependent measure variance accounted by family of origin, current relationship, and financial clusters

	Time 1			Time 2		
	Trauma symptoms	Attachment	Self-esteem	Trauma symptoms	Attachment	Self-esteem
Family of origin	23%	-	-	9%	-	-
Relationship	8	41	29	47	55	19
Financial	9	17	18	90	72	60

power shift (which measures dyadic power changes after violence), dominance/isolation, and length of relationship. Twenty-nine per cent of self-esteem scores at Time 1 were accounted for by relationship variables: length of the relationship, power differential, physical abuse by the partner, and intermittency of abuse.

Relationship variables did best at accounting for attachment at Time 2 (55% of the variance). This was a composite variable comprised of dominance/isolation, power differential, and intermittency. Trauma symptoms at Time 2 had 47% of their variance accounted for by current relationship variables, suggesting a delayed effect of relationship trauma on symptom onset. Both dominance/isolation and total physical abuse were instrumental in this regression.

Financial variables had little effect on post-relationship scores at Time 1 but had a strong effect at Time 2. A composite financial variable measuring the wife's percentage of contribution to child support, likelihood of partner's financial support, employment, partner's contribution to family income, and total family income accounted for 90% of the variance in trauma symptoms at Time 2. The strongest effects were for child support and partner's contribution. This composite financial variable also accounted for 72% of the variance in attachment scores at Time 2 and for 60% of the variance for self-esteem scores.

Finally, a discriminant function analysis was run on the most-attached and least-attached women in B group at Time 2 using all available predictor variables. A five-variable composite explained 76% of the variance in attachment and correctly classified 85.3% of the women according to strength of attachment. The main contributors to this composite variable were dominance/isolation, intermittency, total physical abuse by partner, emotional abuse, and power shift.

Discussion and Conclusions. While the influence of relationship variables on attachment, self-esteem, and trauma following relationship dissolution is complex, some findings clearly emerged. First, we found that variables assessing relationship dynamics, particularly intermittency of abuse and changes in power due to the battering (power shift), were strong predictors of post-separation attachment.

Prior studies have not attempted to assess these dynamic features of relationships. For example, Follingstad, Brennan, Hause, Polek, and Rutledge (1991) had a group of battered women rate both past relationship violence and current physical and psychological symptoms. Results indicated that the number and severity of symptoms was predicted by the frequency of abuse. In the present study, the overall *CTS* (frequency of abuse) score did relate to both trauma symptoms and attachment, but it was a relatively weak contributor compared to intermittency of abuse. Follingstad et al. did not assess intermittency or changes in the power dynamic.

Similarly, Strube's (1988) conclusion that economic variables are stronger predictors of leaving/staying out of abusive relationships than are relationship variables may have to be qualified. Although economic variables contributed strongly to all dependent measures at Time 2 in our study, the discriminant function analysis of attachment revealed relationship variables as the main predictors of attachment status at Time 2. (Attachment was not directly assessed in prior studies.) Indeed, although the reality of financial pressure at Time 2 in influencing attachment affect and trauma symptoms for the partner cannot be underestimated, it must be placed in perspective. One hundred per cent of our sample interviewed at Time 2 said that economic factors did not cause them to contemplate returning, and only 33% said they had ever even considered this.

The intermittency of abuse, a central concept of traumatic bonding theory, not only contributed to the composite predictor variable but also had a high, significant individual correlation with attachment at both times. In fact, the strongest associations at Time 1 were between intermittency and attachment (also partner's violence [*CTS*] and negative self-esteem). These results are summarized in Figure 7.3. If the information presented in Figure 7.3 is compared to that in Figure 5.5, it might be concluded that borderline men generate the highest levels of traumatic bonding in their partners.

As described earlier in this chapter, traumatic bonding theory (Dutton & Painter 1981) postulates that when a woman finally leaves an abusive relationship, her immediate fears may begin to subside and her hidden attachment to her abuser may begin to manifest itself. Emotionally drained and vulnerable, she can become susceptible to her partner's

Figure 7.3

Factors contributing to persistence of attachment, trauma symptoms, and low self-esteem

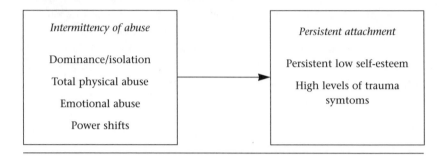

loving, contrite pressure to return. As the fear subsides and the needs previously fulfilled by her husband increase, the woman may suddenly and impulsively decide to give the relationship another chance. Our study verified this process: relationship variables (i.e., intermittent abuse and dominance/isolation) impact on the woman's attachment system with a delayed effect. Their impact on attachment became stronger, rather than weaker, with time. This supports Dutton and Painter's (1981) elastic band analogy, in which the woman figuratively leaves the relationship with an elastic band tied between her and her partner; the longer she is away, the greater the stretch and the greater the pressure – until one day it snaps her back. The strength of relationship variables in predicting attachment underscores their importance in understanding the post-relationship functioning of battered women.

Although only 9% of the battered women had returned to live with their partners at Time 2, 51% had had some form of contact (17% reported that this was sexual) with them (although it is important to remember that the predominant reason given for continued contact related to their children.) This suggests that a variety of forms of attachment survive the process of separation.

This notion of attachment being strengthened by intermittently good and bad treatment is counter-intuitive and still beyond the ken of the average jury member (Ewing & Aubrey 1987). Hence, part of the role of expert witnesses who testify in battered woman self-defence cases (which we will discuss later in this chapter) is to clarify the role of traumatic bonding in contributing (along with threats from the batterer, financial pressures, etc.) to the overall difficulty battered women have in leaving abusive relationships.

Traumatic bonding also has implications for therapists working with battered women. Making the phenomenon explicit to the woman allows her to know what to expect throughout the process and enables her not to infer from her detachment difficulties that there are any special relationship features between her and her batterer. Over time, the increase in the undertow pulling her back to her batterer will be accompanied by an increase in positive memories and a decrease in negative memories. Providing consistent reminders of the factual aspects of the violence can

---

Focus
The Battered Woman Syndrome

According to Walker (1979a, 1984) and Douglas (1987), the battered woman syndrome is comprised of the following signs and symptoms:
(1) Exposure to a relationship with repeated intermittent abuse (sign)
(2) Consequently, the victim experiences:
Primary Complex
 (a) trauma symptoms: anxiety, hyperarousal, flashbacks (re-experiencing the trauma), intrusive recollections, psychic numbing
 (b) lowered self-esteem, learned helplessness (self-destructive coping responses to the violence)
Secondary Complex
 (c) idealization of the abuser ('he's really sweet underneath,' 'he's trying to change')
 (d) denial of danger ('things aren't that bad,' 'I think I can anticipate [and control] his outbursts')
 (e) suppression of anger ('I'm not angry with him')

Note: After the danger passes the woman's anger usually surfaces.

---

help to offset memory changes associated with delayed increases in the traumatically formed bond.

Study 2: Traumatic Bonding and the Battered Woman Syndrome
The Battered Woman Syndrome. Since its initial description by Walker (1979a, 1984), the battered woman syndrome has been widely discussed (Douglas 1987; Schuller & Vidmar 1992) and has been used as a basis for

self-defence in cases where battered women have killed their abusers (Thyfault, Browne, & Walker 1987). Walker (1979a) initially described a three-stage battering cycle (tension build-up, battering, contrition). Victim reactions to this repetitive abuse and its anticipation included psychophysiological stress, lowered self-esteem, and learned helplessness, all of which undercut motivation to leave the abusive relationship.

Douglas (1987) defined the battered woman syndrome as 'a collection of specific characteristics and effects of abuse on the battered woman' (p. 40). She subdivided the characteristics into three major categories: (1) the traumatic effects of victimization by violence, (2) learned helplessness deficits resulting from the violence and others' reactions to it, and (3) self-destructive coping responses to the violence.

Douglas argued that the effects of violence victimization were similar or identical to those for post-traumatic stress disorder: learned helplessness, re-experiencing of the trauma, intrusive recollections, generalized anxiety, lowered self-esteem, and social withdrawal. She also identified two apparently opposite emotional responses as common symptoms: psychic numbing (or reduced responsiveness to the world) and generalized hyper-arousal (such as exaggerated startle responses). These responses are believed to be related to cumulative exposure to the abuse stressor. Douglas did not attempt to quantify the abuse stressor per se, nor did she attempt to specify the essential dimension of spouse-abuse trauma.

In addition, Douglas (1987) described a secondary complex of abuse sequelae, including idealization of the abuser, denial of danger, and the victim's suppression of her own anger. These responses, also common in the trauma literature (van der Kolk 1987), are viewed as coping responses that occur under extreme duress. For example, in developing traumatic bonding theory Dutton and Painter (1981) cited Anna Freud's (1942) description of 'identification with the aggressor' (see Chapter 6) as an explanation of how battered women, amongst others, cope with long-term relationships with potentially lethal others. The idealization of the abuser is related to the strength of the continued attachment to him after relationship termination (Dutton & Painter 1981).

The concept of intermittency of abuse refers to the fact that the onset of positive treatment is contiguous with the cessation of negative treatment. In abusive relationships, negative treatment typically precedes positive treatment. What is essential in order to generate attachment is the extremity of both good treatment and maltreatment, and the temporal juxtaposition of one extreme to the other (usually maltreatment followed immediately by good treatment). While the onset of negative treatment may be predictable, this predictability may be unrelated to extremity or to temporal juxtaposition. Dutton and Painter (1981) argued that intermittency (or periodicity), not predictability, was the main contributor to the battered woman syndrome and to traumatic attachment.

Schuller and Vidmar (1992) have written a critical assessment of the battered woman syndrome from the perspective of its use as a self-defence plea. They have raised two issues. The first is that the cycle of violence cited originally by Walker (1984) as descriptive of the stressor is not always present. Walker's data revealed, for example, that only 65% of her cases demonstrated a tension-building phase and that only 58% demonstrated a contrition phase. Schuller and Vidmar concluded that 'not all couples go through the cycle of violence nor is there a universal time frame for the cycle' (p. 280). Second, the internal reliability of the symptoms comprising the syndrome has not been empirically verified. As the authors put it, how internally reliable are the symptoms of battered woman syndrome and how much do they covary?

With the same data set reported above, Susan Painter and I attempted to address these questions by assessing the interconnectedness (correlations) amongst three major sequelae of the battered woman syndrome (trauma symptoms, self-esteem deficits, and traumatic bonding [Dutton & Painter 1981]) in order to establish whether they constituted a syndrome. We also attempted to examine the role of predictability of abuse in the presentation of these three sequelae by asking respondents four questions pertaining to whether or not they could predict abusive outbursts from their partners. As part of their description of the first, worst, and last incidents of abuse, they were asked if they could tell their partners were going to become abusive. In addition, they were asked if their partners went through predictable and abrupt shifts in mood and became suddenly angry. These questions were combined to form an eight-point scale of predictability.

Results

Intercorrelations of Dependent Measures. Table 7.3 shows intercorrelations of the three main dependent variables (attachment, self-esteem, and trauma symptoms) within a particular time period. Significant correlations were found between all pairs of the three dependent measure scales at Time 1. Women who had low self-esteem at Time 1 tended to have significantly more trauma symptoms and to feel significantly more attached to their ex-mates than did those who had high self-esteem.

The three main dependent measures again correlated significantly at Time 2, with trauma symptoms and self-esteem being even more strongly

Table 7.3

Intercorrelations of dependent measures within a time period

	Attachment	Self-esteem
Time 1		
trauma symptoms	.39[c]	-.22[a]
attachment		-.27[a]
Time 2		
trauma symptoms	.49[c]	-.62[c]
attachment		-.36[b]

[a] $p < .05$
[b] $p < .01$
[c] $p < .001$

Table 7.4

Intercorrelations of Time 1 and Time 2 dependent measures

	Time 2		
Time 1	Trauma symptoms	Attachment	Self-esteem
Trauma symptoms	.48[c]	.27[b]	-.36[b]
Attachment	.34[b]	.68[c]	-.17
Self-esteem	-.16	-.07	.27[a]

[a] $p < .05$
[b] $p < .01$
[c] $p < .001$

related than they were at Time 1. Again, women who had low self-esteem at Time 2 tended to have significantly more trauma symptoms and to feel significantly more attached to their former partners than did those with high self-esteem.

Table 7.4 shows the intercorrelations of Time 1 with Time 2 measures, which were taken six months later. Despite the lengthy interval between Time 1 and Time 2, each dependent measure taken at Time 1 correlated significantly with its counterpart measure taken at Time 2. Note that although attachment shows the largest drop in score size between times, the Time 2 scores are still highly correlated with the Time 1 scores. In this sense, Time 2 attachment is predictably about 73% of the Time 1 attachment score.

Table 7.5

Intercorrelations of dependent measures within a time period by group

	Battered		Emotionally Abused	
	Attachment	Self-esteem	Attachment	Self-esteem
Time 1				
Trauma symptoms	.39[c]	-.22[a]	.44[b]	-.40[a]
Attachment		-.28[a]		-.21
Time 2				
Trauma symptoms	.55[c]	-.67[c]	.41[b]	-.56[b]
Attachment		-.48[b]		-.17

[a] $p < .05$
[b] $p < .01$
[c] $p < .001$

Table 7.5 shows the intercorrelations of the dependent variables at Time 1 and at Time 2, broken down separately for the B and EA groups, respectively. For the B group, significant correlations were found between all pairs of the three dependent measure scales at both Time 1 and at Time 2. For the EA group, *TSC-33* scores correlated significantly with attachment (+.44) and self-esteem (-.40). However, unlike the B group, the EA group showed no significant correlation between attachment and self-esteem (-.21). This pattern was repeated at Time 2. For battered women, the three sequelae of battering measured in this study were significantly intercorrelated. This significant intercorrelation exhibits durability for up to six months. Women in this sample did find their partners' behavior predictable (generating mean scores on predictability of 5.7 out of a possible 8), but predictability and intermittency of abuse were not related ($r = .11$ ns).

Predictability of Abuse. Surprisingly, unlike power shift and intermittency, predictability of abuse was not a strong predictor variable in this study.

Discussion and Conclusions. This discussion addresses both the results described immediately above and those reported in the previous section. The women in this study reported three aspects of the battered woman syndrome: high rates of trauma symptoms, lowered self-esteem, and heightened paradoxical attachment to the batterer. These effects were all significantly intercorrelated, thus forming a syndrome, or complex, that persisted for at least six months, despite their remaining outside their prior relationships.

In addition, these effects were significantly related to the extremity of the battering and to the intermittency of positive-negative treatment. Examination of trauma symptom scores for the emotionally abused group revealed that patterns at Time 1 changed somewhat when physical assault did not recur. The EA group did not experience a significant negative correlation between attachment and self-esteem, but other intercorrelations remained significant (as was the case with the battered group). The pattern which was seen in emotionally abused women at Time 1 was repeated at Time 2.

The trauma symptoms experienced by women in our sample include heightened anxiety, dissociation, depression, and sleep disturbance. Almost half the variance in these symptoms was attributable to relationship variables (i.e., the severity and intermittency of psychological abuse, domination, and battering) as much as six months after its dissolution.

Composite distress or battered woman syndrome scores (comprised of persistent attachment to the abuser, trauma symptoms, and low self-esteem) for these women were largely accounted for by dominance/isolation, intermittency of abuse, total physical abuse, emotional abuse, and power shift (losses in power to the woman and increases in power to the man following abuse). Hence, a direct link is established between these abuse factors and post-relationship distress as assessed by a composite battered women syndrome score. The power of these relationship variables in correctly predicting post-relationship distress (91.3% of subjects were correctly classified into distress categories) speaks to this link. In effect, the totality of symptom scores comprising the battered woman syndrome is affected by the severity of physical abuse, the intermittency of maltreatment and good treatment, dyadic power shifts from the man to the woman, and emotional abuse. It is suggested that each of these contributors be thoroughly assessed in court cases involving battered women.

Intermittency of Abuse versus the Cycle of Violence Explanation for the Battered Woman Syndrome

Criticisms of the battered woman syndrome (e.g., Schuller & Vidmar 1992) have focused on its perceived connection to the cycle of violence described by Walker (1979a 1984), which is not present in all battering relationships. The present data suggest that intermittency of abuse, not a battering cycle per se, is a major determinant of the battered woman syndrome. Whereas a cycle of violence perspective describes violence as going through predictable (and mood-driven) cycles, the term intermittency, as defined in this research, simply indicates that extreme positive and negative behaviors occur with temporal contiguity; they need be neither cyclical nor predictable.

While women in our sample did find their partners' behavior predictable (generating mean scores on predictability of 5.7 out of a possible 8), predictability and intermittency were not significantly correlated. Indeed, predictability did not correlate significantly with any extremity measures of negative or positive behaviors. It was intermittency, not predictability, that forecast post-relationship distress. In fact, intermittency's effect on attachment grew stronger over time.

It appears that it is the extremity and juxtaposition of positive and negative behaviors that contribute to the battered woman syndrome. Intermittency may be cyclical, as in the case of abusive men with borderline personality organization (Dutton 1994a; Dutton & Starzomski 1993); but, whether it is or not, it nonetheless influences attachment, trauma, and self-esteem.

Clearly, more empirical work needs to be done on the battered woman syndrome. Herman (1992) describes trauma effects as a dialectic process characterized by extreme affective states ('floods of intense, overwhelming feeling and arid states of no feeling at all' [p. 47]). This study did not attempt to assess affective reactions such as psychic numbing or hyperreactivity, and little is known about the experiences shaping these apparently opposite emotional responses.

The present study also did not examine learned helplessness (Walker 1979a), an acquired motivational deficit thought to undercut attempts to leave the batterer. However, since our sample was contacted after leaving their partners, they may, ipso facto, have not demonstrated this effect as strongly as did battered women still in abusive relationships. It is sampling problems such as these that continue to make the empirical study of the aftermath of battering problematic. However, for the variables studied, self-esteem, attachment, and trauma symptoms respond similarly to such features of prior abuse as intermittency and power differentials. These abuse features, along with the extremity of the abuse, constitute an important part of the assessment of battering dynamics.

Battered Woman Self-Defence Cases

When abuse victims become perpetrators of violence, the legal defence usually hinges on what is called the *battered woman self-defence*, which attempts to demonstrate to the jury how a past history of abuse, the difficulties involved in the woman trying to leave (including, where applicable, the man's threats against her and her children if she were to do so), and the psychological reality of living in permanent fear can provide the determination of *imminent danger* that is the cornerstone of self-defence pleas. Schuller and Vidmar (1992) point out that a finding of self-defence requires the defendant to establish that she had a reasonable apprehension of imminent death or grievous bodily harm from her partner at the time of the killing, and, further, that the force she used was a necessary response.

In the majority of cases the battered woman does not attack during a beating but, rather, at a later time, when *imminent threat* may not be apparent to an outside observer. This delay between the partner's assault and the eventual response can render the immediacy of the threat questionable under the narrow temporal conception of traditional self-defence laws.

The violence that battered women face is continual and at the hands of an intimate partner rather than those of a stranger. The laws of self-defence were developed with the notion of two equally strong strangers in mind. Psychologists have to instruct juries on how a battered woman's situation differs from this legal prototype. Furthermore, psychologists appearing as expert witnesses in court must address possible misconceptions about battered women, such as their being masochistic and being able to leave if they really wanted.

Ewing and Aubrey (1987) found that jury members of both genders held stereotyped beliefs about battered women. Two-thirds of the authors' mock jurors (71% of the women and 57% of the men) believed that a battered woman can simply leave her batterer. Fifty per cent of all women subjects and 34% of the men believed that women who stay in abusive relationships are somewhat masochistic. Ewing and Aubrey concluded: 'These results suggest that women are much more likely than men to subscribe to these stereotypes' (p. 263). Demographically, the least sympathetic juror in a battered woman self-defence case is a woman over the age of fifty-one.

Follingstad, Polek, Hause, Deaton, Bulger, and Conway (1989) had college student samples read fictitious prototypical battered women self-defence cases. Subjects heard one of three levels of violence portrayed and heard one of two sets of judge's instructions: not guilty by reason of self-defence (NGRSD) or not guilty by reason of insanity (NGRI). Subjects decided on a verdict and completed a questionnaire giving their reasons for it.

The judge's instructions had a strong effect on the outcome: self-defence instructions produced more not guilty verdicts. Verdicts were also influenced by the subjects' view of the severity of the past beatings, the testimony of the expert witness, the subjects' feelings about the woman using a weapon, and the subjects' own histories of abuse (abuse victims were more lenient with the woman defendant).

Schuller (1992) also examined the effect of expert testimony on jury verdicts in battered woman self-defence cases. She had subjects read the transcript of a homicide trial involving a battered woman who had killed her husband. They received either no expert testimony (control), expert testimony presenting general research findings on the battered woman syndrome (general expert condition), or testimony in which the expert supplemented this general information with the opinion that the defendant fit the battered woman syndrome (specific expert condition).

The presence of the specific expert, compared to the control, led to interpretations that were more consistent with the woman's account of what happened. These interpretations, in turn, were related to more lenient verdicts. The interpretations included being more likely, in the expert conditions, to view the woman as fearing for her life on the morning of the homicide. In addition, the defendant was viewed as significantly more trustworthy and credible in the expert conditions. The verdicts were more likely to be manslaughter than murder.

Kasian, Spanos, Terrance, and Peebles (1993) used a simulated trial format with videotapes depicting the trial of a battered woman who killed her husband. The trial proceedings included opening statements from the judge, prosecutor, and defence, then three witnesses for each side who underwent both direct and cross-examination. It concluded with closing arguments from both defence and prosecution and the judge's charge to the jury. The expert witness was depicted as a psychiatrist. Two different pleas were examined: automatism (that the battered woman killed while in a dissociative state brought on by the battering) and self-defence (that the battering had created a reasonable belief in the battered woman that her husband would kill her). Expert witness testimony again had an effect on both the perceptions and the verdicts of the mock jurors. The automatism plea was more successful than was the self-defence plea.

In a second experiment, the authors used a psychological self-defence plea, as suggested by Ewing (1987, 1990) and as criticized by others (Morse 1990). Psychological self-defence means that the battered women used force to prevent 'gross and enduring impairment of her psychological functioning' (Ewing 1987:79). Again, the automatism plea resulted in more acquittals than did the psychological self-defence plea, although psychological self-defence did better than did self-defence. It does not appear that the authors had their experts speak specifically to the issue of imminent danger. Nor did they have experts appear for both sides, as is usually the case in real trials. Abuse severity strongly affected the advantages of self-defence pleas. This finding was replicated in all studies reported above.

Assaulted Women and the Criminal Justice System

The overall picture that emerges from the literature on victimization is as follows: the immediate psychological consequences of being a victim of severe assault are (amongst others) depression, confusion, lack of motivation, anxiety, anger, and guilt. One implication of this post-assault profile is that strong support from the criminal justice system is required if legal action is to proceed. It is unrealistic to expect a person in the traumatized state described above to take the initiative in laying charges. In the next chapter we will examine the outcome of police-initiated intervention. At this point, however, I would argue that the victim of wife assault who is experiencing depression, inertia, and confusion is in no condition to overcome bureaucratic hurdles in proceeding with charges. Furthermore, since her anxiety state is high and the use of intimidation by her husband as a means of getting her to drop the charges is frequent, an additional advantage accrues to police-initiated charges: the victim cannot be cajoled into dropping the charges since she is not responsible for their initiation.

Women who subsequently refuse to testify against their husbands decrease, but do not eliminate, the probability of their being convicted. As shall be seen in Chapter 8, the probability of conviction drops from 83% to 27.5% when the victim does not cooperate with the prosecution (Lerman 1981), but the criminal justice system itself can increase the probability of victim cooperation (Dutton 1981a). A first step in this direction requires that criminal justice professionals understand the victimology of assaulted women and relinquish stereotyped explanations for their post-assault behavior.

Angela Browne (1987) wrote a classic text entitled *When Battered Women Kill*. In this book, Browne examined the multiplicative forces combining to drive battered women to kill their abusers. Browne and Williams (1989) found that battered women's homicides were related to criminal justice system resource availability. US states that had more domestic violence legislation and other resources for battered women (e.g., shelters, crisis lines, support groups) than did others had lower rates of female-perpetrated partner homicide. The increase in resources was associated with a 25% decrease in such homicides between 1976 and 1984. This decline began in 1979, at about the time that domestic violence legislation and extralegal resources for abused women were coming into place (Browne & Dutton 1990). One conclusion that could be drawn is that an effective criminal justice system response not only protects battered women, it lowers the rate of homicide against abuse-perpetrators.

Chapter Summary and Conclusions

This chapter has examined how victims of abuse can become traumatically bonded to their victimizers, suffering from a psychological condition called the battered woman syndrome. This occurs through intermittent reinforcement patterns of abusive and conciliatory behavior. The empirical evidence supports the conclusion that dynamic features of the relationship (abusiveness, intermittency, etc.) strongly affect the syndrome of emotional consequences experienced by the victim. We also examined the use of the battered woman syndrome as a self-defence plea in court and the role and need for expert witness testimony in these cases.

In order to help these women break free from these powerful bonds, we need to reconsider our criminal justice and treatment approaches. Criminal justice professionals must recognize the psychological issues facing intimately assaulted women – the complex factors that often make following through with charges and testimony extremely difficult. New approaches must be developed to aid them through this process.

Mental health professionals also need to recognize the power of traumatic bonding in order to better understand and help their clients. Assaulted women may want to return to their husbands once their initial shock subsides. With the wearing off of that shock, the traumatically established bonds again become salient. This is a period when extensive emotional support is required. Such support should include generating an understanding in the victim of the emotional consequences of traumatic bonding in order to help her to understand her present feelings and to aid her resistance.

As has been seen, intermittently abusive relationships take a huge emotional toll on the victim, lowering her self-worth and creating high rates of trauma symptoms while maintaining her troublesome attachment to the perpetrator. Many post-battering effects are mistakenly attributed to personality traits which the victim has always had; in reality, these traits show only the psychic erosion caused by repeated abuse.

8
The Criminal Justice Response to Wife Assault

The proper design of public policies requires a clear and sober under-standing of the nature of man and, in particular, of the extent to which that nature can be changed by plan.

– J.Q. Wilson, *Thinking About Crime*

Several results and conclusions from earlier chapters converge on the issues of police intervention in family violence. In Chapter 1 we learned that about 10.2% of women are assaulted by their husbands and about 6.8% are assaulted repeatedly (Schulman 1979; Straus, Gelles, & Steinmetz 1980). Of the women who are assaulted, about 14.5% call the police (Schulman 1979; Straus & Gelles 1985). Hence, about one in six assaults (using the Severe Abuse Index of the Straus *CTS* as the criterion) is reported to police. This report rate implies, first of all, that a limit is imposed on criminal justice effectiveness as a solution to wife assault. The criminal justice system cannot deal effectively with crimes that are both private and unreported.

As we shall see later in this chapter, the single greatest impediment to a more effective criminal justice response to wife assault is the victim's fail-ure to report the event to the police. If the assault is severe, and the vic-tim is traumatized, then some of the psychological consequences of assault described in the last chapter may prevent the victim from taking effective self-protective actions. As shall be seen, however, many victims of wife assault do not define the event as a crime and, for this reason, may fail to report it to the police. Nevertheless, the one-in-six report statistic also suggests that the police, more than any other outside agency, will come into contact with the greatest number of wife assaults, perhaps 14.5% of all committed assaults. If the state is to generate policy for diminishing the incidence of wife-assault, such policy will need to focus on police procedure for intervention.

As a society we tend to dismiss the seriousness of violence between intimates. Shotland and Straw (1976) found that third-party perceptions about the seriousness of violence and the utility of intervention were strongly reduced by the knowledge that the violence occurred between intimates. Since the police share many of the perceptions and attitudes of the socializing culture (Rokeach, Miller, & Snyder 1971; Dutton 1986b), these perceptual issues may affect their choice of action in *clearing* domestic disturbance calls (i.e., disposing of the call through arrest, mediation, or getting one party to temporarily leave [see Ford 1987]). In this chapter, we will examine how police make such decisions.

We learned in Chapter 6 that when the situational determinants of a victim remaining with her abusive husband are unclear, third-party observers make victim-blaming attributions that may preclude their taking action to help her. And we learned in Chapter 7 that the immediate post-assault trauma of victims might make them depressed, upset, confused, and uncertain about the efficacy of criminal justice action. When we add to this the uncertainty that police feel when intervening in family matters, we begin to perceive the complexity of domestic dispute intervention from the police perspective. Police are charged with the responsibility of determining the best strategy (i.e., arrest, leave, mediate, etc.) for domestic disputes where assault may or may not have occurred, where the conflict might appear to have subsided, and where the victim may seem uninterested or opposed to charging her husband. Furthermore, the informal working knowledge of the police may suggest that assaulted women inevitably fail to come to court, so that charging the male is believed to be futile. Finally, since a real and unpredictable danger exists for the police officer in a small minority of domestic disputes, all these decisions will have to be made in the presence of a certain amount of danger and anxiety.

The issue of what the police can and should do to prevent repeat wife assault has been a major concern of both psychologists and criminologists since the mid-1970s. In 1991, the American Society of Criminology held a panel discussion on the state of the research to date, and the results were published in a special issue of the *American Behavioral Scientist* (1993, vol. 36). In this chapter we will review the studies bearing on this debate.

The Police and Wife Assault: Early Studies

Seminal psychological contributions to police intervention in family conflict were designed to improve their decisionmaking and communication abilities. Bard developed an experimental program with the New York Police Department in 1967 that was designed to diminish *iatrogenic violence*, that is, violence accidentally triggered by the police (Bard 1971;

Bard, Zacker, & Rutter 1972). Bard held the pioneering view that police officers served a preventive function in that they could reduce the likelihood of future crime by proper handling of current family conflict. His system trained officers how to use arbitration, mediation, and negotiation to manage crisis situations. The trained officers were then assigned to a high-crime precinct in the Harlem area of New York and responded to all its domestic disturbance calls.

Bard established an ongoing case discussion system between the officers and psychologists for the duration of the two-year program. At the conclusion of the program, the project managers claimed that the training had produced decreases in injuries to officers and a reduction in the incidence of domestic disturbances (presumably by diminishing repeat calls). However, these claims have been disputed by others.

Liebman and Schwartz (1973) argued that Bard's data indicated a higher percentage of repeat calls were received in an adjacent control district. Furthermore, family homicides and assaults increased in the experimental district and decreased in the control district. The highly publicized claim that injuries decreased for trained officers was based on no injuries to officers in the experimental district and on one injury to an officer in the control district. The controversy over the Bard project highlighted the early issues that surrounded police intervention in domestic disturbances: Could such interventions be carried out so that the police would be safer, and could the police decision about how to 'clear' the disturbance call reduce future repeat calls?

Stereotypes in the Perception of Wife Assault

The furore over Bard's statistics obscured a second important outcome of his project: It furnished a huge data base on the characteristics of domestic disputes from the police perspective. A select group of 18 officers operating in biracial pairs reported the characteristics of 1,388 domestic disturbance calls in Harlem (Bard & Zacker 1974). On these calls, an assault was alleged 36% of the time by the victim and was confirmed by the police 29% of the time. The most commonly reported immediate cause of conflict was infidelity. The police reported the use of physical force by citizens or by themselves in only 1% of 1,388 disputes studied. The alleged assailants appeared to have been drinking in 30% of the cases, but in only 4.3% were they judged by police to have been drunk. The police perceived alcohol to be primary in the origin of the dispute in only 14% of the cases.

In order to generalize these findings, a second study was conducted in Norwalk, Connecticut, in 1972 (Zacker & Bard 1977). Norwalk, in contrast to Harlem, is a white middle-class community considered to be socio-economically representative of a large number of cities and townships in the US. In 1972, from 4:00 PM to midnight, Norwalk (population 79,113) recorded 2,298 disturbance calls, or 6.3 per night. The data base for the study consisted of police self-reports (on a 'Third-Party Intervention Form') for 344 disputes. Although 246 of these were for people in long-term relationships and 148 were for relatives, a specific category for husband-wife disputes was not reported.

Zacker and Bard (1977) reported that assaults occurred in one-third of these 344 disputes (44% of all disputes between relatives, 25% between non-relatives), and that they were more likely to occur between family members. Family disputes in Norwalk were more likely to be assaultive than were family disputes in Harlem (44% vs. 30%). Again, alcohol was used by one or the other disputant 34.4% of the time, and attending officers reported that such use was unrelated to whether or not an assault had occurred. Interestingly, Zacker and Bard reported that the Norwalk police had trouble believing this finding about alcohol and assault, even though it was based on their own data. Since Zacker and Bard did not report what percentage of disputes attended resulted in reports being filled out by police, there is no way to know if their sample suffers from selective attrition in police reporting.

This caveat notwithstanding, the work of Bard and Zacker provided some interesting systematic data on domestic disturbance at the police level: first, that assaultiveness, at least assaultiveness that was brought to police attention, was higher in a middle-class white area than it was in a working-class black area – a contradiction of the stereotyping of family disturbance; and second, that the durability of police working knowledge (e.g., that alcohol causes most domestic disturbances) – in the face of contradictory evidence that they themselves collected – suggests that mere reporting of the facts in police training will not be persuasive when those facts contradict the dogma of police ideology (Dutton 1986b).

Can Police Prevent Repeat Wife Assault?

A second prominent study of police response to domestic disputes was conducted for the Police Foundation in 1977 by Marie Wilt (in Detroit) and Ron Breedlove (in Kansas City). This study began by analyzing the arrest records of homicide and assault participants for the years 1970 and 1971. The characteristics of the homicides, aggravated assaults, and the participants were analyzed based on interviews by police and project personnel and on Disturbance Profile Cards filled out by officers responding to domestic disturbances. In addition, the number of police responses to the address of participants in a homicide and/or assault for the two years prior to the arrest were recorded. Data from the Disturbance Profile Cards indicated that the best predictors of homicide/assault were the presence of a gun in the household, a history of prior disturbances, and the presence of alcohol. Unfortunately, the police return rate for these cards was only 5%, making the generalizability of these findings questionable. Analysis of the data on prior police response indicated that 90% of the homicide and 85% of the aggravated assault participants had at least one prior police response to their address, and 50% of both homicide and aggravated assault participants had five or more police responses.

The Wilt and Breedlove study was cited as indicating the preventive policing potential of domestic disturbance calls, since the possibility of avoiding subsequent violent crime might have been realized if the police had acted more effectively in the first place. However, as we shall see below, just what is considered to be more effective is debatable. Also, the Wilt and Breedlove study was retrospective in nature, working back from a crime-identified sample. Hence, it does not tell us what percentage of police responses to domestic calls do not result in repeat violence. We are, in effect, looking only at the interventions that subsequently had an undesirable outcome. In determining police policy, prospective studies that examine long-term effects of police practice are required in order to establish the incidence of desirable/undesirable outcomes as a function of the mode of intervention.

Policy Changes and Training

An examination of the impact of policy on the actual practice of responding to domestic disturbance calls was made by Levens and Dutton (1980). Baseline measures of police practices were obtained by analyzing 174 hours of taped calls from citizens to police in order to determine how they should be categorized. Figure 8.1 demonstrates these categories and the percentages of calls falling into each.

Police officers were requested to fill out research reports on each family dispute they attended. Police time and contact records were examined for all relevant police activity, and field observations were made of a subset of dispute interventions. Baseline data were collected for a six-month period (January to June 1975). At the end of this period, the chief of police announced a more aggressive policy of intervention for family disputes, including intensive training for recruits, in-service training for veteran officers, and training of dispatch communications personnel. Follow-up data were collected in July and August 1976, at which point 40% of the street force had received training.

Figure 8.1

Telephone requests for police assistance and breakdown of dispatches into service and law enforcement (Levens & Dutton 1980)

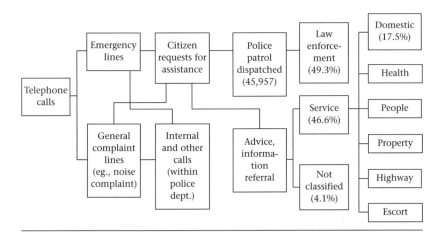

Baseline measures indicated that 17.5% of all calls to police were for family disputes, and that 13.5% were specifically for husband-wife disputes. These calls generally increased in frequency towards the end of the week and were greatest from 7:00 PM to 1:00 AM. Analysis of police dispatch records yielded a subsample of 283 domestic disputes (family, neighbour, landlord, or tenant) and 96 husband-wife disturbances for which police presence was requested. Surprisingly, police attended only 47.9% of these calls. Callers who did not receive police service were either told their problem was not a police matter or were given quasi-legal advice. Police dispatch probability was analyzed by type of information given by the caller. Mention of weapons increased the dispatch probability to .78, mention of violence to .61, mention of alcohol to .59. Dispatch probabilities were unaffected by time of day or availability of officers. Levens and Dutton concluded that the low dispatch probabilities reflected a negative police attitude towards domestic dispute intervention.

A more recent examination of the process of screening calls for police intervention has been undertaken by Manning (1992). Some of Manning's findings replicate the Levens and Dutton results reported above. Manning found that call-screening was common for all computer-assisted dispatch (CAD) systems, and that, historically, family violence calls had been typologized as low-priority misdemeanours deserving little police interest. Twenty-five years of improvement in information technology had done little to 'alter the quality of police response to reported incidents or order problems' (p. 45).

However, Manning's study also demonstrates the ambiguity of many domestic violence messages received by police departments and the working rules developed by operators to screen actionable calls. For example, if the operator concludes that the caller is dreaming, hallucinating, drunk, or on drugs, the call may be treated differently than would a 'normal' call. Essentially, operators want the following information: the location of the incident, the character of the location (house, bar, etc.), description of the problem (e.g., domestic), actions involved (hitting, threats, etc.), to whom or to what those actions are directed (e.g., spouse), incident number, and potential for escalation.

In a follow-up after a stated policy change on domestic dispute intervention, Levens and Dutton (1980) studied data on 117 domestic dispute requests for service taken in 1976 and found a substantial increase in police willingness to respond, with a dispatch probability of 78.6% (which was significantly higher than the 47.9% obtained in the 1975 measure). Apparently, the policy change had an effect on the likelihood of dispatching cars.

In order to ascertain whether the effects of training and policy change influenced the police handling of the calls, observational measures were combined with self-report measures of what police did when they attended the call (Dutton 1981a; Dutton & Levens 1977). Training significantly increased the use of mediation and referral techniques and made police less likely to remove one party for the evening. There were no differences in arrest rates (which were around 6% of all calls attended) between trained and untrained police.

The use of arrest as a strategy of choice for police handling of husband-wife disputes has been a topic of some controversy. Recent research on the police and domestic disturbances has focused on the decision criteria that determine whether or not an alleged assaultive husband will be arrested.

Police Decisions to Arrest for Wife Assault

Is there a prima facie case for police arrest on domestic disturbance calls? We know from the Bard and Zacker (1974) study that police witness assaults on 29% to 33% of the domestic disturbances they attend. Furthermore, the victims of these assaults are disproportionately women (95%) (Berk et al. 1981). The women victims are injured in 36% of all domestics attended by police and require medical attention 17% of the time (Jaffe & Burris 1982). Clearly, then, domestic disturbance calls do present a category of calls that have a high violence potential. We also know from the Schulman (1979) and Straus, Gelles, and Steinmetz (1980) surveys that the likelihood of repeat violence is high (66% without police intervention). Furthermore, in a study that we will review below, Sherman and Berk (1984) found that recidivist assault within six months has a 28% to 37% likelihood when police attend and do not make an arrest.

Combining these findings, a case can be made for police arrest for putative wife assault. If one objective of the criminal justice system is to prevent recurrent violence, then the means of handling husband-wife disputes is important – for such disputes constitute a source of considerable repeat violence. This being the case, it is instructive to examine those studies that have attempted to determine how police make the decision whether or not to make an arrest on domestic disturbance calls. Three types of methodology have been used to examine such decisions: having police specify how they would respond to hypothetical scenarios; reconstructing arrest decisions from information on police reports; and examining police behavior under real intervention conditions.

Hypothetical Scenarios

Loving and Farmer (1980) gave questionnaires to 130 police officers of assorted ranks from sixteen police agencies. Police responded that they would make an arrest in domestic violence situations if a crime had been committed or if the likelihood of recurring violence was high. In rating the importance of factors influencing their decision to arrest, they mentioned, in decreasing order of importance, the following: commission of a felony, serious injury to the victim, use of a weapon, use of violence against the police, likelihood of future violence, previous legal action against the assailant, previous injury to victim or damage to property, and the presence of an alcohol- or drug-intoxicated assailant. Factors that would lead police to refrain from making an arrest – in decreasing order of importance – were: a refusal by the victim to press charges, the victim's tendency to drop charges, and lack of serious injury. Of course, as Loving and Farmer point out, there is no way of knowing, on the basis of this study, whether these factors would be given similar weight under actual intervention conditions. The risk of officers providing what they perceive to be socially desirable responses pervades studies of this sort (see, for example, Rosenthal 1969).

Waaland and Keeley (1985) devised simulated police reports (seventy-one descriptions of cases) containing seven informational cues: the man's occupational status, history of wife assault, assailant's behavior towards the officers, extent of the victim's injuries, drinking by the assailant, drinking by the victim, and verbal antagonism of the assailant by the victim. With the exception of occupational status, three levels of each cue were presented in fifty-six unique combinations (order of information was randomized with a few restrictions). Twenty-six patrol officers in Oregon were asked to make judgments of both the husband's and wife's responsibility for the incident and to assign one of four possible legal outcomes for the offender.

Waaland and Keeley found that officers believed an abusive husband to be more responsible than his wife, but the judgment of this responsibility varied widely. Victim antagonism and victim drinking influenced police judgments of responsibility, but judgments of responsibility did not influence police decisions to arrest. Decisions to arrest were most strongly influenced by victim injuries (which accounted for 85% of the variance in composite arrest decisions). The assailant's behavior towards investigating officers and his assaultive history made smaller but significant contributions to arrest decisions.

Waaland and Keeley considered the social desirability issue in their study, noting that officers report basing their intervention decisions primarily on legal information (i.e., extent of victim injuries). Not coincidentally, the state of Oregon had recently adopted legal standards for domestic intervention at the time data were collected. These new legal standards may have influenced officers to appear to be going by the book. Interestingly, despite the high probability of social desirability influences, very low arrest rates were obtained in this study. Although 36% of the victims were depicted as severely injured, half the officers did not prescribe arrest under these conditions. Multiple bruises and blackened eyes were not considered sufficient causes for legal action, although such evidence explicitly defines unlawful assault under Oregon law.

Not all studies that use a hypothetical example seem to suffer from socially desirable responding. Ford (1987) provided such a hypothetical example to 439 law enforcement officers in Indiana and correlated their self-reported likelihood of arrest to a variety of attitudes and stereotypes about victims of wife assault. Ford's hypothetical example contained sufficient grounds to establish probable cause (in the opinion of judges, prosecutors, and defence attorneys). Only 20% of officers, however, indicated a greater than 50/50 chance that they would arrest under these circumstances. Since the state policy mandated arrest where reasonable and probable grounds existed, this 20% rate certainly does not represent the police providing a researcher with a procedurally correct answer. Factors that contributed most heavily to police disinclination to arrest were their perceptions that the couple was in a continuing relationship and that the woman had not made a serious effort to leave. In weighing the conflicting stories given by the hypothetical man and woman at the scene, the notion that 'if things were as bad as she says, why doesn't she leave?' influenced police perceptions of the existence of probable cause. Police who were most likely to report they would arrest tended to do so because of their perception that violence would recur.

Observational Studies

The most obvious way to circumvent the social desirability issues raised by hypothetical studies is through direct or indirect observation of actual police practice. Indirect observation means the examination of police records and the reconstruction of their arrest decision through multivariate analysis on the information provided on the records.

Berk and Loseke (1980) used this method, examining 262 official police reports on domestic disturbance interventions, and generated a multiple regression model to predict whether or not police would arrest in these cases. The variable that had the greatest weight in predicting whether or not the police would arrest was the victim's willingness to sign a citizen's arrest warrant. The next most powerful predictors were: (1) alcohol use or intoxication by the male and (2) allegations of violence by the victim. Neither injuries to the victim nor property damage had any significant effect on arrests. In addition, when the victim was the person who called the police, arrest rates dropped. Berk and Loseke do point out that the injuries variable approached significance ($p = .08$), and that a more sensitive measure of severity of victim injuries may have produced a significant result. They concluded that police intervention decisions do not appear to centre on the collection of evidence for proof of legal violations but, rather, are the outgrowth of a subjective theory that the officer forms about the causes of the domestic dispute.

To a certain extent, this subjective theory begins to develop before the officer arrives at the scene, fuelled by personal beliefs about male-female violence and the dispatcher's descriptions of the current situation. Berk and Loseke suggest that when the police arrive they begin to look for signs that verify their theory of what caused the conflict. The researchers propose, as have others (Dutton 1981a; Bennett-Sandler 1975), that police intervention decisions are not pure products of legal requirements or departmental policy but, rather, are the result of an admixture of personal attitudes and informal occupational norms that combine with more formalized policy. Hence, altering police intervention practice would require not only specific policy directives but also changes in recruitment and training, the attitudinal objectives of which are buttressed by systemic support from prosecution and judges (Dutton 1986b).

On the whole, direct observational methods tend to support these conclusions. Furthermore, they avoid a weakness in indirect observational techniques. Police reports that provide the data base for such techniques may be after-the-fact reconstructions of incidents (intended by the police officer to justify actions that he or she has already taken) rather than accounts of what actually occurred in the encounter.

An early field observation of police intervention was conducted by Black (1979) on data collected in 1966. Field observations of 108 domestic dispute interventions involving married couples revealed that, although sixty-five cases involved violence, only thirteen arrests were made. Black reported that police acted in a coercive fashion with black and working-class couples and in a conciliatory fashion with white middle-class couples. However, his data may not represent contemporary police practice.

Worden and Pollitz (1984) examined direct reports of trained observers who witnessed 167 domestic disturbances in twenty-four different police departments as part of a Police Services Study conducted at Indiana University. Worden and Pollitz corroborated results from Berk and Loseke's indirect study. Both studies found that probability of police arrest increased substantially with the woman victim's promise to sign a warrant, with the male's appearance of having been drinking, and with the woman's allegations of violence. Both studies also found that arrest did not increase if one disputant had been injured. Worden and Pollitz also confirmed the findings that disrespectful behavior towards the police increases the likelihood of arrest. Observers coded citizen behavior into categories such as apologetic, sarcastic, disrespectful, and hostile. The disrespectful category increased the probability of arrest by .43.

Worden and Pollitz also attempted to relate police attitudes to their arrest decisions. They divided police into crime-fighter and problem-solver categories on the basis of their agreement or disagreement with the item 'police should not have to handle calls that involve social or personal problems where no crime is involved.' Agreement with this item had little effect on arrest decisions, since arrest was infrequent in any case.

Smith and Klein (1984) had trained civilians ride on 900 patrol shifts and observe 5,688 police-citizen encounters in 24 metropolitan US areas. Of these, 433 involved an interpersonal dispute, with the dispute being in progress when the police arrived. For methodological reasons, 100 of these cases were omitted, leaving a data base of 333. It should be pointed out that these were not all husband-wife or even male-female disputes. For these 333 cases, arrests were made by police 15.3% of the time. The main determinants of arrest in this study were: (1) the complainant's statements that she/he wanted an arrest, (2) the demeanour of the offender, (3) whether the offender had been drinking, and (4) the socioeconomic status (SES) of the area in which the house was located. The arrest rates by SES were as follows: high status: 5.5%, middle status: 1.9%, low status: 21.2%.

Among factors that had no effect on the decision to arrest were: (1) the race of the parties involved, (2) whether or not one party was injured, and (3) whether or not weapons were involved. Arrest was less likely in domestic disputes than it was in non-domestic disputes, but the difference was not significant. The authors concluded that the police appeared reluctant to arrest in both domestic and non-domestic disputes.

What is discomfiting from a policy perspective is the apparent lack of weight given to victims' injuries by police, and their indifference towards ascertaining whether assaults are isolated incidents or part of a continuing series of violent incidents. If habitual assault is occurring, the likelihood increases of future violence, victim injury, and repeat demands on police service. From a decisionmaking perspective, information about these factors seems essential. On the other hand, the man's demeanour towards the police is relatively irrelevant to likely recidivism and is probably given too much weight.

The police decision about arrest versus other alternatives initiates a chain of criminal justice policy decisions about wife assaulters. The objective of arrest decisions is to prevent wife assault from recurring. How might this objective best be achieved? What constellation of decisions by police, prosecutors, and judges might operate to reduce recidivist assault? To these questions we now begin to formulate an answer by discovering what is commonly done in cases of wife assault.

Dutton (1987b) performed a stepwise analysis of the slippage between the occurrence of the assault, the reporting of the assault, the official detection of the assault, the making of an arrest decision, and a court conviction with punishment. What are the conditional probabilities at each step of this process?

The Objective Probability of Being Detected and Punished

The Probability of Wife Assault Being Reported to Police

First let us consider the probability of detection, given that wife assault has occurred. We will refer to this as p(detection); that is, given an event of wife assault has occurred, what is the probability that it will be detected by the criminal justice system? This is made up of the probability of the event being reported (p[reporting]) and the system taking the report seriously enough to investigate and write an official report.

By reviewing survey data (e.g., Schulman 1979 and Straus & Gelles 1985) that asked respondents if they had reported the conflict tactics used against them to the police, Dutton (1987b) determined that the overall likelihood of a serious assault (defined as items N to R on the *CTS*) being reported to the police was 14.5%.

The Probability of Police Attendance

However, police response is not always forthcoming for all reported events. By reviewing studies of police response rates, Dutton (1987b) determined that the average attendance rate for 1976 was 78.6%. The resulting p(detection/event) is (14.5% x 78.6%) or 11.5%. While this result involves combining data from different jurisdictions (and we have no way of knowing how representative these jurisdictions are), those data sources represent an estimate of the victim's likelihood of reporting and the police likelihood of attending, using the best empirical studies available.

The Probability of Police Report

One could argue that p(reporting) x p(attending) do not yet constitute detection, which requires that an event be formally registered in a system. For the criminal justice system, this registration takes the form of a police report. If police view a family dispute as not serious and feel overworked with report writing, the likelihood of that event being recorded will be low. Only through reconstructing calls for service, police dispatches, and subsequent reports would it be possible to determine whether police attended but failed to write a report.

Levens and Dutton (1980) performed this type of analysis and concluded that police wrote reports on 16.5% of the family dispute calls they attended. Given Bard and Zacker's (1974) finding that assaults occurred in 29% to 33% of family dispute calls attended by police, this suggests a further failure to officially detect an event because of overlooking the assault or considering it unworthy of a report. The effect on p(detection/event) is to further lower p(detection) by a factor of (16.5/31), which represents the percentage of events reported over an estimate of the total number of attendances where an event occurred. Hence, p(detection/event) equals 6.1% (the product of p[reporting] x p[police attending] x p[report being issued] or 14.5% x 78.6% x 16.5%/31%).

It could be argued that a police report is not necessary for subsequent criminal justice action to occur. Police have frequently advised women to initiate legal proceedings on their own by laying charges with a prosecutor or justice of the peace (Fields 1978). However, the likelihood of self-initiated charges proceeding is extremely slight. Field and Field (1973) examined 7,500 requests for prosecutors to issue warrants for wife assault in Washington, DC. Less than 200 were issued. Parnas (1973) found that of 5,057 self-initiated requests for warrants only 323 were issued. Some studies (Hogarth 1980) also revealed a catch-22 for putative complainants: no proceedings would be initiated as a matter of policy by justices of the peace without a police report. The Field and Field and Parnas studies suggest a p(warrant/request) of only .04. If we assumed that every woman who called the police when assaulted by her husband (and who did not receive assistance in the form of police attendance and a formal report) initiated proceedings on her own, detection in the form of a formal warrant would still be only marginally improved (1.1% of all reported events). Hence, if we combined police-initiated and self-initiated formal reports, p(detection/event) would be 6.5%.

The relevance of this 6.5% figure is that it gives us a rough indication of the percentage of wife assaults that are publicly recorded by the police. In other words, in 93.5% of assaults against wives, the assault remains a private event with respect to the criminal justice system. We turn our attention now to the next step in the criminal justice system.

Arrest for Wife Assault

P(arrest/detection) refers to the action taken by police when attending family dispute calls. Again, the evidence argues for a winnowing process whereby most attended calls do not result in arrest. Arrest rates vary in the observational studies done on police,[1] but a weighted average across several empirical studies is 7.3% (Black 1979; Meyer & Lorimer 1979; Emerson 1979; Levens and Dutton 1980; Worden and Pollitz 1984).

Of course, not all domestic disturbances result in assaults. Two ways of estimating whether prima facie evidence exists for an assault having occurred are: (1) by estimating the percentage of victims injured in domestic altercations (although accidents may happen, the accidental nature of the injury is probably best decided by the court) and (2) by direct observation.

Direct observation studies estimate assault rates on domestic disturbance calls to be about 34.5% (Bard and Zacker 1974; Zacker and Bard 1977; Jaffe and Burris 1982; Berk, Berk, Loseke, & Rauma 1983). Given the arrest rate of 7.3% based on the cumulative studies reported above, a discrepancy exists between the percentage of cases in which prima facie evidence for arrest exists and the percentage of cases in which an arrest is made. The probability of an arrest being made – given that police detected prima facie evidence for arrest – is 21.2%. Since we estimated the probability of detection to be 6.5%, the probability of arrest would be 1.4% (see Figure 8.2).

Figure 8.2

Conditional probabilities at each step of the criminal justice process (Dutton 1987b)

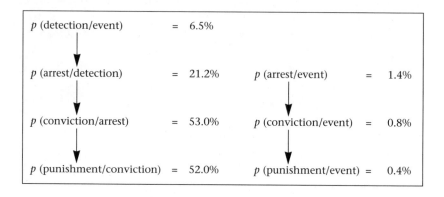

Conviction for Wife Assault

Given that an arrest is made, will the case wind up in court? Dutton's (1987b) review of several empirical studies found that the probability of the case going to court is about 67% (Schulman 1979; Lerman 1981; Jaffe, Wolfe, Telford, & Austin. 1986; Ferraro & Boychuk 1992). Sometimes battered women, through an admixture of pressure from their partners, traumatic bonding-induced loyalty, and/or fear of reprisal, succumb to their partners' pleas to convince prosecutors either that they will not testify or that they will be hostile witnesses. In such cases, if other evidence for a conviction is lacking, the prosecution may decide not to proceed.

If the case is tried in court, what happens? Could incorrigible repeat wife assaulters be made less likely to repeat their crimes if they were punished by the courts? Much has been written about the unwillingness of courts to convict for wife assault (Fields 1978; Parnas 1973; Lerman 1981). Parnas's (1973) study indicated that p(arrest/conviction) was practically zero in Chicago's Court of Domestic Relations. In recent years, court policy has changed in many jurisdictions and prosecutors have developed practices to maximize victim cooperation (Dutton 1981a; Lerman 1981). Empirical studies of court dispositions, however, have usually been performed in jurisdictions with exceptional awareness about wife assault and, consequently, have developed experimental programs that have included court-outcome studies as a component of evaluation. Dutton (1987b) reviewed court outcomes in Westchester County, New York; Seattle, Washington; London, Ontario; and Vancouver, British Columbia.

The combined estimate of p(arrest/conviction) for these four jurisdictions is .53 (a weighted mean based primarily on the Seattle data).[2] However, in many cases conviction leads merely to a discharge or to probation. If we consider incarceration or fines as punishing outcomes, and probation, suspended sentences, and/or batterers' therapy as less-punishing outcomes, then p(punishment/conviction) is only about .52. If we accept these data as providing rough estimates of conviction and punishment, respectively, and if we keep in mind that the p(arrest/event) is approximately 1.4%, it would follow that p(punishment/event) would be .53 x .52 x .014 (again, the product of all probabilities [see Figure 8.2]). *For every 100 wife assaults, about 14 are reported, 6 are detected, 1.5 arrests are made, .75 men are tried, .49 men are convicted, and .24 men are punished with a jail sentence or a fine.* Furthermore, since the conviction and punishment data are drawn mainly from one progressive program – that which is located in Seattle – they may over-represent p(punishment/arrest).

In addition, punishment is rarely severe; average sentences for first convictions typically involve probation with conditions attached (Lerman 1981), such as the man not contacting the woman, not drinking, and attending treatment for assaultiveness. This punishment rate of 0.5% is lower than is the percentage of men who constitute incorrigible wife assaulters. This clearly suggests that, at least with respect to such assaulters, improved criminal justice policy should involve increased arrest rates, better identification of such offenders, and special sentencing designed to reduce their recidivism.

If aggregate reduction in recidivism is the goal of policy, what happens in court is relatively unimportant compared to the police response. Courts are limited by police arrest rates, and, as long as only 21.2% of cases with prima facie evidence for assault result in arrest, they will encounter a much smaller population of potential recidivists than actually exists and will have a correspondingly smaller impact on aggregate reduction of recidivist assault. From a policy point of view, the primary slippage is in reporting, which is a public-education issue; the secondary slippage is in police under-arresting, which is a police-training issue.

Prosecution and Restraining Orders
An elaborate study of the effects of prosecutorial policy was conducted by Ford and Regoli (1992). Using a randomized design with 678 cases in Indiana, they tested which of four policies – no prosecution, pretrial diversion, prosecution, and rehabilitation – was most effective in reducing future recidivism. They found that prosecutors' actions could have a dramatic effect on recidivism. The simple act of accepting the charges and

proceeding through the initial hearing decreased future acts of violence. Surprisingly, this effect held even if the victim was later allowed to drop the charges.

Of the four treatment conditions, allowing women to drop the charges resulted in the lowest percentage of new reports of violence in a six-month follow-up period (26% versus 35% in the other three categories). The authors speculated that empowering the victim may be more important than maintaining prosecution to the point of court conviction. Below, we will consider whether an unintended effect of arrest is not deterrence per se but victim empowerment.

A related question about criminal justice system policy is whether temporary restraining orders, which legally forbid the man to come within a specified distance of the woman, have any effect (see Finn [1991] for an extended discussion of the legal aspects of this issue). Chaudhuri and Daly (1992) investigated the experiences of women who received temporary restraining orders (TROs) in New Haven, Connecticut. There, as in many other jurisdictions, violation of a TRO is sufficient basis for an arrest. The researchers found that TROs had some deterrent value. Although their sample was small, they found that 11 of 30 men violated the TRO (34%). Factors that increased the probability of violation were the man having a prior record (which put the violation rate to 100%!), abusing alcohol (48%), or being unemployed (83%). The authors viewed the TRO as having extralegal spinoffs in terms of victim empowerment. This theme, which also was raised by Ford and Regoli (1992) above, is one that will resurface in the studies we review below.

Wife Assault versus Other Crimes
Is it possible to determine whether the criminal justice response is less aggressive towards wife assault than it is towards other crimes? Certainly, at first glance, the studies we have just reviewed reveal a strong filtering effect which results in the majority of detected events not leading to arrest or conviction. Based on the observational studies of police intervention into domestic disputes, the finding that police arrest in only 21.2% of the cases where prima facie evidence for arrest exists suggests that the arrest option may be under-utilized, especially since some evidence now exists to show that arrest decreases recidivist assault (Jaffe et al. 1986; Sherman & Berk 1984).

Comparison of the winnowing effect of the criminal justice system in response to wife assault as opposed to other crimes is complicated by some methodological issues. Both the National Criminal Justice Survey (NCJS) and the Canadian Urban Victimization Survey (CUVS) compared reporting rates to police for spouse assaults and other crimes (see Chapter 1). The NCJS found that the reporting rate was higher for spouse assault (54.8%) than it was for other assaults (44.9%). Similarly, the CUVS found report rates for spouse assault to be 36% while that for stranger assault was 22%, for sexual assault 26%, and for robbery 44%. If we accept the caveat that much spouse assault may not be reported as crime, the resulting figures do not suggest an under-reporting of spouse assault. As we have described above, both the NCJS and CUVS were crime surveys and required the respondents to perceive an aggressive action by their spouses as criminal. Not all violent acts by spouses are necessarily defined as crimes by the victims.

In a US national victim survey reported by Hood and Sparks (1970), the overall report rate for 121 crimes was 49%. The only strong result to appear from these data is that victims seem more willing to report crime in the US than they do in Canada. Overwhelmingly, the most frequent reason for not reporting spouse assault given on the NCJS survey was that it was a private matter (70.9%); only 9% reported fear of reprisal as a reason for not reporting an assault. On the CUVS 59% of respondents feared reprisal. Obviously, the criminal justice system can do very little about unreported crimes. When crimes are reported, however, some interesting comparisons develop.

Table 8.1

Police responses to wife assault versus other crimes

	Wife assault (Dutton 1987b)	Other crimes (Hood & Sparks 1977)
(a) Reported incidents attended by police	79%	77%
(b) Police make arrests (if a)	21	20
(c) Trials (if b)	67	42
(d) Convictions (if c)	53	52

Hood and Sparks (1970) found that police responded to 77% of reported crimes, while Levens and Dutton (1980) found that police responded to only 53.8% of family dispute calls where assault was a possibility. This difference may, of course, merely reflect a police tendency to respond after the fact rather than an under-response to family violence. However, on 145 calls monitored by Levens and Dutton where violence was reported as already having occurred, the police response rate was still only 61%. After a policy change, however, the attendance rate on domestic dispute calls increased to 78.6%.

Hood and Sparks (1970) found that police made arrests in 20% of the cases where they attended and decided that a crime had been committed. Our review of observational studies of police handling of family disputes concluded that police made arrests in 21.2% of cases where evidence of a crime (assault) was obvious to a third-party observer. Hood and Sparks (1970) found that trials resulted in 42% of wife-assault arrests, while our review concluded that 67% of such arrests came to trial. Hood and Sparks (1970) found that 52% of cases coming to trial resulted in convictions, while our review found that 53% of such cases resulted in convictions.

What can we conclude from this? First, that the winnowing effect of the criminal justice system is about the same for wife assault as it is for other crimes. Given that the event is reported, the police are about as likely to attend (78.6% vs. 77%), arrest (21.2% vs. 20%), and obtain a conviction (53% vs. 52%) for wife assault as they are for other crimes. This is not to argue that the police response to wife assault is sufficient but merely to point out that available evidence suggests that police do not single out wife assault as being less actionable than are other crimes. The well-known police dislike of handling domestics (Dutton 1981c) does not appear to alter their performance.

Ferraro and Boychuk (1992) compared the court's response to intimate versus non-intimate assaults in order to ascertain whether the criminal justice system response to the former was lenient. Their argument was that the legal system reinforces patriarchal authority along with distinct race and class boundaries. They reasoned from this analysis that intimate violence would be punished less, not merely because it represents a sexual hierarchy but because intimate assaults are typically between persons who are racially and socially homogeneous. They examined decisions to prosecute in Maricopa County, Arizona, in 1987 and 1988, and they concluded that crimes of violence, whether against an intimate or a non-intimate, were treated leniently. The authors argue that 'hidden in the rhetoric about getting tough on domestic violence is the faulty assumption that nondomestic violence is treated as a serious crime' (p. 222). Their data suggested otherwise: prison time, jail time, and restitution were all higher for intimate violence than they were for non-intimate violence. When violence is committed against people of the same race or social class, it is treated leniently whether or not it is intimate violence. The authors conclude that, 'given this information, it is not likely that calls to treat domestic violence as a crime will result in more and harsher punishment for men who beat their wives' (p. 223).

When an assault is viewed as a crime, criminal justice action is comparable to what it is for other crimes, including non-intimate assault. However, when we examine the aftermath questions of surveys on family conflict rather than the aftermath questions of surveys on crime (i.e., Schulman 1979; Straus, Gelles, & Steinmetz 1980; Straus & Gelles 1985), we see that the tendency to report potentially arrestable assaults is low: Schulman found a 17% report rate for severe aggression items on the *CTS*, and Straus (personal communication, 1986) found a 10% report rate in his national survey (only 27/533 of severe aggression actions were reported to the police). The main impediment to a more comprehensive handling of wife assault by the criminal justice system is the tendency of victims to view their assaults in non-criminal terms.

Does Arrest Reduce Future Assaults?

The central assumption underlying the above studies is that arrest is the best way to reduce recidivism. Several empirical studies have attempted to determine whether or not this is true.

Jaffe et al. (1986) examined police records and conducted interviews with wives of men arrested for wife assault. Their interviews included *CTS* assessments of the men's use of violence for one-year periods prior to and following arrest. When police charged a man with wife assault, significant decreases in post-charge violence occurred, whether measured by the number of new contacts he had with police in the ensuing year or by his wife's report of his use of violence. Specific violent acts against wives were reduced by two-thirds for the year following arrest compared to the year preceding arrest. Unfortunately, Jaffe et al. did not specify the exact nature of contacts with police, so we do not know whether re-arrest occurred.

Sherman and Berk (1984) provided some evidence that recidivism may be reduced for men who are arrested. Three hundred and fourteen men involved in instances of misdemeanour wife assault attended by the Minneapolis police were, for a six-month period, randomly assigned to the following treatments: arrest, separation, or mediation. The recidivism of arrested men was significantly lower (13% repeated assaults, according to police reports; 19% repeated assaults, according to interviews with wives) than was the recidivism of men who received other resolution treatments. Corresponding recidivism rates for separation and mediation were 26% and 18%, respectively, for police reports and 28% and 37%, respectively, for wives' reports.[3] Sherman and Berk did not report whether the trial had been completed or was pending for the arrested men, whether and how many couples had broken up, or whether the assaultive males knew their wives were being interviewed every two weeks by social scientists.

What makes the Sherman and Berk evidence impressive (apart from the randomized design) is that the reduced recidivism rate (if we accept that it was not produced by these unreported factors) seems to have been produced largely with repeat offenders. Eighty per cent of the victims in their study had been previously assaulted at least once by the suspects in the prior six months. This result suggests that for that small subgroup of men who were repeat offenders without police intervention (probably about 2.5% [Schulman 1979; Straus et al. 1980]), a possibility of recidivism reduction exists (at least for a six-month period) if arrest does occur (only 19% of this group assaulted their wives after having been arrested).

The Minneapolis experiment had as great an impact on social policy as did any other experiment ever conducted (Gelles 1993). Within a matter of months after the data were released, police departments across North America began to adopt mandatory arrest policies for cases of marital assault. With mandatory arrest, the police officer must arrest the presumed perpetrator whenever reasonable and probable grounds exist for believing an assault has occurred.

However, attempts to replicate the Minneapolis study in other cities have provided mixed results. Dunford, Huizinga, and Elliott (1990) obtained an ambiguous result in Omaha: in comparison with separation and/or mediation, arrest neither reduced nor increased subsequent violence. There was some evidence for lowered recidivism in one experimental group: men who were not present when the police attended and who had arrest warrants issued against them scored lower on the prevalence and frequency of repeat offending than did men who were present.

Hirschell, Hutchinson, Dean, Kelley, & Pesackis (1990) replicated the police experiment in Charlotte, North Carolina, adding police-issued citations as a fourth treatment option and employing the entire patrol division in round-the-clock and city-wide sampling for the full duration of the project. The investigators' conclusion was that 'arrest of spouse abusers is neither substantially nor statistically a more effective deterrent to repeat abuse than either of the other two responses (separation or mediation) examined in the study' (p. 154)

In Milwaukee, Wisconsin, Sherman and his colleagues (1992) addressed the question of whether arrest works to reduce recidivism only for certain kinds of offenders. The Milwaukee experiment was conducted from 1987 to 1988 in order to assess the use of arrest for misdemeanour domestic battery. (At that time, Milwaukee had a city-wide policy of mandatory arrest for such assaults.) Sherman et al. examined 1,200 cases in a sample that was 91% male, 76% black, 64% non-married, 55% unemployed, and in which 32% had a prior arrest for wife assault. Police responding to wife assault calls deemed the call eligible for the experiment if the victim was not seriously injured, the perpetrator was on the scene, and no warrants existed for his arrest. Experimental treatments included *warning* (suspect not arrested but read a warning of arrest if police have to return), *short arrest* (suspect arrested, booked, and released, typically within two hours), and *full arrest* (suspect arrested, booked, and eligible for release on $250 bail). These treatments were randomized within all eligible cases. Outcome measures were ensured by subsequent police hotline reports to local battered women's shelters for each case of wife assault (whether or not they could make an arrest). Arrests, offence reports, and victim interviews were also used as data sources (78% of contacted victims were interviewed).

Using all of these data sources, the authors composed a time-at-risk index. They found that arrest did not differentially cause couples to break up. The arrested men cohabited with their partners after arrest as much as did the non-arrested men. The initial effect created by arrest was the suppression of recidivism. For thirty days after the presenting incident, the prevalence (proportion of cases with one or more incidents) of repeat violence reported in the victim interviews was substantially lower than was that reported in the arrest groups. However, at about seven to nine months after the presenting incident, the arrest and non-arrest recidivism curves cross over, and, from that point on, the arrest group has a *higher* rate of recidivism than does the non-arrest group. In other words, for this sample, the long-term effect of arrest was to increase the rate of repeat violence. This increase is small in magnitude but is consistent across all measures of repeat violence. The arrested group averaged 124 days before repeating, whereas the warned group averaged 160 days. Hotline data showed a statistically significant long-term escalation effect resulting from arrest (but only for the 'short-arrest group'). The authors conclude that police departments with policies of releasing arrestees within three hours of arrest might want to reconsider this policy.

The persons for whom arrest backfired in the long term were socially marginal (defined by the authors as unemployed and/or high-school dropouts). While arrest deterred those who were most likely to conform socially, it escalated those who were less likely to so conform into higher frequencies of domestic violence. When 'the majority of domestic violence incidents responded to by police involve unemployed suspects, then mandatory arrest fails to produce the greatest good for the greatest number' (Sherman et al. 1992:160). Replications in Omaha and Colorado Springs confirmed these findings. In general, the authors conclude that in areas where urban problems are great and marginality high, arrest may be contra-indicated. In other words, when general social constraints have broken down, arrest 'in a vacuum' will not reduce recidivism in wife assault cases. *Arrest only works for men who have something to lose by being arrested.*

Obviously, the Sherman et al. (1992) study raises large and complex issues for those who make criminal justice system policy. If these results are generalizable, it would mean that mandatory arrest and release policies could endanger certain groups of women in the long term. Hotline follow-ups among the unemployed, for example, were 19.4% higher in the short arrest category than they were in the warning category.

Yet the Sherman et al. data require some further consideration. For one thing, in those groups for which arrest decreased the size of repeat hotline calls (employed, white, and married), the size of the decrease was substantial (31% to 35%). In all other groups (except the unemployed), increases in calls were minimal (e.g., with unmarried groups it was a 2.7% increase, with blacks it was a 3.3% increase). In other words, the gains from arrest, summed across all groups, outweigh the losses.

A second point about the Sherman et al.(1992) study is that, like the Sherman and Berk (1984) study, the authors never report what happened to the subjects after arrest. Were the charges dropped? Did they go to court? Did they get convicted? Were they referred to mandatory treatment groups? Without this information, we wind up treating arrest as though it occurred in a vacuum, when in reality it is just one link in a chain of events. As we shall see below, these criminal justice system outcomes make a difference in long-term recidivism reduction.

Recidivism Reduction
Looking at aggregate data on all wife assaulters, the largest contributor to the prevention of recidivist wife assault is some constellation of extralegal factors that prevents one-third of men who have assaulted their wives from repeating the act within a year. In all surveys reported in Chapter 1, the proportion of single assaults to repeat assaults is 1:2. For some reason, in about one-third of the cases surveyed, families who do not call the police do not experience repeat assault. We can speculate that the reasons for cessation might include feelings of guilt or remorse, as reported by some men in treatment for wife assault (Dutton 1986b), but they might also include their wives' reactions to assaults. Many men volunteer for

treatment groups because their wives have threatened to leave if assaults recur (Dutton 1986a).

The Sherman and Berk (1984) and Jaffe et al. (1986) studies reported above suggest that arrest per se reduced recidivism, although the population of assaultive males who come to the attention of the police is probably only about 14.5% of the entire population of wife assaulters (Schulman 1979; Straus & Gelles 1985). Nevertheless, from the perspective of social policy, the police are the outside agency that encounters the greatest number of assault offenders and victims. All further criminal justice contact, whether through courts, probation, or court-mandated treatment groups, reaches a much smaller population of putative recidivists than do the police. As we shall see in the next chapter, court-mandated treatment for wife assaulters appears to reduce recidivism (Dutton 1987b). However, only half the men who appear in court are convicted, and even fewer have mandatory treatment attached as a condition of their probation.

Thus, from the perspective of reducing aggregate recidivism, treatment groups show initial indications of success but reach a much smaller target population than do the police. The most effective means of reducing recidivism might be to increase arrest rates up to the level reported for prima facie evidence for assault in observational studies. The main historical argument against increased arrest rates has been the danger of flooding the courts with the process of plea bargaining to lesser charges (Wilson 1983). However, this would probably have little effect in cases of wife assault, where, as we have seen, severe penalties are rare and probation is the most frequent outcome of conviction.

Fagan (1989) has argued that the central mechanism that precludes recidivism is an equalization of power in the male-female relationship. Citing data from his own study and from a study by Lee Bowker (1983), Fagan points out that fear of divorce and fear of relationship loss were mentioned more frequently as factors that enabled batterers to desist than was fear of legal sanction. Furthermore, Bowker's subjects (battered women) reported that social disclosure of the assaults worked as well as did legal intervention in getting their husbands to stop their assaultive behavior.

Cessation, Fagan concludes, occurs when legal or extralegal factors diminish power imbalances in the family and raise the costs of repeat assault for the husband.[4] When wife assault is disclosed to informal groups or to police, a variety of psycho-social mechanisms are initiated:
(1) The victim may discover that assault is more common than she formerly believed and, as a consequence, may stop blaming herself for the assault (see Chapter 6).

(2) The husband may learn that others consider his assaultive behavior illegal or unacceptable.

(3) The husband may learn that his wife has the power to disclose his unacceptable behavior to others who can sanction or punish him.

Whether or not the husband fears re-arrest, these psychosocial factors may reduce recidivist assault. Clearly, studies (such as Sherman & Berk 1984) that assume deterrence to be the operant mechanism when reduced recidivism occurs are overlooking the potential impact of these alternative psychosocial mechanisms.

Deterrence

Could the criminal justice system deter wife assault through more aggressive responding? *Deterrence* refers to the state's ability to diminish the incidence of a prohibited action through legal threats which clearly indicate that the cost of the action would be greater than would any benefits that might derive from it (Andenaes 1974; Blumstein, Cohen, & Nagin 1978; Ehrlich 1979; Zimring & Hawkins 1973). While considerable disagreement exists in the literature about whether criminal justice deterrence of violent crime has or has not been demonstrated by crime incidence studies (National Research Council [US] 1978; Wilson 1983; Phillips & Hensley 1984; Gibbs 1985), some agreement exists as to the minimal conditions which must exist in order for criminal justice to serve as a deterrent. The efficacy of legal threat in deterring prohibited actions requires that the criminal justice system generate perceived certainty, severity, and swiftness of punishment (Wilson 1983). Furthermore, where gains from the prohibited action are great (as in illegal drug sales), or where the action is impulsive and not reasoned, deterrence is unlikely (Wilson 1983).

General deterrence refers to a state's ability to control or to minimize the incidence of a prohibited act in a general population (e.g., the total number of wife assaults in a specific jurisdiction and time period). *Specific deterrence* refers to a state's ability to prevent or to minimize recidivism in a population that has already committed at least one prohibited act. If states publicized new, more severe punishments for wife assault, and if large-sample victim surveys revealed a diminution in first-time offenders after such a crackdown, then claims for the latter's general effectiveness as a deterrent could be made. If actual procedures for rendering swift and certain punishment demonstrated to first-time offenders that the state was treating their prohibited action more seriously than they expected, with an ensuing decrease in their rate of recidivism, specific deterrence could be claimed. Clearly, for general deterrence to occur, the probability of the assault being detected by the authorities must be high enough to generate the belief in the general population that ensuing punishment is highly probable. As Ross et al. (1982) has shown, such has not been the case with the deterrence of drunk driving.

Subjective Contributors to Recidivism Reduction

As our review above demonstrates, objectively, detection of wife assault has a low probability. However, deterrence research has begun to focus on subjective perceptions of likelihood of punishment (Gibbs 1985; Williams & Hawkins 1984).

Wilson (1983) has criticized using an exclusively objective approach to evaluating the criminal justice system's capacity to deter. He questions such an analysis's assumption about a person's knowledge and/or ability to estimate the probability of being caught. Wilson describes how recidivist offenders frequently belong to a criminal subculture that has extensive informal knowledge of criminal justice system operation. They know which judges will give which sentences for which crimes. They know, in effect, how to beat the system.

One could argue, however, that subjective estimates of the likelihood of punishment could also operate in the opposite direction. For example, the criminal justice system could have a placebo effect if objective probabilities of punishment were low but potential lawbreakers believed otherwise. As Wilson points out in his discussion of the Sherman and Berk (1984) study, short-term specific deterrence for the arrested husbands may have occurred because a sudden, conspicuous change in police behavior cued an aggressive criminal justice system response. He argues that, since few of the men in this group were subsequently punished with a fine or with incarceration, the police action of arrest, in and of itself, may have provided a signal for future system intervention.

It is obviously difficult to ascertain the wife assaulter's subjective perception of the probability of his being punished. Based on the Schulman (1979) and Straus et al. (1980) surveys it is reasonable to conclude that, through some admixture of socialization and general deterrence, the majority of men (89.8%) do not assault their wives. Furthermore, of the 10% of men who assault their wives once, 33% to 37% (3.3% of all men) do not repeat within a year (Schulman 1979:20; Straus et al. 1980:41). Since only 14.5% of women in the Schulman and Straus and Gelles samples who reported being assaulted called the police (Schulman 1979), the 33% to 37% cessation rate is probably due to factors other than concern about punishment by the criminal justice system.

Guilt, remorse, shame, or related emotional reactions (see Martin 1977; Walker 1979a; Dutton & Hemphill 1992) produced by the assaultive event or the victim's threat to leave the relationship if assault recurs could account for the drop in recidivism. If this is so, we must also account for the failure of these mechanisms in the 6.7% of men who are repeatedly assaultive (2.8% severely so). We shall return to this consideration below. The possibility of cessation (Fagan 1989) or reduced recidivism, in any event, would be restricted to this very small percentage of men who are repeat wife assaulters and who are most likely to come to the attention of the criminal justice system.

We do not know, at present, whether men arrested for wife assault do not repeat because of fear of re-arrest or whether the original arrest served the didactic function of demonstrating to them that wife assault was unacceptable behavior. Data is required on the subjective perceptions of men arrested for wife assault, including their projections of the likelihood of re-arrest should they repeat assault and a determination of the extent of their self-punishing reaction to the assault. The impact of these data on eventual likelihood of repeat assault would be highly instructive.

A first step in this direction is some data reported by Dutton, Hart, Kennedy, and Williams (1992). Using a questionnaire developed by Williams and Carmody (1987), which asks respondents to estimate the likelihood and perceived severity of each of a list of sanctions should they commit wife assault, the authors compared responses for two non-arrested (Kennedy & Dutton 1989; Williams & Carmody 1986) and one arrested sample of men (Dutton & Strachan 1987b). The results are presented in Table 8.2.

By multiplying the perceived likelihood and severity of a variety of consequences if they were to re-offend, a *sanction weight* was derived for such possible outcomes of assault as arrest, divorce, and so forth. These sanctions were categorized as legal (arrest, etc.) and extralegal (or informal). Men who had not been arrested for wife assault estimated extremely low weights for legal sanction. Men who had been violent but never arrested estimated even lower legal sanctions (for obvious reasons – it had never happened to them). Men who had been arrested estimated significantly higher legal sanctions than did those who had not been arrested, but they also estimated higher informal sanctions if they were ever to re-offend. In other words, they not only thought it was likely that the police would intervene, but that if they were to commit wife assault again, their partners could pick up the phone and call the police anytime, that the police would believe them, and that they would be more likely to leave (divorce).

The finding that inflated estimates of legal sanction follow arrest is, of course, not surprising. However, that inflated estimates of informal

Table 8.2

Sanction weights derived from arrest and non-arrest of repeat offenders

	Williams & Carmody (1986)		Kennedy & Dutton (1989)		Dutton & Strachan (1987b)
	Non-violent	Repeat violence	Non-violent	Violent	Arrested
n =	1,533	93	344	44	27
Partner would retaliate	6.7	8.7	10.5	6.8	21.4
Partner would call police	n/a	n/a	15.9	6.6	54.5
Arrest	19.0	17.9	17.0	6.8	64.7
Partner would divorce	29.6	25.3	30.4	19.1	52.2
Social condemnation	47.7	34.0	46.2	33.6	40.5
Lose self-respect	n/a	n/a	61.6	48.9	58.3

sanction follow arrest is interesting and is consistent with Fagan's notion that arrest might redress a power imbalance in the family. But as we saw in Chapter 5, not all abusive couples are male dominant (Coleman & Straus 1992). This leads to the question, so far unanswered, of whether arrest works best on couples that are male dominant. On female dominant couples, it may heighten the male's sense of powerlessness – an original cause of his assaultiveness (see also Babcock et al. 1993). Whether these couples also represent the boomerang effect seen with Sherman et al.'s (1992) marginal group is not presently known.

Sherman and Berk (1984) reported that 31% of their sample of wife assaulters had prior arrests for crimes against persons (only 5% for wife assault). Unfortunately, they did not analyze for the impact of prior history on subsequent likelihood of recidivism. (Were the 19% of arrested males who again assaulted their wives males with the greatest prior contact with – thus the least fear of – criminal justice intervention?). If we bear in mind that only 6.7% of men repeatedly assault their wives (2.8% severely so) (Schulman 1979; Straus et al. 1980), then, clearly, these recidivist assaulters should be the target of criminal justice intervention.

Sherman and Berk (1984) reported that in their sample of wife assaulters, 80% had assaulted their wives in the previous six months but only 5% had been arrested for it. Once arrested, however, only 19% repeated the assault in the next six months. Considering these aggregate data, arrest may function to signal increased state interventions above and beyond any objective probability of future detection, arrest, or punishment. Furthermore, arrest may serve a didactic function of indicating that the state considers wife assault to be a crime. We do not know from the Sherman and Berk data whether the recidivism reduction observed for the arrested group is due to deterrence or to some other factor. As described above in the Dutton et al. (1992) study, arrest also serves: to teach perpetrators that society considers their acts to be wrong; to correct a power imbalance in a family; to bring awareness of their behavior (and thus social sanctions) to their social circle; and so on. These other functions of arrest could lead to recidivism reduction whether or not the men believed punishment for repeat assault was likely. Only research on the subjective estimates of consequences for future assault would disentangle these explanations. Clearly, we need research that relates subjective estimates of punishment to likelihood of recidivism.

Some, but not all, wife assaults are impulsive acts, performed in states of high physiological and emotional arousal (Dutton, Fehr, & McEwan 1982). By definition, such actions do not fall under the rational self-interest assumptions of deterrence theory. However, many wife assaults are deliberate and involve carefully choosing the time, place, and parts of the body to be injured (Gelles 1975). This obviously indicates that rational process is not always absent. That recidivism reduction can occur with some wife assaulters is supported by the Sherman and Berk (1984) study, which indicated that 81% of assaultive males could monitor and control their assaultive behavior for a six-month period post-arrest. The remaining 19% need further incentive and assistance in order to monitor and to control their behavior.

The Role of Court-Mandated Treatment

At present, a variety of court-mandated treatment groups have been developed to provide assistance based on social learning notions of development and maintenance of aggressive behavior patterns (Bandura 1979). Bandura (1979) describes the psychological mechanisms that allow reprehensible conduct to recur (see Chapter 3 for a detailed review). While arrest may challenge all of these mechanisms of self-justification, they are further challenged through court-mandated treatment. Indeed, a primary objective of such treatment (as we shall see in Chapter 9) is to directly undermine such cognitive, habit-sustaining mechanisms in assaultive males (Ganley 1981; Dutton 1981c).

A second objective of such confrontation is to challenge the belief held by some convicted wife assaulters that their arrests were unjust. To the extent that a wife assaulter believes that (1) his wife's injuries were minimal, or (2) she was to blame for the conflict, or (3) his use of violence was justified, to such an extent is he likely to view his subsequent arrest and conviction as unjust. Most treatment formats confront these beliefs (Eddy & Meyers 1984; Browning 1984).

A third objective of treatment is to enable wife assaulters to improve their ability to detect the warning signs of their own violence (e.g., increased arousal, anger) and to develop a more elaborate set of behaviors for managing violence-evoking situations. The empirical question for such treatment is whether these improved cognitive and behavioral abilities, when linked with the belief that future assault will lead to punishment, can decrease recidivism for a treatment population.

Power and Beliefs

Men who repeatedly assault their wives gain from their use of violence both personal feelings of power (Novaco 1976) and a feeling of having gained control of a conflict that felt unmanageable prior to the violence (Sonkin, Martin, & Walker 1985). These are not the type of gains typically considered by deterrence theory. For most men, these gains are expensive, since they are obtained through the use of conduct (Bandura 1979; Stark & McEvoy 1970) which erodes the quality of the marital relationship. It is indicative of the power of these informal social controls that most men eschew wife assault, and that only a small group repeat the act. For these repeaters, arrest and surveillance serve to reduce their recidivism rate (Sherman & Berk 1984), and court-mandated treatment seems to lower the likelihood of repeat assault (Dutton 1987b) below the level generated by arrest and conviction alone.

Nevertheless, our assessments of the impact of criminal justice interventions with wife assault remain rather piecemeal, and solid conclusions await a more systematic, long-term study. In particular, subjective belief systems of offenders need to be scrutinized as an important mediator between objective system change and subsequent recidivism rates. Specifically, we need to know more about the impact of various intervention strategies on perception of risk of arrest, and we also need to know under what psychological circumstances such perception may govern the behavior of the assaulter. Instead of using broad demographic variables such as race or employment to investigate recidivism, it may be more fruitful to examine couple dynamics – specifically, power shifts as a by-product of criminal justice system process, whether it be the issuing of a TRO, arrest, or prosecution. Many studies reviewed above (Chaudhuri & Daly 1992; Ford & Regoli 1992; Fagan 1989; Dutton et al. 1992) suggested that shifts in couple power may mitigate recidivist assault and may illuminate the contradictions in the Sherman et al. (1992) results.

Chapter Summary and Conclusions

In this chapter we have reviewed the literature on police response to domestic disturbance calls. Since the police come into contact with family violence more than does any other government agency, they have the potential to make the greatest impact on the detection and cessation of future violence. In reviewing these studies, we found that about one-third of all husband-wife domestic disturbances led to an assault, and, contrary to the beliefs of the police themselves, alcohol was only a causative factor in about 14% of domestic disturbances.

Police decisions to arrest when on domestic disturbance calls seem to give too little weight to victim injuries and too much weight to the demeanour of the alleged assailant. However, given that the assault is defined by the victim as a crime and is reported as such, the criminal justice system processes the case just as it does other crimes. One could make the point that, given the aggressor-victim relationship (being under the same roof, in a continuing relationship), perhaps the criminal justice

response should be more aggressive, since the likelihood of repeat violence is higher in this situation than it is in a situation in which those
involved are strangers.

We have argued in this chapter that some qualified support exists for
the deterrence of future assault through the police use of arrest, and we
have further suggested that coupling arrest with mandatory treatment is a
promising policy strategy for the greater reduction of recidivism. Finally,
the results of the many replications of the original Minneapolis study
underscore the finding that arrest does not work for men with nothing to
lose by being arrested. What can men lose through arrest? They can lose
their jobs, if they are gainfully employed (hence, as we see unemployment increase, so we may see the power of arrests decrease); they can lose
status within their friendship group (as subcultural values become more
condemning of wife assault, the effect of arrest might increase – but the
success of government programs in influencing subcultural values is
unclear); they can lose their self-respect and/or the respect of their wives
(but marginal men [as Sherman et al. called them] may already have lost
this, leaving them with nothing more to lose through arrest). The point,
again, is that arrest cannot compensate for qualities lost through social
attrition, and it cannot serve as a panacea for general social control (see
also Wilson 1983).

9
The Treatment of Wife Assault

In the last chapter we showed that court-mandated treatment of wife assault was making an essential contribution to the criminal justice objective of reducing recidivism. Treatment, it was argued, provides a means through which repeat wife assaulters can learn alternative skills for conflict management, improve their ability to detect and express anger, and have the negative consequences of their violence made salient to them. This latter cognitive shift occurs through a direct therapeutic challenge to the cognitive mechanisms (e.g., minimizing, rationalizing, denying responsibility) that support reprehensible conduct (Bandura 1979). We described these mechanisms in Chapter 3, and in Chapter 4 we provided an empirical study that described how they are implemented by wife assaulters. We have argued that the didactic function of arrest may be to provide a major challenge or confrontation to these cognitive mechanisms. In this chapter, we will examine how therapy extends this process of reframing the assaulter's interpretation of anger-inducing events.

Treatment Philosophy
In order to devise a form of therapy to be used as a condition of probation for men convicted of wife assault, certain sets of requirements must be met. First, the therapeutic form will have to have a philosophical base that is compatible with criminal justice philosophy. If, for example, criminal justice philosophy emphasizes personal responsibility for action, a treatment philosophy with a similar orientation is recommended.

In some areas of human conduct, a division exists between legal philosophy (which stresses individual responsibility) and social science philosophy (which stresses situational determinism) (see Fincham and Jaspars 1980; Dutton 1981b). Social learning theory, while acknowledging the formative role of situational events in shaping habit patterns, nevertheless stresses choice and responsibility for individual action. The therapist, then, must repeatedly challenge statements by the client that his violence was caused by an external force (his wife's behavior being a typical example), a short-term situational occurrence (being drunk), or an uncontrollable predisposition (a bad temper, uncontrollable arousal, a drinking problem). In each case the therapist reminds the client that his wife did not force him to hit her, that other men get drunk and do not become violent, and that he may have been either violent when sober or drunk and non-violent. The point of this exercise is to get the client to acknowledge that his violence involves elements of choice, and that he has greater ability to control it than he has formerly acknowledged.

Figure 9.1 represents an event-anger-aggression model that demonstrates the points of choice at which therapeutic modification of clients' perceptions is aimed. It demonstrates a conceptual model for the event-aggression link that is influenced by the learning process in four ways:

(1) The appraisal of the event as maliciously intended or threatening seems to be a learned process.
(2) The affective reaction to the consequent arousal may be shaped by sex-role socialization or other learned factors.
(3) The mode of behavioral expression of anger represents a learned habit.
(4) The choice of a target for abuse seems also to be learned.

Descriptions of therapy with assaultive males (e.g., Ganley 1981; Gondolf 1985a; Sonkin, Martin, & Walker 1985; Edelson & Tolman 1992) outline the variety of techniques that are used in treatment groups to generate the learning of new perceptions and behaviors. These include having the men keep anger diaries in which they log the instigators (i.e., events that made them angry), analyses of violent events discussed in their treatment groups, discussions of emotional reactions to specific behaviors of others in their treatment groups (or empathy-building), and relaxation exercises (while imagining anger-provoking situations).

While the emphasis and form of these therapeutic practices may vary from group to group, the objective that they serve remains constant: they demonstrate to the clients how their use of violence is a learned behavior sustained by their own perceptions. This presents the possibility of learning alternative behaviors which have less destructive consequences. Many men come to treatment for assaultive behavior with the belief that their violence is immutable. Having a therapist confront their interpretation of their wives' motives, their denial of emotions other than anger, and their refusal to use other behaviors to express anger gradually develops their perception that alternatives to violence are possible.

Clinical descriptions of men who are court-mandated to attend such treatment groups (Ganley 1981; Sonkin et al. 1985) underscore the need

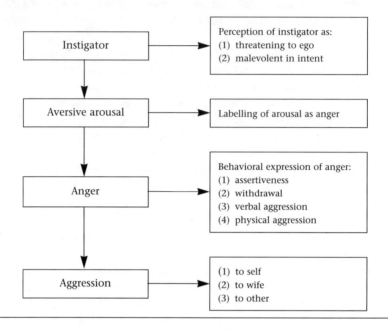

Figure 9.1

Cognitive mediators of instigator-aggression relationship

for highly structured, confrontational techniques. These men are described as cognitively rigid and unassertive, with strong tendencies to externalize blame for their behavior. They rarely have experience in psychological treatment groups (unless involved in alcohol treatment programs) and typically have had little interest in considering the possibility of personal change. Hence, highly directive treatment and the provision of motivation-builders is required.

Since many court-directed treatment programs are short-term in nature (i.e., three to six months), therapeutic priorities must be selected carefully. It is unlikely, for example, that a man socialized into a macho working environment is going to embrace a feminist view of male socialization during weekly treatment sessions, especially when he returns to a work milieu that is philosophically contradictory to a feminist perspective (cf. Ptacek 1984). However, demonstrating to him that his sex-role expectations may differ from his wife's and teaching him skills to negotiate these differences are not necessarily incompatible with his social milieu. Accordingly, we favour using anger-management techniques that can be adapted to a variety of social milieux rather than attempting to generate ideological changes that may be incompatible with a client's background and needs. It is important for therapists to base their work on individual assessments of each of their clients – for reducing these people to broad social categories may prevent therapists from hearing what they have to say.

Cognitive-Behavioral Therapies for Anger

Cognitive-behavioral therapies are based on three fundamental assumptions: (1) that cognition affects behavior, (2) that cognition may be monitored and altered, and (3) that behavior change can be generated through changing cognitions (Dobson and Block 1987). Stemming from a growing body of 1970s literature emphasizing the role of cognition in anxiety (Lazarus and Averill 1972) and depression (Beck 1976), and from a dissatisfaction with the results of long-term psychodynamically oriented psychotherapy (Eysenck 1969; Rachman & Wilson 1980), cognitive behavioral treatment began to be applied to a wide variety of affective and behavioral disorders (Dobson and Block 1986). These included problems with self-control (Mahoney and Thoreson 1979), anxiety (Meichenbaum 1977), depression, (Beck 1976); and anger (Novaco 1975).

Novaco's (1975) application of cognitive-behavioral therapy to anger management focused on the interrelationship of autonomic and cognitive determinants. As described in Chapter 3, Novaco also emphasized the positive functions served by anger arousal: it energizes behavior and serves both expressive functions (advertising potency and determination) and defensive functions (overriding feelings of anxiety, vulnerability, and ego threat). If anger serves this variety of functions, then therapy must include alternative means for clients to satisfy each of them. This is not always easily accomplished in short-term therapy. For example, if anxiety and vulnerability increase as a result of a client's learning to reinterpret his anger in these new emotional terms, he may need to learn strategies for dealing with these alternative – and male sex-role dissonant – feelings. However, his time in therapy may not be sufficient to permit this. A less ambitious therapeutic objective may be the development of awareness in the client that other feelings can be mislabelled as anger.

Novaco's (1975) anger management treatment was designed to alter clients' anger-enhancing cognitions. Figure 9.2 presents his treatment focus. If we refer back to Figure 9.1, Novaco's techniques would apply to all four learned aspects of the stimulus-response chain. In social learning terms, anger management attempts to modify both the perception of the instigators to aggression and the cognitive regulators of aggression.

In order to achieve the five objectives listed in Figure 9.2, Novaco first assessed the impact of various provocations on clients by means of an

Figure 9.2

Novaco's (1975) anger management approach

1. Changing clients' perception of the aversive stimulus or incident from a personal affront to a task that requires a solution.

2. Teaching clients to use their own arousal as a cue for nonaggressive coping strategies.

3. Increasing clients' perceptions that they are in control of themselves in provoking circumstances.

4. Teaching clients to dissect provocation sequences into stages, with self-instructions for managing each stage.

5. Teaching relaxation techniques to enable clients to reduce anger-arousal.

anger inventory containing ninety provocation incidents (Novaco 1975). Clients rated on a five-point scale how angry they would feel if they had been involved in these incidents. Analysis of reactions to the anger inventory items generated provocations that clients then role-played. Novaco (1975) reported that his treatment techniques successfully allowed subjects to lower self-report anger scores and physiological indices associated with anger (i.e. systolic and diastolic blood pressure and galvanic skin response scores). In addition, subjects demonstrated improved scores on interpersonal reactions to provocation (i.e., constructive action scores increased while verbal and physical antagonism scores decreased).

While these results are promising, they were obtained under role-playing conditions that lent themselves to subjects occasionally cooperating in order to verify experimental hypotheses (Orne 1969). However, even if these *demand characteristics* (that cue subjects to the nature of the experimental hypotheses) were involved in Novaco's assessment, they still demonstrate that when angry clients want to lower their anger they can do so. They can effectively improve their affective, physiological, and interpersonal responses to provocation. Novaco also tried to offset the artificial nature of role-playing provocations by conducting direct-experience laboratory provocations (unsuspected personal affronts that would be perceived as real-life provocations). However, given that his subjects were wired for physiological measurement, the deceptive nature of this design is questionable.

Novaco reports comparisons of various partial treatment groups (e.g., groups concentrating on cognitive control alone, relaxation training alone, etc.) in an effort to ascertain which components had the greatest effect on improved anger management. Subjects themselves reported that the most important aspect of treatment was task orientation when faced with a provocation. Task orientation requires clients to define the situation as one requiring a solution rather than an attack, and it directs attention away from internal stimuli associated with anger. The automatic perception of a provocation as a personal affront begins to change as clients learn that not becoming demonstrably angry does not mean that they have to give up their positions or back down. In other words, increased assertiveness is possible when anger is controlled.

Treatment Groups for Wife Assaulters

The development of treatment groups to specifically work with wife assaulters was pioneered by Anne Ganley (Ganley and Harris 1978; Ganley 1981). Ganley developed her treatment program from a social-learning orientation (similar to that developed in Chapter 3) which focused on improving the poor conflict-resolution skills learned by wife assaulters in their family of origin. In such families violence is often the only means of dealing with conflict-generated anger because listening skills are poor, verbal problem-solving skills are poor, and emotional self-disclosure is equated with loss of control. As a step towards rectifying these deficits, Ganley included assertiveness training as part of her treatment model.

Typically, Ganley's groups focus not only on physical abuse but on verbal, sexual, and property abuse as well. Since the abuse takes place in the context of an intimate relationship with a woman, the man's perceptions about women, his wife, and the meaning of intimacy must all be explored. In particular the extent to which the man uses violence as a form of control must be assessed. For some wife assaulters this is its primary function, while for others violence is reactive (either to a felt insurmountable conflict or to alleviate an internal tension state [as described in Chapter 5]).

Ganley viewed battering as a learned tension-reducing response that occurred in the family setting because that was the safest place to commit acts of violence without being punished and because batterers stereotypically viewed themselves as the absolute rulers of their homes. Ganley described the tendency of batterers to deny or to minimize their violence and abuse as well as to externalize it by holding others responsible for it. She recommended confrontation as a therapeutic strategy for dealing with these forms of the neutralization of self-punishment. She also developed a highly structured treatment format that stressed personal accountability. Exercises such as maintaining an anger diary emphasized the need for personal responsibility in that it required the constant monitoring of anger.

Batterers also tended to express as anger emotions such as hurt, anxiety, excitement, sadness, guilt, humiliation, and helplessness. Ganley's treatment program develops their motivation to change by helping them identify negative feelings other than anger. Men may use anger to ward off chronic emotional scripts of guilt, shame, or depression; they must learn how to identify and better cope with these emotions.

Anger diaries help the man to identify the instigators of his anger and his physical and cognitive responses to it. Men list the 'triggers' (instigators) of their anger (i.e., what another person did or said to anger them), how angry they became (on a ten-point scale), how they knew they were angry (physiological responses, etc.), their 'talk up' (i.e., what they said to themselves to increase their anger), and their 'talk down' (what they said to themselves to calm themselves down). Men list the 'triggers' as objective recordings of events. They are taught to be specific, not to make assumptions about others' motives, and to record only what they saw or heard.

This exercise forces them to analyze how frequently they impute negative motives to others and the extent to which these assumptions generate anger. Comparisons of the 'trigger' and 'talk up' columns emphasize the interpretative or subjective quality of their anger responses (since the 'talk up' column generally contains blaming statements that serve to increase the man's self-generated anger). 'Talk down' or anger-decreasing statements have to be taught to most men. Through changing men's self-statements from those assessing external blame to those acknowledging internal feelings, such statements serve both to improve their ability to detect anger cues and to generate self-control. For a complete description and examples of anger diaries, the reader is referred to Sonkin and Durphy (1982) or to Sonkin, Martin, and Walker (1985). When men are in treatment groups and are consistently completing anger diaries, the latter are used as a step towards assertiveness training.

Bower and Bower (1976) develop assertiveness by getting clients to verbalize a DESC script. DESC is an acronym for *describe, express, specify,* and *consequences*. Clients are asked to describe what behaviors in others bother them, to express how these behaviors make them feel, to specify what new behaviors they want, and to express the positive consequences for others if they perform these behaviors. This assertiveness exercise becomes a first step in teaching clients to negotiate interpersonal differences.

The bridge from the anger diary to the DESC script is built as follows: The 'triggers' from the anger diary (specific acts or statements) provide the 'describe' portion of the DESC script. The specificity learned in keeping an anger diary helps the man to focus his verbal statements on a behavior rather than on a predisposition of the other. The 'talk down' column (statement of feeling) then becomes the 'express' part of the DESC script. Hence, the anger diary provides the first half of an assertive statement, often an improvement in communication without the 'specify' and 'consequence' portions. These latter steps teach the man to assert what changes he wants and what changes he is willing to make in order to bring them about.

Thus men are led to develop a problem-oriented or negotiation approach to the communication of anger. After rehearsal and practice in the treatment group, men are encouraged to continue with couples communication therapy. It should be emphasized that we recommend such treatment only when the man's use of violence is under control. The communication aspect of treatment is designed to improve the conflict climate of the wife assaulter's primary relationship once his wife no longer feels at risk for further violence.

Motivation to Change

As mentioned above, men who come to treatment for wife assault, particularly those who are court-mandated, may have no prior experience with treatment groups. The thought of disclosure of personal problems in front of other men is discomfiting. Denying and minimizing abuse is commonplace, as is blaming the victim, the criminal justice system, or any other external source in order to ward off personal responsibility for violence. (Recall Bandura's schema for neutralization of self-punishment in Chapter 3 and Dutton's study of perpetrators' accounts of their own violence in Chapter 4). How, then, do we motivate these men to work at reducing their violence?

Prochaska, DiClemente, and Norcross (1992) present a model of the change process applied to addictive behaviors. Figures 9.4 and 9.5 outline their stages of change.

Prochaska et al. describe the empirical studies of change for a wide variety of addictive behaviors. Based on these studies, most people do not successfully maintain their gains on their first attempts at change; rather, a type of spiral process occurs where gains and relapses follow each other as people progress from stage one to stage four.

Figure 9.3

Anger diary based on a DESC (describe, express, specify, and consequences) script

Anger Diary

Name _____

Date _____

Date of Event	Trigger	How Anger Known	Rating (1-10)	Self Talk Talk-Up	Self Talk Talk-Down
Nov. 17	WIFE KEPT BOTHERING FRIEND OF SON BY REPEATEDLY ASKING HIM QUESTIONS ABOUT A BOOK HIS FATHER WROTE.	STARTING FEELING MORE UP TIGHT THE MORE SHE WENT ON.	4	WHY DOESN'T SHE LEAVE THE POOR KID ALONE. WHY DOESN'T SHE JUST SHUT UP AND WATCH THE MOVIE LIKE EVERYONE ELSE.	I FEEL ANGRY ABOUT THE WAY SHE'S TREATING THIS KID BUT MAKING A SCENE ABOUT IT IN FRONT OF THE KIDS WILL ONLY BRING ME DOWN TO HER LEVEL.
Nov. 18	WIFE CONTINUALLY NAGGING AT ME + POINTING HER FINGER IN MY FACE	NECK + BACK FELT TENSE + HAD EMPTY FEELING IN GUT.	7	THIS BITCH IS PUSHING ME TO THE LIMIT ONCE AGAIN. WHY CAN'T SHE BACK OFF AND TRY TO WORK THINGS OUT QUIETLY.	I FEEL REALLY MAD BUT I WON'T LOOSE CONTROL. I BETTER GET AWAY FOR AWHILE AND HOPE THINGS COOL DOWN.
Nov. 19	WIFE NOT HELPING WITH ANYTHING AROUND THE HOUSE BECAUSE SHE SAYS SHE IS SICK.	FELT UNUSUALLY NERVOUS + UP TIGHT	3	THE ONLY REASON SHE FEELS SO SICK IS BECAUSE SHE DRANK ALL WEEKEND AND NOW I HAVE TO PAY FOR IT ONCE AGAIN BY HAVING MORE WORK TO DO.	I'M GETTING ANGRY AGAIN FOR THE SAME OLD REASON HER DRINKING. DON'T LET IT GET TO YOU. THINGS WILL HAVE TO IMPROVE OR OUR RELATIONSHIP WON'T LAST.

(Continued on next page)

Figure 9.3 (continued)

Anger Diary

Name ————————————————

Date ————————————————

Date of Event	Trigger	How Anger Known	Rating (1-10)	Self Talk Talk-Up	Self Talk Talk-Down
Nov. 30	FINDING OUT WIFE HAD GONE OUT AND NOT COME HOME ALL NIGHT	FELT MY ADRENALIN START TO FLOW AND STARTED MOVING AROUND HOUSE AT A QUICK PACE	4	SHE'S DONE IT AGAIN. GONE OUT WITHOUT AS MUCH AS A NOTE OR PHONE CALL TO SAY WHERE SHE IS. THAT BITCH DOESN'T GIVE A SHIT ABOUT MY FEELINGS.	THIS ISN'T THE FIRST TIME OR I MIGHT REALLY GET WORRIED. I'M SURE SHE WILL SHOW UP TOMORROW SO I MIGHT AS WELL GO BACK TO BED. ACTUALLY I FEEL RELIEVED THAT SHE ISN'T HERE.
Dec. 1	WIFE STARTED YELLING AT ME— WHY DIDN'T YOU LEAVE ME A NOTE TO SAY WHERE YOU WERE. CALLED ME AN ASSHOLE, ETC. THEN TOLD ME NOT TO TOUCH THE FRYING PAN TO MAKE DINNER BECAUSE EVERYTHING BELONGED TO HER. SAW BOTTLE OF RUM ON COUNTER.	ENTIRE BODY BECAME TENSE AND STOMACH GOT VERY UPSET.	9	THAT FUCKING BITCH. HOW DARE SHE QUESTION + TALK TO ME LIKE THIS WHEN SHE DISAPPEARED LAST NIGHT WITHOUT AN EXPLANATION. SHE'S DRUNK AND I'M FED UP WITH HER-PERIOD.	TIME OUT! GET OUT OF HERE NOW SHE'S PUSHING ME BEYOND MY CONTROL. GET AWAY FROM HER NOW!
Dec. 2.	BARGING IN. HOUSE DRUNK LATE AT NIGHT AND STARTED YELLING NOT TO COME NEAR HER THEN SMACKED ME WITH HER HAND RIGHT IN THE LEFT EYE.	MUSCLES BECAME TENSE + FACE BECAME HOT.	7	WHAT A FUCKING NERVE. I'VE NO INTENTION OF GOING ANYWHERE NEAR HER JUST GO TO BED AND PASS OUT. I DON'T WANT ANYTHING TO DO WITH YOU	I'M FURIOUS WITH HER BUT I'M NOT GOING TO RETALIATE OR I'LL BE THE ONE TO PAY FOR ALL THIS SHIT SHE'S CAUSING.

Source: Provided by a client in the Assaultive Husband's Project

Figure 9.4

Prochaska, DiClemente, and Norcross's (1992) stages of change

1. *Precontemplation.* No intention to change, no recognition of his lack of awareness of the problem. Family and close friends are aware of the problem.

2. *Contemplation.* Awareness of the problem and serious thought about overcoming it, but no action plan. ('Knowing you want to go [to treatment] but not quite ready yet,' p. 1103).

3. *Preparation.* Intending to take action. Some minor attempts but no substantial behavioral change.

4. *Action.* Overt behavioral change with successful modification from one day to six months (depending on the prior frequency of the behavior).

5. *Maintenance.* Work to prevent relapse and consolidate the gains from action.

Figure 9.5

A spiral model of the stages of change (Prochaska, DiClemente & Norcross 1992)

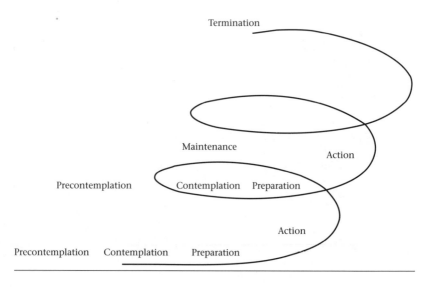

When we apply this analysis to wife assaulters, the following conclusions seem reasonable:

(1) Wife assault is a form of addictive behavior that the man has learned to use habitually in ego-threatening or stressful conflict.

(2) Men who enter treatment are anywhere from the precontemplative stage to the action stage.

(3) Denying and minimizing are similar to the underawareness reported by Prochaska et al.

Unfortunately, Prochaska et al.'s conclusion is that some form of relapse is almost inevitable for men who are trying to quit for the first time and who have entered therapy in the earlier (precontemplation-contemplation) stages. This would describe almost all court-mandated assaultive men. Again, we must wonder whether it is realistic to expect court-mandated men to become violence-free immediately after a sixteen-week treatment group.

Prochaska et al. also suggest that different forms of treatment might work better at different stages of treatment. For example, consciousness-raising is important at the precontemplation stage, whereas reinforcement management is more important at the action stage. In court-mandated groups, a detailed examination of the range of abusive acts (physical, emotional, sexual, property, and pet) constitutes part of consciousness-raising. Men frequently comment on how their abuse was much more frequent and pervasive than they had formerly thought. (Another form of consciousness-raising is to get the men to attend to the language they use to describe women, especially when they are angry. What does this language [which typically focuses on the woman as a 'whore' or 'slut'] tell us about the deeper images they have of women?) Reinforcement management would include redefining power from control of the other to self-control (and rewarding the latter).

The stages and processes used by Prochaska et al. enabled them to predict, with 93% accuracy, which patients would drop out of therapy prematurely. We will consider below the question of whether treatment groups actually work. According to the analysis just presented, it might be naive to expect court-mandated men who are forced into treatment in the precontemplative stage to become totally violence-free by the end of their therapy.

Sex-role Socialization, Power, and Group Processes

While anger recognition and improved communication skills provide the essence of therapy for assaultive males, other issues also constitute an important adjunct to this treatment. Since treatment is for male-female violence, the contribution of sex-role socialization to setting the stage for violence is important. Male socialization both narrows the range of acceptable emotions (Fasteau 1974; Pleck 1981) and creates occasionally unrealistic expectations about family roles. This can be a source of chronic conflict in a relationship (Coleman & Straus 1986). Treatment must address these issues and attempt to develop empathy for the victims of violence (see Edelson & Tolman 1992).

One way to develop empathy is to have assaultive males describe their own experiences as victims of parental abuse. Exploring the feelings connected to these experiences in the group, and explicitly relating them to their wives' experiences as victims, can serve to strengthen empathy. In our treatment groups, the discussion of parental abuse has usually been a very emotional experience – one in which strong group cohesiveness is developed. For many of our clients, this may be the first time in their lives that they have discussed these painful experiences.

Treatment should also include an attempt to have males think about power in a different way. A man typically enters treatment thinking about power vis-à-vis his wife in an adversarial fashion: his gain is his wife's loss and vice versa. The therapist encourages each man to view power in interdependent terms; that is, by diminishing his wife he loses a vital partner, whereas by accepting her empowerment he actually gains. This is done by making clear the personal losses he sustains as a result of violence towards his wife (e.g., her emotional and sexual withdrawal, mistrust, and chronic anger towards him). By repeatedly yoking the couple's gains and losses, the concept of power interdependence becomes clear. In this way, an objective of feminist therapy is addressed by a means less threatening than confronting the man's attitudes about sexual politics.

This is not to say that confrontation does not occur in anger management groups – it does. For one thing, men will confront each other over sexist attitudes. Any generalized attitude to an entire social category, however, usually has some basis in negative personal experiences. By confronting the feelings, both behavioral and attitude changes can occur. We do this, in part, by having the men write a personal 'violence policy,' to make clear when violence is justified, when is it not, and why. This tends to clarify a personal code and the reasons that sustain it. The point, though, is that attitudinal confrontation and change must be accompanied by affective change through a sense of acting in one's own interest. Diminishing chronic intimate conflict becomes incorporated as a form of self-interest. The interests of the self and the partner are thus intertwined.

Feminist approaches to therapy tend to work towards a recognition that violence is used to maintain the power imbalance in a patriarchal society, and that such an imbalance is unhealthy and unproductive for all concerned. However, to attempt to change assaultive men's attitudes about patriarchy in a *limited* therapeutic time period can be ineffective. Instead, it can offer an opportunity to cast responsibility for their behavior onto the social system rather than onto themselves. Furthermore, many assaultive males feel powerless; trying to convince them that they are powerful and controlling can backfire therapeutically.

What therapy *can* do is to clarify the negative consequences of any individual's attempts to achieve greater power solely through control of another person and the positive consequences of sharing that power and of finding non-coercive lifestyles that lead to a feeling of empowerment. Strangely, empowerment issues, so important for battered women, are also therapeutically relevant to wife assaulters. As assaultive men find alternative methods of feeling inner power, their need for power over their wives is diminished (see Ng [1980] for an extended discussion of this distinction). Thus, the assaultive male moves closer to a feminist perspective but on an individual, rather than on a systems, level.

Finally, since treatment for assaultive males usually occurs in a group setting, group process issues (Yalom 1975) are also important. Most clinical texts describe assaultive males as being isolated (Ganley 1981; Sonkin et al. 1985). They frequently feel anxious about describing personal problems and feelings in front of other men. Therapists engage in considerable bridge-building by explicitly connecting the experiences of men in the groups in order to establish camaraderie and a sense of safety in self-disclosure.

On the other hand, the therapist cannot allow group cohesiveness to generate mutual protection vis-à-vis denying and minimizing violence. Since men in these groups may have a shared sense of outrage at the 'injustice' of arrests for what they consider to be minimal acts, they may try to feed each other's tendency to blame the victims, women in general, or the criminal justice system. The therapeutic objective is to allow resentments to be expressed in the group while still confronting the men's perceptions of blame. Having a reformed client, or clients, participate in group sessions can be extremely useful in diffusing the individually confrontational role the therapist would otherwise have to assume.

Regardless of whether the therapist operates alone or with reformed clients when confronting individuals in the group, if some or all of the clients perceive the challenges as attacks, group polarization can occur as a form of defence. The therapist must make it clear that confrontation is used to help each individual accept responsibility for his actions and to learn new ways to manage conflict; they are not used to attack or to judge.

Individual versus Systems Approaches to Treatment

Considerable controversy surrounds the choice of a treatment approach for wife assault. Treatment programs for assaultive males view violence as a response learned by an individual during his ontogenetic development. The habit of reacting to conflict with violence is seen as an individual predisposition. The therapeutic implication is that the individual aggressor must be treated to learn how to control his use of violence prior to couples therapy or family systems therapy, which teaches the family how to deal constructively with conflict. Since couples therapy frequently includes negotiation and mediation aspects, a woman who feels threatened and unsafe cannot negotiate without preserving a power imbalance that makes true negotiation impossible.

A view of wife assault that assumes assaulters ontogenetically learn the use of violence predicts that assaultive males would be violent across relationships and that their violence would manifest itself whenever a set of instigators appeared. The type of abusive personality profile described in Chapter 5 would be an example of this tendency. Rounsaville (1978) reported that 39% of assaultive males in his study (n = 31) had prior violent relationships (this finding, however, was based on interviews with the women).

Kalmuss and Seltzer (1986) present data from the 1975 national survey (Straus et al. 1980) which address the question of whether predispositional perspectives or family systems perspectives more adequately describe the transrelationship incidence of spouse abuse. Kalmuss and Seltzer compared intact families (both spouses married for the first time), remarried families (one or both spouses divorced but no children from prior marriages), and reconstituted families (one or both divorced and children from prior marriages). Predispositional explanations would predict, Kalmuss and Seltzer argue, that individuals who are violence-prone would manifest violence trans-situationally. Since divorced couples are approximately ten times as likely to have used violence (Levinger 1966) than non-divorced couples, predispositional explanations would predict increased violence rates for remarried families over and above intact families.

Family systems approaches view structural stress as a major contributor to violence and, hence, would predict that reconstituted families would be more violent than would intact or remarried families (on the assumption that the complex structure and role confusion would increase the likelihood of violence). The national survey data tended to support a predispositional view: contrasts in violence incidence between intact and remarried families were significant, contrasts between remarried and reconstituted families were not. Hence, Kalmuss and Seltzer conclude that structural variables do not increase the likelihood of spouse abuse, while an inferred predisposition towards violence (based on the status of being divorced) does.

Kalmuss and Seltzer controlled for exposure to violence in the family of origin and found that their results persisted. Remarried adults who observed no physical aggression between their parents are still almost twice as likely to be involved in spouse abuse as are similar adults in intact families. They suggest that behavioral repertoires that include violence may not necessarily be rooted in early childhood experiences but may originate in the adults' first marriages.

Family systems approaches (Giles-Sims 1983; Neidig & Friedman 1984) view wife assault from an interactive (microsystem) rather than from an intrapsychic perspective. The rules of the family system that define what behavior is acceptable, the power imbalances of that system, and the personal resources of individual members that provide a basis for exchange are viewed as major contributors to family violence. Giles-Sims (see Chapter 2) acknowledges that 'victims may inadvertently be reinforcing the violent behavior' (1983:33), a perspective supported in the child abuse literature by the interactive studies of Patterson and his colleagues (reviewed in Chapter 2).

Patterson, Cobb, and Ray (1972), for example, observed parents' reinforcement of the violence of their highly destructive boys. These parents were not aware of providing reinforcements, and Giles-Sims suggests that the same may be true for battered women. Pagelow (1984) describes how some of these reinforcers include a low likelihood of retaliation, an acceptance by the weaker partner of battering as a proper response to stress, and an intense traditional ideology (e.g., that the woman shouldn't leave the marriage no matter how destructive it is, that she has a responsibility to save the man from his own excesses, etc.). All of these lead, in effect, to the assaultive male avoiding punishment for his violence.[1]

Neidig and Friedman (1984) begin their description of their couples treatment program with the statement that 'abusive behavior is a relationship issue but it is ultimately the responsibility of the male to control physical violence' (p. 1). Their view is that approaches that attribute total responsibility to either party lead to blaming, which only compounds the problem. It does so, according to these authors, by beginning a chain of retributive strategies by the victim and the aggressor, whereby each tries to get even for the other's most recent transgression. A systems approach avoids blaming by getting couples to think of the causes of violence from a circular-feedback, rather than from a linear, perspective. This leads to constructive interventions in the escalating process, permitting each partner to accept a portion of responsibility.

Having said that, however, Neidig and Friedman assign 'ultimate responsibility to the male for controlling violence' (p. 4), as both parties are usually not equal in physical strength. For some readers, this may suggest an artificial separation of responsibility from blame. If a man is responsible for his violence, then why is he not to blame if he acts violently? One answer may be that his violence occurred in a state of high arousal, when he perceived no alternatives to the actions he took.[2] In therapeutic terms, a couples approach and an individual approach have a fundamental disagreement: the couples approach tries to reduce blame, and the individual approach tries to increase responsibility.

The decision of whether an individual or a couples approach is best may depend on the client. If a man has a history of violence in several relationships with women, he may be a conflict-generator. Certainly, the abusive personality profiled in Chapter 5 requires extensive therapeutic work at an individual level before couples treatment seems viable. Also, as some therapists have shown (Richter 1974), single persons are capable of generating entire interaction patterns within families on the basis of their individual pathologies. Richter describes how a paranoid personality who holds power in a family can generate a shared paranoia in the entire family system. I expect that men with abusive personalities are conflict-generators in all intimate relationships, regardless of the personalities or conflict styles of their female partners. Many such men present for treatment with histories of multiple short-term relationships. Of course, such men may also pick women with their own backgrounds of abuse victimization and personality disorders. I recommend obtaining detailed social histories of clients and their partners prior to embarking on a systems approach, especially in view of the Kalmuss and Seltzer (1986) findings reported above. If a male batterer has a history of violence with women that predates his current relationship, or if he has strong indicators of an abusive personality, then couples treatment may not be advisable. Where the female feels threatened by the male's violence potential, or where violence is still recent, couples therapy might be delayed until the man has successfully completed an anger management program and is violence-free for a lengthy period. In general, where the violence and conflict seem specific to the present relationship, couples treatment may be more useful after the man has successfully completed anger treatment.

Are Treatment Groups Effective?

Since the late 1970s there has been a proliferation of court-mandated treatment groups for men convicted of wife assault. Browning (1984) and Eddy and Meyers (1984) provide descriptive profiles on numerous treatment programs for assaultive males. Both reviews outline referral processes, treatment procedures, and funding issues for such programs; and both agree on the need for an evaluation of treatment effectiveness.

Treatment groups for wife assaulters originated from public pressure on the criminal justice system to respond more effectively to the problem of wife assault (e.g., US Commission on Civil Rights 1978 and Standing Committee of Health, Welfare, and Social Affairs [Canada] 1982). As Dutton (1981a) pointed out, the hopes for such groups were twofold. First, the groups were seen as a means of improving protection for women who opted to remain in relationships with husbands who would not seek treatment voluntarily. Second, by providing a viable sentencing option for judges, treatment groups could create a salutary ripple effect throughout the criminal justice system by making judges more willing to convict, prosecutors more willing to proceed with cases, and police more willing to proceed with charges. Clearly, both of these hopes were based on the expectation that treatment groups would be effective.

Furthermore, since incarceration for a first offence of wife assault is unlikely (Lerman 1981; Dutton 1987b), treatment groups represent an addendum to probation that could provide convicted men with a means for managing anger (see Novaco 1975). The hazard of treatment groups lies in their offering false hope. If men remain at risk for violence despite treatment, then their wives may be imperiled while falsely believing that their husbands are cured. Therapists who offer treatment to abusive men have an obligation to educate their partners as to the realistic chances of improvement. Offender treatments for other behavioral problems have had mixed results (Shore and Massimo 1979; Gendreau and Ross 1980). Clearly, there is a need to assess the effectiveness of court-mandated treatment for wife assault.

Attempts at assessing treatment programs have not been as systematic or thorough as one might expect. Given the potential stake in these programs from a policy perspective, a thorough evaluation seems obligatory. Deschner (1984) evaluated the effects of teaching anger-control skills to nine groups of battering spouses. She reported data on 58 clients (32 women and 26 men) who completed intakes and at least 4 treatment sessions. Treatment included training in anger recognition, time out procedures, cognitive techniques, and assertiveness training. Pre-post anger measures were taken using anger self-reports to imagined anger-arousing scenes. The post-measures were taken four months after treatment completion. Clients also completed the *Taylor-Johnson Temperament Analysis* (1980), which assesses mood transition.[3]

Deschner reported that anger-control training was effective in increasing battering couples' anger management skills and in reducing the intensity and frequency of their disputes. However, as Deschner pointed out, these results were all based on self-report data and may have been biased by the clients' wish to please the researchers. Clients want to believe that the treatment in which they have just invested time will be successful, and they want the therapist to believe this as well. Separation of the evaluator from the therapist becomes an important component of an effective evaluation design.

Maiuro, Cahn, Vitaliano, and Zegree (1986) also reported results of an anger-control program for batterers conducted at Harborview Hospital in Seattle. This program also had a cognitive-behavioral basis, with techniques based on Novaco's work. The evaluation compared 63 batterers (treated for 18 weeks and having independently documented histories of domestic violence) with 26 untreated controls (wait-listed for treatment and matched to the batterers on demographic variables and general level of disturbance). The pre-post measures included the *Buss-Durkee Hostility Inventory* (Buss & Durkee 1957), the *Hostility and Direction of Hostility Questionnaire* (Caine, Foulds, & Hope 1967), the *Beck Depression Inventory* (Beck 1967), assertiveness scales, and anger-aggression scales completed by their spouses. Maiuro et al. reported significant differences between groups on all measures. The wait-list controls showed no decreases, while the treated men showed significant decreases on the anger/hostility measures, the depression measure, and the spouse-based ratings of anger and aggression. The treatment group also evidenced significant increases in assertiveness compared to the control group. Maiuro et al. concluded that specialized anger-control treatment could be effective in modifying psychological and behavioral variables related to battering.

Saunders and Hanusa (1984) reported evaluation data on twenty-five men who completed twenty sessions of a cognitive-behavioral treatment comprised of assertiveness training, relaxation training, and cognitive restructuring. They reported decreases in depression and threats from female competence but no significant drop in anger-scale scores. Actually, there was a decrease reported in pre-post anger scores (on a modified version of the Novaco anger scale). When social desirability scores (attempts by subjects to look good in their responses, measured by the *Marlowe-Crowne Social Desirability Scale*) were used to adjust anger scores, however, the significant differences disappeared. This emphasizes once again the problem with relying exclusively on self-report measures of treatment effectiveness.

Pirog-Good and Stets (in press) used a recidivism measure to evaluate group success. This was done by surveying leaders of treatment groups for batterers in the US and reporting recidivism rates for seventy-two such programs. They found from their survey that, of every 100 men who enrol in treatment programs for batterers, 60 complete the program. Of these 60, 42 to 53 do not return to battering in the year following treatment. Thus, the success rate in absolute terms is 79%. However, this study has two major problems associated with it. The first is that the recidivism measure was not systematic but was based on the educated estimates of (program) administrators; these personal estimates, as the authors admit, can be unreliable. The second is that no controls exist; hence, we do not know what percentage of non-recidivists would have stopped battering without treatment.

What Constitutes Effective Treatment?

The effect size of treatment (Rosenthal 1983) for wife assaulters can be established by estimating what percentage of men would not repeat assault *without* treatment. The difference between the treated and untreated rates is the effect size of treatment. Schulman (1979) and Straus et al. (1980) reported that single events of severe violence occurred for about 33% of couples reporting physical assaults, and that repeated events of assault occurred for 66% of couples. Should we consider this 33% the target baseline for treatment? There is a problem in doing this: the Straus and Schulman data were collected on the general population, whereas men who report for treatment, either through the courts or at their wives' behest, are more extreme cases and, typically, have longer histories of violence than would be found in a general population sample. In our treatment group (the Assaultive Husbands Program) the men's use of physical aggression, whether assessed by their own or by their wives' reports, puts them in the top 1% of population scores for violence. Any effective reduction with this population may seem, to the therapist, like a success. Another point to consider in assessing group effectiveness is that frequency of violence rates vary greatly for men in treatment, so pre-post individual comparisons should be made that compare post-treatment behavior to each man's pre-treatment individual frequency rate.

How might we establish a baseline against which to judge treatment group success? A major problem in assessing wife assault treatment effects has been the lack of a baseline measure of recidivism for a matched group of untreated offenders. In the absence of randomized designs, the next best comparison group would be a group of males demographically similar to the treated group, with similar arrest patterns and (if available) similar patterns of frequency of wife assault. The Sherman and Berk (1984) study reported an attempt to evaluate the specific deterrence effects of arrest for misdemeanour wife assault with men who had had criminal justice contact. Their six-month follow-up of 161 domestic disturbances – where police contact occurred – indicated an overall recidivism rate of 28.9% and a 19% recidivism rate for men who were arrested. Eighty per cent of the perpetrators had chronic assault histories. Hence, the Sherman and Berk study allows us to estimate expected recidivism for those under surveillance (e.g., on probation) after criminal justice intervention. Specifically, if a treated population has been arrested prior to treatment we might expect a 19% recidivism rate in the first six months.

For a variety of reasons, it is extremely difficult to conduct a randomized experiment that assigns assaultive men to control and experimental conditions by chance. Many service providers would be concerned with the ethics of refusing treatment to a designated control subject. If the man re-offended, could the victim sue the criminal justice agency for putting her at risk? Could his defence lawyer argue that his client never received the treatment to which he was entitled? However, until a randomized design experiment is conducted we will never know for sure if treatment really works. What has been carried out in lieu of a randomized design experiment are several comparisons between groups of wife assaulters who have received treatment and matched groups of wife assaulters (i.e., having similar histories of assault, arrest, and conviction) who have not received treatment. For example, Dutton (1987a) scrutinized police records of a group of fifty men for up to three years post-conviction. During the same period, records for fifty-nine men arrested, convicted, and treated for wife assault were examined. Demographic comparisons with the treated and untreated groups were virtually identical and were similar to groups of men studied by Sherman & Berk (1984).

The treatment program consisted of four months of court-mandated group therapy that included cognitive behavior modification, anger management, and assertiveness. Men in the evaluated treatment program met in groups of eight for three hours each week. Three measures of use of violence against wives were obtained in this study. First, police information records were examined, which showed all court appearances, including convictions. These records constitute the official recidivism rate for the treated and untreated groups. To provide longitudinal pre-post assessments of the use of violence by treated men, other measures of wife

Table 9.1

Characteristics of treated and untreated wife assaulters

	Sherman & Berk (1984)	Dutton (1987a)	
		Untreated	Treated
n =	205	50	50
Age	32	34	35
% unemployment	60%	48%	45%
% with prior assault	31%	28%	27%
Assault on wife in six months prior to arrest	80%	80%	80%
Recidivism rate: within 6 months	13%[a]	16%	4%
within 2.5 years	n/a	40%	4%

[a] 13% based on police reports; 19% based on wives's reports

assault were obtained by having men in treatment and their wives independently fill out the Straus (1979) *CTS* (Form N) for a period prior to and following treatment.

The *CTS* measures were only obtainable, however, for men who had undergone treatment. Hence, they provide pre-post data on the rate of assault, but they do not allow us to unambiguously attribute any changes to treatment per se. Diminution of the use of violence could be due to arrest, arrest and conviction, arrest, conviction and treatment, maturation, or regression towards the mean (Campbell 1969). While the use of both official recidivism and self-report measures partially offsets the problems of interpretation associated with the use of either one alone, it does not yet constitute an ideal evaluation design, as we will discuss below. Both the treated (*n* = 50) and the untreated (*n* = 50) males in this study had been convicted of wife assault and had had similar histories of assault. The untreated group had a total of forty prior assaults; the treated group had a total of forty-four prior assaults.

The decision to include men in treatment is made primarily by their probation officers and secondarily by their therapists. Considerations for the probation officers often include mundane issues such as whether a convicted man has employment that makes the treatment location accessible. Other men are untreated simply because their probation orders expire before spaces in treatment groups are available. Therapists base treatment decisions on the men's willingness to participate, although even recalcitrant men are often taken on a trial basis. For the fifty untreated men in the Dutton (1987a) study, forty-two were not treated due to practical considerations and eight were rejected by the therapists as unsuitable for treatment. In trying to match the treated and untreated groups, however, we can say with confidence that they are similar both demographically and in their pre-conviction records of violence. However, systematic psychological assessment was not performed, so we cannot rule out potential differences between groups with respect to psychological profiles. For the purposes of this study, treated men were defined as those who had completed treatment; untreated men were defined as those who had been interviewed for the group but who had completed fewer than four sessions of treatment. The post-interview follow-up period was assessed in 1985 and varied from three years (for men who had been interviewed in 1982) to six months (for more recent intake interviews [X = 2.0 years]).

Results of Police Data

The untreated group repeated assaults in 20/50 cases; the treated group in 2/50 cases. This difference was statistically significant (p < .001). In other words, treatment improves the nonrecidivist success rate from 60% to 96%, according to police records.

Furthermore, it is instructive to note that for the untreated group, 9/20 recidivist assaults were of an extremely serious variety and were classified as assault causing bodily harm. This typically indicated the use of a weapon and/or extreme injuries to the victim and was comparable to *aggravated assault*. However, a note of caution must accompany this apparent escalation in severity of crimes. It is not clear from police records whether it reflects an actual increase in severity of assault or a refusal of the prosecution to plea bargain to lesser charges when dealing with a repeat offender (see Repucci and Clingempeel 1978).

Sherman and Berk (1984) reported that 13% of their arrested group (n = 54) generated new police reports of wife assault within six months. Our untreated group generated new police reports 16% of the time (8/50) in the same six months. However, when the post-treatment assessment period was extended to 2.5 years (average 1.5 years), this increased to 40%. Arrest may have a short-term deterrent effect (see the Sherman et al. 1992 study reported in the Chapter 8), but treatment may lead to a long-term reduction of recidivism due to the men learning different skills for handling anger.

Self-Reports and Wives' Reports

Sixty-four per cent of treated men were married throughout treatment and follow-up (n = 37). These men and their wives were administered the Straus *CTS*. Data on men's pre-treatment conflict resolution were collected by having them fill in a *CTS* for violence for a period of one year prior to their arrest and conviction. Their wives filled out a *CTS* within five weeks of the beginning of their husbands' treatment; this also assessed violence which had occurred during the preceding year. Post-treatment data were collected by having men and their wives independently fill out a *CTS* at a point ranging from six months to three years after treatment completion (average two years). All data were then adjusted to yearly rates.

Each spouse was asked to rate the frequency with which each item or conflict tactic was used, both by them and by their spouses, in the time period specified. The frequency scale ranges from zero (never) to six (more than twenty times). Using Straus's regular scoring system, which involves summing the frequency ratings over the items, a range of scores from 0 to 48 is possible for all violence items and from 0 to 30 for severe violence items. Means for husband and wife ratings of annual rates of husband's use of violence are presented in Table 9.2.

Results of Self-Reports and Wives' Reports. For this subsample of thirty-seven couples, both husbands' self-reports and wives reports of husbands' violence show significant pre-post drops. Treated husbands still used acts of severe violence an average of 1.7 times a year (wives' report), down from an average of 10.6 times a year. Thirty-one of the 37 wives (84%) reported no acts of severe violence since termination of treatment. Intercorrelations of husbands' and wives' reports of the former's use of violent acts improved significantly from a pre-treatment score of .63 to a post-treatment score of .81. Reports of use of verbal aggression were similar to reports of use of severe violence. Based on both husbands' reports and wives' reports, overall rates of use of verbal aggression dropped after treatment. However, eight wives reported increases in verbal aggression.

The results of this study constituted a first step towards a conclusive assessment of long-term effects of treatment for wife assault. Clearly, the design could offer only tentative conclusions in this direction. While both police reports, self-reports, and wives' reports of male violence showed significant post-treatment drops, a variety of problems existed with the interpretation of these results. Police reports typically overlook the *chiffre noire* or 'hidden statistic' for wife assault, since only a small percentage end up in the filing of charges. However, this small percentage of assaultive males still places a considerable demand on police and court

Table 9.2

Husbands' and wives' mean ratings of husbands' annual use of violence before and after treatment

		Subscale range	
		Pre-treatment scores	Post-treatment scores
Dutton (1987a) sample			
Husband's rating (of own violence) (*n* = 37)	Verbal abuse (0-36)	23.9	12.8
	All violence (0-48)	13.4	4.6
	Severe violence (0-30)	5.5	1.1
Wife's rating (of husband's violence) (*n* = 37)	Verbal abuse (0-48)	28.3	13.9
	All violence (0-30)	21.3	6.1
	Severe violence (0-30)	10.6	1.7
Jaffe, Wolfe, Telford, & Austin (1986) sample[a]			
		Pre-arrest	Post-arrest/no treatment
Wife's rating (of husband's violence) (*n* = 61)	Verbal abuse (0-48)	18.32	13.56
	All violence (0-48)	24.17	9.19
	Severe violence (0-30)	n/a	n/a

[a] Jaffe et al. used a modified version of the CTS. Their raw data have been transformed to simplify direct comparisons.

resources in most jurisdictions. A 36% reduction in recidivism for the charged group would constitute a substantial conservation of criminal justice resources. Self-reports run the risk of being self-serving in that they may under-report violence (Browning and Dutton 1986). Men who have been convicted of wife assault once may be especially loath to report new assaults to interviewers because of anxiety about re-arrest. Wives' reports of husband violence might suffer from a similar unwillingness either to involve their husbands once again in the criminal justice system or to admit that the therapy group failed. Interviewers were careful to explain to wives that their reports of husbands' post-treatment violence would not generate criminal justice action, and that therapy was not expected to terminate all husband violence. However, there is no way of knowing if this was universally believed.

Even if one accepted that an amalgam of police, self-report, and wife-report data generated rough indices of husband violence, other interpretative problems existed. Since men were not allocated at random to treatment and no-treatment conditions, we could not attribute differences in outcome to treatment per se. Although the treated and untreated groups were roughly matched on demographic factors and pre-treatment arrest patterns for violence, other systematic differences between the groups could exist.

Interestingly, none of the treated husbands used violence during a wait-list period between the intake interview and the onset of treatment (based on both self- and wives' reports). This period varied from a few weeks to three months. This suggests that, at a point where criminal justice action (court conviction) is still salient, and where further scrutiny of the use of violence (treatment) is anticipated, assaultive males can monitor and control their use of violence. This finding suggests (as did the Sherman and Berk results) that surveillance is a useful means of diminishing the rate of wife assault with men who have something to lose from another assault conviction. Typically, such men simply avoid conflict with their wives during their probationary period. When probation is over, however, and since they have not yet learned anger management and conflict resolution techniques, we might expect their violence to flare up again. Viewed from this perspective, treatment becomes a means of instilling self-surveillance when long-term surveillance by the criminal justice system becomes a practical impossibility.

Since this initial matched-group evaluation, numerous other evaluations of treatment groups have been performed. Rosenfeld (1992) presented an overview of the results of twenty-six such evaluations, including eleven evaluations of untreated or dropout offenders. For untreated offenders the recidivism rate, according to police reports, goes from 16% at six months (Dutton 1987a), to 20% at one year (Waldo 1988), to 40% at 2.5 years (Dutton 1987a). The overall recidivism for untreated men is 23.4%, for men who dropped out of treatment it is 29%, and for men who complete treatment it is 8.4%. Hence, based on several studies, treatment seems to diminish police measures of recidivism by about 66% (8.4/23.4). This result should be viewed as positive by criminal justice system professionals.

Table 9.3

Rosenfeld's (1992) review of 26 treatment evaluations

	Recidivism by:	
	Wife's report	Police report
Treated	33.0%	8.4%
Dropouts	47.3	29.0
Untreated	n/a	23.4

When we turn to wives' reports of recidivism we find that 33% of the wives of men who completed treatment reported some post-treatment violence, whereas 47.3% of the wives of dropouts reported such violence. (The 16% figure in the Dutton study seems low because we counted only Severe Assaults on the *CTS*, reasoning that they were the ones most likely to be injurious and to require repeat police presence.)

Despite his data, Rosenfeld concluded that 'men arrested but not referred to treatment appear to resume their violent behavior no more frequently than men arrested and treated' (1992:221). It seems to me that his data do not support that negative conclusion. Rosenfeld did err in a few places in his analysis. For example, he presented the recidivism figure in my untreated group as 20% when it was 40% (p. 215), leading to an underestimate of the recidivism rate in untreated men. He also described my untreated group as more treatment-resistant because they had more prior arrests (it was only .8 versus .88 in the two groups) and because some men had been untreated due to extreme resistance and denial (only 8 of 50). These interpretations lead me to be concerned that he may have been trying more to make a case against treatment groups than to objectively read the data. However, despite these criticisms, Rosenfeld is correct in his contention that a serious need exists for a design through which men convicted of wife assault are assigned at random to treatment or non-treatment conditions.

As judges occasionally attach public service conditions to probation orders, a case could be made for participation in an evaluation study as a condition of probation for untreated men. In addition to a randomized design to circumvent the cumbersome matching made necessary in this study, all men entering treatment should undergo thorough psychological assessments. With a large stake in the outcome of treatment groups for wife assaulters, we need to know the conditions under which they are successful and for which men they are most appropriate.

In an attempt to answer this question, Dutton, Bodnarchuk, Kropp, Hart, Ogloff, & Starzomski (1994) assessed sixty-five men treated in the Assaultive Husbands Program, both before and after treatment. The men's self-reports of *BPO* (as described in Chapter 5) correlated significantly with their self-reports of abusiveness post-treatment (+.53, $p < .001$) and with their wives' report of the men's abusiveness (.49, $p < .01$). In fact, 51% of the variance in women's post-treatment reports of abusiveness could be accounted for by the men's *BPO* score. Hence, BPO, a deep-seated aspect of personality, is associated with poor post-treatment prognosis.

However, all is not lost. Not only did average abusiveness (as reported by wives on the *TMWI*) (see Chapter 5) drop significantly after treatment, but the men's *BPO* scores dropped significantly as well! Men who completed the test had average scores of 68 before treatment, 62 after.

Given the limited success of other forms of offender treatment (Shore and Massimo 1979; Gendreau and Ross 1980), some criminal justice officials are generally sceptical about the success of treatment for wife assaulters. They tend to view a false dichotomy between treatment approaches and law-and-order approaches to violence, when in actuality both have the same objective: to prevent repeat violence. As we saw in Chapter 8, incarceration for first-time wife assaulters is very rare – unless the assaults were extremely violent and caused serious injuries. Although 33% to 60% of these men will probably not re-offend (Schulman 1979; Straus 1977a; Sherman and Berk 1984), proponents of treatment groups have argued that wife assaulters require therapeutic intervention in order to alter their habitual methods of dealing with conflict through the use of violence (Ganley 1981).

The results of the studies reviewed by Rosenfeld (1992) tend to support this view and argue, I believe, for arrest/treatment combinations in order to diminish recidivist wife assaults. Through this model, arrest serves both a didactic and a deterrent function in showing the man that wife assault is unacceptable and will be punished by the state. The treatment group then provides the opportunity for the man to learn new responses to the interchanges with his wife that formerly generated violent behavior. In this sense, treatment and law-and-order approaches to wife assault operate symbiotically to reduce future violence. Of course, such interventions will never end the broader problem of wife assault, for, as we have seen, only a small percentage of assaults get as far as criminal justice system intervention and treatment. Treatment groups 'work' for most men who complete them, but they cannot be a panacea for a social problem.

Chapter Summary and Epilogue

In this chapter we have developed a treatment philosophy for wife assaulters that holds men responsible for their use of violence and helps them to analyze and control their anger. We have traced the development of such a cognitive-behavioral treatment program and reviewed evidence for its success, both with men with general anger problems and with wife assaulters.

We have examined the controversy over individual as opposed to family systems approaches to the treatment of abusers and have argued that, since the empirical evidence suggests that individuals with conflict-generating habits transfer them from one family to another (Kalmuss & Seltzer 1984), family systems approaches may occasionally err by emphasizing the current family system while disregarding the history of the relationships between the family's individual members. Detailed historical assessment might allow the detection of individual conflict-generators whose intrapsychic problems manifest themselves interpersonally in the contemporary family. Ignoring this possibility is unfair to other family members in that it makes them share responsibility for the intrapsychic pathology of one dominant member.

Feminist therapy errs in the other direction, viewing all male violence as a result of the systematic domination of women. Feminist therapy calls for treatment which attempts to resocialize men, even though this resocialization may be at odds with their primary socializing milieu and world view. If this is the case, such attempts are likely to backfire. Feminist approaches to therapy seem to assume that because men have greater objective sociopolitical and economic power than do women, their violence is used in the protection of this power. In my therapeutic experience, assaultive males frequently feel completely powerless. That they earn more money than their wives is irrelevant to them. That they feel incapable of living up to the economic demands of raising their families, winning arguments with their wives, fulfilling their goals, or earning as much as their co-workers are what is salient to their views of themselves as powerless. Clearly, there is a vast discrepancy between objective power and subjective feelings of powerlessness (see also Ng 1980).

Anger management-assertiveness treatment falls philosophically into a middle ground between feminist and family systems approaches. It uses a philosophy of personal responsibility that is compatible both with criminal justice philosophy and with the values of the broader culture in which it is nested. In that sense, it is a conservative approach, seeking to change individuals to fit systems rather than seeking to change social systems in general. It is an essentially pragmatic approach, a band-aid that requires buttressing by other therapeutic forms and by constant action for social change.

We have presented a review of the outcome of several such treatment programs. What is sorely needed is a repeated, randomized evaluation. If such an evaluation reaffirmed the results of the studies to date, we would argue strongly for the implementation of arrest/treatment strategies in order to reduce recidivist assault. However, for ethical and practical reasons, such a design is difficult to implement. For example, withholding treatment for men who need it because they fall by chance into a 'control group' is not favoured by therapists, probation officers, or judges and may be featured by the man's defence lawyer should he re-offend.

10
The Future

When we profess to believe in deterrence and to value justice, but refuse
to spend the energy and money required to produce either, we are send-
ing a clear signal that we think safe streets, unlike all other public goods,
can be had on the cheap. We thereby trifle with the wicked, make sport
of the innocent, and encourage the calculators. Justice suffers, and so
do we all.

– J.Q. Wilson, *Thinking About Crime*

How will the current generation's children deal with conflict in their marriages when they reach adulthood? Will they be more violent than contemporary adults? Will incidence rates for wife assault increase during the
next decade? Two lines of analysis converge on these questions. One line
examines the demographic structure of society and predicts how violence
rates may increase or decrease as a result of baby booms and other demographic factors that affect the structure of contemporary and future society. A second line of analysis examines the effects of current family dysfunction on the probability of dysfunction in the next generation. We
know, for example, that approximately 40% of today's children will witness their parents divorce by age sixteen (Bumpass 1984), and that
Levinger's (1966) analysis of court records for divorce applicants found
that 36.8% of the wives cited physical aggression by their husbands. Even
amongst non-divorced families, we know from the surveys reported in
Chapter 1 that 8.7% to 12.6% of families report acts of severe abuse. How
would the witnessing of abuse affect a child? What prognostications can
we make about the adult conflict-resolution behavior of these child witnesses?

Effects on the Child Witness of Observing Violence
In the 1975 US national survey, Straus, Gelles, and Steinmetz (1980)

describe what they call the social heredity of family violence – that is, the learning of violence in the family of origin. In order to ascertain whether such learning occurred, Straus et al. compared husbands whose parents had not been violent towards each other to husbands who reported at least one incident of violence between their parents. Men who had seen parents physically attack each other were almost three times more likely to have hit their own wives during the year of the study than were men who had not seen this. In fact, about one out of three had done so (35%) compared with one out of ten (10.7%) of the men with non-violent parents. These statistics were virtually identical for women. Women whose parents were violent had a much higher rate of hitting their own husbands (26.7%) than did women whose parents were non-violent (8.9%). The scale of violence towards spouses rose steadily with the violence these people observed between their own parents. Sons of the most violent parents had wife beating rates 1000% greater than did those of non-violent parents, and daughters of violent parents had a 600% greater rate of abusing their husbands than did those of non-violent parents.

Straus et al. argue that the family of origin is where people first experience violence and learn its emotional and moral meaning. For most, this experience occurs through being a victim of violence;[1] for others it occurs through the observation of parental violence. Straus et al. describe the unintended lessons of such violence: (1) that those who love you are also those who hit you, (2) that hitting other members of the same famil is morally acceptable, and (3) that violence is permissible when other things don't work. Being hit as a teenager clearly makes people more prone to spouse assault: people who experienced the most punishment as teenagers had spouse-beating rates four times greater than did those whose parents did not hit them. Straus et al. concluded by reporting a double-whammy effect: When people both experience violence from a parent themselves and witness interparental violence, they are five to nine times more likely to be violent than are people who experience neither type of violence.

Rosenbaum and O'Leary (1981) obtained comparison data for twenty violent couples with a group of twenty non-violent couples. The authors reported that abusive husbands were more likely than were non-abusive husbands to have been victimized by parental physical abuse and to have witnessed parental violence. They did not report covariation between the two. The significant between-group difference for witnessing violence occurred regardless of whether they used the wives' reports of husbands' family backgrounds or the husbands' self-reports.

Kalmuss (1984) reviewed prior studies on effects of observing father-mother violence and found mixed results, which she attributed to methodological inconsistencies in the research. Some studies, for example, examined the cognitive consequences of witnessing parental violence (Ulbrich & Huber 1981) rather than effects on violent actions per se. Others failed to distinguish behavioral effects due to victimization from those due to witnessing and also failed to disentangle the two dependent behavioral variables involved: likelihood of aggression and likelihood of victimization.

Furthermore, effects of interparental aggression may be contingent upon the role of the same-sex parent. If children model the behavior of the same-sex parent, we would expect sons to show increased aggression when they witnessed father-mother aggression. We would expect daughters who witnessed such aggression to be at increased risk for victimhood. These effects should be reversed for mother-father aggression. Using the data from the 1975 US national survey (Straus et al. 1980), Kalmuss established that 15.8% of her respondents had witnessed parental hitting and that 62.4% had themselves been hit by parents while in their teens.

By correlating these responses with *CTS* scores for their adult relationships, Kalmuss was able to generate the following findings: witnessing parental hitting and being hit as a teenager are both related to severe husband-wife (and wife-husband) aggression. However, for both types of aggression, the stronger effect comes from witnessing parental hitting (which doubles the odds of husband-wife aggression). As with the Straus et al. (1980) study, Kalmuss reports a double-whammy effect: the odds of husband-wife aggression increase dramatically when sons both observe and are victimized by parental aggression.

Modelling of Aggression

Kalmuss concludes that two types of modelling occur for parental aggression. *Generalized modelling* communicates the acceptability of aggression between family members and increases the likelihood of *any form* of family aggression in the next generation. *Specific modelling* occurs when individuals reproduce the particular types of family aggression to which they were exposed. *Intergenerational modelling*, Kalmuss concludes, involves more specific than generalized modelling, in that severe marital aggression is more strongly related to witnessing parental aggression than it is to being victimized by it.

It is not clear how Kalmuss arrives at the conclusion that witnessing involves the specific more than the general modelling mechanism, especially given her further finding that there is no evidence for sex-specific learning of aggression. Exposure to fathers hitting mothers increases the likelihood of both husband-wife and wife-husband aggression in the next generation – neither is specified by sex. In other words, both sons and daughters are more likely to be victims and perpetrators of violence when they have witnessed parental hitting. This latter finding is consistent with social learning findings that challenge the notion that children are more likely to imitate same-sex parents (Bandura 1973; Hetherington 1965).

As Kalmuss points out, however, her study has two limitations: first, as with most studies of this sort, it is based on retrospective accounts, which may be reconstructed to justify current use of marital aggression; second, the data report on only one member of a current couple, and it is not known whether the results would change as a function of his or her partner's experience with parental violence.

A later study by Kalmuss and Seltzer (1986) partially rectified this latter problem. In this study (cited in Chapter 9), Kalmuss and Seltzer examined continuity in the use of violence across relationships (first and second marriages) and concluded that evidence supported the notion that individual characteristics gave a better account of the use of violence than did current family structure. They also concluded, however, that a repertoire of marital violence was not necessarily rooted in early childhood experience but frequently originated in the first marriage and maintained itself in new relationships.

How can we sum up these findings? The weight of evidence, it seems, suggests that witnessing violence in families of origin strongly increases the odds of using violence in adult relationships. This learning is not sex-specific but occurs about equally for men and women and independently of the sex of the aggressor parent. Self-taught aggression also occurs and carries over to new relationships from that in which it was learned.

Immediate Effects of Witnessing Parental Violence

We do not know, of course, whether the modelling effects described above are examples of simple imitation or whether witnessing interparental violence produces other negative psychological consequences that act as mediating variables for adult aggression. Carlson (1984) estimated that about 3.3. million children in the US witness interparental violence every year. The research of Peter Jaffe and David Wolfe, among others, has indicated a variety of adjustment problems for children who witness violence.

Wolfe, Jaffe, Wilson, and Zak (1985) evaluated the behavioral problems of 198 children from violent and non-violent families. The CTS was used to assess violence, and the Achenbach *Child Behavior Checklist* was used to assess the children's behavioral problems. Half of the children were from transition houses. Interviews with the mothers established whether the children had witnessed violence, but the study did not report scales to indicate the extent of exposure. The amount of violence witnessed had significant effects on diminished social competence and behavioral problems, but this effect was mediated by maternal stress. Over one-quarter of the children assessed had behavioral problems which fell into the clinical range. These children tended to have been exposed to a higher frequency of violence and to have experienced more negative life events than did the others. Additionally, the maternal stress variable accounted for 19% of the variance in child behavior problems.

Jaffe, Wolfe, Wilson, and Zak (1986a) reported that adjustment problems associated with being exposed to interparental violence (defined as having been in visual or auditory range of the parents during violent conflicts at least once in the previous year) seemed more severe for boys than for girls. Boys displayed a higher degree of both externalizing symptoms (e.g., argumentativeness, bullying, temper tantrums) and internalizing symptoms (e.g., withdrawal, attention deficits). General social competence was impaired and all the above problems were significantly associated with the degree of violence witnessed. Girls from abusive homes were described as demonstrating internalizing symptoms related to depression and anxiety. Boys, however, also showed heightened signs of inadequacy, dependency, anxiety, and depression. The authors raised the question of whether these behaviors, in addition to violence, were modelled by abusive fathers.

Jaffe, Wolfe, Wilson, and Zak (1986b) compared victims of child abuse with children who had witnessed interparental violence. The profiles of behavioral problems in the two groups were quite similar. *Child Behavior Checklist* scores indicated that witnessing interparental violence was as harmful as was experiencing physical abuse. However, as the authors point out, common factors, such as family stress, abrupt home changes, inadequate child management, and parental separations, existed for both groups. Also, the abused and the witness samples may have had as much as a 40% overlap. Nonetheless, they conclude that exposure to family violence is a major factor in determining child problem behavior. Interestingly, some of the problem areas identified by Jaffe et al. (1986b) for this sample of children from violent homes, such as exaggerated dependency and impulse control problems, have also been identified as common in populations of wife assaulters (Ganley 1981).

Jaffe, Wolfe, and Wilson (1990) reviewed several studies on the effects of witnessing parental battering and found a constellation of associated behavioral problems in the children. These included lower social competence, shyness, depression, conduct problems (irritability, impulsivity), school phobia, poorer academic performance, and attention deficits. Hilberman and Munson (1977-8) also found a variety of health-related issues for children who had witnessed interparental abuse, including headaches, stomachaches, diarrhoea, ulcers, intestinal difficulties, asthma, enuresis, insomnia, sleepwalking, and nightmares. Many of these trauma symptoms are also found in abusive males (Dutton 1994c).

Dutton (1994b) argued that witnessing abuse and/or experiencing abuse can have two broad effects on the child: first, it can provide the opportunity to model physical aggression as described by Kalmuss (1984), leading to a behavioral repertoire of aggressive actions; second, it can lead to the development of what Dutton (1994b) calls the *abusive personality* – that is, the type of personality described in Chapter 5. Having an abusive personality sets the stage for intimate abusiveness by creating repeated dysphoric states or internal aversive stimuli that one learns to extinguish through abusive explosions (see Figure 5.9).

Of course, not all children who witness or experience abuse become abusive. Other factors somehow interact with these early experiences to determine whether or not the child will grow up to be an abusive adult. And once an adult, cultural and relationship factors continue to interact with the individual's personality style (as we described in Chapter 3 and Chapter 5).

Dating Violence

As Kalmuss (1984) pointed out, many of the conflict resolution strategies used throughout life are developed through trial and error in the first intimate relationship. In this sense, premarital violence, as assessed by levels of violence in dating couples, may be viewed as an omen of things to come. In a review of empirical studies on dating violence, Hotaling and Sugarman (1986) found that about a third of both men and women reported expressing violence during dates. The incidence rates in these studies varied greatly, however, because some took only direct violence as a measure while others assessed both expressed and implied (threatened) violence. Also, as with other areas of intimate violence, it was unclear whether men were more violent (Lane & Gwartney-Gibbs 1985; Makepeace 1983), whether violence was similar across genders (Marshall & Rose 1990), or whether women were more violent (Arias, Samios, & O'Leary 1987; Riggs, O'Leary, & Breslin 1990; Bookwala, Frieze, Smith, & Ryan 1992). Although the more recent, better designed, and larger sample studies have tended to find that women express more violence than do men, it must be remembered that there is usually a considerable difference between the damage resulting from male as opposed to female violence. Therefore, it is possible that female violence may have different intentions than does male violence (e.g., it may not be intended to physically injure or terrify).

Attempts to determine predictors of dating violence have been mixed: on the one hand many of the predictors for wife assault that we examined in Chapter 5 also apply to dating violence. Riggs et al. (1990), for example, found that personality variables that they defined as aggressive personality and dominant personality both contributed strongly to a discriminant function of aggressive and non-aggressive men. But too many studies use what I call *quasi-tautological* variables in their predictions. By this, I mean that the predictor and the criterion variables are too similar. For example, Riggs et al. found that a history of fighting predicted current aggression, and Marshall and Rose (1990) found that use of violence was predicted by receipt of violence.

Tontodonato and Crew (1992) studied dating violence in a sample of 847 college undergraduates in a US midwestern university. For males, the strongest linear correlation with use of violence was parental separation (-.25), followed by drug use (+.20), and approval of violence (+.16). As we have mentioned above, the latter attitudinal measure may be a result of justifying prior violence rather than a predictor per se. Violence in the family of origin was not strongly related to dating violence in this study, although witnessing parent-parent violence was correlated (+.11) with using violence.

Smith and Williams's (1992) study of 1,353 high school students in North Dakota found that students from abusive households showed significantly higher rates of dating violence than did students from non-abusive households. The increases due to abusiveness in the family of origin appeared highest for the more severe forms of violence. Also, severe violence rates for these high schoolers were about five times the general population rate found by Straus et al. (1980).

Bookwala et al. (1992) found that 'receipt of physical violence from one's partner emerged as the largest predictor of expressed dating violence for both men and women' (p. 297). This variables seems quasi-tautological because the predictor variable is practically the same as the dependent variable. What is of greater interest is what generates the violence in these couples in the first place. Could it be predicted before they start to fight?

In the Riggs et al. study the largest pre-relationship contributor to dating violence was personality (aggressiveness, dominance), followed by stressful life events; in the Bookwala et al. study the strongest predictor of male dating violence was adversarial sexual beliefs (but as we have described above, it is not known whether these beliefs were a cause, or developed as a consequence, of conflicted intimate relationships). In the other studies only attitudes and parental treatment were examined, so personality variables do not emerge.

Regardless of explanatory weaknesses in these studies, what is of the greatest importance is the finding that assault rates for dating couples were much higher than were those for the general adult population (described in Chapter 1). Whereas lifetime incidence for couples in the national surveys were in the 19% to 28% range (see Table 1.1.), the rates reported for dating couples are in the 40% to 50% range (Marshall & Rose 1990; Bookwala et al. 1992). Does this finding mean that wife assault rates will increase again in the future? Or are the rates, like most crime indicators, simply reflective of age-determined peaks that will drop as this population ages? In the next section we examine an analysis that takes developmental stage, population demographics, and social learning factors into consideration in order to predict trends in assaultiveness.

Demographic Trends

Turner, Fenn, and Cole (1981) developed a social-psychological analysis of violent behavior that begins with the social learning analysis we developed in Chapter 3. Social learning analyses attempt to explain the development and maintenance of violent habits in *individuals*. To predict changes in incidence rates in *aggregates*, Turner et al. combined their social learning analysis with a demographic analysis.

They argue that certain demographic groups are at risk for various violent crimes. Homicide, for example, is most frequently committed by males between the ages of 18 and 24 (modal age = 21). When structural changes occur in a population, the relative proportion of males falling into this age category can fluctuate. As the number of males falling into the 18- to 24-year category increases, the homicide rate should increase. In North American society a postwar baby boom saw increases in the birth rate for each year from 1947 to 1957, when the birth rate began to decline. Hence, 1957 represents the zenith of a disproportionately large age cohort that was thirty years old in 1987, will be forty in 1997, and so on. Other factors being equal, we should witness increases in crimes associated with high-risk age groups as this disproportionately large cohort matures. As baby boomers reach and pass the age of risk for specific crimes, the rate for those crimes should rise and then fall.

Turner et al. provide demographic analyses of marriage, divorce, homicide, and unemployment that suggest increases in youth violence are greatest when a relatively high proportion of the population falls into the high-risk age category and an economic downturn occurs generating a feeling of relative deprivation in this group. Historically, the last two periods of relative deprivation (1930-5 and 1970-5) demonstrated increased probabilities of homicide.

Turner et al. (1981) reason that young males, ceteris paribus, are likely to have socially learned responses of aggression in response to aversive stressors. Economic downturns occurring just when these males are expected to enter the labour market constitute a major aversive stressor. Hence, population demographics interact with economic indicators, learned behaviors to stress, and age-relevant social expectations (e.g., to get a job) to influence rates of violence. When unemployment is high in general, or when a high percentage of young males are forced out of the labour market by such phenomena as more women entering the work-force, the result is the existence of a large group whose members: (1) are likely to have learned aggression as a response to stress and (2) are currently experiencing economic stress. When a relatively high proportion of males in the high-risk category exists in conjunction with these other two factors, violence rates climb. Turner et al. claim that between 1925 to 1970, homicides (rate/100,000 population) were due to fluctuations in relative deprivation and changing birth rates.

If we examine the demographic profile of wife assaulters based on a variety of studies (Rounsaville 1978; Dutton & Browning 1988; Jaffe & Burris 1982; Sherman & Berk 1984) where the subject populations come from differing sources (e.g., the criminal justice system, wives in shelter houses, self-referred, etc.), the median age for wife assaulters seems to be thirty-one. This means that if we assume marriage rates to be fairly steady, the peak year for wife assault, according to a demographic analysis, should have been 1988. That was the year that the greatest number of at-risk males should have been married. According to Turner et al.'s analysis, the peak of wife-assault incidence in 1988 would have been preceded by an increase caused by annual increases in the proportion of at-risk males and increases in the marriage rate between 1975 and 1985.

A further examination of temporal trends was performed by Grasmick, Blackwell, Bursik, & Mitchell (1993). They conducted two surveys, one in 1982 and the other in 1992, that measured perceived threats of shame, embarrassment, and legal sanctions for 'physically hurting someone on purpose.' In a study somewhat reminiscent of what Dutton, Hart, Kennedy, & Williams (1992) reported in Chapter 8, these authors sampled 350 respondents in Oklahoma City and found that threat of legal sanction did not increase between 1982 and 1992, although legal remedies had strengthened. Perceived shame, on the other hand, did increase, although this was primarily due to age; that is, the adult population had aged as described above, with the baby-boom cohort being more prominent in 1982 and in decline in 1992 (when they were thirty-five or older). Grasmick et al. found whether age had a direct effect on perception of shame for violence (as did being male and being unmarried). Males, unmarried and young, perceived the least shame as a result of violence. This result was essentially duplicated for embarrassment. Unfortunately for our purposes, Grasmick et al. did not specify that it was intimate violence they were assessing, so it is difficult to ascertain how the respondents imagined the scenario to which they replied. Their result underscores, however, the necessity of changing the perception of younger males so that interpersonal violence is perceived as shameful rather than as romantic.

A Comparison of the 1975 and 1985 US National Surveys

In 1985 Straus and Gelles again supervised a US national survey of family violence. A national probability sample of 6,002 households was obtained through telephone interviews conducted by Louis Harris and Associates (Straus & Gelles 1985). The sample criteria were broadened in this survey to include not only married or cohabiting couples but any household with an adult over eighteen who was divorced or separated in the two years prior to the survey. The response rate for this survey was 84%. For the sake of comparability, Straus and Gelles (1985) compared data from an 1985 subsample of 3,520 married/cohabiting couples with their 1975 sample.

As we noted in the previous section, a social demographic analysis would lead to a prediction of an increase in wife assault between 1975 and 1985, as the number of males in the at-risk age category of age thirty-one increases (up to a peak in 1988). However, husband-to-wife violence declined from 1975 to 1985. Rates of husband-wife violence on the Physical Violence Scale of the *CTS* dropped from 12.1 to 11.3, and rates on the Severe Violence Scale dropped from 3.8 to 3.0 (a 21% decrease). There was a slight (non-significant) increase in wife-husband violence. Hence, the data appear to contradict the prediction made by social demographers.

However, prior to disconfirming social demographic theory, we should consider some alternative explanations for the 1975 to 1985 results. Straus and Gelles (1985) point out that the 1975 survey was a face-to-face interview, and that the 1985 survey was a telephone interview. Studies comparing telephone to in-person interviewing (Groves & Kahn 1979) indicate that major differences in results rarely occur as a function of the method used. However, Straus and Gelles speculate that respondents would feel freer to report the issue of family violence to an anonymous telephone interviewer than to an in-person interviewer. This should lead to increases in reporting and, hence, if we accept Straus and Gelles's argument, suggests that the obtained decrease may have been even larger than what appeared in the data (to offset the expected increase generated by the shift in method). Unfortunately, we do not know for certain what the effect of the shift in method may have been. One could speculate that if rapport is established in an in-person interview, freedom to report may increase. We have found in interviews with wives of clients for court-mandated therapy that incidence reporting increases once trust and rapport are established.

A second methodological difference is that the telephone survey produced a 20% higher completion rate than did the 1975 in-person survey. If we assume that people who refuse to participate may be more violent than those who do participate, then the telephone survey screened out fewer violent people and correspondingly should have produced increased incidence rates. Again, if this is true, the decline obtained may under-represent the true decline.

Unfortunately, these results of methodological differences are based on speculation. At this point, the safest conclusion may be that the 21% decrease found in the 1985 survey is far larger than could be accounted for by methodological differences in in-person and telephone surveys (Groves & Kahn 1979). A third US national survey was conducted in 1992 (Straus & Kantor 1994). This survey found a continuation of the 'trend' established between 1975 and 1985. That is, severe assaults by husbands continued to decrease from a rate of 38 (per thousand) in 1975 to 30 in 1985 to 19 in 1992. The authors controlled for age, SES, and ethnic composition, so these variables could be ruled out as 'causes' of the continued drop. It is not known, however, whether the drop constitutes a reporting effect or an actual change in incidence. Why then, contrary to the prediction of social demographers, might wife assault have decreased in the last decade?

From Societal Indicators to Individual Pathology

Attempting to predict how an individual will behave based on aggregate socioeconomic or demographic indicators has been termed the *ecological fallacy* by Dooley and Catalano (1984). In extending the work of psychologist Barbara Dohrenwend, Dooley and Catalano have examined the impact of aggregate indicators on unemployment, economic stress, and so forth on individual pathology. Their interest was sparked by the uncritical linking of unemployment rates with increases in suicide, homicide, and psychiatric admissions.

In reviewing the literature on panel studies that address the issue of change in symptoms over time as a function of job loss or length of unemployment, Dooley and Catalano found very mixed results. Typically, job loss is followed by an increase in symptoms (e.g., health problems, mental health problems). However, several studies found no clear effects, and some found counterintuitive improvements. The majority of studies that did find worsening of symptoms found relatively modest associations between economic stressors and symptoms. Catastrophic outcomes, such as suicide or psychiatric-admission, were extremely rare.

Dooley and Catalano devised a cross-level approach to studying the issue that allowed them to divide the variability in an individual-level disorder measure into several possible sources: (1) pre-existing individual characteristics (age, sex, social economic status, etc.), (2) non-economic stressful life events, (3) stressful economic life events, and (4) the economic environment at the aggregate level as well as all interactions between (1), (2), (3), and (4).

Dooley and Catalano conducted a series of trend surveys by telephone over a five-year period with a minimum of 500 respondents per survey. In total, over 8,000 respondents answered their questionnaire from 1978 to 1982. The surveys included comprehensive measures of stressful events and symptoms at two different times for each subject. The impact of the economy on symptoms was extremely moderate, to say the least. The best predictor of symptoms at Time 2 was symptoms at Time 1. And when the variance in Time 2 symptoms accounted for by Time 1 symptoms was partialled out, economic life events accounted for only 1% of the remaining variance. Dooley and Catalano concluded that the economy is related to symptoms by more than one pathway. A poor economic climate has a small direct effect on symptoms primarily for those in the workforce. It also has a small indirect effect in that it creates an increase in the number of undesirable economic events for middle-status persons. These undesirable economic events are fairly strongly related to symptoms.

The implications of Dooley and Catalano's analysis for wife assault are as follows: Demographic and economic factors probably are not good predictors of wife assault incidence rates. More sophisticated causal models will need to be developed in order to identify variables that may moderate or enhance the impact of sociodemographic or economic variables on assaultive behavior. At present we have not empirically established what such moderating variables might be, although our hunch is that two candidates would be ontogenetically learned conflict-resolution habits and microsystem features, such as subculture membership. At present, very little is known about the interaction of the abusive personality with sociodemographic factors. However, with regard to microsystem features, the increase in women in the workforce suggests a trend towards diminished economic inequality between men and women, and, as Coleman and Straus (1986) have shown, relatively egalitarian marriages tend to be less violent than do non-egalitarian marriages.

Straus and Gelles (1985) make the argument that raising public consciousness about family violence may also lead to decreased incidence. They argue that child abuse, which shows the greatest increase in public acceptance as a serious social problem, also shows the greatest decrease in incidence from 1975 to 1985. This increased awareness both influences the personal definition of what constitutes unacceptable behavior and the perceived consequences for transgressions. This latter factor, which we dealt with in an earlier chapter, includes the subjective perception of punishment and, by implication, notions of general deterrence. Publicity surrounding new police policy for wife assault has occurred in many US states and Canadian provinces during the last decade. To date, no systematic assessment of the impact of this policy on the perceptions and behavior of at-risk males has been made, although such an assessment is clearly important.

The Community Response to Wife Assault
We have argued that criminal justice system policy, no matter how well implemented, can only deal with a small proportion of wife assault cases, and that, when men become marginalized, criminal justice system responses have diminished deterrence value. We have also argued that values such as family privacy place a limit on how involved the state can be in detecting family violence. Some strategy is needed that protects family privacy while maximizing our ability to prevent wife assault.

Some examples of new prevention strategies are beginning to surface. Jaffe, Sudermann, Reitzel, and Killip (1992) reported the results of a large-scale primary prevention program for high school students. The program included an intervention (i.e., a large group auditorium presentation, including videos on wife assault and speakers from the police department, knowledgeable professionals such as individuals from a treatment program for batterers and local transition houses, an abuse survivor, and a presentation by a local theatre company). Myths and facts about wife assault were addressed in the auditorium presentation. Classroom discussion was then facilitated by professionals from counselling centres (for women, children, and men), the police, and woman's shelters. The entire intervention comprised one and a half hours for the auditorium presentation and one hour for the classroom discussion. Students' attitudes, knowledge, and behavioral intentions were assessed prior to the intervention, immediately afterwards, and six weeks later. Significant, positive attitudes, knowledge, and behavioral changes were found post-test. The majority of these were maintained at a delayed follow-up.

Sex differences, which the authors attributed to male defensiveness, existed (although the bulk of the differences reported had to do with power-sharing in relationships and could be interpreted as differential gender interest). Both males and females reported an equal likelihood of intervening with an abusive male friend. Also of interest was the authors' report that a small group of male students showed a backlash effect (negative responses to the intervention). The authors speculate that this group may already have been behaving abusively and recommended a primary prevention program that would begin before adolescence. I would think that the members of this group might also be prime candidates for a secondary intervention program. In other words, these are the boys who might be considered at risk for long-term repeat abusiveness. It is in this very area (secondary prevention) that our policies are weakest. We do not know what to do between primary (for everybody) and tertiary (for those who have already offended) prevention. It is at this point that violence prevention and civil liberties clash. A way has to be found to provide these boys with positive role models for intimacy.

Hospital programs are another method of community involvement. Since the groundbreaking work of Stark, Flitcraft, and Frazier (1979), it has become evident that hospital emergency wards see a lot of battered women. Many cities have developed programs to sensitize emergency-ward personnel so that the detection of battering-induced trauma may be improved. Grunfeld (1993) reports the results of one such program at Vancouver General Hospital. Such programs can be another point of community entry into domestic violence.

Churches are another source of potential community contact, although, as Johnson (1992) discovered, many denominations will experience ambivalence towards addressing family violence issues. Over 80% of ministers surveyed indicated that the mass media were their main sources of information regarding domestic violence. Martin (1989) found significant variation in the clergy's reports of incidence of spouse-abuse counselling. Although different counselling practices could account for some of this variation, Martin raises the question of whether reported variation correlates with denominational attitudes towards family violence. Clergy who reported giving advice provided information about shelters and treatment groups, and they suggested calling the police if the violence recurred.

A Last Word

The future of wife assault is unclear. On the negative side are the disturbing rates of violence in dating relationships. Given the enormous difficulties involved in generating social change, the decrease in general rates from 1975 to 1992 provides some optimism. One would like to see further decreases reported in a 1995 survey.

In fifteen years, family violence has infiltrated public consciousness as a legitimate social problem, and this phenomenon, in and of itself, may serve to make battered women feel that they are not alone (and not the cause) of their husbands' violence. In 1982 a man in our treatment group appeared on local television and described his problem with violence towards his wife. By so doing, he enabled a private behavior to be identified as a public problem.

It is clear from contrasting crime victim surveys with conflict tactics surveys that many victims of wife assault still do not define the violence committed on them as criminal or as requiring state intervention. The assumption made by many battered women that husband-wife violence is particular to their relationships leaves them with a sense of personal blame vis-à-vis their own victimization. Publicizing wife assault as a social problem diminishes this tendency towards self-blame. It brings wife assault out of the closet, allowing both victims and aggressors to accept it as a problem behavior capable of modification. This process diminishes the terrifying isolation that constitutes the everyday existence of both victims and aggressors.

On the other hand, the data from the dating violence studies indicate that much work still needs to be done with a younger generation that appears to be violence-prone. The type of primary prevention work done by Jaffe et al. (1992) and reported above is a start. I believe that we need to discover an effective secondary prevention program for boys at risk in order to supplement this work. When we recall that a small percentage of men with a discernable abusiveness profile are responsible for a large amount of repeat abuse throughout their lifetimes (see Chapters 1 through 5), the need for stronger secondary prevention becomes obvious.

In this book we attempt to develop a perspective on wife assault that is essentially social psychological. We present some paradoxes about men who assault their wives: although they have a number of features in common (e.g., strong motives for power, poor assertiveness, exaggerated anxieties about control and intimacy), they also present great variation in their individual etiologies. And although they are aggressors, they are also victims – victims of their past exposure to violence and their present alienation from themselves. We have attempted to apply these same standards to the analysis of battered women: they are not masochistic – they do not remain because they enjoy being victimized by violence.

Women use violence as much as do men (but with a much less destructive effect), and some of the same social factors – particularly observation of interparental violence – influence the use of violence in both women and men. Extreme power imbalances in current adult relationships make both men and women more violent. Male violence is by far the greater social problem because it has more severe consequences; but, in explaining the development of violent behavior, in many instances the same rules, with the same results, apply to women.

This conclusion will not sit well with people who hold tightly to some currently popular perspectives on wife assault. Feminists, in particular, may object to these conclusions – but they should not. Feminism has long argued that socialization shapes the behavior of males and females. I have argued that social factors do indeed shape both male and female violence. Both males and females can learn to be violent through observation and both react violently to power imbalances in primary relationships.

Sociobiologists might perceive my approach to the origins of wife assault as a dismissal of their position. Although I do not dismiss all that sociobiological theory has to offer, I am convinced that the overwhelming weight of evidence supports the view that violence in intimate relationships is a learned phenomenon, and that it has more to do with attachment and the metaphorical meaning we read into primary relationships than it does with contributions to the gene pool.

Police and criminal justice officials may feel I have been too critical of their practices, but I stand by my conclusion that police arrest rates for wife assault are too low and that arrests are made for the wrong reasons. If the police want to be professional in their orientation to their job, they must consider factors that achieve objectives (such as diminishing recidivist violence) rather than personal factors (the demeanour of a husband on a disturbance call) in their decisionmaking.

Arrest-treatment combinations are not a complete solution to the problem of wife assault, but they are probably the best solution we currently have. Arrest remains the primary means available to the state to keep wife assaulters from denying that they have behavioral problems with consequences for others. Treatment should ensure that an assaulter recognize the unacceptability of his behavior and that he be provided with the means to change it. And, if it is to be successfully integrated into the criminal justice process, then treatment should be based on a philosophy that is consistent with criminal justice views of personal responsibility.

Unless it wants to engage in a losing tug-of-war between socializing influences, treatment should also recognize the flexibility, or lack thereof, of the cultural parameters within which attitude and behavior change can be effected for each individual.

Treatment programs should try to obtain objectives that include the non-violent expression of anger, the recognition that intimate relationships require an interdependent orientation towards the distribution of power, and the recognition that assaultive behavior will impact on children. Most assaultive males feel a sense of guilt about their use of violence and do not want their children to be violent.

Eventually, all social institutions must address the problem of family violence. Churches, mosques, and synagogues must address it openly and directly. Schools must teach the art of non-violent conflict resolution. And the media must act responsibly in their depiction of the many kinds of violence they present to their audiences.

Finally, we have tried to convey a sense of the enormous research still needed in the area of wife assault. We need to know more about the attributions made by aggressive males about the actions of others and how these attributions fuel anger and violence. We need to know for whom therapy is (or is not) effective and how subjective perceptions and beliefs of assaultive males both sustain their habits of violence and provide a means for change. This research requires collaboration amongst psychologists, sociologists, feminists, and criminologists; and it should be integrated around a common practical theme – how best to stop wife assault.

Notes

Chapter 2: Explanations for Wife Assault

1 This conclusion, of course, is based on the assumption that factors from each level directly influence the likelihood of wife assault. As we shall see in Chapter 7, however, the path from societal 'causes' to individual reactions is complicated by indirect causal chains. Causal modelling techniques such as LISREL (Joreskog 1979) make the statistical assessment of such indirect pathways possible and may be required for the eventual test of nested ecological models.

Chapter 3: The Social Psychology of the Wife Assaulter: The Theory

1 Portions of 'Severe Wife Assault and Deindividuated Violence' are reprinted, by permission, from *Victimology* (1982), *7*(13): 1-4.

Chapter 4: The Social Psychology of the Wife Assaulter: The Research Studies

1 Data for fifty-four of the men reported here were collected by Jim Browning and constituted his doctoral dissertation. An earlier report on these fifty-four men is reported in Dutton and Browning (1988). The author, Brenda Gerhard, Andrew Gotowiecz, Hamida Hajee, Sally Harrison, Stephen Hart, and Catherine Strachan collected and analyzed data on the additional assaultive males.

2 Browning and Dutton (1986) found that wives of assaultive husbands report about twice as much husband-wife violence as do their husbands (for Serious Violence Subscale items on the Straus *CTS*). Except where weapons are implicated, husband-wife correlations on specific items are in the +.32 to +.57 range, indicating considerable disparity in recall of violence.

3 Originally, the pictures used represented a variety of gender relationships (male-male, male-female, female-female). The results of this original test indicated that between-group differences on the need for power seemed to occur only when the pictures depicted male-female relationships (Browning 1983). A second experiment was run (Dutton & Strachan 1987a) using five male-female pictures, in which both the setting and relationship were ambiguous. It is the results from this latter experiment that we report below.

4 The raters demonstrated agreement with expert scoring (rho = .87, category agreement on power imagery = .93) on 60 test stories (Winter 1973).

5 The Bonferroni method of correcting alpha for experiment-wise error was used (see Harris 1975).

6 For a more detailed report on these findings, see Dutton and Strachan (1987a).

7 For a complete description of this experiment, see Browning (1983) or Dutton and Browning (1988).

8 The power variable was chosen as a between-subjects variable because it would appear less realistic if the actors were to switch from dominant to submissive for a given viewer than to be merely arguing over different issues. In addition, since there are only two power conditions (either male or female dominant), this approach allows for a more efficient use of participants.

9 Since these analyses all involved at least one repeated measures factor of the univariate ANOVA to test the assumption of symmetry (i.e., that the orthogonal polynomials for any within factor were independent and had equal variance [see Anderson 1958; Dixon, Brown, Engleman, Frane, Hill, Jennrich, & Joporek 1981]). If the sphericity test were significant, adjustments would be made to the within-factor degrees of freedom via a procedure outlined by Greenhouse and Geisser (1959).

10 Where noted, $p < .01$ or more.

11 Where noted, $p < .01$ or more.

12 Where noted, $p < .01$ or more.

13 Where noted, $p < .01$ or more.

14 The Assaultive Husbands' Project is a treatment program for wife assaulters which has operated in Vancouver since 1982 under funding from the Ministry of the BC Attorney-General.

15 Where noted, $p < .01$ or more.

16 Where noted, $p < .01$ or more.

17 $X^2 = 4.07$, $df = 4$, n.s.

18 Where noted, $p < .01$ or more.

19 Where noted, $p < .01$ or more.

Chapter 5: The Abusive Personality

1 Oldham et al. (1985) report on the scale's intrascale consistency, interscale relationships, its relationship to BPD differential diagnosis, and the application of the scale to differing theories of borderline personality organization and its DSM-IIIR Axis 2 definition. Cronbach's alpha for the BPO subscales are Identity Diffusion .92, Primitive Defenses .87, Reality Testing .84. We replicated these scores in our current sample. We also correlated BPO scores with the C scale of the Millon Clinical Multiaxial Inventory (version 2) (MCMI-II) as a validity check (Millon 1981).

2 Siegel reports the results of a factor analysis of this scale and its reliability, of its subscales (alphas = .51 to .83), and of the scale as a whole (alpha equal to .84 and .89 for two separate samples). The scale was validated by correlation with other, conceptually similar, anger inventories.

3 Analysis of the internal consistency of the five subscales indicated reasonable reliability with an average subscale alpha of .71 and a total alpha for the TSC-33 of .89 (Briere & Runtz 1989).

4 Factor analyses support the inclusion of these two factors. In the sample considered in this study, Cronbach's alpha for the dominance/isolation subscale was .82, and for the emotional/verbal subscale it was .93.

5 The EMBU was originally developed in Sweden and has been translated and widely used with English-speaking subjects (Gerslma, Emmelkamp, & Arrindell 1990). The psychometric properties of the English version were developed by Ross, Campbell, and Clayter (1982).

6 The *RSQ* was created from items drawn from Hazan and Shaver's (1987) attachment measure, Bartholomew and Horowitz's (1991) Relationship Questionnaire, and Collins and Read's (1990) Adult Attachment Scale. The *RSQ* attachment scores show convergent validity with interview ratings of the four attachment patterns (Griffin & Bartholomew 1994).

Chapter 6: Effects on the Victim

1 Kalmuss (1984) reported an analysis of Straus et al.'s (1980) national survey data which demonstrated that witnessing father-mother violence increased the likelihood of daughters being both victims and perpetrators of violence in their own marriages (the same was true for sons). Kalmuss argues that intergenerational transmission of marital aggression is not sex-specific, and she questions the assumption that children would be more likely to model the same-sex parent than they would the opposite-sex parent. Kalmuss's analysis raises important questions about modelling effects. Why, for example, would some girls become victims and others become perpetrators of violence, when both have witnessed father-mother violence? Observational influences may interact with other ontogenetically developed traits or habits to produce eventual behavioral outcomes of witnessing violence.

Chapter 7: Traumatic Bonding

1 Kitson (1982) reports the psychometric qualities of the scale, including an alpha of .80.
2 Since the composite scale was new, we performed an item-whole correlation for each item and retained items that had correlations over .55 ('I feel I will never get over the breakup'). Chronbach's alpha for the entire 20-item scale was .92. 3.
3 The *Rosenberg Self Esteem Scale* (1965) has reported alphas of .77 and .88 (Robinson, Shaver, & Wrightsman 1991).

Chapter 8: The Criminal Justice Response to Wife Assault

1 Estimates of arrest rates obtained through victim interviews or police reports vary even more and seem less reliable than do observational studies. Roy's (1977) survey of women in crisis centres revealed that 90% reported no arrest by police when one was requested. However, Schulman (1979), in his victim survey, found that victims reported a 41% arrest rate by police (with an additional 16% rate of police obtaining a warrant). Schulman's estimate is based on a rather small *n* of seventy-six incidents, however.

Bell (1985) found that 45% of 128,171 domestic disputes reported to Ohio police between 1979 and 1981 resulted in injuries or death to the victims. Offenders were arrested in only 14% of these cases. Bell's data base consisted of incidents reported to police (and sheriffs), and, although it is not clear from his methodology section, these incidents were presumably recorded on a report form which he then sampled. Bell's data are consistent with the observational studies described (albeit more extreme in the discrepancy between injured victims and arrests).

Similarly, Berk and Loseke (1980) reported a 38.5% arrest rate for 262 domestic disturbances reported by police. However, when their entire unrefined sample is considered to include incomplete police reports and so on, the arrest rate drops to 14%. Since selection factors influence what incidents get reported by police, we believe that observational studies constitute the best measure of incidence of victim injuries.

2 Police and other criminal justice professionals occasionally argue that aggressive prosecution of wife assault is futile because the victims will not cooperate with the prosecution. There is a kernel of truth to this complaint. The court study by the Battered Women's Project of the Seattle City Attorney's Office (Lerman 1981) found that 596 wife assault charges led to 495 convictions (an 83% conviction rate) when the victims cooperated. When the victims did not cooperate, the conviction rate fell to 27.5% (143/520). What this statistic does not tell us, however, is what role the criminal justice system can play in generating victim cooperation.

Dutton (1981a), in reviewing innovative court programs for wife assault, found that in jurisdictions where the prosecution operated to maximize the protection of the victim (such as in Santa Barbara, California) and to dispel her fears and confusions about the criminal justice process, victim cooperation with the prosecution was 90%.

3 It appears difficult to reconcile this drop in recidivism with the Wilt and Breedlove (1977) finding that 90% of subsequent felonious wife assault charges in Kansas City occurred in households visited at least once by police (who merely separated the assailant and victim on the prior occasion). Wilt and Breedlove's study has been interpreted as evidence that recidivism with increasing severity is likely when mere separation occurs, whereas Sherman and Berk generate a steep drop in recidivism based solely on separation.

Wilt and Breedlove's data are retrospective, working backwards from a pool of eventual felonious wife assault cases and, therefore, cannot generate a baseline estimate of recidivism. On the other hand, Sherman and Berk's data, with the ambiguous nature of the two-week follow-up interviews, may underestimate recidivism rates when the assailant does not suspect surveillance by authorities.

4 Coleman and Straus (1986) found that violence was greatest in husband-dominant and wife-dominant families, less in shared-responsibility families, and least in egalitarian families. Fagan's power equalization hypothesis might work for families that were husband-dominant before police intervention, but it does not explain intervention effects on wife-dominant families.

Chapter 9: The Treatment of Wife Assault

1 This perspective raises, of course, the thorny issue of who has the responsibility of punishing the male for his violence. Perhaps a less problematic question is whether the victim is responsible for her own future safety. If one answers in the affirmative, then she is responsible for self-protective actions such as leaving, taking refuge, and so on. For the variety of reasons we have described in Chapters 6, 7, and 8, these options are not always available to battered women.

2 If he does not live up to his responsibility, we tend to hold him culpable; he is to blame. We make a negative judgment about his lack of responsibility. As therapists we try to teach increased self-control and responsibility for violence to clients. The limit of personal responsibility is one's perception of choice. If a battered woman perceives that her husband will kill her if she leaves, we do not blame her for staying in an abusive relationship. She does not perceive that she has a choice. This may also be true for the assaultive male: he may not perceive that he has a choice. Altering his perceptions makes that choice more visible and, hence, increases his responsibility. If a man refuses to get help for a chronic abuse problem, then regardless of what caused the problem originally, he is to blame for his refusal to reform.

3 Male clients in Deschner's study reported post-treatment decreases in dominance on the Taylor-Johnson scale, while female clients reported decreases for depression.

Chapter 10: The Future

1 Straus et al. (1980) report that physical punishment of children is commonplace and seems to have been consistently so (based on retrospective reports) for the last two generations. Grandparents seem to have hit parents as much (37.3%) as those parents now hit their children.

References

Abelson, R.P. & Levi, A. (1985). Decision-making and decision theory. In G. Lindzey & E. Aronson (eds.), *Handbook of social psychology* (3rd ed.). Vol. 1 (pp. 231-310). New York: Random House

Achenbach, T.M. & Edelbrock, C.S. (1983). *Manual for the child behavior checklist and revised child behavior profile.* Burlington, VT: University Associates in Psychiatry

Adams, D. (1988). Treatment models of men who batter: A profeminist analysis. In K. Yllo & M. Bograd (eds.), *Feminist perspectives on wife abuse* (pp. 176-99). Beverly Hills: Sage

Adler, A. (1966). The psychology of power. *Journal of Individual Psychology, 22,* 166-72

Ainsworth, M.D.S., Blehar, M.C., Waters, E., & Wall, S. (1978). *Patterns of attachment: A psychological study of the strange situation.* Hillsdale, NJ: Erlbaum

Akiskal, H.S. (1992). Delineating irritable and hyperthymic variants of the cyclothymic temperament. *Journal of Personality Disorders, 6*(4), 326-42

Alexander, P.C. (1992). Application of attachment theory to the study of sexual abuse. *Journal of Consulting and Clinical Psychology, 60*(2), 185-95

Allen, J.G. & Hamnsher, J. H. (1974). The development and validation of a test of emotional styles. *Journal of Consulting and Clinical Psychology, 42*(5), 663-8

Allen, V. & Greenberger, D. (1978). An aesthetic theory of school vandalism. In E. Wenk & N. Harlow (eds.), *School crime and disruption.* Davis, CA: Responsible Action (International Dialogue Press)

American Psychiatric Association. (1981). *Diagnostic and statistical manual of the mental disorders* (3rd edition). Washington, DC: Author

– (1987). *Diagnostic and statistical manual of the mental disorders* (3rd edition, revised). Washington, DC: Author

Amsel, A. (1958). Role of frustrative non-reward in non-continuous reward situations. *Psychological Bulletin, 55,* 102-19

Andenaes, J. (1974). *Punishment and deterrence.* Ann Arbor: University of Michigan Press

Anderson, T.W. (1958). *An introduction to multivariate statistical analysis.* New York: Wiley

Aquirre, B.E. (1984). Why do they return? Abused wives in shelters. Paper presented at the Second National Family Violence Researchers Conference, Durham, NH

Arias, I., Samios, M., & O'Leary, K.D. (1987). Prevalence and correlates of physical aggression during courtship. *Journal of Interpersonal Violence, 2,* 82-90

Babcock, J.C., Waltz, J., Jacobson, N., & Gottman, J.M. (1993). Power and violence: The relation between communication patterns, power discrepancies, and domestic violence. *Journal of Consulting and Clinical Psychology, 61*(1), 40-50

Bandura, A. (1973). *Aggression: A social learning analysis*. Englewood Cliffs, NJ: Prentice-Hall
– (1977). Self-efficacy: Towards a unified theory of behavioral change. *Psychological Review, 84*, 191-215
– (1979). The social learning perspective: Mechanisms of aggression. In H. Toch (ed.), *Psychology of crime and criminal justice* (pp. 298-336). New York: Holt, Rinehart & Winston
Bard, M. (1971). Iatrogenic violence. *Police Chief, 38* (January), 16-17
Bard, M. & Zacker, J. (1974). Assaultiveness and alcohol use in family disputes: Police perceptions. *Criminology, 12*(3), 281-92
Bard, M., Zacker, J., & Rutter, E. (1972). *Police family crisis intervention and conflict-management: An action research analysis* (Report No. NI 70-068). New York: US Department of Justice
Baron, R.A. (1971a). Aggression as a function of magnitude of victim's pain cues, level of prior anger arousal, and aggressor-victim similarity. *Journal of Personality and Social Psychology, 18*, 48-54
– (1971b). Magnitude of victim's pain cues and level of prior anger arousal as determinants of adult aggressive behavior. *Journal of Personality and Social Psychology, 17*, 236-43
Bartholomew, K. (1990). Avoidance of intimacy: An attachment perspective. *Journal of Social and Personal Relationships, 7*, 147-78
Bartholomew, K. & Horowitz, L.M. (1991). Attachment styles among young adults: A test of a four-category model. *Journal of Personality and Social Psychology, 61*(2), 226-44
Bateson, G. (1972). *Steps to an ecology of mind*. New York: Ballantine
Baum, A., Fleming, R., & Singer, J.E. (1983). Coping with victimization by technological disaster. *Journal of Social Issues, 39*(2), 119-40
Baum, A. & Singer, J.E. (1980). Applications of personal control. *Advances in environmental psychology*. Vol. 2. Englewood Cliffs, NJ: Erlbaum
Beasley, R. & Stoltenberg, C.D. (1992). Personality characteristics of male spouse abusers. *Professional Psychology: Research and Practice, 23*, 310-17
Beck, A.T. (1967). *Depression: Clinical, experimental, and theoretical aspects*. New York: Harper & Row
– (1976). *Cognitive theory and the emotional disorders*. New York: International Universities Press
Becker, E. (1973). *The denial of death*. Glencoe, IL: Free Press
Bell, D.J. (1985). Domestic violence victimization: A multiyear perspective. Paper presented at the American Society of Criminology Meeting, San Diego, CA
Belsky, J. (1980). Child maltreatment: An ecological integration. *American Psychologist, 35*(4), 320-35
Belsky, J. & Nezworski, T. (1988). Clinical implications of attachment. In J. Belsky & T. Nezworski (eds.), *Clinical implications of attachment* (pp. 3-17). Hillsdale, NJ: Erlbaum
Bennett-Sandler, G. (1975). Structuring police organizations to promote crisis management programs. Paper presented at the Symposium on Crisis Management in Law Enforcement, National Conference of Christians and Jews and California Association of Police Trainers, Berkeley, California
Berk, R.A., Berk, S.F., Loseke, D.R., & Rauma, D. (1981). Mutual combat and other family violence myths. In D. Finkelhor, R.J. Gelles, G.T. Hotaling, & M.A. Straus (eds.), *The dark side of families: Current family violence research* (pp. 197-212). Beverly Hills, CA: Sage
Berk, S.F. & Loseke, D.R. (1980). 'Handling' family violence: Situational determinants of police arrest in domestic disturbances. *Law and Society Review, 15*(2), 317-46

Berlyne, D.E. (1967). Arousal and reinforcement. In D. Levine (ed.), *Nebraska Symposium on Motivation* (pp. 1-132). Lincoln: University of Nebraska Press

Bettelheim, B. (1943). Individual and mass behavior in extreme situations. *Journal of Abnormal and Social Psychology, 38,* 417-52

Bigelow, R. (1972). The evolution of co-operation, aggression and self-control. In J.K. Cole & D.D. Jensen (eds.), *Nebraska symposium on motivation* (pp. 1-58). Lincoln: University of Nebraska Press

Black, D. (1979). Dispute settlement by the police. Unpublished manuscript, Yale University

Blackstone, W. (1987). *Commentaries on the laws of England.* in E. Pleck, Domestic tyranny: The making of American social policy against family violence from colonial times to the present. New York: Oxford University Press

Bland, R. & Orn, H. (1986, March). Family violence and psychiatric disorder. *Canadian Journal of Psychiatry, 31,* 129-37

Blood, R. Jr. & Wolfe, D. (1960). *Husbands and wives: The dynamics of married living.* Glencoe, IL: Free Press

Blumstein, A., Cohen, J., & Nagin, D. (1978). *Deterrence and incapacitation: Estimating the effects of criminal sanctions on crime rates.* Washington, DC: National Academy of Sciences

Bologna, M.J., Waterman, C.K. & Dawson, L.J. (1987). Violence in gay male and lesbian relationships: Implications for practitioners and policy makers. Paper presented at the Third National Conference of Family Violence Researchers, Durham, NH

Bookwala, J., Frieze, I.H., Smith, C, & Ryan, K. (1992). Predictors of dating violence: A mulitvariate analysis. *Violence and Victims, 7*(4), 297-311

Bower, G.H. (1990). Awareness, the unconscious and repression: An experimental psychologist's perspective. In J. Singer (ed.), *Repression and dissociation: Implications for personality theory, psychopathology and health* (pp. 209-31). Chicago: University of Chicago Press

Bower, S.A. & Bower, G.H. (1976). *Asserting yourself: A practical guide for positive change.* Reading, MA: Addison-Wesley

Bowker, L.H. (1983). *Beating wife beating.* Lexington, MA: Lexington

Bowlby, J. (1969). *Attachment and loss.* Vol. 1, *Attachment.* New York: Basic

– (1973). *Attachment and loss.* Vol. 2, *Separation.* New York: Basic

– (1977). The making and breaking of affectional bonds. *British Journal of Psychiatry, 130,* 201-10

– (1980). *Attachment and loss.* Vol. 3, *Loss, sadness and depression.* New York: Basic

Briere, J. & Runtz, M. (1989). The trauma symptom checklist (TSC-33): Early data on a new scale. *Journal of Interpersonal Violence, 4*(2), 151-62

Bronfenbrenner, U. (1977). Toward an experimental ecology of human development. *American Psychologist, 32*(6), 513-31

– (1979). *The ecology of human development.* Cambridge, MA: Harvard University Press

Browne, A. (1987). *When battered women kill.* New York: Free Press

– (1992). Violence against women by male partners. *American Psychologist, 48*(10), 1077-87

Browne, A. & Dutton, D.G. (1990). Escape from violence: Risks and alternatives for abused women. In R. Roesch, D.G. Dutton, & V.F. Sacco (eds.), *Family violence: Perspectives on treatment, research and policy* (pp. 67-92). Burnaby, BC: Institute on Family Violence

Browne, A. & Williams, K. (1989). Exploring the effects of resource availability and the likelihood of female-perpetrated homicides. *Law and Society Review, 23*(1), 75-94

Browning, J.J. (1983). Violence against intimates: Toward a profile of the wife assaulter.

Unpublished doctoral dissertation, University of British Columbia, Vancouver, BC
– (1984). *Stopping the violence: Canadian programmes for assaultive men.* Ottawa: Health and Welfare Canada
Browning, J.J. & Dutton, D.G. (1986). Assessment of wife assault with the conflict tactics scale: Using couple data to quantify the differential reporting effect. *Journal of Marriage and the Family, 48,* 375-9
Bugenthal, M.D., Kahn, R.L., Andrews, F., & Head, K.B. (1972). *Justifying violence: Attitudes of American men.* Ann Arbor, MI: Institute for Social Research
Bulman, R.J. & Wortman, C. (1977). Attributions of blame and coping in the 'real world.' Severe accident victims react to their lot. *Journal of Personality and Social Psychology, 35,* 351-363
Bumpass, L. (1984). Children and marital disruption: A replication and update. *Demography, 21,* 7-82
Burgess, R. (1978). Child abuse: A behavioral analysis. In B. Lakey & A. Kazdin (eds.), *Advances in child clinical psychology.* New York: Plenum
Burgess, A.W. (1983). Rape Trauma Syndrome. *Behavioral Sciences and the Law, 1*(3), 97-113
Burman, B., Margolin, G., & John, R.S. (1993). America's angriest home videos: Behavioral contingencies observed in home reenactments of marital conflict. *Journal of Consulting and Clinical Psychology, 61*(1), 28-39
Burt, M.R. (1980). Cultural myths and supports for rape. *Journal of Personality and Social Psychology, 38*(2), 217-30
Buss, A.H. & Durkee, A. (1957). An inventory for assessing different kinds of hostility. *Journal of Consulting Psychology, 21,* 343-9
Caesar, P.L. (1986). Men who batter: A heterogeneous group. Paper presented at American Psychological Association, Washington DC
Caine, T.M., Foulds, G.A., & Hope, K. (1967). *Manual of hostility and direction of hostility questionnaire (HDHQ).* London: University of London Press
Campbell, D.T. (1969). Reforms as experiments. *American Psychologist, 24,* 409-29
Campbell, J. (1992). Prevention of wife battering: Insights from cultural analysis. *Response, 14*(3), 18-24
Campbell, J.C. (1987). Making sense of the senseless: Women's attributions about battering. Paper presented at the Third National Family Violence Research Conference, Durham, NH
Caplan, N. & Nelson, S.D. (1973, March). On being useful: The nature and consequences of psychological research on social problems. *American Psychologist, 28*(3), 199-211
Caplan, P. (1984). The myth of women's masochism. *American Psychologist, 39*(2), 130-9
Carlson, B.E. (1984). Children's observations of interpersonal violence. In *Battered women and their families: Intervention strategies and treatment programs.* New York: Springer
Chaudhuri, M. & Daly, K. (1992). Do restraining orders help? Battered women's experience with male violence and legal process. In E.S. Buzawa & C.G. Buzawa (eds.), *Domestic violence: The changing criminal justice response.* Westport, CN: Auburn House
Clanton, G. & Smith, L. (1977). *Jealousy.* Englewood Cliffs, NJ: Prentice-Hall
Cohn, E.S. & Giles-Sims, J. (1979). Battered women: Whom did they blame? Paper presented at the meeting of the Eastern Psychological Association, Philadelphia, PA
Coleman, D.H. & Straus, M.A. (1986). Marital power, conflict, and violence in a nationally representative sample of American couples. *Violence and Victims, 1*(2), 141-57
– (1992). Marital power, conflict and violence in a nationally representative sample of American couples. In M.A. Straus & R.J. Gelles (eds.), *Physical violence in American*

families (pp. 287-300). New Brunswick: Transaction

Collins, N.L. & and Read, S.J. (1990). Adult attachment, working models and relationship quality in dating couples. *Journal of Personality and Social Psychology, 58,* 644-63

Conway, F. & Siegleman, J. (1978). *Snapping: America's epidemic of sudden personality change.* New York: Dell

Crawford, M. & Gartner, R. (1992). *Woman killing: Intimate femicide in Ontario, 1974-1990.* Women's Directorate, Ministry of Social Services, Toronto, ON

Crowne, D.P. & Marlowe, D.A. (1960). A new scale of social desirability independent of psychopathology. *Journal of Consulting Psychology, 24,* 349-54

Daly, M. (1973). *Beyond god the father.* Toronto: Fitzhenry & Whiteside

– (1978). *Gyn/ecology: The metaethics of radical feminism.* Boston: Beacon

Daly, M., Wilson, M., & Weghorst, S.J. (1982). Male sexual jealousy. *Ethology and Sociobiology, 3,* 11-27

Daly, M. & Wilson, M. (1988). *Homicide.* New York: Aldine

Darwin, C. (1871). *The descent of man and selection in relation to sex.* Vol. 1. London: Murray

– (1872). *The expression of emotion in man and animals.* London: Murray

Davidson, T. (1977). Wife beating: A recurring phenomenon throughout history. In M. Roy (ed.), *Battered women: A psychosociological study of domestic violence* (pp. 1-23). New York: Van Nostrand

– (1978). *Conjugal crime: Understanding and changing the wife-beating pattern.* New York: Hawthorn

de Reincourt, A. (1974). *Sex and power in history.* New York: Delta.

Deschner, J. (1984). *The hitting habit: Anger control for battering couples.* New York: Free Press

Deutsch, H. (1944). *The psychology of women.* Vol. 1. New York: Grune & Stratton

Diener, E. (1976). Effects of prior destructive behavior, anonymity and group presence on deindividuation and aggression. *Journal of Personality and Social Psychology, 33*(5), 497-507

Dixon, W.J., Brown, M.B., Engelman, L., Frane, J.W., Hill, M.A., Jennrich, R.J., & Joporek, J.D. (1981). *BMPD statistical software.* Berkeley, CA: University of California Press

Dobash, R.E. & Dobash, R.P. (1978). Wives: The appropriate victims of marital assault. *Victimology, 2,* 426-42

– (1979). *Violence against wives: A case against the patriarchy.* New York: Free Press

– (1984). The nature and antecedents of violent events. *British Journal of Criminology, 24*(31), 269-88

Dobson, K.S. & Block, L. (1987). Historical and philosophical bases of the cognitive-behavioral therapies. In K.S. Dobson (ed.), *Handbook of cognitive-behavioral therapies.* New York: Guilford

Dooley, D.G. & Catalano, R. (1984). The epidemiology of economic stress. *American Journal of Community Psychology, 12*(4), 387-409

Douglas, M.A. (1987). The Battered Woman Syndrome. In D.J. Sonkin (ed.), *Domestic violence on trial: Psychological and legal dimensions of family violence* (pp. 39-54). New York, NY: Springer

Dunford, F.W., Huizinga, D., & Elliott, D.S. (1990). The role of arrest in domestic assault: The Omaha police experiment. *Criminology, 28*(2), 183-206

Dutton, D.G. (1977). Domestic dispute intervention by police. *Proceedings of the United Way Symposium on Domestic Violence,* Vancouver, BC

– (1981a). *The criminal justice system response to wife assault.* Ottawa: Solicitor General of Canada, Research Division

– (1981b). A nested ecological theory of wife assault. Paper presented at the Canadian Psychological Association, Toronto

– (1981c). Training police officers to intervene in domestic violence. In R.B. Stuart (ed.), *Violent behavior*. New York: Brunner/Mazel

– (1983). Masochism as an 'explanation' for traumatic bonding: An example of the 'fundamental attribution error.' Paper presented at the meeting of the American Orthopsychiatric Association, Boston

– (1985). An ecologically nested theory of male violence towards intimates. *International Journal of Women's Studies, 8*(4), 404-13

– (1986a). Wife assaulters' explanations for assault: The neutralization of self-punishment. *Canadian Journal of Behavioral Science, 18*(4), 381-90

– (1986b). The public and the police: Training implications of the demand for a new model police officer. In J. Yuille (ed.), *Police selection and training: The role of psychology* (pp. 141-58). Amsterdam: Nijhof

– (1987a). The outcome of court-mandated treatment for wife assault: A quasi-experimental evaluation. *Violence and Victims, 1*(3), 163-75

– (1987b). The criminal justice response to wife assault. *Law and Human Behavior, 11*(3), 189-206

– (1988). *The domestic assault of women: Psychological and criminal justice perspectives.* Allyn & Bacon: Boston

– (1994a). Behavioral and affective correlates of Borderline Personality Organization in wife assaulters. *International Journal of Law and Psychiatry, 17*(3), 265-77

– (1994b). The origin and structure of the abusive personality. *Journal of Personality Disorders, 8*(3), 181-91.

– (1995c). Trauma symptoms and PTSD profiles in perpetrators of abuse. *Journal of Traumatic Stress*

Dutton, D.G. & Aron, A. (1989). Romantic attraction and generalized liking for others who are sources of conflict-based arousal. *Canadian Journal of Behavioral Science, 21*(3), 246-57

Dutton, D.G., Bodnarchuk, M., Kropp, R., Hart, S., Ogloff, J., & Starzomski, A. (1994). An initial evaluation of the impact of personality variables on wife assault treatment outcome. Vancouver: BC Institute of Family Violence

Dutton, D.G. & Browning, J.J. (1988). Concern for power, fear of intimacy, and aversive stimuli for wife assault. In G.T. Hotaling, D. Finkelhor, J.T. Kirkpatrick, & M.A. Straus (eds.), *Family abuse and its consequences: New directions in research* (pp. 163-75). Newbury Park, CA: Sage

Dutton, D.G., Fehr, B., & McEwen, H. (1982). Severe wife battering as deindividuated violence. *Victimology, 7*, 13-23

Dutton, D.G., Hart, S.D., Kennedy, L.W., & Williams, K.R. (1992). Arrest and the reduction of repeat wife assault. In E.S. Buzawa and C.G. Buzawa (eds.), *Domestic violence: The changing criminal justice response* (pp. 111-27). Westport, CT: Auburn House

Dutton, D.G. & Hemphill, K.J. (1992). Patterns of socially desirable responding among perpetrators and victims of wife assault. *Violence and Victims, 7*(1), 29-39

Dutton, D.G. & Levens, B.R. (1977). Domestic crisis intervention: Attitude survey of trained and untrained police officers. *Canadian Police College Journal, 1*(2), 75-92

Dutton, D.G. & McGregor, B.M.S. (1991). The symbiosis of arrest and treatment for wife assault: The case for combined intervention. In M. Steinman (ed.), *Redefining crime: Responses to spouse abuse* (pp. 131-54). Lincoln: University of Nebraska Press

Dutton, D.G. & Painter, S.L. (1980). *Male domestic violence and its effects on the victim.* Ottawa: Health and Welfare Canada

– (1981). Traumatic bonding: The development of emotional attachments in battered

women and other relationships of intermittent abuse. *Victimology, 6,* 139-55
– (1993a). Emotional attachments in abusive relationships: A test of Traumatic Bonding Theory. *Violence and Victims, 8*(2), 105-20
– (1993b). The Battered Woman Syndrome: Effects of severity and intermittency of abuse. *American Journal of Orthopsychiatry, 63*(4), 614-22
Dutton, D.G. & Ryan, L. (1994). Antecedents of Borderline Personality Organization in wife assaulters. Unpublished manuscript
Dutton, D.G., Saunders, K., Starzomski, A., & Bartholomew, K. (1994). Intimacy-anger and insecure attachment as precursors of abuse in intimate relationships. *Journal of Applied Social Psychology, 24*(15), 1367-86
Dutton, D.G. & Starzomski, A. (1993). Borderline Personality Organization in perpetrators of psychological and physical abuse. *Violence and Victims, 8*(4), 327-38
– (1994). Psychological differences between court-referred and self-referred wife assaulters. *Criminal Justice and Behavior: An International Journal, 21*(2), 203-22
Dutton, D.G. & Strachan, C.E. (1987a). Motivational needs for power and dominance as differentiating variables of assaultive and non-assaultive male populations. *Violence and Victims, 2*(3), 145-56
– (1987b). The prediction of recidivism in a population of wife assaulters. Paper presented at the Third National Family Violence Conference, Durham, NH
Dutton, M.A. (1992). *Empowering and healing the battered woman.* New York: Springer
Easterbrook, J. (1959). The effect of emotion on the utilization and organization of behavior. *Psychological Review, 66,* 183-201
Eddy, M.J. & Meyers, T. (1984). *Helping men who batter: A profile of programs in the U.S. Texas Council on Family Violence,* Arlington, Texas
Edelson, J.L. & Tolman, R.M. (1992). *Intervention for men who batter: An ecological approach.* Newbury Park, CA: Sage
Ehrenreich, B. (1983). *The hearts of men.* New York: Anchor/Doubleday
Ehrlich, I. (1975). The deterrent effect of capital punishment: A question of life and death. *American Economic Review, 65,* 397-412
Elbow, M. (1977). Theoretical considerations of violent marriages. *Social Casework, 58,* 515-26
Elias, N. (1978). *The history of manners.* New York: Pantheon
Elliott, F. (1977). The neurology of explosive rage: The episodic dyscontrol syndrome. In M. Roy (ed.), *Battered women: A psychosociological study of domestic violence.* New York: Van Nostrand
Emerson, C.D. (1979, June). Family violence: A study by the LA County Sheriff's Department. *Police Chief* (June) 48-50
Eth, S.E. & Pynoos, R.S. (1985). *Post-traumatic stress disorder in children.* Washington, DC: American Psychiatric Association Press
Ewing, C.P. (1987). *Battered women who kill: Psychological self-defense as legal justification.* Lexington, MA: D.C. Heath
– (1990). Psychological self-defense: A proposed justification for battered women who kill. *Law and Human Behavior, 14,* 579-94
Ewing, C P. & Aubrey, M. (1987). Battered women and public opinion: Some realities about the myths. *Journal of Family Violence, 2,* 257-64
Eysenck, H. (1969). *The effects of psychotherapy.* New York: Science House
Fagan, J. (1989). Cessation of family violence: Deterrence and dissuasion. In L. Ohlin & M. Tonry (eds.), *Family violence.* Chicago: University of Chicago Press
Fallaci, O. (1981). *A man.* New York: Simon and Schuster
Farberow, N. (1980). *The many faces of suicide.* New York: McGraw-Hill
Fasteau, M.F. (1974). *The male machine.* New York: McGraw-Hill

Fattah, E.A. (1981). The victimization experience and its aftermath. *Victimology: An International Journal, 6*(1-4), 29-47

Faulk, M. (1974). Men who assault their wives. *Medicine, Science and the Law, 14,* 180-3

Felson, R. & Ribner, S. (1981). An attributional approach to accounts and sanctions for criminal violence. *Social Psychology Quarterly, 44,* 137-42

Ferraro, K.J. & Boychuk, T. (1992). The court's response to interpersonal violence: A comparison of intimate and nonintimate assault. In E.S. Buzawa & C.G. Buzawa (eds.), *Domestic violence: The changing criminal justice response* (pp. 209-26). Westport, CN: Auburn House

Feshback, S. (1970). Aggression. In P.H. Mussen (ed.), *Carmichael's manual of child psychology.* Vol. 2. New York: Wiley

Field, M.H. & Field, H.F. (1973). Marital violence and the criminal process: Neither justice nor peace. *Social Service Review, 47,* 221-40

Fields, M. (1978). Wife beating: Government intervention policies and practices. In US Commission on Civil Rights, *Battered women: Issues of public policy* (pp. 228-87). Washington, DC: US Government Printing Office

Fincham, F. & Jaspars, J. (1980). Attribution of responsibility from man the scientist to man as lawyer. *Advances in Experimental Social Psychology, 13,* 81-138

Finn, P. (1991). Civil protection orders: A flawed opportunity for intervention. In M. Steinman (ed.), *Woman battering: Policy responses.* Cincinatti: Anderson

Fischer, C. (1982). *To dwell amongst friends: Personal networks in town and city.* Chicago: University of Chicago Press

Fiske, D.W. & Maddi, A.R. (1961). A conceptual framework. In D.W. Fiske & S.R. Maddi (eds.), *Functions of varied experience.* Homewood, IL: Dorsey

Fleming, J.B. (1979). *Stopping wife abuse.* Garden City, NY: Anchor

Flynn, E.E. (1986). Victims of terrorism: Dimensions of the victim experience. In E. Fattah (ed.), *The plight of crime victims in modern society.* London: Macmillan

Follingstad, D.R., Brennan, A.F., Hause, E.S., Polek, D.S, & Rutledge, L.L. (1991). Factors moderating physical and psychological symptoms of battered women. *Journal of Family Violence, 6*(1), 81-95

Follingstad, D.R., Hause, E.S., Rutledge, L.L., & Polek, D.S. (1992). Effects of battered women's early responses on later abuse patterns. *Violence and Victims, 7*(2), 109-28

Follingstad, D.R., Polek, D.S., Hause, E.S., Deaton, L.H., Bulger, M.W., & Conway, Z.D. (1989). Factors predicting verdicts in cases where battered women kill their husbands. *Law and Human Behavior, 13*(3), 253-69

Ford, D.A. (1987). The impact of police officers' attitudes toward victims on the disinclination to arrest wife batterers. Paper presented at the Third National Family Violence Conference, Durhamn, NH

Ford, D.A. & Regoli, M.J. (1992). The preventive impacts of policies for prosecuting wife batterers. In E.S. Buzawa & C.G. Buzawa (eds.), *Domestic violence: The changing criminal justice response* (pp. 181-208). Westport, CN: Auburn House

Freud, A. (1942). *The ego and the mechanisms of defense.* New York: International Universities Press

Freud, S. (1938). Three contributions to the theory of sex. In A. A. Brill (ed.), *The basic writings of Sigmund Freud.* New York: Random House

Frieze, I.H. (1979). Perceptions of battered wives. In I.H. Frieze, D. Bar-Tal, & S. Carroll (eds.), *New approaches to social problems.* San Francisco: Jossey-Bass

Fromm, E. (1941). *Escape from freedom.* New York: Avon

– (1973). *The anatomy of human destructiveness.* New York: Fawcett

Ganley, A. (1980, March). Interview: Whatcom County Counseling and Psychiatric Center. Bellingham, WA

– (1981). *Participant's manual: Court-mandated therapy for men who batter – A three day workshop for professionals.* Washington, DC: Center for Women Policy Studies

– (1989). Integrating feminist and social learning theories of aggression. In L. Caesar & K. Hamberger Caesar (eds.), *Treating men who batter: Theory, practice and programs.* New York: Springer

Ganley, A. & Harris, L. (1978). Domestic violence: Issues in designing and implementing programs for male batterers. Paper presented at the 86th annual convention of the American Psychological Association, Toronto

Gaquin, D.A. (1977). Spouse abuse: Data from the National Crime Survey. *Victimology, 2*(3-4), 632-42

Garbarino, J. (1977). The human ecology of child maltreatment: A conceptual model for research. *Journal of Marriage and the Family, 39,* 721-36

Gayford, J.J. (1975). Wife battering: A preliminary survey of 100 cases. *British Medical Journal, 301,* 194-7

Geen, R.J. (1970). Perceived suffering of the victim as an inhibitor of attack-induced aggression. *Journal of Social Psychology, 81,* 209-16

Geen, R.J., Rakosky, J.J., & Pigg, R. (1972). Awareness of arousal and its relation to aggression. *British Journal of Social and Clinical Psychology, 11,* 115-121

Gelles, R.J. (1972). *The violent home: A study of physical aggression between husbands and wives.* Beverly Hills: Sage

– (1974). *The violent home: A study of physical aggression between husbands and wives.* Newbury Park, CA: Sage

– (1975). Violence and pregnancy: A note on the extent of the problem and needed services. *The Family Co-ordinator, 24,* 81-6

– (1976). Abused wives: Why do they stay? *Journal of Marriage and the Family, 38,* 659-68

– (1978). Violence towards children in the United States. *American Journal of Orthopsychiatry, 48,* 580-92

– (1993). Constraints against family violence: How well do they work? *American Behavioral Scientist, 36*(5), 575-86

Gelles, R.J. & Straus, M.A. (1979). Determinants of violence in the family: Toward a theoretical integration. In W. Burr, R. Hill, I.l. Nye, & I. Reiss (eds.), *Contemporary theories about the family.* Vol. 1. New York: Free Press

– (1988). *Intimate violence.* New York: Simon and Shuster

Gendreau, P. & Ross, R. (1980). Correctional potency: Treatment and deterrence on trial. In R. Roesch & R. Corrado (eds.), *Evaluation and criminal justice policy.* Beverly Hills: Sage

Gerslma, C., Emmelkamp, P.M.G., & Arrindell, W.A. (1990). Anxiety, depression and perception of early parenting: A meta-analysis. *Clinical Psychology Review, 10,* 251-77

Gibbs, G. (1985). Deterrence theory and research. *Nebraska Symposium on Motivation, 33,* 87-130

Giles-Sims, J. (1983). *Wife battering: A systems theory approach.* New York: Guilford

Goldman, P. (1978). Violence against women in the family. Unpublished master's thesis, McGill University, Faculty of Law

Gondolf, E.W. (1985a). *Men who batter: An integrated approach for stopping wife abuse.* Holmes Beach, CA: Learning Publications

– (1985b). Anger and oppression in men who batter: Empiricist and feminist perspectives and their implications for research. *Victimology, 10*(l-4), 311-24

– (1987). Who are those guys? A typology of batterers based on shelter interviews. Paper presented at the Third National Conference for Family Violence Researchers, Durham, NH

– (1988). *Battered women as survivors: An alternative to treating learned helplessness.*

Lexington, MS: Lexington

Goode, W.G.J. (1971). Why men resist. *Dissent*, 181-93

Gould, S.J. (1983, June). Genes on the brain. *New York Review of Books*, p. 5

Grasmick, H.G., Blackwell, B.S., Bursik, R.J., & Mitchell, S. (1993). Changes in perceived threats of shame, embarrassment, and legal sanctions for interpersonal violence 1982-1992. *Violence and Victims*, 8(4), 313-26

Greenglass, E.R. (1982). *A world of difference: Gender roles in perspective*. Toronto: Wiley

Greenhouse, S.W. & Geisser, G. (1959). On methods in the analysis of profile data. *Psychometrika*, 24, 95-112

Griffin, D. & Bartholomew, K. (in press). Testing a two-dimensional model of adult attachment: A latent variable approach. *Journal of Personality and Social Psychology*

Griffin, D.W. & Bartholomew, K. (1994). The metaphysics of measurement: The case of adult attachment. In K. Bartholomew & D. Perlman (eds.), *Advances in personal relationships*. Vol. 5, *Attachment processes in adulthood* (pp. 17-52). London: Jessica Kingsley

Grossmann, A.L. (1989). Avoidance as a communicative strategy in attachment relationships. Paper presented at the Fourth World Association of Infant Psychiatry and Allied Disciplines, Lusanne, Switzerland

Groves, R.M. & Kahn, R.L. (1979). *Surveys by telephone: A national comparison with personal interviews*. New York: Academy

Grunfeld, A. (1993). *Identification, assessment, care, referral and follow-up of women experiencing domestic violence in emergency department treatment*. Interim progress reports to Health and Welfare Canada, Ottawa

Gunderson, J.G. (1984). *Borderline personality disorder*. Washington, DC: American Psychiatric Press

Haft, W.L. & Slade, A. (1989). Affect attunement and maternal attachment: A pilot study. *Infant Mental Health Journal*, 10, 157-72

Hamberger, K.L. & Hastings, J.E. (1991). Personality correlates of men who batter and non-violent men: Some continuities and discontinuities. *Journal of Family Violence*, 6(2), 131-47

– (1986). Characteristics of male spouse abusers: Is psychopathology part of the picture? Paper presented at American Society of Criminology, Atlanta, GA

Hare, R.D. (1965a). Psychopathy, fear, arousal, and anticipated pain. *Psychological Reports*, 16, 499-502

– (1965b). Temporal gradient of fear arousal in psychopaths. *Journal of Abnormal Psychology*, 442-5

– (1968). Psychopathy, autonomic functioning and the orienting response. *Journal of Abnormal Psychology*, 73, 1-24

Harlow, H.F. & Harlow, M. (1971). Psychopathology in monkeys. In H.D. Kinnel (ed.), *Experimental psychopathology*. New York: Academic Press

Harris, R.J. (1975). *A primer of multivariate statistics*. New York: Academic Press

Hart, S.D., Dutton, D.G., & Newlove, T. (1993). The prevalence of personality disorder amongst wife assaulters. *Journal of Personality Disorders*, 7(4), 328-40

Hastings, J.E. & Hamberger, L.K. (1988). Personality characteristics of spouse abusers: A controlled comparison, *Violence and Victims*, 3(1), 5-30

Hathaway, S.R. & McKinley, J.C. (1967). *MMPI Inventory Manual*. New York: Psychological Corporation

Hawkins, D. (1986). *Homicide among Black Americans*. New York: University Press of America

Hazan, C. & Shaver, P. (1987). Conceptualizing romantic love as an attachment process. *Journal of Personality and Social Psychology*, 52, 511-24

Helzer, J.E., Robins, L.N., & McEvoy, L. (1987). Post-Traumatic Stress Disorder in the general population. *New England Journal of Medicine, 317*(26), 1630-4

Henderson, M. & Hewstone, M. (1984). Prison inmates' explanations for interpersonal violence: Accounts and attributions. *Journal of Consulting and Clinical Psychology, 52*(5), 789-94

Hendrick, J. (1977, January 29). When television is a school for criminals. *TV Guide*, 4-10

Herman, J.L. (1992). *Trauma and recovery*. New York: Basic

Hetherington, E.M. (1965). A developmental study of the effects of sex of the dominant parent on sex-role preference, identification and imitation in children. *Journal of Personality and Social Psychology, 2*, 188-94

Hilberman, E. (1980). Overview: The 'wife beater's wife' reconsidered. *American Journal of Psychiatry, 137*(ll), 1336-47

Hilberman, E. & Munson, K. (1977-78). Sixty battered women. *Victimology, 2*, 460-70

Hirshell, J.D., Hutchinson, I.W., Dean, C.W., Kelley, J.J., & Pesackis, C.E. (1990). Charlotte Spouse Assault Replication Project: Final report. Unpublished manuscript cited in Gelles, R.J. (1993)

Hogarth, J. (1980). Battered wives and the justice system. Unpublished manuscript, University of British Columbia, Faculty of Law

Hokanson, J.E., Willers, K.R., & Koropsak, E. (1968). Modification of autonomic responses during aggressive interchange. *Journal of Personality, 36*, 386-404

Holmes, T.H. & Rahe, R.H. (1967). The social readjustment rating scale. *Journal of Psychosomatic Research, 11*, 213-18

Hood, R. & Sparks, R. (1970). *Key issues in criminology*. New York: McGraw-Hill

Hotaling, G.T. & Sugarman, D.B. (1986). An analysis of risk markers in husband to wife violence: The current state of knowledge. *Violence and Victims, 1*(2), 101-24

Hunt, J.M., Cole, M.W., & Reis, E.E.A. (1958). Situational cues distinguishing anger, fear, and sorrow. *American Journal of Psychology, 71*, 136-51

Hunt, M. (1959). *The natural history of love*. New York: Alfred A. Knopf

Huston, T.L. (1983). Power. In H.H. Kelley, E. Berscheid, A. Christensen, J.H. Harvey, T.L. Huston, G. Levinger, E. McClintock, L.A. Peplau, & D.R. Peterson (eds.), *Close Relationships*. New York: W.H. Freeman

Huxley, A. (1980). *The human situation*. Great Britain: Granada/Triad

Island, D. & Letellier, P. (1991). *Men who beat the men who love them*. New York: Harrington Park

Izard, C.E., Dougherty, F.E., Bloxom, B.M., & Kotsch, W.E. (1974). *The differential emotions scale: A method of measuring the subjective experience of discrete emotions*. Nashville: Vanderbilt University

Jacob, J, (1975). Family interaction in disturbed and normal families: A methodological and substantive review. *Psychological Bulletin, 82*, 33-65

Jaffe, P. (1982, February). *Testimony before Standing Committee on Health, Welfare and Social Affairs* (pp. 27-15). Ottawa: House of Commons

Jaffe, P. & Burris, C.A. (1982). *An integrated response to wife assault: A community model*. Ottawa: Research Report of the Solicitor General

Jaffe, P., Sudermann, M., Reitzel, D., & Killip, S.M. (1992). An evaluation of a secondary school primary prevention program on violence in intimate relationships. *Violence and Victims, 7*(2), 129-54

Jaffe, P., Wolfe, D. A., Telford, A., & Austin, G. (1986). The impact of police charges in incidents of wife abuse. *Journal of Family Violence, 1*(1), 37-49

Jaffe, P., Wolfe, D., Wilson, S.K., & Zak, L. (1986a). Family violence and child adjustment: A comparative analysis of girls' and boys' behavioral symptoms. *American Journal of Psychiatry, 143*, 74-7

– (1986b). Similarities in behavioral and social maladjustment among child victims and witnesses to family violence. *American Journal of Orthopsychiatry, 56*(1), 142-6

Jaffe, P., Wolfe, D. & Wilson, S.K. (1990). *Children of battered women.* Newbury Park, CA: Sage

Janoff-Bulman, R. (1979). Characterological versus behavioral self-blame: Inquiries into depression and rape. *Journal of Personality and Social Psychology, 37,* 1798-809

Janoff-Bulman, R. & Lang-Gunn, L. (1985). Coping with disease and accidents: The role of self-blame attributions. In L.Y. Abramson (ed.), *Social-personal influence in clinical psychology.* Vol. 5. Hillsdale, NH: Erlbaum

Jones, E.E. & Nisbett, R.E. (1971). The actor and the observer: Divergent perceptions of the causes of behavior. In E.E. Jones, D. Kanouse, H.H. Kelley, R.E. Nisbett, S. Valins, & B. Weiner (eds.), *Attribution: Perceiving the causes of behaviors.* Morristown, NJ: General Learning Press

Joreskog, K. (1979). Statistical estimation of structural models in longitudinal development investigations. In J. Nesselroode & P. Baltes (eds.), *Longitudinal research in the study of behavior and development.* New York: Academic Press

Jorgenson, D.O. & Dukes, F.O. (1976). Deindividuation as a function of density and group membership. *Journal of Personality and Social Psychology, 34*(1), 24-9

Kahneman, D.S. & Tversky, A. (1973). On the psychology of prediction. *Psychological Review, 80,* 237-51

Kalmuss, D.S. (1984, February). The intergenerational transmission of marital aggression. *Journal of Marriage and the Family, 46,* 11-19

Kalmuss, D.S. & Seltzer, J.A. (1986). Continuity of marital behavior in remarriage: The case of spouse abuse. *Journal of Marriage and the Family, 48,* 113-20

Kalmuss, D.S. & Straus, M.A. (1982, May). Wife's marital dependency and wife abuse. *Journal of Marriage and the Family, 44,* 277-86

Kardiner, S.H. & Fuller, M. (1970). Violence as a defense against intimacy. *Mental Hygiene, 54*(2), 310-15

Karen, R. (1990). *Becoming attached.* New York: Warner

Kasian, M. & Painter, S. (1992). Frequency and severity of psychological abuse in a dating population. *Journal of Interpersonal Violence, 7*(3), 350-64

Kasian, M., Spanos, N., Terrance, C.A., & Peebles, S. (1993). Battered women who kill: Jury simulation and legal defenses. *Law and Human Behavior, 17*(3), 289-312

Katz, J. (1988). *Seductions of crime.* New York: Basic

Kelley, H.H. & Stahelski, A.J. (1970). Errors in perception of intentions in a mixed-motive game. *Journal of Experimental Social Psychology, 6,* 379-400

Kempe, C.H., Silverman, F.N., Steele, B.F., Droegemueller, W., & Silver, H. (1962). The battered child syndrome. *Journal of the American Medical Association, 181,* 107-12

Kempe, R.S. & Kempe, C.H. (1978). *Child abuse.* Cambridge, MA: Harvard University Press

Kendrick, D.J. & Cialdini, R. (1977). Romantic attraction: Misattribution vs. reinforcement explanations. *Journal of Personality and Social Psychology, 36*(6), 381-91

Kennedy, L.W. & Dutton, D.G. (1989). The incidence of wife assault in Alberta. *Canadian Journal of Behavioral Science, 21*(1), 40-54

Kernberg, O. (1977). The structural diagnosis of borderline personality organization. In P. Hartocollis (ed.), *Borderline personality disorders: The concept, the syndrome, the patient* (pp. 87-121). New York: International Universities Press

Kim, K. & Cho, Y. (1992). Epidemiological survey of spouse abuse in Korea. In E. Viano (ed.), *Intimate violence: Interdisciplinary perspectives.* Washington, DC: Hemisphere

Kitson, G.C. (1982, May). Attachment to the spouse in divorce: A scale and its application. *Journal of Marriage and the Family, 44,* 379-93

Kobak, R. & Sceery, A. (1988). Attachment in late adolescence: Working models, affect regulation, and representations of self and others. *Child Development, 59,* 135-46

Konecni, V.J. (1975). Annoyance, type and duration of postannoyance activity, and aggression: The 'cathartic effect.' *Journal of Experimental Psychology, 104*(1), 76-102

Lane, K.E. & Gwartney-Gibbs, P.A. (1985). Violence in the context of dating and sex. *Journal of Family Issues, 6,* 45-59

Langer, E. (1983). *The psychology of control.* Beverly Hills, CA: Sage

Lazarus, R.A. & Averill, J.R. (1972). Emotion and cognition: With special reference to anxiety. In C.D. Spielberger (ed.), *Anxiety: Current trends in theory and research.* Vol. 2. New York: Academic

Lerman, L.G. (1981). Prosecution of spouse abuse: Innovations in criminal justice response. Washington, DC: Center for Women Policy Studies

Lerner, M. (1977). The justice motive in social behavior. *Journal of Social Issues, 45,* 1-50

Leuba, C. (1955). Toward some integration of learning theories: The concept of optimal stimulation. *Psychological Reports, 1,* 27-33.

Levens, B.R. & Dutton, D.G. (1977). Domestic crisis intervention: Citizens' requests for service and the Vancouver Police Department response. *Canadian Police College Journal,* 1, 29-50

– (1980). *The social service role of the police: Domestic Crisis Intervention.* Ottawa: Solicitor General of Canada

Levenson, R.W. & Gottman, J.M. (1983). Marital interaction: Physiological linkage and affective exchange. *Journal of Personality and Social Psychology, 45,* 587-97

Levinger, G. (1966). Sources of marital dissatisfaction among applicants for divorce. *American Journal of Orthopsychiatry, 36,* 803-7

Levinson, D. (1989). *Family violence in a cross-cultural perspective.* Newbury Park, CA: Sage

Lewin, K. (1951). *Field theory in social science.* New York: Harper & Row

Lewin, K., Lippitt, R., & White, R. (1947). An experimental study of leadership and group life. In T.M. Newcombe & E.L. Hartley (eds.), *Readings in social psychology.* New York: Holt, Rinehart, & Winston

Leyens, J.P., Camino, L., Parke, R.D., & Berkowitz, L. (1975). Effects of movie violence on aggression in a field setting as a function of group dominance and cohesion. *Journal of Personality and Social Psychology, 32,* 346-60

Lie, G. & Gentlewarrior, S. (1991). Intimate violence in lesbian relationships: Discussion of survey findings and practice implications. *Journal of Social Service Research, 15*(1-2), 41-59

Lie, G., Schilit, R., Bush, J., Montague, M., & Reyes, L. (1991). Lesbians in currently aggressive relationships: How frequently do they report aggressive past relationships? *Violence and Victims, 6*(2), 121-35

Liebman, D.A. & Schwartz, J.A. (1973). Police programs in domestic crisis intervention: A review. In J. Snibbe & H. Snibbe (eds.), *The urban policeman in transition.* Springfield, IL: Charles C. Thomas

Lion, J. (1977). Clinical aspects of wife battering. In M. Roy (ed.), *Battered women: A psychosociological study of domestic violence.* New York: Van Nostrand Reinhold

Loftus, E. (1993). The reality of repressed memories. *American Psychologist, 48*(5), 518-37

Lorenz, K. (1937). The companion in the bird's world. *Auti, 54,* 245-73

Loving, N. & Farmer, M. (1980). *Police handling of spouse abuse and wife beating calls: A guide for police managers.* Police Executive Research Forum, Washington, DC

Maccoby, E.E. & Jacklin, C.N. (1974). *The psychology of sex differences.* Stanford, CA: Stanford University Press

MacLeod, L. (1980). *Wife battering in Canada: The vicious circle.* The Canadian Advisory Council on the Status of Women: Canadian Government Publishing Centre

Mahler, M. (1971). A study of the separation-individuation process and its possible application to borderline phenomena in the psychoanalytic situation. *Psychoanalytic Study of the Child, 26,* 403-24

Mahler, M., Pine, F., & Bergman, A. (1975). *The psychological birth of the human infant.* New York: Basic

Mahoney, M.J. & Thoreson, C.E. (1979). *Self-control: Power to the person.* Monterey, CA: Brooks/Cole

Main, M., Kaplan, N., & Cassidy, J. (1985). Security in infancy, childhood and adulthood. In I. Bretherton & E. Waters (eds.), Growing points of attachment theory and research. *Monographs of the Society for Research in Child Development, 50*(1-2), serial no. 109, 60-106

Main, M. & Weston, D.R. (1982). Avoidance of the attachment figure in infancy: Descriptions and interpretations. In C.M. Parkes and J. Stevenson-Hinds (eds.), *The place of attachment in human behavior.* London: Tavistock

Maiuro, R.D., Cahn, T.S., Vitaliano, P.P., & Zegree, J.B. (1986). Anger control treatment for men who engage in domestic violence: A controlled outcome study. Paper presented at the annual convention of the Western Psychological Association, Seattle, WA

Makepeace, J.M. (1981). Courtship violence among college students. *Family Relations, 30,* 97-102

Mandler, G. (1975). *Mind and emotion.* New York: Wiley

Manning, P.K. (1992). Screening calls. In E.S. Buzawa & C.G. Buzawa (eds.), *Domestic violence: The changing criminal justice response* (pp. 41-58). Westport, CN: Auburn House

Marascuilo, L.A. & Levin, J.R. (1983). *Multivariate statistics in the social sciences: A researcher's guide.* Belmont, CA: Wadsworth

Margolin, G. (1984). Interpersonal and intrapersonal factors associated with marital violence. Paper presented at the Second National Family Violence Research Conference, Durham, NH

Marlatt, G.A. & Rohsenow, D.J. (1980). Cognitive processes in alcohol use: Expectancy and the balanced placebo design. In N.K. Mello (ed.), *Advances in substance abuse: Behavioral and biological research – a research annual.* Vol. 1 (pp. 159-99). Greenwich, CT: JAI

Marshall, L.L. (1992). Development of the Severity of Violence Against Women Scales. *Journal of Family Violence, 7*(2), 103-21

Marshall, L.L. & Rose, P. (1990). Premarital violence: The impact of family of origin violence, stress and reciprocity. *Violence and Victims, 5,* 51-64

Martin, D. (1977). *Battered wives.* New York: Kangaroo

Martin, S.E. (1989). The response of the clergy to spouse abuse in a suburban county. *Violence and Victims, 4*(3), 217-25

Maslach, C. (1974). Social and personal bases of deindividuation. *Journal of Personality and Social Psychology, 29*(3), 411-25

Mathes, E.W. & Severa, N. (1981). Jealousy, romantic love and liking: Theoretical considerations and preliminary scale development. *Psychological Reports, 49,* 23-31

Mathes, E.W., Philips, J.T., Skowran, J., & Dick III, W.E. (1982). Behavioral correlates of the interpersonal scale. *Educational and Psychological Measurement, 42,* 1227-31

McClelland, D. (1975). *Power: The inner experience.* New York: Halstead

Meichenbaum, D. (1977). *Cognitive behavior modification.* New York: Plenum

Meloy, J.R. (1988). Violent and homicidal behavior in primitive mental states. *Journal of the American Academy of Psychoanalysis, 16,* 381-94

Meyer, C.B. & Taylor, S.E. (1986). Adjustment to rape. *Journal of Personality and Social Psychology, 50*(6), 1226-34

Meyer, J.K. & Lorimer, T.D. (1979). *Police intervention data and domestic violence: Exploratory development and validation of prediction models.* Bethesda, MA: National Institutes of Mental Health and Kansas City, MO, Police Department

Milgram, S. (1974). *Obedience to authority.* New York: Harper & Row

Mill, J.S. (1869). *The subjection of women.* Introduction by Stanton Coit. London: Longmans

Millon, T. (1981). *Disorders of personality, DSM-III: Axis II.* New York: Wiley

– (1992). Millon clinical Multiaxial inventory: I and II. *Journal of Counseling and Development, 70*(3), 421-6

Mishler, E.G. & Waxler, N.E. (1968). *Interaction in families: An experimental study of family processes and schizophrenia.* New York: Wiley

Mones, P. (1991). *When a child kills: Abused children who kill their parents.* New York: Simon and Schuster

Morse, S.J. (1990). The misbegotten marriage of soft psychology and bad law: Psychological self-defense as justification for homicide. *Law and Human Behavior, 14,* 595-618

Murstein, B.I. (1978). *Exploring intimate lifestyles.* New York: Springer

National Research Council, US (1978). *Deterrence and incapacitation.* Washington, DC: National Academy of Sciences

Neidig, P.H. & Friedman, D.H. (1984). *Spouse abuse: A treatment program for couples.* Champaign, IL: Research Press

Neidig, P.H., Friedman, D.H., & Collins, B.S. (1986). Attitudinal characteristics of males who have engaged in spouse abuse. *Journal of Family Violence, 1*(3), 223-34

Ng, S.H. (1980). *The social psychology of power.* New York: Academic Press

NiCarthy, G. (1982). *Getting free: A handbook for women in abusive relationships.* Seattle, Washington: Seal Press

Nielsen, J.M., Eberle, P., Thoennes, N., & Walker, L.E. (1979). Why women stay in battering relationships: Preliminary results. Paper presented at the annual meeting of the American Sociological Association, Boston

Nisbett, R. & Ross, L. (1980). *Human inference: Strategies and shortcomings of social judgment.* Englewood Cliffs, NJ: Prentice-Hall

Notarius, C.I. & Johnson, J.I. (1982). Emotional expression in husbands and wives. *Journal of Marriage and the Family, 44,* 483-92

Novaco, R. (1975). *Anger control: The development and evaluation of an experimental treatment.* Lexington, MA: Lexington

– (1976, October). The functions and regulation of the arousal of anger. *American Journal of Psychiatry, 133*(1), 1124-8

Ochberg, F.M. (1988). *Post-traumatic therapy and victims of violence.* New York: Brunner\Mazel

Ofshe, R. (1989). Coerced confessions: The logic of seemingly irrational action. *Cultic Studies Journal, 6,* 1-15

Okun, L. (1986). *Woman abuse: Facts replacing myths.* Albany, NY: State University of New York Press

Oldham, J., Clarkin, J., Appelbaum, A., Carr, A., Kernberg, P., Lotterman, A., & Haas, G. (1985). A self-report instrument for Borderline Personality Organization. In: T.H. McGlashan (ed.) *The Borderline: Current empirical research.* The Progress in Psychiatry Series (pp. 1-18). Washington, DC: American Psychiatric Press

Orne, M. (1969). Demand characteristics and the concept of quasi-controls. In R. Rosenthal & R. Rosnow (eds.), *Artifact in behavioral research.* New York: Academic Press

Orwell, G. (1949). *1984.* New York: Harcourt Brace

Pagelow, M. (1984). *Family violence.* New York: Praeger

– (1993). Response to Hamberger's comments. *Journal of Interpersonal Violence, 8,* 137-139

Painter, S.L. (1985). Why do battered women stay? Theoretical perspectives. *Highlights: Newsletter of the Canadian Psychological Association.* Old Chelsea, PQ: Canadian Psychological Association

Parke, R. & Collmer, C. (1975). Child abuse: An interdisciplinary review. In E.M. Hetherington (ed.), *Review of child development research.* Vol. 5. Chicago: University of Chicago Press

Parnas, R.I. (1973). Prosecutorial and judicial handling of family violence. *Criminal Law Bulletin, 9,* 733

Patterson, G.R. (1979). A performance theory for coercive family interactions. In R. Cairns (ed.), *Social interaction: Methods, analysis, and illustrations.* Hillsdale, NJ: Erlbaum

– (1981). *Families of antisocial children: An interactional approach.* Eugene, OR: Catalia

Patterson, G.R., Cobb, J.A., & Ray, R.S. (1972). A social engineering technology for retraining families of aggressive boys. In H.E. Adams & P.J. Unikel (eds.), *Issues and trends in behavior therapy.* Springfield, IL: Charles C. Thomas

Patterson, G.R., Littman, R.A., & Brickner, W. (1967). Assertive behavior in children: A step toward a theory of aggression. *Monographs of the Society for Research in Child Development, 32*(5), serial no. 133

Patterson, M.L. (1976). An arousal model of interpersonal intimacy. *Psychological Review, 83*(3), 235-45

Perlmuter, L.C. & Monty, R.A. (eds.). (1979). *Choice and perceived control.* Hillsdale, NJ: Erlbaum

Perris, C., Jacobsson, L., Lindstrom, H., von Knorring, L., & Perris, H. (1980). Development of a new inventory for assessing memories of parental rearing behavior. *Acta Psychiatrica Scandinavica, 61,* 265-74

Peters, E. (1985). *Torture.* New York: Blackwell

Phillips, D.P. & Hensley, J.E. (1984, summer). When violence is rewarded or punished: The impact of mass media stories on homicide. *Journal of Communication, 34*(3), 101-16

Pirog-Good, M.A. & Stets, J. (in press). Recidivism in programs for abusers. *Victimology*

Pistole, M.C. (1989). Attachment in adult romantic relationships: Style of conflict resolution and relationship satisfaction. *Journal of Social and Personal Relationships, 6,* 505-10

Pizzey, E. (1974). *Scream quietly or the neighbours will hear.* London: Penguin

Platt, J. (1973). Social traps. *American Psychologist, 28,* 641-51

Pleck, E. (1987). *Domestic tyranny: The making of American social policy against family violence from colonial times to the present.* New York: Oxford University Press

– (1989). Criminal approaches to family violence, 1640-1980. In L. Ohlin and M. Tonry (eds.), *Family violence: Crime and justice – A review of the research.* Vol. 2, (pp. 19-58). Chicago: University of Chicago Press

Pleck, J.H. (1976). Male threat from female competence. *Journal of Clinical and Consulting Psychology, 44,* 608-13

– (1981). *The myth of masculinity.* Cambridge, MA: MIT Press

Pollack, S. & Gilligan, C. (1982). Images of violence in thematic apperception test stories. *Journal of Personality and Social Psychology, 42,* 159-67

Porter, C.A. (1983). Blame, depression and coping in battered women. Unpublished doctoral dissertation, University of British Columbia

Prochaska, J.O., DiClemente, C.C., & Norcross, C.C. (1992). In search of how people change: Applications to addictive behaviors. *American Psychologist, 47*(9), 1102-14

Ptacek, J. (1984). The clinical literature on men who batter: A review and critique. Paper presented at the Second National Conference for Family Violence Research, University of New Hampshire, Durham, NH

Rachman, S.J. & Wilson, G.T. (1980). *The effects of psychological therapy* (2nd ed.). Oxford: Pergamon

Rajecki, P., Lamb, M., & Obmascher, P. (1978). Toward a general theory of infantile attachment: A comparative review of aspects of the social bond. *The Behavioral and Brain Sciences, 3*, 417-64

Rathus, S.A. (1973). A 30-item schedule for assessing assertive behavior. *Behavior Therapy, 4*, 498-596

Reid, J.B. & Patterson, G.R. (1976). The modification of aggression and stealing behavior of boys in the home setting. In E. Ribes-Inesta & A. Bandura (eds.), *Analysis of delinquency and aggression*. Hillsdale, NJ: Erlbaum

Reid, J.B., Patterson, G.R., & Loeber, R. (1981). The abused child: Victim, instigator or innocent bystander? In D.J. Bernstein (ed.), *Response structure and motivation*. Nebraska Symposium on Motivation. Lincoln/London. University of Nebraska Press

Repucci, N.D. & Clingempeel, W.G. (1978). Methodological issues in research with correctional populations. *Journal of Consulting and Clinical Psychology, 46*, 727-46

Revitch, E. & Schlesinger, L.B. (1981). *Psychopathology of Homicide*. Springfield, IL: Charles C. Thomas

Richter, H. (1974). *The family as patient*. New York: Farrar, Straus, & Giroux

Riggs, D.S., O'Leary, K.D., & Breslin, F.C.. (1990). Multiple correlates of physical aggression in dating couples. *Journal of Interpersonal Violence, 5*(1), 61-73

Robins, L.N., Helzer, J.E., Croughan, J., Williams, J.B.W., & Spitzer, R.L. (1981). *The NIMH Diagnostic Interview Schedule, Version III*. Washington, DC: Public Health Service

Robinson, J.P., Shaver, P.R., & Wrightsman, L.S. (1991). *Measures of personality and social psychological attitudes*. San Diego: Academic Press

Rokeach, M., Miller, M.G., & Snyder, J.A. (1971). The value gap between police and policed. *Journal of Social Issues, 27*(2), 155-71

Rosenbaum, A. & O'Leary, K.D. (1981). Marital violence: Characteristics of abusive couples. *Journal of Consulting and Clinical Psychology, 41*, 63

Rosenbaum, M.E., & deCharms, R. (1960). Direct and vicarious reduction of hostility. *Journal of Abnormal and Social Psychology, 60*, 105-11

Rosenberg, M. (1965). *Society and the adolescent self-image*. Princeton, NJ: Princeton University Press

Rosenfeld, B.D. (1992). Court-ordered treatment of spouse abuse. *Clinical Psychology Review, 12*, 205-26

Rosenthal, R. (1969). Interpersonal expectations: Effects of the experimenter's hypothesis. In R. Rosenthal & R.L. Rosnow (eds.), *Artifact in Behavioral Research*. New York: Academic Press

– (1983). Assessing the statistical and social importance of the effects of psychotherapy. *Journal of Consulting and Clinical Psychology, 51*(1), 4-13

Ross, M.W., Campbell, R.L., & Clayter, J.R. (1982). New inventory of measurement of parental rearing patterns: An English form of the EMBU. *Acta Psychiatrica Scandinavica, 66*, 499-507

Rounsaville, B. (1978). Theories in marital violence: Evidence from a study of battered women. *Victimology, 3*(1-2), 11-31

Rounsaville, B., Lifton, N., & Bieber, M. (1979). The natural history of a psychotherapy group for battered wives. *Psychiatry, 42*(1), 63-78

Roy, M. (1977). *Battered women: A psychosocial study of domestic violence*. New York: Van Nostrand

Rubonis, A.V. & Bickman, L. (1991). Psychological impairment in the wake of disaster:

The disaster-psychopathology relationship. *Psychological Bulletin 109*(3), 384-99

Rule, B.G. & Leger, G.L. (1976). Pain cues and differing functions of aggression. *Canadian Journal of Behavioral Science, 8,* 213-33

Rule, B.G. & Nesdale, A.R. (1976). Emotional arousal and aggressive behavior. *Psychological Bulletin, 83,* 851-63

Russell, J. & Mehrabian, A. (1974). Distinguishing anger and anxiety in terms of emotional response factors. *Journal of Consulting and Clinical Psychology, 42,* 79-83

Ryan, W. (1971). *Blaming the victim.* New York: Vintage

Sage, W. (1976, October). The war on the cults. *Human Behavior,* 40-9

Sales, E., Baum, M., & Shore, B. (1984). Victim readjustment following assault. *Journal of Social Issues, 40*(1), 117-36

Sanders, G.A. & Baron, R.A. (1977). Pain cues and uncertainty as determinants of aggression in a situation involving repeated instigation. *Journal of Personality and Social Psychology, 32,* 495-502

Saulnier, D. & Perlman, D. (1981). Inmates attributions: Their antecedents and effects on coping. *Criminal Justice and Behavior, 8,* 159-72

Saunders, D. (1989). Cognitive and behavioral interventions with men who batter: Application and outcome. In P.L. Caesar and L.K. Hamberger (eds.), *Treating men who batter: Theory, practice and programs* (pp. 77-99). New York: Springer

– (1992). A typology of men who batter women: Three types derived from cluster analysis. *American Journal of Orthopsychiatry, 62*(2), 264-75

Saunders, D.G. & Hanusa, D.R. (1984). Cognitive-behavioral treatment for abusive husbands: The short-term effects of group therapy. Paper presented at the Second National Conference on Family Violence Research, Durham, NH

Schachter, S. & Singer, J. (1962). Cognitive, social and physiological determinants of emotional state. *Psychological Review, 69,* 379-99

Schein, E. (1971). *Coercive persuasion.* New York: Norton

Scheppele, K.L. & Bart, P.B. (1983). Through women's eyes: Defining danger in the wake of sexual assault. *Journal of Social Issues, 39*(2), 63-81

Schram, D. (1978). Rape. In R. Chapman & M. Gates (eds.), *The victimization of women.* Beverly Hills, CA: Sage

Schuller, R.A. (1992). The impact of battered woman syndrome evidence on jury decision processes. *Law and Human Behavior, 16*(6), 597-620

Schuller, R.A. & Vidmar, N. (1992). Battered woman syndrome evidence in the courtroom. *Law and Human Behavior, 16*(3) 273-91

Schulman, M. (1979). *A survey of spousal violence against women in Kentucky.* Washington, DC: US Department of Justice, Law Enforcement

Scott, J.P. (1963). The process of primary socialization in canine and human infants. *Monographs of the Society for Research in Child Development,* 28:46-58

Sears, R.R., Maccoby, E.E., & Levin, H. (1957). *Patterns of child rearing.* Evanston, IL: Row, Peterson

Seay, B., Alexander, B., & Harlow, H.F. (1964). Maternal behavior of socially deprived rhesus monkeys. *Journal of Abnormal and Social Psychology, 69,* 345-54

Seligman, M.E. (1975). *On depression, development and death.* San Francisco: Freeman

Selzer, M.L. (1971). The Michigan Alcoholism Screening Test: The quest for a new diagnostic instrument. *American Journal of Psychiatry, 127,* 89-94

Shainess, N. (1977). Psychological aspects of wife battering. In M. Roy (ed.), *Battered women: A psychosocial study of domestic violence.* New York: Van Nostrand

Shaver, P., Hazan, C., & Bradshaw, D. (1988). Love as attachment: The integration of three behavioral systems. In: R.J. Sternberg and M. Barnes (eds.) *The psychology of love* (pp. 68-99). New Haven, CT: Yale University Press

Sherman, L.W. & Berk, R.A. (1984). The specific deterrent effects of arrest for domestic assault. *American Sociological Review, 49,* 261-72

Sherman, L.W., Schmidt, J.D., Rogan, D.P., Smith, D.A., Gartin, P.R., Cohn, E.G., Collins, D.J., & Bacich, A.R. (1992). The variable effects of arrest on criminal careers: The Milwaukee domestic violence experiment. *Journal of Criminal Law and Criminology, 83*(1), 137-61

Shields, N.M. & Hanneke, C.R. (1983). Attribution processes in violent relationships: Perceptions with violent husbands and their wives. *Journal of Applied Social Psychology, 13,* 515-27

Shields, N.M., McCall, G.J., and Hanneke, C.R. (1988). Patterns of family and non-family violence: Violent husbands and violent men. *Violence and Victims, 3*(2), 83-96

Shore, M. & Massimo, J.V. (1979). Fifteen years after treatment: A follow up study of comprehensive psychotherapy. *American Journal of Orthopsychiatry, 49*(2), 240-5

Short, J.F., Jr. (ed.). (1968). *Gang delinquency and delinquent subcultures.* New York: Harper & Row

Shotland, L. & Straw, M. (1976). Bystander response to an assault: When a man attacks a woman. *Journal of Personality and Social Psychology, 34*(5), 990-9

Siegel, J.M. (1986). The multidimensional anger inventory. *Journal of Personality and Social Psychology, 51*(1), 191-200

Silver, R.L., Boon, C., & Stones, M.L. (1983). Searching for meaning in misfortune: Making sense of incest. *Journal of Social Issues, 39*(2), 83-103

Silverman, L.H. & Weinberger, J. (1985). Mommy and I are one: Implications for therapy. *American Psychologist, 40*(12), 1296-308

Simeons, W. (1962). *Man's presumptuous brain.* New York: Dutton

Slavin, M. (1972). The theme of feminine evil: The image of women in male fantasy and its effects on attitudes and behavior. Unpublished doctoral dissertation, Harvard University, MA

Smith, D.A. & Klein, J.R. (1984). Police control of interpersonal disputes. *Social Problems, 31*(4), 468-81

Smith, J.P. & Williams, J.G. (1992). From abusive household to dating violence. *Journal of Family Violence, 7*(2), 153-65

Smith, M. (1990). Patriarchal ideology and wife beating: A test of feminist hypothesis. *Violence and Victims, 5*(4), 257-73

Smith, P. & Chalmers, D.L. (1984). Does sheltering help abused women? Paper presented at the annual meeting of the Canadian Sociology and Anthropology Association, Guelph, ON

Snell, J.E., Rosenwald, P.J., & Robey, A. (1964). The wifebeater's wife. *Archives of General Psychiatry, 2,* 107-13

Snyder, D.K. & Fruchtman, L.A. (1981). Differential patterns of wife abuse: A data-based typology. *Journal of Consulting and Clinical Psychology, 49,* 848-85

Snyder, D.K. & Scheer, N.A. (1981). Predicting disposition following brief residence at a shelter for battered women. *American Journal of Community Psychology, 9,* 559-66

Solicitor General of Canada. (1985). Canadian Urban Victimization Survey. *Female Victims of Crime.* Bulletin no. 4. Ottawa

Solomon, R.L. (1980). The opponent-process theory of acquired motivation: The costs of pleasure and the benefits of pain. *American Psychologist, 35*(8), 691-712

Sonkin, D.J. (1987). The assessment of court-mandated male batterers. In D.J. Sonkin (ed.), *Domestic violence on trial: Psychological and legal dimensions of family violence* (pp. 174-96). New York: Spring

Sonkin, D.J. & Durphy, M. (1982). *Learning to live without violence: A handbook for men.* San Francisco: Volcano

Sonkin, D.J., Martin, D., & Walker, I.E. (1985). *The male batterer: A treatment approach.* New York: Springer

Sorenson, S.B. & Telles, C.A. (1991). Self-reports of spousal violence in a Mexican-American and a non-Hispanic white population. *Violence and Victims, 6*(1), 3-15

Spanier, G. (1976). Measuring dyadic adjustment: New scales for assessing the quality of marriage and similar dyads. *Journal of Marriage and the Family, 3,* 15-28

Spence, J.T. & Helmreich, R.L. (1978). Masculinity and Femininity: The psychological dimensions, correlates and antecedents. Austin: University of Texas Press

Spieker, S.J. & Booth, C. (1988). Maternal antecedents of attachment quality. In J. Belsky & T. Nezworski (eds.), *Clinical implications of attachment* (pp. 95-135). Hillsdale, NJ: Erlbaum

Sroufe, A. & Fleeson, J. (1986). Attachment and the construction of relationships. In W. Hartup & Z. Rubin (eds.), *Relationships and development* (pp. 55-71). Hillsdale, NJ: Erlbaum

Standing Committee on Health, Welfare, and Social Affairs. (1982). *Report on violence in the family: Wife battering.* House of Commons, Ottawa

Stark, E., Flitcraft, A., & Frazier, W. (1979). Medicine and patriarchal violence: The social construction of a private event. *International Journal of Health Services, 9*(3), 461-93

Stark, R. & McEvoy, J. (1970). Middle-class violence. *Psychology Today, 4*(6), 107-12

Steiner, G. (1981). *The futility of family police.* Washington, DC: Brookings Institute

Steinmetz, S.K. (1977). *The cycle of violence: Assertive, aggressive and abusive family interaction.* New York: Praeger

Stets, J. & Straus. M. (1990). Gender differences in reporting marital violence and its medical and psychological consequences. In M. Straus & R. Gelles (eds.), *Physical violence in American families.* New Brunswick, NJ: Transaction

Stewart, A. & Rubin, Z. (1976). The power motive in the dating couple. *Journal of Personality and Social Psychology, 34,* 305-9

Straus, M.A. (1973). A general systems theory approach to a theory of violence between family members. *Social Science Information, 12*(3), 105-25

– (1976). Sexual inequality, cultural norm and wife beating. *Victimology, 1,* 54-76

– (1977a). Wife beating: How common and why? *Victimology, 2*(3-4), 443-59

– (1977b). Violence in the family: How widespread, why it occurs and some thoughts on prevention. In *Family Violence: Proceedings from Symposium, United Way of Greater Vancouver.* Vancouver BC

– (1977c). Societal morphogenesis and intrafamily violence in cross cultural perspective. *Annals of the New York Academy of Sciences, 285,* 718-30

– (1979). Measuring family conflict and violence: The Conflict Tactics Scale. *Journal of Marriage and the Family, 41,* 75-88

– (1980). Victims and aggressors in marital violence. *American Behavioral Scientist, 23*(5), 681-704

– (1986). Domestic violence and homicide antecedents. *Bulletin of the New York Academy of Medicine, 62*(5), 446-65

– (1992a). The National Family Violence Surveys. In Straus, M.A. & Gelles, R.J. (eds.), *Physical Violence in American Families* (pp. 3-14). New Brunswick, NJ: Transaction

– (1992b). Measuring intrafamily conflict and violence: The Conflict Tactics Scale. In Straus, M.A. & Gelles, R.J. (eds.), *Physical violence in American families* (pp. 29-45). New Brunswick, NJ: Transaction

– (1992c). The Conflict Tactics Scale and its critics: An evaluation and new data on validity and reliability. In Straus, M.A. & Gelles, R.J. (eds.) *Physical Violence in American Families* (pp. 49-71). New Brunswick, NJ: Transaction

Straus, M.A., Gelles, R.J., & Steinmetz, S. (1980). *Behind closed doors: Violence in the*

American family. Garden City, NY: Anchor/Doubleday

Straus, M.A. & Gelles, R.J. (1985, November). Is family violence increasing? A comparison of 1975 and 1985 national survey rates. Paper presented at the American Society of Criminology, San Diego, CA

– (1986). Societal change in family violence from 1975 to 1985 as revealed by two national surveys. *Journal of Marriage and the Family, 48*, 465-79

– (1990). *Physical violence in American families: Risk factors and adaptations to violence in 8,145 families*. New Brunswick, NJ: Transaction

Straus, M.A. & Kantor, G.K. (1994). Change in spouse assault rates from 1975 to 1992: A comparison of three national surveys in the U.S. Paper presented at the 13th World Congress of Sociology, Bielefeld, Germany

Strentz, T. (1979, April). Law enforcement policy and ego defenses of the hostage. *FBI Law Enforcement Bulletin, 2*

Strube, M. (1988). The decision to leave an abusive relationships: Empirical evidence and theoretical issues. *Psychological Bulletin, 104*(2), 236-50

Strube, M.J. & Barbour, L.S. (1983). The decision to leave an abusive relationship: Economic dependence and psychological commitment. *Journal of Marriage and the Family, 45*, 785-93

– (1984). Factors related to the decision to leave an abusive relationship. *Journal of Marriage and the Family, 46*(4), 837-44

Summers, M. (1928). *Malleus maleficarum*. London: Pushkin

Symonds, M. (1975). Victims of violence: Psychological effects and aftereffects. *American Journal of Psychoanalysis, 35*, 19-26

– (1980). The 'second injury' to victims and 'Acute responses of victims to terror.' *Evaluation & Change*. Special issue, 36-41.

Symons, D. (1980). *The evolution of human sexuality*. Cambridge, MA: Cambridge University Press

Tannahill, R. (1980). *Sex in history*. New York: Stein and Day

Tannenbaum, P. & Zillmann, D. (1975). Emotional arousal in the facilitation of aggression through communication. *Advances in Experimental Social Psychology, 8*, 150-88

Taylor, G.R. (1954). *Sex in history*. New York: Vanguard

Taylor, S.P. & Epstein, S. (1967). The measurement of autonomic arousal. *Psychosomatic Medicine, 29*, 514-25

Taylor-Johnson Temperament Analysis Manual. (1980). Los Angeles: Psychological Publications

Terr, L. (1991). Childhood traumas: An outline and overview. *American Journal of Psychiatry, 148*(1), 10-20

Teske, R.H. & Parker, M.L. (1983). *Spouse abuse in Texas: A study of women's attitudes and experiences*. Huntsville, TX: Criminal Justice Center, Sam Houston State University

Thyfault, R.K., Browne, A., & Walker, L.E.A. (1987). When battered women kill: Evaluation and expert witness testimony techniques. In D.J. Sonkin (ed.), *Domestic violence on trial: Psychological and legal dimensions of family violence* (pp. 71-85). New York: Spring

Tift, L.L. (1993). *Battering of women*. Boulder, CO: Westview

Timmerman, J. (1981). *Prisoner without a name, cell without a number*. New York: Vintage

Tinbergen, N. (1951). *The study of instinct*. London: Oxford University Press

Toch, H. (1969). *Violent men: An inquiry into the psychology of violence*. Chicago: Aldine

Tolman, R.M. (1989). The development of a measure of psychological maltreatment of women by their male partners. *Violence and Victims, 4*(3), 159-77

Tontodonato, P. & Crew, B.K. (1992). Dating violence, social learning theory, and gender: A multivariate analysis. *Violence and Victims, 7*(1), 3-14

Tuchman, B.W. (1984). *The march of folly*. New York: Knopf

Turner, C., Fenn, M., & Cole, A. (1981). A social psychological analysis of violent behavior. In R.B. Stuart (ed.), *Violent behavior: Social learning approaches*. New York: Brunner/Mazel

Ulbrich, P. & Huber, J. (1981). Observing parental aggression: Distribution and effects. *Journal of Marriage and the Family, 43*, 623-31

United States. Bureau of the Census. (1979). *Social and economic characteristics of the older population: 1978*. Current Population Reports, series P-23, no. 85. Department of Commerce, Washington, DC: US Government Printing Office

– Commission on Civil Rights. (1978). *Battered women: Issues of public policy*. Washington, DC: US Government Printing Office

– Department of Justice. (1980). *Intimate victims: A study of violence among friends and relatives*. Washington, DC: US Government Printing Office

van der Kolk, B. (1987). *Psychological trauma*. Washington, DC: American Psychiatric Press

Waaland, P. & Keeley, S. (1985). Police decision-making in wife abuse: The impact of legal and extralegal factors. *Law and Human Behavior, 9*(4), 355-66

Wahler, R.G. (1980). The multiply entrapped parent: Obstacles to change in parent child problems. In J.P. Vincent (ed.), *Advances in family intervention, assessment and therapy*. Greenwich, CT: JAI

Waldo, M. (1988). Relationship enhancement counseling groups for wife abusers. *Journal of Mental Health Counseling, 10*, 37-45 Walker, L. (1978). Psychotherapy and counseling with battered women. Paper presented at the American Psychological Association

– (1979a). *The battered woman*. New York: Harper & Row

– (1979b). Treatment alternatives for battered spouses. In J.R. Chapman & M. Gates (eds.), *The victimization of women*. Beverly Hills, CA: Sage

– (1984). *The Battered Woman Syndrome*. New York: Springer

– (1989). Psychology and violence toward women. *American Psychologist, 44*(4), 695-702

Walters, R.H. & Brown, M. (1963). Studies of reinforcement of aggression. III. Transfer of responses to an interpersonal situation. *Child Development, 34*, 563-71

Watson, R.I. (1973). Investigation into deindividuation using a cross-cultural survey technique. *Journal of Personality and Social Psychology, 25*(3), 342-5

Weiss, R.S. (1982). Attachment in adult life. In C. Parkes and J. Steveson-Hinde (eds.), *The place of attachment in human behavior* (pp. 171-84). New York: Basic

Weisz, A.E. & Taylor, R.L. (1970). American presidential assassination. In D.N. Daniels, M.F. Gilula, & F.M. Ochberg (eds.), *Violence and the struggle for existence*. Boston: Little, Brown

White, G.L. (1977). The social psychology of romantic jealousy. *Dissertation Abstracts International, 37*(10), 5449-B

– (1980). Inducing jealousy: A power perspective. *Personality and Social Psychology Bulletin, 6*, 222-7

White, G.F., Katz. J., & Scarborough, K.E. (1992). The impact of professional football games upon violent assaults on women. *Violence and Victims, 7*(2), 157-71

Whitehurst, R.N. (1971). Violence potential in extramarital sexual responses. *Journal of Marriage and the Family, 33*, 683-91

Widom, C. (1989). Does violence beget violence? A critical examination of the literature. *Psychological Bulletin, 106*, 13-28

Williams, K. & Carmody, D. (1986). Wife assault: Perceptions of sanctions and deterrence. Unpublished manuscript. University of New Hampshire

Williams, K. & Hawkins, R. (1984). Perceptual research on general deterrence: A critical review. Paper presented at American Society for Criminology, Cincinnati, OH

Wilson, E.O. (1975). *Sociobiology*. Cambridge: Harvard University Press
– *On human nature*. Cambridge: Harvard University Press
Wilson, J.Q. (1983). *Thinking about crime*. New York: Basic
Wilt, G.M. & Breedlove, R.K. (1977). *Domestic violence and the police: Studies in Detroit and Kansas City*. Washington, DC: Police Foundation
Winter, D.G. (1973). *The power motive*. New York: Free Press
Wolfe, D., Jaffe, P., Wilson, S., & Zak, L. (1985). Children of battered women: The relation of child behavior to family violence and maternal stress. *Journal of Consulting and Clinical Psychology, 53*, 657-65
Wolfgang, M.E. & Ferracuti, F. (1967). *The subculture of violence*. London: Tavistock
Worden, R.E. & Pollitz, A. (1984). Police arrests in domestic disturbances: A further look. *Law & Society Review, 18*(1), 105-19
Wortman, C. (1976). Causal attributions and personal control. *New Directions in Attribution Research, 1*, 23-52
Wynne-Edwards, V.C. (1962). *Animal dispersion in relation to social behavior*. Edinburgh & London: Oliver & Boyd
Yalom, T.D. (1975). *The theory and practice of group psychotherapy*. New York: Basic
Yarrow, M.R., Campbell, J.D. & Burton, R.V. (1970). Recollections of childhood: A study of the retrospective method. *Monographs of the Society for Research in Child Development, 35*(15), serial no. 138
Yllo, K. & Straus, M. (1990). Patriarchy and violence against wives: The impact of structural and normative factors. In M. Straus & R. Gelles (eds.), *Physical violence in American families* (pp. 383-99). New Brunswick, NJ: Transaction
Zacker, J. & Bard, M. (1977). Further findings on assaultiveness and alcohol use in interpersonal disputes. *American Journal of Community Psychology, 5*(4), 373-83
Zimbardo, P.G. (1969). *The human choice: Individuation, reason and order vs. deindividuation, impulse and chaos*. Nebraska Symposium on Motivation, University of Nebraska Press
Zimbardo, P.G., Haney, C., & Banks, W.C. (1972, April 8). A Pirandellian prison: The mind is a formidable jailer. *New York Times Magazine*, 38-60.
Zimring, F.E. & Hawkins, G.J. (1973). *Deterrence: The legal threat in crime control*. Chicago: University of Chicago Press
Zuckerman, M. (1979). *Sensation-seeking: Beyond the optimal level of arousal*. Hillsdale: NJ: Erlbaum
Zuckerman, M., Lubin, B., Vogel, L., & Valerius, E. (1964). Measurement of experimentally induced affects. *Journal of Consulting Psychology, 28*(5), 418-25

Subject Index

Author Index

Set in Stone by Val Speidel

Printed and bound in Canada by D.W. Friesen & Sons Ltd.

Copy-editor: Joanne Richardson

Proofreader: Nancy Pollak